Costing and Budgetary Control

R. C. McEntegart, B.Sc., F.C.A.

POLYTECH PUBLISHERS LTD STOCKPORT

First published in 1980

Set in 10 pt Times series by
Bury Phototypesetting Limited, Peel Mills, Bury, Lancashire
and printed in Great Britain by
Ashworths Print Services, Peel Mills, Bury, Lancashire

Contents

Preface

The aim of this book is to provide a foundation course in Cost Accounting, which is suitable for a wide range of students. It follows a familiar path, introducing first the essential language and ideas of the cost accountant's model of the firm. This is followed in part two by chapters which deal mainly with aspects of control, including budgeting and standard costing, control of working capital and capital expenditure. Part three introduces decision making in the firm and includes chapters on linear programming and capital budgeting.

The style of the book is to present the essential features of each topic in a simple direct approach which is intended to avoid an over elaborate treatment of providing too many alternatives. In this way it is hoped that the student, obviously new to the subject, will obtain a clear grasp of the essentials on which to build at later stages of study. The introductory chapter starts on the well-trodden ground of the double-entry model, which should enable the reader to proceed with confidence. Immediately after this he moves on to a study of cost behaviour, thus gaining on early insight into the concepts of cost which are so necessary for the correct study of many features of Cost Accounting.

The full text has been designed as a one year course for full-time students of accounting who are undertaking their first course in Costing. It will be equally useful for part-time students undertaking an equivalent course over a longer time span. Students on advanced courses of Management would find it a useful guide to the subject as preliminary reading at a number of points in their studies.

The plan of the chapters is not intended to be a blueprint for all users and individual tutors may wish to adapt it to their own preferences and the needs of their students.

There are over two hundred examples to be worked. The standard pattern for each chapter is five questions with answers, five questions without answers and one seminar problem. Questions $1-5$ of each chapter have been specifically designed to cover points in the text. Questions $6-10$ have been chosen from past examination papers of the main accounting bodies. These are largely taken from foundation examinations, but a good number have been included from the professional stages, either to add an extra challenge or because the subject matter is not examined in the early stages. The seminar problems are intended to provide the basis for a weekly small group teaching occasion. The answers to questions $6-10$ and the seminar problems are provided in a separate book available to tutors.

Terminology used throughout has been chosen so as to familiarise the student with terms used both in British and American texts.

My grateful thanks are due to Mr. S. Keers for his helpful criticisms of an early draft. Needless to say he has to be completely exonerated from blame for all the blemishes which have remained or crept in during the later stages. Mrs. Muriel Shingler deserves thanks and congratulations for making such a good job of typing from very poor originals.

I would like to acknowledge the permission to use past examination papers given by the Association of Certified Accountants, the Institute of Chartered Accountants in England and Wales and the Institute of Cost and Management Accountants.

R. C. McEntegart
June 1980

Chapter 1

The Cost Accounting Model

A fundamental part of an accountant's work in industry, has always been to operate what is referred to today as the accounting model. This comes in many forms including an extended version which provides the basis for cost accounting. This book sets out to explain the cost model's basic features, since these are the key to all the cost systems employed in a modern industrial society.

At the present time the cost accounting model is a simple one in terms of mathematical techniques. Based as it is, on the concepts of doubly-entry accounting, no rules higher than arithmetic ones are required for the most part. However, there are areas where relatively more advanced mathematics are needed if the best information is to be provided. These developments have been included in the appropriate sections. It can be expected that in the future, the mathematical dimension of accounting will grow. Nonetheless, the current style of cost accounting will be with us for many years to come.

This simplicity of mathematical thought is overlain by a complexity of requirements and volume of events. The sheer number of transactions in a firm has created such data handling problems, that a specialised industry has emerged to cope with the demand to process this raw data efficiently. This complexity of requirements calls for a variety of forms of analyses and output. Whether these should be met by incorporating the means of satisfaction into the system, or whether periodic special exercises should be mounted, is part of the skill that a cost accountant has to acquire. As an example sales may be analysed according to geographical areas, product types, means of distributions, agencies and possibly in other ways. The cost accountant is responsible for designing the system to give the required results most efficiently in terms of service and cost.

Purposes of Cost Accounting

It would be possible to produce a lengthy list of purposes for which costs are collected and analysed. To do so would be to give a summary of the points to be covered in this book. On the grounds that this could be more confusing than helpful at this early stage, such a list will be avoided and instead, two broad areas will be discussed. These are control and decision making.

Control means the managerial supervision of ongoing operations. This includes profit and loss statements for short intervals of time, both for the whole firm and segments of the firm, as well as reports on product and departmental costs. It will be seen later that these results are most helpful when set against standards.

Standards and figures from the past are also useful when assessing the future. All decisions on future courses of action involve making estimates of future revenues and costs. In turn, the estimates are frequently projections of historic costs, adapted to expectations about the future.

Variations in Cost Accounting

There are probably as many costing systems as there are firms. Fortunately, this is not a cause for excessive alarm, since a set of basic features can be identified. It is not intended to describe in minutiae all the possible variants, but to concentrate on discussing a system which is assumed to be sufficiently common to all manufacturing firms. Where necessary, alternative procedures will also be included.

Manufacturing firms have been chosen as the norm, because they constitute a considerable sector of the economy and this makes the study of them important. Also costing as applied to manufacture can be adapted for use in all other forms of organisation. Small manufacturers, retailers and wholesalers use less elaborate forms, since the nature of their activities allows this. Service organisations adapt according to their own particular needs. Hospitals are an example. For some purposes hospital authorities want to use figures of cost per patient per day, and in so doing are developing their own units of measurement. As students advance in their studies and their careers they will need to read specialist works on costing, relating to particular industries and services.

Trading Firms

By this term is meant firms which buy goods in a finished states for sale without any further processing. Such firms produce the familiar profit and loss statement shown in Figure 1.1.

	£'000		£'000
Opening stock	100	Sales	1,600
Purchases	1,200		
	1,300		
Closing stock	200		
Cost of goods sold	1,100		
Gross Profit	500		
	1,600		1,600
Wages	150	Gross Profit	500
Selling expenses	100		
Administration expenses	50		
Finance expenses	50		
Net profit	150		
	500		500

Figure 1.1 Profit and Loss Statement.

The recording system for this calculation of profit is usually very simple. Mainly, it needs to control information on purchases and sales in order to conduct the payment and collection of money efficiently. The inclusion of total sales and purchases in the statement shown contributes towards the calculation of the gross profit. This calculation is completed by measuring the amount in money terms, by which the stock-in-trade has increased or decreased. In other words, the figure of gross profit is derived from the difference between sales and the cost of those sales. Further, this figure for the cost of goods sold is obtained from purchases and opening and closing stocks.

How does such a firm know its opening and closing stock positions? The physical quantities at the two points in time can be counted and valued according to some principle based on current accounting conventions. Alternatively, the movements in and out of the place of business can be recorded in detail. In the first method, in order to calculate profit it is necessary to count and value the stock. The second method provides a perpetual record of stock on hand and, provided it is accurate, the profit can be stated without a physical stock count.

Whichever method is employed is a matter for judgement in individual cases. Judgement would normally call for a balance between opposing benefits and costs. Physical stock-takes are usually big jobs relative to the resources of the firm and are not undertaken lightly. It is probable that the cost of the count and evaluation would exceed the cost of maintaining the perpetual stock records if the former were carried out on more than a quarterly basis. Against this is the fact that the perpetual records make monthly profit reporting possible and as a business grows in size and complexity this facility becomes more desirable. If the nature and size of the business are simple it is almost certainly an advantage to keep the cost of recording down and to rely on easily obtainable statistics to report on periodic progress. Once this simplicity is lost a perpetual inventory or stock record is required.

Manufacturing Firms

If one moves from the retailing or wholesaling sector to the manufacturing one, does this automatically call for a change from reliance on physical stock count to perpetual stock recording? No, the answer still depends upon the balance of advantage between extra cost and the usefulness of the additional information required. In the simple manufacturing situation it may well be best to keep the recording of stock movements to a basic record of relationships with suppliers. However, within the manufacturing sector of an industrial economy it is the case that the firms responsible for the majority of production have no such problem of balance. For these firms it is essential that the records should contain all movements of stock, from the raw material state to the finished product. From these records, or cost accounting model as we have referred to it, a statement of profit for any reasonable period can be prepared. The norm for such a period is four

4

weeks or a calender month. Anything shorter than four weeks involves too much approximation in arriving at figures. A longer period reduces the degree of estimation, but lengthens the period during which a firm may be without important control information. Nothing said here in relation to profit reporting should imply that weekly statistics are not important or that controlling action cannot be taken in the absence of profit reports. Clearly, the contrary is true. Weekly figures for orders received etc. are of paramount importance and along with other key controls form the basis of continuous decision taking.

The Flow of Costs Illustrated

What has been said for far can be illustrated with a simple example of a manufacturing process. In this case the manufacture of pencils. The procedures shown here are not the only ones available for a costing system. Alternatives will be examined in later chapters and the differences highlighted and evaluated. See Figure 1.2.

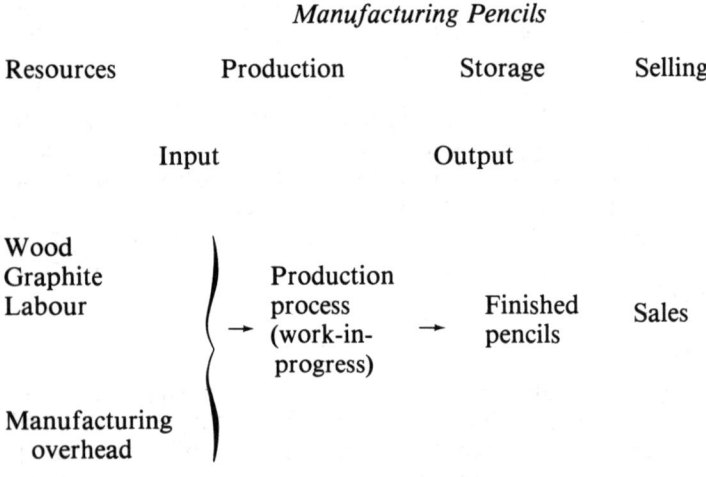

Manufacturing Pencils

| Resources | Production | Storage | Selling |

Input   Output

Wood
Graphite
Labour

Production process (work-in-progress)

Finished pencils

Sales

Manufacturing overhead

Fig. 1.2 Selling and administration overheads

This diagram of the physical flows of material and labour can be matched by a diagram of cost flows. This is shown in Figure 1.3.

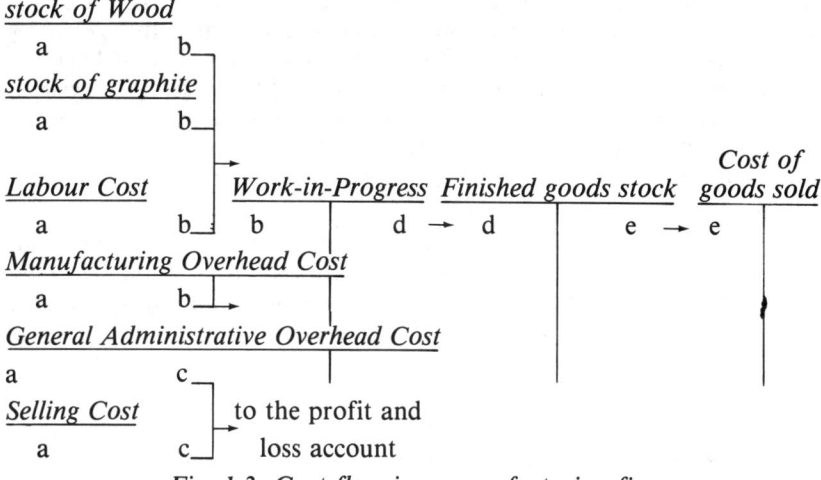

Fig. 1.3. Cost flow in a manufacturing firm.

Transfers to Work-in-Progress

The system of recording the cost flow is shown as a simplified form of T accounts. The accounts on the left record the payments for the resources to be used in making the pencils. Thus all the accounts are debited 'a'. These are wood and graphite which are the raw materials of the process. Labour is the cost of the work force operating the productive process. Manufacturing overheads use such costs as repairing the machinery, heating and lighting the factory, organising the work flow. General administrative overheads are a fairly small category including such items as company secretarial expense and legal fees. Selling overhead costs are salesmen's salaries, commissions, expenses and other forms of support to the selling effort. Later these categories will be defined more rigorously and others added.

Transfers between these accounts and the work-in-progress have been labelled 'b'. In the case of the wood and graphite the physical movement is matched by paper work in the form of stores issue notes. These are completed when the raw material is taken from the storage place and put into production. Initially quantities only are included and prices are added later. The balance of the account at any time gives the value to be attributed to the stock of raw material on hand.

The labour cost is similarly transferred to production, but here there is no concern with valuing a stock. In practice the collection of labour costs is more complicated than stated here and is explained more fully in Chapter 4.

Manufacturing overhead costs are collected on the debit side and charged to production in the usual double-entry manner, by crediting manufacturing overhead and debiting work-in-progress. Two points should be made here. The manufacturing overhead account is a control account, backed up by individual accounts for all the goods and services included. The second point is that the rate of collection of the overhead costs is not likely to be the same as the rate of transfer to production. For example, the electricity charge is likely to be received quarterly, whereas consumption will need to be charged on a monthly basis if monthly profit reporting is desired. Furthermore, electricity is one of a class of overheads which vary seasonally and management policy will probably be to iron out these seasonal variations, to help with their own comparisons of results for different periods.

Administrative and selling overheads are not transferred to work-in-progress, but straight to the trading and profit and loss account. They are not judged to be sufficiently closely related to manufacture to justify their inclusion as part of the cost of making the product.

Work-in-Progress to Finished Goods

As and when a quantity of goods, in this case pencils, are completed, they are physically transferred to a store of the finished product. In many cases of manufacture the goods are immediately shipped to customers, but few firms achieve this for all of their production. In the diagram of the flow of costs, the value for the transfer is denoted by 'd'. This is the usual product of quantity times price. As usual the quantity involved is ascertained straight forwardly. The price is more of a problem. One solution would be to measure the costs input for a period, measure the quantity manufactured and divide to arrive at a unit cost for transfer.

Month X.

Raw material consumed	£X
Labour	2X
Manufacturing overhead	X
	£4X
Production in units	Y
Cost/unit	£4x/Y

This illustrates one possible method, without entering any complications such as opening and closing stocks and adjustments for price-level changes. Chapter 3 contains a description of different pricing procedures and their implications.

Finished Goods to Cost of Goods Sold

The movement of the finished good to the customer is recorded by a set of documents which form the basis of despatch notes, invoices and cost of goods sold. Again the value of the transfer is quantity multiplied by price. Under current cost accounting for example, the price will be the replacement cost of the goods at the date of consumption, which will normally be at the date of delivery to the customer.

Profit Measurement

The final double entries are from 'cost of goods sold' account to the 'trading and profit and loss' account, and from 'sales' also to 'trading and profit and loss'. This gives the gross profit on manufacturing and trading. The gross profit is then reduced to the net profit by deduction of the administrative and selling expenses already referred to above.

Illustration in Detail

The student will find it in his best interest to work through the following detailed example. The first section gives the opening position of the company and a set of summarised results for a quarter. Each of these is given a distinguishing letter of the alphabet. The second section gives the corresponding journal entries, with the same identifying letters. The third section gives the accounting entries. Finally, the figures are brought together in the form of profit and loss and balance sheet statement.

The best way to follow the example, is to read the first item of section one and examine the corresponding entry in section two. Repeat this for each entry through to the end. Next perform a similar task for sections two and three.

Bankfield Limited

Section 1

The starting position of Bankfield Limited at 1st January 19X5 is given by the following balances:

	£		£
Fixed Assets	60,000	Share Capital	100,000
Depreciation	5,000		
	55,000		
Cash	45,000		
	100,000		100,000

During the three months to 31st March 19X5, total transactions and transfers amounted to the following aggregated figures:

(a) Purchases of material from suppliers on credit amounted to £110,000. These were analysed between raw materials (£100,500) and manufacturing overheads (£9,500).

(b) Services such as security guards and management consultancy were also received on a credit basis. These amounted to £13,000 and were entirely classed as manufacturing overheads.

(c) Wages and salaries paid amounted to £135,000 for all personnel, that is for all direct labour and other labour engaged in manufacturing, administration or selling. £100,000 was paid in cash and £35,000 and deducted for income tax, etc.

(d) Goods and services other than wages were also obtained in return for a direct payment of cash. Detailed analysis is as follows:

Manufacturing overhead	£4,000
Administration overheads	£5,000
Selling overheads	£8,000

(e) Throughout the period raw materials were issued from stores to the work-in-progress, at prices giving a total value to the transfers of £74,500. In addition some materials were issued for such purposes as repairs to production machinery. This amounted to £13,000 and would be classed as manufacturing overhead.

(f) The analysis of the wages and salaries paid, as provided by the wages and salaries office was:

Work-in-progress	£112,000
Manufacturing Overhead	8,500
Administration Overhead	5,000
Selling Overhead	9,500
	£135,000

(g) The manufacturing overheads have to be added to the cost of production, without allowing seasonal variations to distort results. The method used to transfer overheads into work-in-progress is based on averages for volume of production and incidence of the expenses. It has been forecast for the period to which these figures relate, that for every £1 paid to the direct labour, there will be 50p of manufacturing overhead. Using this predetermined ratio, the manufacturing overheads absorbed by production in the period will be £112,000 × ½ = £56,000.

(h) The value attached to output transferred from the production department to the finished goods can be arrived at according to many variations of formulae based on output and costs. In this case the finished product was transferred at a value of £220,000.

(i) As a result of sales contracts, goods are delivered to customers. It is necessary to record this to show both the sales value and the cost of goods which have been sold. Proceeds from sales amounted to £230,000, and the corresponding cost of goods sold amounted to £200,000.

(j) Overhead expenses accumulated as a result of analysing all cash and credit expenses are not exhaustive. One example of an overhead expense not resulting from current cash or credit items is the depreciation of fixed assets. In this example the total depreciation charge amounted to £5,000 for the period. £4,000 of this related to production plant and equipment and £1,000 to assets used in the selling function.

(k) Cash received from debtors amounted to £104,000.

(l) Payments to creditors in the period amounted to £80,000.

(m) During the period prices had been rising, necessitating a series of adjustments to bring the figures to current costs. These were

Raw materials	£600
Work-in-Progress	£1,000
Finished goods	£1,000

(n) Finally, the fixed assets have to be adjusted to show current costs. Using an approved index, the company will show the assets at a net replacement cost of £54,000 at the end of the period. The net asset account will be as shown.

Assets Account (Gross less depreciation)

	£		£
Starting balance	55,000	Depreciation for period	5,000
Revaluation reserve	4,000	Closing balance	54,000
	59,000		59,000

Assume that the transfer of £4,000 to the reduction reserve is the net result of increasing the gross asset figure by £5,000 and charging £1,000 backlog depreciation.

Section 2

These transactions and transfers can be summarised in journal entry form, using the same identifying letters.

	Dr.	Cr.
(a) Raw materials	100,500	
Manufacturing overheads	9,500	
Creditors		110,000
Materials and supplies received.		
(b) Manufacturing overheads	13,000	
Creditors		13,000
Services received.		
(c) Wages control	135,000	
Cash		100,000
Deductions		35,000
Gross wages paid in cash after deductions for tax etc.		
(d) Manufacturing overhead control	4,000	
Administration overhead control	5,000	
Selling overhead control	8,000	
Cash		17,000
Analysis of cash payments for goods and services.		
(e) Work-in-progress control	74,500	
Manufacturing overhead control	13,000	
Raw materials		87,500
Analysis of materials issued.		

(f) Work-in-progress control	112,000	
Manufacturing overhead control	8,500	
Administration overhead control	5,000	
Selling overhead control	9,500	
Wages control		135,000
(g) Work-in-progress control	56,000	
Manufacturing overhead control		56,000
Overheads absorbed to work-in-progress using the predetermined rate of 50% of direct labour.		
(h) Finished goods	220,000	
Work-in-Progress		220,000
(i) Cost of goods sold	200,000	
Finished goods		200,000
Transfer of finished goods to customers at cost		
Debtors	230,000	
Sales		230,000
Transfer of finished goods to customers at selling prices.		
(j) Manufacturing overhead control	4,000	
Selling overhead control	1,000	
Provision for depreciation		5,000
(k) Cash	104,000	
Debtors		104,000
Receipts from debtors.		
(l) Creditors	80,000	
Cash		80,000
Payments to creditors.		
(m) Raw materials	600	
Work-in-progress	1,000	
Finished goods	1,000	
Revaluation reserve		2,600
Adjustments to account for price-level changes		
(n) Fixed assets	5,000	
Provision for depreciation		1,000
Revaluation reserve		4,000

These journal entries are the basis of the figures debited and credited to the individual accounts. In practice a firm has a number of procedures for recording these original entries, so that what is here presented as a single primary record would be spread over a number of different recording routines.

Section 3

Using the same initial letters again, the amounts can now be shown in account form.

Share Capital			Fixed Assets			Cash			
	(−) 100,000					(−) 45,000	(c)	100,000	
			(−) 60,000			(k) 104,000	(d)	17,000	
			(n) 5,000				(e)	80,000	

Raw Materials			Work-in-Progress			Finished Goods		
(a) 100,500	(e) 87,500		(e) 74,500	(h) 220,000		(h) 220,000	(i) 200,000	
(m) 600			(f) 112,000			(m) 1,000		
			(g) 56,000					
			(m) 1,000					

Manufacturing o/h			Administration o/h			Selling o/h		
(a) 9,500	(g) 56,000		(d) 5,000			(d) 8,000		
(b) 13,000			(f) 5,000			(f) 9,500		
(d) 4,000						(j) 1,000		
(e) 13,000								
(f) 8,500								
(j) 4,000								

Wages and Salaries			Wage and Salary Deductions			Provision for Depreciation		
(c) 135,000	(f) 135,000			(c) 35,000			(−) 5,000	
							(j) 5,000	
							(n) 1,000	

Cost of Goods Sold						Sales		
(i) 200,000							(i) 230,000	

Debtors			Revaluation Reserve			Creditors		
(i) 230,000	(k) 104,000			(m) 2,600		(l) 80,000	(a) 110,000	
				(n) 4,000			(b) 13,000	

Only reference letters and figures are shown. In addition it is normal to show dates and cross references to other accounts and the journal reference. In our case, the letters act as the journal references.

A profit statement and balance sheet can be prepared from these accounts in the usual way. There is one unusual feature, however, that must be highlighted. It concerns the manufacturing overhead account, which shows a credit balance of £4,000. How should this be interpreted and handled?

As regards interpretation, it represents the difference between overhead costs recorded and overheads added to the cost of work-in-progress. This difference arises because the amount absorbed by work-in-progress is based on an estimate. This makes a standing monthly charge for items which are seasonal and which are often charged to the firm at longer intervals than a month. Figure 1.4 reproduces the manufacturing overhead account from the example given earlier in this chapter.

Manufacturing Overhead Account

Creditors:		Transfer to work-in-progress:	
for materials	9,500	50% of direct labour	
for services	13,000	$= \frac{1}{2}$ 112,000	56,000
Cash for services	4,000		
Raw material	13,000		
Indirect wages	8,500		
Depreciation of			
plant and equipment	4,000		
Balance	4,000		
	56,000		56,000
		Balance b/f	4,000

Fig. 1.4.

Many of these debits will be for regular monthly amounts, but a significant number will be seasonal, charged to the company at other than monthly intervals or else somewhat sporadic in their impact. To overcome these problems of season and slowness in collection, the monthly charge is made as an estimate. The usual process is to relate the overhead to an activity such as labour, which is fundamental to the production process and for which quick and accurate information is available. In this example the method used was to take the ratio of manufacturing overhead cost to direct labour cost. The figure arrived at from past experience and future expectations was 50p per £1 of direct labour. A fuller examination of absorption methods will be made in chapter 5.

The method of handling the difference between actual and absorbed cost depends upon the circumstances. In this case the period under review is a quarter and one would expect a balance on the account at the end of the period. During later quarters the cumulative difference should move towards nil. A valid treatment in these circumstances, for this quarter, is to carry forward the balance on manufacturing overhead control, in the expectation that it will be eliminated during the rest of the year.

The appropriate financial statements can be prepared from the accounts of the illustration. (Figure 1.5).

Bankfield Limited
Manufacturing, Trading & Profit & Loss Account
For the Quarter Ended 31.3.19X5

	£	£
Sales		230,000
Cost of Goods Sold		200,000
Gross Profit		30,000
Selling Expenses	18,500	
Administrative Expenses	10,000	28,500
Net Profit		1,500

Fig. 1.5.

Bankfield Limited
Balance Sheet — 31.3.19X5

		£			£
Share Capital		100,000	Fixed Assets:		65,000
Add profit		1,500	Depreciation		11,000
		101,500			54,000
Revaluation reserve		6,600			
Current Liabilities:			Current Assets:		
Creditors	43,000		Raw Materials	13,600	
Wage Deductions	35,000		Work in Progress	23,500	
Bank Overdraft	48,000		Finished Goods	21,000	
		126,000	Debtors	126,000	184,100
Manufacturing					
Overheads (bal.)		4,000			
		238,100			238,100

The £35,000 wage deductions are amounts owing to such bodies as the Inland Revenue for P.A.Y.E. If the illustration had been extended to include some payments of these, then the wage deductions would have been shown at a reduced amount and the bank overdraft correspondingly enlarged.

A more detailed presentation of the profit statement would show the cost of manufacture for the period, the cost of finished goods manufactured and the cost of goods sold. An example of the format is given in figure 1.6.

Open stock of raw materials	X
Add: purchases	XX
	XX
Deduct: closing stock	X
Materials used	XX
Direct labour	XX
Material overhead	XX
Cost of manufacture	XXX
Increase/decrease in work-in-progress	X
Cost of goods manufactured	XXX
Increase/decrease in finished goods	X
Cost of goods sold	XXX

Fig. 1.6. Alternative form of manufacturing statement.

Separate Cost and Financial Accounts

Most firms today operate their accounting system along the lines just described. However, this has not always been so and, in the past, cost accounts were usually kept separately from the financial ones. To a large extent this was a duplication of work, but was often convenient and justified. With the development of data processing aids the justification has really disappeared, based as it was on the need for two teams to be working simultaneously on the same physical records. Where such a system is still used, the two sets of accounts require a link.

This link is provided by the cost ledger control account. In the financial accounts this is a memorandum account only and does not form part of the double-entry. In the cost accounts it is part of the double-entry system.

Using the figures given above in the integrated example, we can illustrate separate cost accounts as follows:

Cost Ledger Control Account

(i) Sales	230,000	(−) Starting balance	Nil
(−) Closing balance	52,600	(a) Raw materials	100,500
		(a) Manufacturing overhead	9,500
		(a) Manufacturing overhead	13,000
		(c) Wages	135,000
		(d) Manufacturing overhead	4,000
		(d) Administration overhead	5,000
		(d) Selling overhead	8,000
		(j) Manufacturing overhead	4,000
		Selling overhead	1,000
		(m) Raw material	600
		(m) Working-in-progress	1,000
		(m) Finished goods	1,000
	282,600		282,600

It would be tedious to repeat all the other accounts. A trial balance extracted before calculating profit would show:

Raw material	13,600	
Work-in-Progress	23,500	
Finished goods	21,000	
Manufacturing expense		4,000
Administration expense	10,000	
Selling expense	18,500	
Cost of goods sold	200,000	
Sales		230,000
Cost ledger control		52,600
	286,600	286,600

To put it simply the cost accounts are a section of the full accounts. Accounts not relevant to the cost process, e.g. debtors, are all collected in the control account.

The two sets of accounts should give the same profit. In practice this is not always the case, because a transaction or adjustment in one set may not be reflected in the other. For example, interest paid on loans may be included in the financial accounts only. Such instances give rise to difficulties and reconciliations are necessary.

Reconciliation of Cost and Financial Accounts

A reconciliation statement for two sets of accounts would take the following form:

		£
Profit per cost accounts:		6,000
Less: stock value adjustment		500
		5,500
Financial items:		
Loan interest		1,000
Profit before appropriation		4,500
Less: Taxation	1,000	
Dividends	1,000	2,000
Retained profit as per financial accounts		2,500

The reconciliation gives examples for each of three main types of entry which can be distinguished. The first category consists of items which are valued differently for internal accounting purposes from external reports. Stock figures in the cost accounts may be on the basis of material, labour and manufacturing cost only, with the financial accounts showing an additional element for administrative overheads.

Expenses which relate to financial items of an interest payment nature are often excluded from cost accounts, whilst being included in the financial ones. Costs and proceeds of transactions not falling within the mainstream of company activities are usually excluded from the cost accounts.

Finally, appropriations of profit are clearly not the concern of the cost accounts and are only included in the financial accounts.

Summary

This chapter started on the familiar ground of an accounting system which relied on physical stock counting and valuation for the information necessary for profit reporting. This was extended in two ways:

1) a system of perpetual inventory or stock recording was introduced in the form of accounts for raw materials, work-in-progress and finished goods.

2) the manufacturing overhead was added to work-in-progress by using a predetermined rate.

The result is a set of accounts which can be used for profit reporting, without recourse to a physical stock check.

The next step is to look more closely at the meaning of costs and the ways in which they may be analysed.

Exercises 1

1.1-1.5. Answers provided.

1.1 The cost accounts of the Oak Company are maintained on an absorption costing basis, as outlined in Chapter 1. The accounts show the following costs for the operations of one period:

	£
Raw materials purchases	10,000
Direct labour cost	25,000
Manufacturing overhead cost	45,000

a) If the opening stock of raw materials were £1,000 and the closing stock were £1,500, what was the cost of production for the period?

b) If the cost of raw materials used were £9,500 and the opening and closing work-in-progress figures were £15,000 and £17,000 respectively, what was the cost of goods manufactured during the period?

c) If the cost of goods manufactured during the period were £77,500 and the opening and closing stocks of finished goods were £10,000 and £8,000 respectively, what was the cost of goods sold during the period?

1.2 The Elm Company maintains control accounts and subsidiary accounts in the following form:

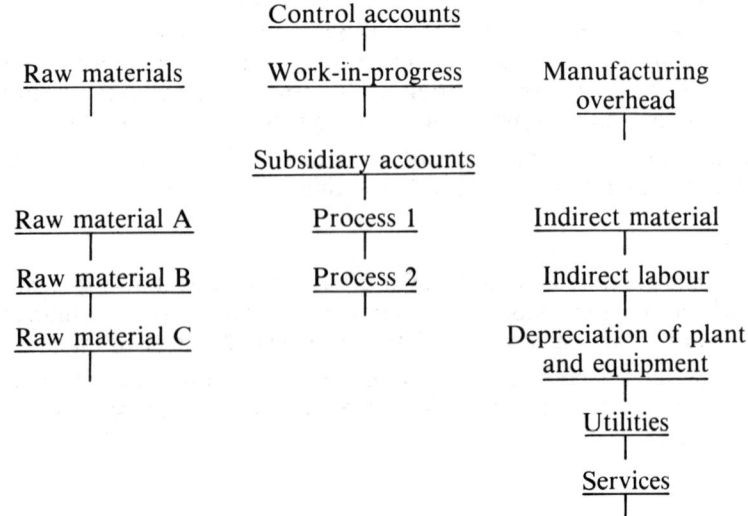

Prepare control account and subsidiary account entries for the following data:

a) Purchase of raw materials:

	A	£2,000
	B	£2,500
	C	£1,200

b) Analysis of raw materials:

amounts requisitioned,	A	£1,000
	B	2,000
	C	400
consumption by process,	1	£1,600
	2	1,800

c) Labour costs:

process 1	£2,000
2	2,500
indirect	2,000

d) Manufacturing overhead:

indirect materials	£500
depreciation	2,500
utilities	2,000

e) Manufacturing overhead absorbed by production:
process 1, 100% of direct labour cost.
process 2, 200% of direct labour cost.

f) Completed work-in-progress:

process 1	£5,000
process 2	6,000

1.3 The Sycamore Company had the following balances in its accounts at the end of a period:

	£
Stocks at close:	
Raw materials	9,000
Work-in-progress	15,000
Finished goods	5,000
Manufacturing overhead supplies	1,000
Purchases — materials	70,000
Purchase returns — materials	1,000
Carriage inwards — materials	1,000
Sales	320,000
Direct Labour	100,000
Indirect labour of manufacture	20,000
Heating and lighting	5,000
Power	15,000
Repairs to factory building	1,000
Factory security	4,000
Administrative expense	15,000
Selling expense	25,000

Opening inventories of all classes were nil.

Required a profit and loss statement for the period, showing the production cost, the cost of goods produced and the cost of goods sold.

1.4 The Plane Company maintains separate financial and cost accounts. For the year 19X5, the financial accounting profit was lower than the figure in the cost accounts by £3,575.

Summary Trading, Profit and Loss Account
per financial accounts

Sales		£300,000
Cost of goods sold		200,000
Gross profit		100,000
Selling expenses	£30,000	
Administrative expenses	20,000	
Financial expenses	5,000	55,000
		45,000

Notes:

a) Depreciation of plant and equipment in the financial accounts was £10,000 calculated on the straight-line basis. In the cost accounts there is an annual charge of half the straight-line calculation plus £0.025 per unit of production.

b) The cost accounts contain a notional rent of £500 for property owned.

c) Financial expenses are not included in the cost accounts.

d) Stock is valued at material and labour in the cost accounts, but also includes manufacturing overhead in the financial accounts.

e) Opening stock consists of 4,000 units, valued as follows:

Material	£2,000
Labour	1,300
Overheads	700
	£4,000

Closing stock consists of 9,000 units, valued as follows:

Materials	£4,500
Labour	3,000
Overheads	1,500
	9,000

Sales in units were 200,000

Required

A reconciliation of the financial and cost accounts.

1.5 The Ash Company had the following Balance Sheet at 1st January 19X5:

1. Starting position – Share Capital $\qquad$ £100,000

    Fixed Assets $\qquad$ 55,000
    Cash $\qquad$ 45,000

    Aggregation of events for 3 months is as follows:

2. Materials from suppliers on credit terms £110,000 of which £100,500 were raw materials and £9,500 were factory overheads.

3. Services such as security guards and consultancy on production methods were also received on a credit basis. They amounted to £13,000.

4. Wages paid amounted to £135,000 for all personnel. Of this, £120,000 was in cash and £15,000 was deducted for P.A.Y.E. etc.

5. Goods and services other than wages were also obtained in return for a direct payment of cash.

    Factory overheads $\qquad$ £4,000
    Selling expenses $\qquad$ 8,000
    Admin. expenses $\qquad$ 5,000

6. Issues of raw materials totalled £36,000 to department A, £38,500 to department B and £13,000 was issued for non-production activities in the factory.

7. Wages paid were analysed according to functions:

    Work-in-progress A $\qquad$ £60,000
    Work-in-progress B $\qquad$ 52,000
    Factory overheads $\qquad$ 8,500
    Selling expenses $\qquad$ 9,500
    Administrative expenses $\qquad$ 5,000
    $\qquad$ £135,000

8. Factory overheads absorbed in the period were department A £22,000 and department B £24,000.

9. The cost of finished goods completed was:

    Department A labour $\qquad$ £58,000
    material $\qquad$ 35,000
    overhead $\qquad$ 21,000 $\qquad$ £114,000

    Department B labour $\qquad$ £31,000
    material $\qquad$ 37,000
    overhead $\qquad$ 23,000 $\qquad$ £111,000

10. Sales were £174,000 and the corresponding cost of sales was £140,000.

11. The depreciation expense (of factory plant and equipment) was £3,000 for the period.

12. Cash received from debtors, £104,000.

13. Payments made to creditors, £30,000.

14. All deductions from wages were paid to the appropriate body.

Required: i) T accounts, Trial Balance, Profit and Loss Account for the three months ended 31 March 10X5 and a Balance Sheet on that date.

ii) What do the account balances at 31 March represent?

Questions 1.6-1.9 Answers not provided

1.6 The following balances were extracted from the records of CFL Ltd. for the months of May 1976:

	May 1 £	May 31 £
Finished Goods Stock	7,298	16,732
Work-in-Progress: Materials	28,480	21,360
Work-in-Progress: Labour	44,500	49,840
Work-in-Progress: Factory Overhead	11,125	12,460
Raw Materials Stock	146,138	114,098

During the month raw materials costing £85,440 were purchased and the direct labour payroll amounted to £149,520.

Included in the issues from Raw Materials Stock were items valued £10,680 which were used for the maintenance of factory premises and plant and machinery.

Factory Overhead is absorbed on the direct labour cost basis, the rate for May 1976 being 25%.

From the foregoing data you are required to write up the accounts referred to above and to show the cost of goods sold during the month. CA(AC2).

1.7 Meklect Limited produce two types of lawnmower, a mechanical model, and an electric model. The company's trading summary for the year recently ended is as follows:

	£	£
Sales		550,000
Direct material and labour	389,000	
Factory Overhead	40,000	
Administration Overhead	30,000	
Marketing Overhead	16,500	
		475,500
Profit		£74,500

The directors consider the profit/sales ratio (13.54%) to be inadequate and have asked you to analyse the trading summary in order to determine the profitability of each of the two models.

Your investigation reveals:

(1) Sales for the year were   £
      5,000 mechanical models   325,000
      3,000 electric models   225,000

(2) Opening stocks of raw material were £45,000 and closing stocks £54,000. Purchases during the year were £324,000.

(3) £150,000 of material was used in the production of mechanical models and the remainder on the electric models.

(4) The piecework labour rate is £10 for a mechanical model and £8 for an electric model.

(5) Included in Factory Overhead are the following costs with indications of the directors' views of their apportionment:

	£	*Mechanical*	*Electric*
Indirect labour	15,000	one-third	two-thirds
Power	6,500	three-fifths	two-fifths
Depreciation	12,600	three-sevenths	four-sevenths

The remaining Factory Overhead is to be apportioned equally.

(6) Administration Overhead includes a computer bureau's charge of £11,000 for producing sales invoices; this charge is to be apportioned according to invoiced sales value; the remaining Administration Overhead is to be apportioned equally to the two models.

(7) Marketing Overhead is to be borne by the two models in proportion to invoiced sales values.

(8) Finished Stocks and Work in Progress were the same at the end of the year as they were at the beginning.

You are required to produce statements to show:

(a) the trading results for each model

(b) The unit cost and profit of each model, analysing cost as follows:
    Direct Material
    Direct Labour
    Factory Overhead
    Administration Overhead
    Marketing Overhead
and to add brief comments which you think may be helpful to the directors. CA(AC2)

1.8 (a) A company operates a financial accounting system and a cost accounting system. Extracts from both final accounts for the year are shown below, from which you are required to prepare a reconciliation statement or account.

The final financial accounts included the following:

	£
Debenture interest	2,000
Interest received	1,000
Discount allowed	8,000
Discount received	3,000
Net profit	57,000

Stock valuations:	Opening stock £	Closing stock £
Raw materials	152,000	198,000
Work-in-progress	66,000	72,000
Finished goods	84,000	87,000

The final cost accounts included the following:

	£
Interest on capital	30,000
Notional rent	20,000
Administration overhead over-absorbed	10,000
Production overhead under-absorbed	15,000
Selling and distribution overhead over-absorbed	14,000

Stock valuations:	Opening stock £	Closing stock £
Raw materials	164,000	187,000
Work-in-progress	61,000	68,000
Finished goods	90,000	94,000

(b) Explain the meaning of:

(i) interest on capital;

(ii) notional rent.

Discuss briefly the reason why the cost accountant may choose to introduce these items into the cost accounts. ICMA(CA1)

1.9 During 1960 Alfred Williams retired from the army and with his gratuity purchased a small retail wool shop which he called by his wife's name. Since then he has run the shop with no assistance other than that from his wife Olive. During 1975 he was asked by the Retail Association of Wool Shops whether he would be prepared to submit his annual accounts, for these to be combined in an anonymous manner with those of other firms, to enable comparisons of trading results to be made.

Mr. Williams agreed and sent along his accounts for the year ended 31st March, 1975, which were as follows:

Olive's Wool Shop

Profit & Loss Account for the year ended 31st March, 1975

Sales		£10,145
Less: Cost of goods sold		6,087
Gross Profit		4,058
Expenses		
Wages	£325	
Rates	125	
Heating and light	370	
Insurance	80	
Advertising, print, stationery	510	
Miscellaneous expense	275	
Depreciation	400	
		2,085
Net Profit (before taxation)		£1,973

The following additional information had to be supplied:

(i) Whether the premises were owned or rented, and if the latter, the amount of the rent.

(ii) Details of the time that the owner and other members of his family spent working in the shop. In their case, Mr. Williams worked for 40 hours each week and his wife for 30.

(iii) Details of equipment used in the shop (cost, date of purchase, estimated life).

(iv) The amount shown on the capital account. This was £4,750 at the commencement of the year in question.

Subsequently Mr. Williams received the following statement of the 'average' accounts for the wool shops contributing to the scheme, with his own results as 'adjusted' by the Association.

		Olive's Wool Shop	*Average Wool Shop*
Sales		£10,145	£12,440
Less: Cost of goods sold		6,087	6,470
Gross Profit		4,058	5,970
Expenses			
Management expenses	£2,000		£1,850
Wages	865		610
Rates	125		120
Heating and light	370		345
Insurances	80		90
Advertising, printing, etc.	510		280
Miscellaneous expenses	275		250
Depreciation	400		400
Interest on capital	475		480
Rent	500		500
		5,600	4,925
Net Profit (*Loss*) (before taxation)		(£1,542)	£1,045

Mr. Williams and his wife were perplexed at these figures, as from their own accounts they had felt that they were doing very well.

Required:

(a) An explanation of the purpose of the exercise and of the reasons for each of the adjustments to the orginal profit statement.

(b) A comparison of the results of Olive's Wool Shop with those for similar shops which indicates those areas which Mr. Williams should investigate. How should Mr. Williams view these individual problem areas in order to improve the overall performance of his business?

CA(MA)

Seminar Problem 1

Proposed sale of the Beech Company

Mr. Wood has been the owner and manager of his own tobacconist, sweets and book-store for over ten years. Currently in his early fifties, he is considering an offer made for his business by a company which operates a chain of similar shops in thriving market towns.

To help in the process of negotiating a price, Mr. Wood has asked you to complete his accounts for the previous year as quickly as possible. As usual, his contribution to this process is a jumble of cheque book stubs, invoices from suppliers, copy invoices for customers and other sundry receipts and records of cash takings.

One of the clerks has compiled a cash record from this and made a note of other relevant information. In addition you have the closing balance sheet from the previous year. This information is given in schedule A.

Schedule A

The Beech Company

Balance Sheet — 31 December 19X4

	£		£	£
Owners Interest	26,150	Fixed Assets:		
		Premises at cost		20,000
Current Liabilities:		Fittings, fixtures,		
Wages	50	equipment at cost	5,000	
Creditors	500	Depreciation	1,000	4,000
		Current Assets:		
		Stock-in-trade	2,000	
		Debtors	200	
		Cash	500	2,700
	26,700			26,700

Cash payments and receipts for 19X5

Receipts:	£	Payments:	£
Cash sales	60,000	Wages	4,000
Debt collection	2,000	Rates	800
		Advertising	200
		Supplies	1,000
		Telephone	500
		Insurance	500
		Miscellaneous expenses	500
		Maintenance	500
		Heat and Light	1,000
		Payments for stock	40,000
	62,000		49,000

Additional information:

1) Amounts due for payment at the end of the year:
   - wages £100
   - creditors for stock 700

2) Receipts due at the end of the year
   - debtors £300
   - insurance refund 50

3) Miscellaneous expenses include £100 for the lease of equipment paid in advance for the quarter beginning 1-January 19X5.

4) Closing stock was independently valued at £1,500.

5) Depreciation of equipment is 20% of the written down value.

Required:

1. A profit and loss account for the year ended 31 December 19X5 and a Balance Sheet on that date.

2. How should Mr. Wood proceed to decide on a fair price for the business?

3. If the chain were to add this store to their group, what sort of cost information would they expect to receive in the future?

Chapter 2

Cost Behaviour — Absorption and Marginal Cost Systems

Chapter 1 expanded the basic accounting model to incorporate continually updated stock accounts for raw material, work-in-progress and finished goods. This chapter will look more closely at the underlying ideas and then go on to explore alternative systems.

Absorption Costing

The name given to the methods described in the preceding chapter is 'absorption costing'. It can alternatively be called 'full costing' and frequently goes by this latter name in the United States of America. It would be inappropriate at this stage to attempt a definition, since some of the terms that would have to be used, have yet to be explained. The succeeding paragraphs contain these necessary explanations, which are then followed by the more formal definition of absorption costing.

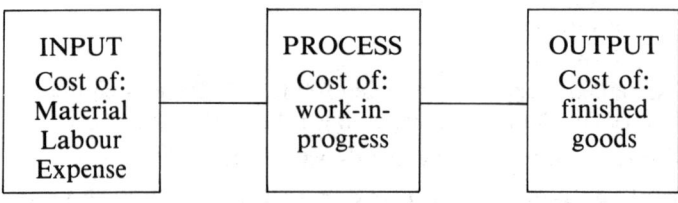

Figure 2.1

Cost

A 'cost' in the accounting sense, is usually taken to mean the expense of following some particular course of action. This can be the payment for some material or wages paid to the labour employed. Additionally it can be some estimated part of the expenditure on assets which are of benefit for a long period, that is depreciation. This idea frequently needs to be modified to suit the types of decisions which are being made with some aid from cost information. From time to time throughout the text new costing terms will be introduced as they become useful.

Input to Production

The nature of the inputs can be classified under three headings: material, labour and expense. Material and labour costs are self-explanatory terms, but a short explanation on expense is worthwhile. The word is used here in a special sense as the cost of some service provided, other than by the firm's own labour force. It also includes the notional cost of the use of assets which are owned by the firm, e.g. depreciation.

In turn the material, labour and expense can be analysed between 'direct production costs' and 'indirect production costs'. Figure 2.2 illustrates this, with the addition of 'prime cost' and 'manufacturing or production overhead' as further costing terms.

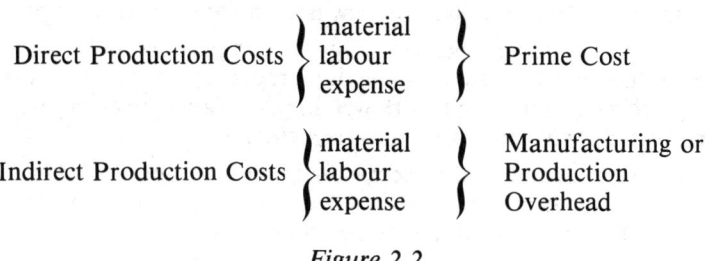

Figure 2.2

Direct Production Costs

A cost is 'direct' in relation to some specified function, e.g. production, if it can be reasonably easily traced to that function and can be closely identified with it. The direct cost of production of bread for example, would include flour and the bakers' wages. An important point to make is that the effort of relating the cost to the product must be worthwhile. Small materials, such as screws, form part of many finished products and are certainly closely identified with them. Nonetheless, the cost of these items would probably be classed as indirect.

Indirect Production Costs

These are less closely identified with the finished product. They include such items as the cost of stationery (material), the salary of a foreman (labour) and the depreciation of factory buildings (expense). The indirect production costs are often called manufacturing or factory overheads. They include all the factory costs up to the point of goods being made ready for distribution. The border of the factory overheads is the cost of a primary package (a cigarette packet) as opposed to a carton of such packets. The former is a production cost and the latter a distribution cost.

Other Indirect Costs

Other indirect costs or overheads may be sub-divided according to their function. A common set is distribution, selling, research, development and administration. These are fairly self-explanatory, although some costs will be borderline cases.

The distribution costs cover the activity of moving the goods from the end of the production line to the point of sale. In appropriate cases this will include the cost of moving goods to storage depots. In specialised cases, such as electricity and gas, the maintenance of the mains and pipe networks will be a distribution cost. Where there are re-usable containers, the reconditioning expense will also be included.

Selling costs include the securing of orders and the process of advertising the product and stimulating demand for it. After sales services where this is free and included as part of the product attraction can also be a selling cost.

Research is the cost of looking for something new. It can be a new product or a new method of production or a new use for some existing by-product.

Development takes its place between research and production. It is the cost of implementing research into a production process and it is often a difficult and costly process. Things that work well in pilot plants, often develop new problems under conditions of full scale production.

The administration costs tend to be residual policy making, organising and controlling costs. Residual in the sense that they cannot be directly associated with one of the functions described above.

Cost of Work-in-Progress and Finished Goods

These are made up from the combined direct and indirect costs of production as they are consumed in the manufacturing process. Generally speaking, the cost attributed to a unit of output is an average one. Whilst it is possible to measure how much direct material has been used in a particular unit manufactured, it is usually quite impossible to measure the cost of such things as the factory manager's salary. Even if it were possible it would be unreasonable to go to the expense of making such a measurement. Hence, as will be seen later, such indirect items are averaged over production. In broad terms the costing system for calculating such average costs can be either jobbing or process costing systems. Briefly, a jobbing system is one in which items or work-in-progress can be identified with the eventual customer or with some specific works order. In the process costing situation such identification is not possible. Clothing manufacturers make to their customers specific orders and employ jobbing systems. Glass is manufacturered and then matched to customer requirements, so that process costing applies. Variants of jobbing systems are batch costing and contract costing. In many cases, hybrid scheme are operated to suit specific sets of circumstances.

Presentation of Accounts

Use of the direct to production/indirect to production split, together with the functional division into production, distribution etc. gives an accounting statement of profit as shown in figure 2.3.

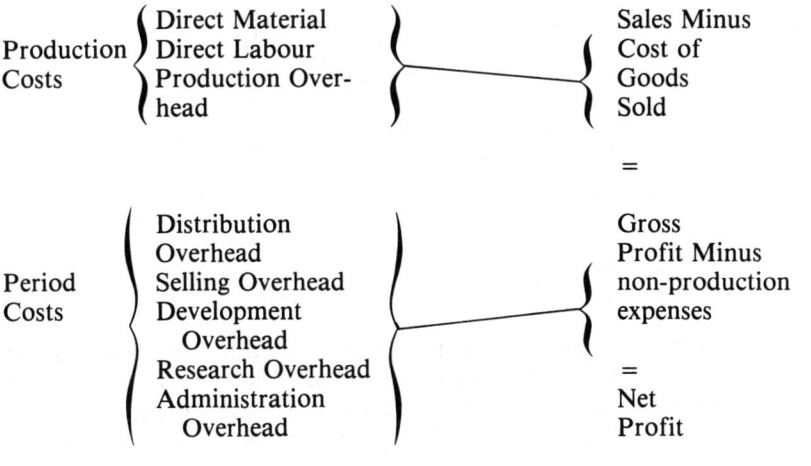

Figure 2.3

Product and Period Costs

In figure 2.3 two more terms are introduced. These are product costs and period costs. The product costs are the ones traced through the production process, and so included in stock values. They are not matched against sales until the period in which they are sold. Period costs are not traced through production and are matched against sales in the period in which they are incurred.

Marginal Costing

Under 'absorption' or 'full' costing the distinction or dichotomy is between costs or production or period costs. Under 'marginal' costing a more fundamental dichotomy is observed, between costs which vary with activity and those which are fixed. Some consideration must now be given to the way in which costs behave as volumes of output and sales change.

Variable Costs

These are the costs which change as the volume of activity changes. Economists regard this change as taking place at different rates as the level of activity increases. As output rises the average variable cost declines as efficiency increases. At higher levels the average variable cost levels off and finally begins to increase as the point of diminishing returns is reached. This being the result of attempting to use facilities excessively.

Accountants accept this view, but work on the basis that firms do not operate at the very low or very high levels of activity. Consequently, the accountant assumes that the average variable cost per unit is constant. This is the same as saying that variable costs vary directly with output.

These alternative viewpoints are illustrated in figures 2.4a and 2.4b.

30

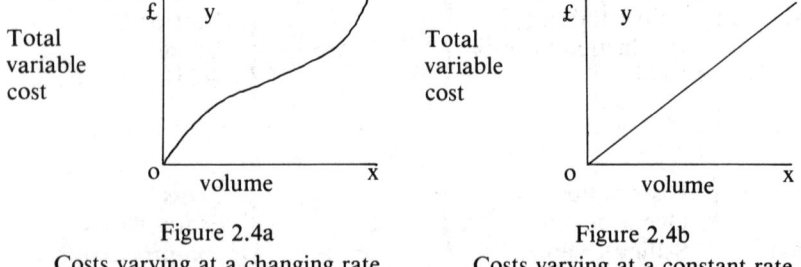

| Figure 2.4a | Figure 2.4b |
| Costs varying at a changing rate | Costs varying at a constant rate |

An example of a variable cost is the material used in a product. Direct labour to production is also frequently regarded as a variable, but this depends on the circumstances of the firm. In an increasing number of cases, the direct labour force is remaining fairly constant over long periods, despite fluctuations in output.

Fixed Costs

In contrast, the fixed costs do not vary with changes in the volume of activity. This is easily depicted as the straight horizontal line in figure 2.5

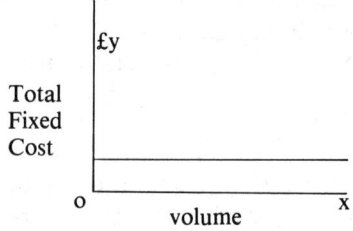

Figure 2.5

Fixed Costs

Examples of fixed costs are found in the provision of manufacturing facilities, such as factory rent and depreciation of machinery. Higher level management costs are another good example, together with programmed costs. These latter are amounts authorised for programmes of advertising, research and development and other overhead items which are independent of production activity.

Unfortunately, the task of classifying costs into these two categories is by no means simple and in practice some fairly arbitrary decisions have to be made. The problem is that costs, in the main, do not behave as simply as in the above diagrams. Any number of cost curves can be drawn to fit special cases. There are two common variants which have to be dealt with, if a system using variable cost concepts is to be adopted. These are semi-variable costs and step costs.

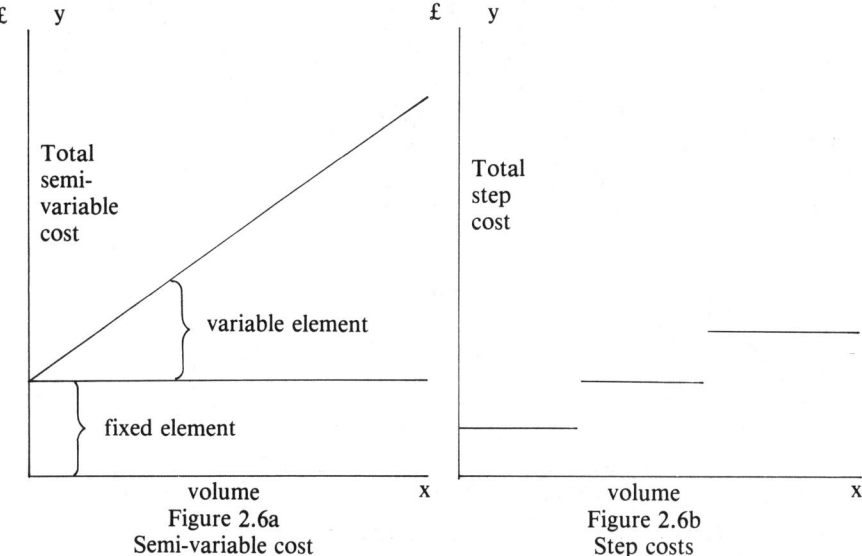

Figure 2.6a
Semi-variable cost

Figure 2.6b
Step costs

Semi-variable costs

These are illustrated in figures 2.6a. The graph shows that they contain both variable and fixed elements.

As the volume of activity increases in figure 2.6a the cost increases linearly, but part of the cost is basically fixed. A production machine hired for a minimum rent plus additional payments related to units of output would fit into this category. Again, this illustration helps to explain the idea, but it should not be allowed to suggest that all semi-variable costs can be analysed so easily. The split of semi variables into variable and fixed elements is not an easy job and will need to be looked at in more detail later.

In figure 2.6b a different type of cost behaviour is shown. These are referred to as step costs. At certain points as volume increases, the cost takes a sudden upward jump. In between these points the cost remains constant. Step costs can approximate either to variable costs or fixed costs in certain circumstances.

Figures 2.7a and 2.7b show this

In figure 2.7a the steps are very short and are insignificant in relation to total costs for a whole business. At any level of volume, it is immaterial which part of the short step is taken as being the cost. Consequently, the steps can be approximated by a straight line. Direct operating labour can exhibit this type of cost. Alternatively, the steps can be long, in which case they may be regarded as fixed. There is one condition for this, each step must extend beyond the lower and upper boundaries of normal activity. In the long run most fixed costs are step costs. One factory can provide the necessary capacity for a considerable period and is an example of a fixed cost. Eventually, increases in productivity and shift-working may no longer

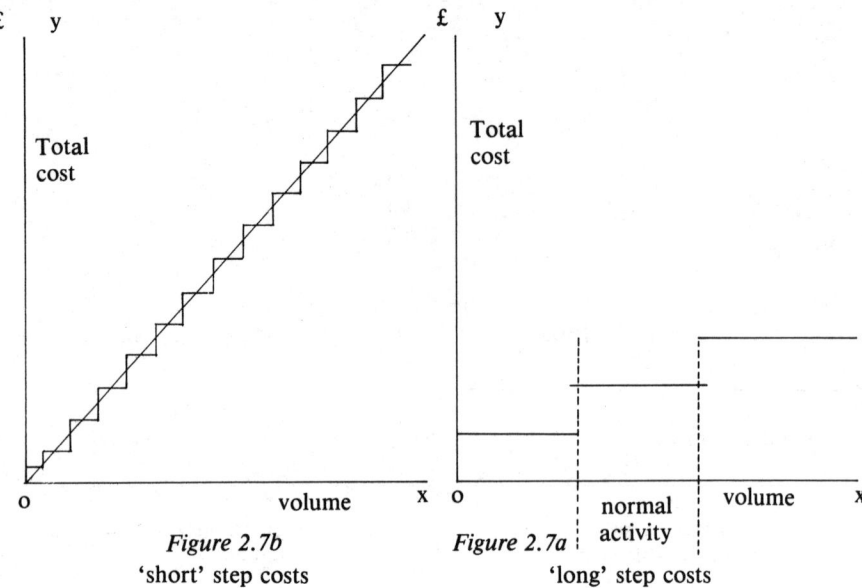

Figure 2.7b
'short' step costs

Figure 2.7a
'long' step costs

be sufficient to raise output as required by sales and a second factory unit would become necessary. In this sense factory rent is a step cost approximated to a fixed cost. There are some step costs which do not straddle the boundaries of normal production (see figure 2.8).

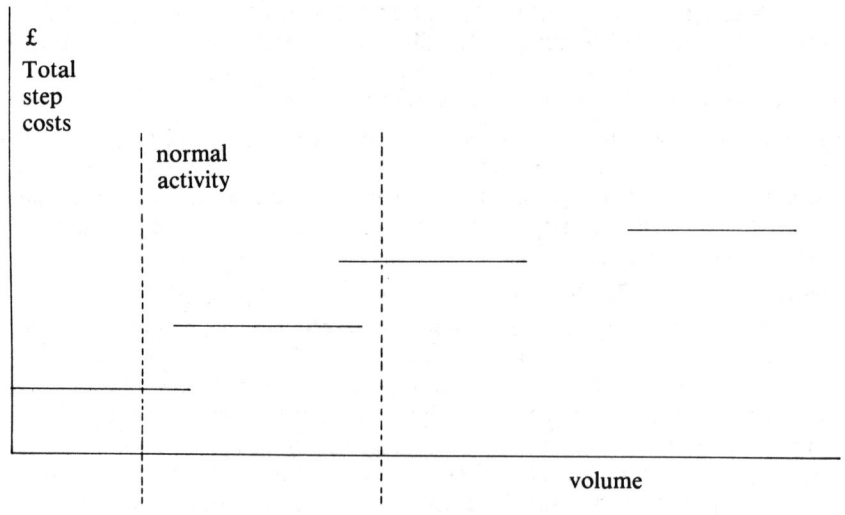

Figure 2.8 Step costs which do not approximate to variable or fixed.

The steps shown in figure 2.8 are of intermediate length in relation to volume. It could be costs of supervision, which will increase as extra volume is provided by additional direct labour. Costs such as these have to be treated without any approximation and dealt with according to the appropriate facts of the case.

Application of variable costs

The analysis of costs into variable or fixed elements forms the basis of marginal costing and distinguishes it from absorption costing. In the United States of America and other countries the term 'variable costing' is used in preference to 'marginal costing'. They do this in order to separate the process from the economists' concept of marginal costs. The accountant is not calculating the cost of each extra unit produced, but is using variable cost as an approximation.

In a variable or marginal costing system the variable costs of production are treated as product costs and the fixed costs of production plus all other costs are treated as period costs. More specifically, in the full costing system the manufacturing overheads charged to stocks of finished goods includes both the variable and fixed elements and, in fact, no attempt is made to separate these elements. In variable costing only the variable manufacturing overheads are added to finished goods costs. See figures 2.9a and 2.9b. It follows that the variable system requires the necessary analysis to be done and that this extra task should be justified in terms of the additional benefits obtained.

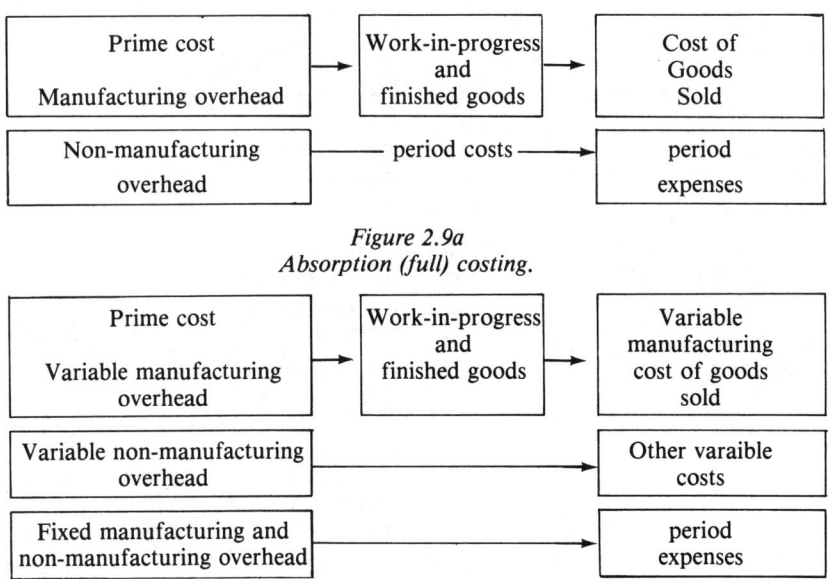

Figure 2.9a
Absorption (full) costing.

Figure 2.9b
Marginal (variable) costing.

Absorption and Marginal Costing – a comparison of results.

One of the benefits resulting from the use of marginal costing is that fluctuations in production from period to period do not affect the reported profit as they do under absorption costing. This is illustrated in figures 2.10 to 2.12 which contain comparative sets of figures under both systems for three successive periods.

The basic data used in the examples are:-

Period 1

Sales — 20,000 units at £8 a unit

Cost of Production — 25,000 units at a variable cost of £5 per unit plus fixed cost of £50,000

Opening stock – nil

Closing stock: – 5,000 units

Administration and selling expenses, variable £3,000 and fixed £8,000

Ignore work-in-progress.

Absorption or Full	£	£	*Marginal or Variable*	£	£
Sales		160,000	Sales		160,000
Cost of Goods Sold:			Variable manufacturing cost of goods sold:		
Opening stock – Cost of goods			Opening stock – Cost of goods produced (variable)		
Produced	175,000	(25,000 units)	$(25,000 \times £5)$	125,000	
Less – closing stock	35,000		Closing stock $(5,000 \times £5)$	25,000	
$(5,000 \text{ units} \times £7)$		140,000		100,000	
Gross Profit		20,000	Add—variable administrative and selling expenses	3,000	103,000
Less administrative & selling expenses		11,000	Contribution to fixed expenses and profit		57,000
			Less – fixed costs:		
			Manufacturing	50,000	
			Administration and selling	8,000	58,000
Net Profit		9,000	Net Loss		1,000

Figure 2.10
Comparison of Absorption (Full) and Marginal (Variable) costing — first period.

The two systems have produced different profit figures for the same period and from the same data. What has happened is that in the absorpotion cost system one fifth of the fixed manufacturing overhead has been included in the closing stock. It has been treated as a product cost. In the marginal cost system, this £10,000 has been set against sales as a period cost.

Moving into the second period, change the data given to show production equal to sales at 20,000 units. Otherwise the figures remain the same. The results are set out alongside each other in figure 2.11.

	Absorption or Full				*Marginal or Variable*	
	£	£			£	£
Sales		160,000		Sales		160,000
Cost of Goods sold				Variable manufacturing of goods sold –		
Opening stock (5,000 units)	35,000			Opening stock	25,000	
Cost of goods Produced	150,000			Cost of goods produced (variable)	100,000	
	185,000				125,000	
Less – closing Stock (5,000 × £7.00)	35,000			Closing stock (5,000 × £5.00)	25,000	
		150,000				100,000
Gross profit		10,000		Add – variable administrative		
Less – administrative and selling expenses		11,000		selling expenses	3,000	103,000
				Contribution to fixed expenses & Profit		57,000
				Less – fixed costs Manufacturing	50,000	
				Administration & selling	8,000	58,000
Net loss		1,000		Net loss		1,000

Figure 2.11

Comparison of Absorption (Full) and Marginal (Variable) costing — second period.

In the second period the results shown are equal. Closing stock has again been valued at £7 per unit. For the final period the production will be reduced to 15,000 units, all other figures remaining the same. Figure 2.12 sets out the results.

Absorption or Full			*Marginal or Variable*		
	£	£		£	£
Sales		160,000	Sales		160,000
			Variable manufacturing		
Cost of goods sold:			cost of goods sold –		
Opening stock	35,000		Opening stock	25,000	
Cost of goods			Cost of goods		
Produced	125,000		produced	75,000	
	£160,000			£100,000	
Closing stock	–	160,000	Closing stock	–	
Gross Loss		nil		£100,000	
			Add-variable		
			administrative &		
Less – administrative and			expenses	3,000	103,000
and selling expenses		11,000	Contribution to		
			fixed expenses &		
			profit		57,000
			Less fixed costs		
			Manufacturing	50,000	
			Administration &		
			selling	8,000	58,000
Net loss		11,000	Net loss		1,000

Figure 2.12

Comparison of Absorption (Full) and Marginal (Variable) costing – third period.

The final period shows a further set of divergent profit figures. Throughout, the marginal cost system has shown a consistent figure. This is because profit is related to sales and is independent of the production volume. The absorption cost system shows a higher profit when production was high relative to sales than when it was low. Essentially the difference between the two systems reduces to a choice of treatment for fixed production or manufacturing overheads.

For the three periods taken together the total profits are the same under either system, that is a total loss of £3,000. This is because the opening stock of the first period and the closing stock of the third period were both nil. It was as though the business had run through its life from start to close. It is possible to conclude from this that over a long period the two methods will give substantially the same results. This is a reasonable conclusion, since firms must balance their production and sales in the long run.

One advantage then, of marginal (variable) costing is that the reported profit is unaffected by imbalance between production and sales. Management is helped by the removal of fluctuations based on stock build up or run down.

A second advantage lies in the usefulness of the contribution concept in making decisions. One simple example will suffice here and a more detailed study will be made later. A report to management is given in figure 2.13.

Product	A	B
	£	£
Sales	750	750
Total variable cost of goods sold	425	725
Contribution to fixed overheads and profit	325	25
Less – fixed costs	225	125
	100	100 (loss)

Figure 2.13
Report on product profitability

A decision has to be made about dropping product B. First it should be said that a lot of commercial considerations will come into the decision – for example does selling product A depend upon the existence of product B in the selling range? The figures show that B is contributing to fixed costs and could usefully be continued whilst a long term appraisal is carried out.

Chapter summary
The beginning of this chapter dealt with the idea of costs being classified between direct or indirect to production. The indirect costs were then sub-divided between functions of production, selling etc. and these were defined.

An alternative approach is to classify costs according to behaviour in relation to some measure of volume. The elements of this classification system were examined.

The first method leads to absorption (full) costing and the second to marginal (variable) costing. The effects of marginal costing on profit reporting were considered. Finally advantages in terms of profit reporting and decision making were claimed for marginal costing.

Exercises 2
2.1-2.5 Answers provided.

2.1 Identify the following costs with the appropriate graph:
   i)   Raw material used in the manufacture of the finished product.
   ii) The hire charge for a piece of equipment, based on a fixed rent plus a standard amount per hour of use.
   iii) Factory rent.
   iv) Supervision costs, where each supervisor controls twenty operators.

v) Salesmen remuneration based on a fixed wage plus 10% commission on the first £1,000 of sales in the period and 15% for sales in excess of £1000.

vi) A utility charged at a fixed rate for the first 5,000 units consumed, £1 per unit for the next 5,000 with a maximum charge of £10,000.

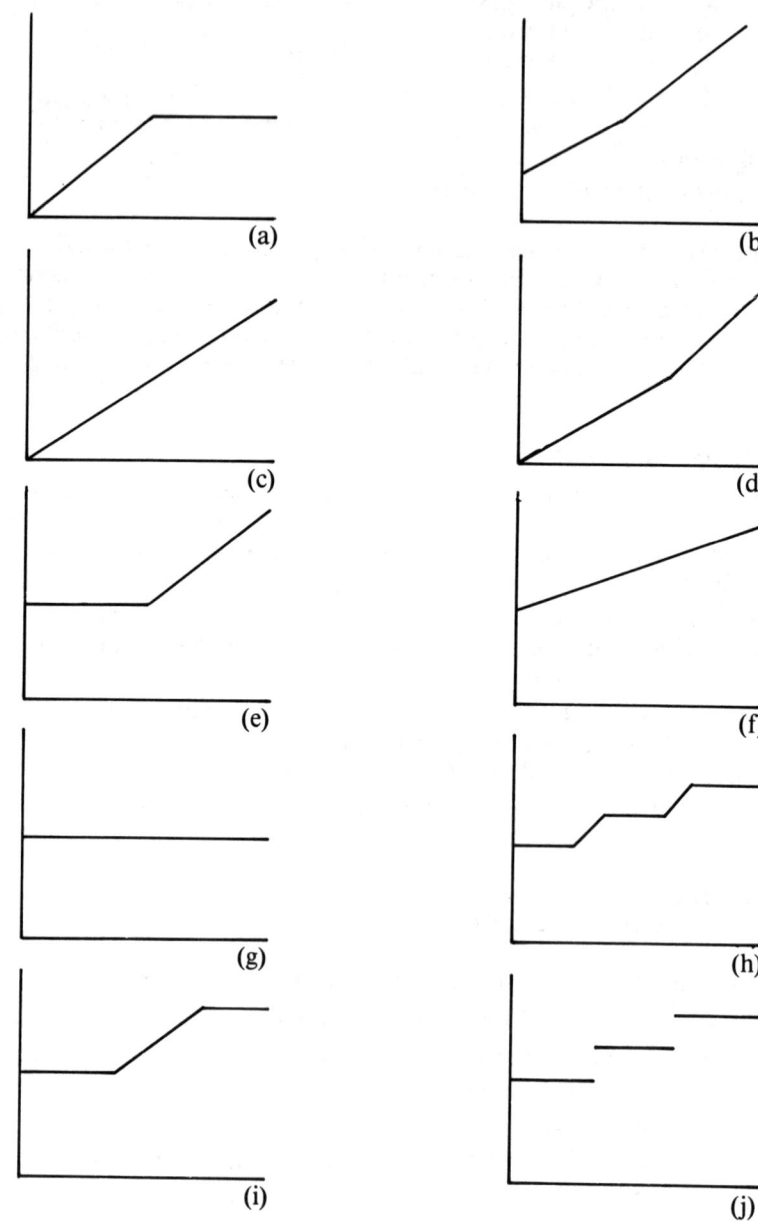

(a) (b) (c) (d) (e) (f) (g) (h) (i) (j)

2.2 Complete the following sentences:
   i)   Factory rates are a _____ cost of factory overhead.
   ii) Supervisory wages are usually _____ of factory overhead.
   iii) Raw materials are a _____ cost of manufacture.
   iv) The factory managers salary is a fixed cost of _____.
   v)   The salemen's commissions are _____ cost of selling.
   vi) In absorption costing the product cost includes _____ factory overhead.
   vii) In marginal costing the fixed cost of manufacturing overhead are treated as _____ costs.
   viii) The alternative name for Absorption costing is _____ and for Marginal costing it is _____.

2.3 From the following partial list of accounts prepare a statement of the variable cost of goods manufactured:

£

Opening stock of raw material	4,000
Purchases of raw material	55,000
Closing stock of raw material	7,000
Wages paid	48,000
Wages accrued at period end.	2,000
Factory overhead (excluding depreciation):	
variable	30,000
fixed	20,000
Depreciation of plant and machinery	
(straight-line basis)	10,000

2.4 From the following information, prepare a profit and loss statement using marginal cost methods:

	units	price £	£
Sales	500,000	3	1,500,000
Raw materials:			
opening stock			8,000
purchases			260,000
closing stock			12,000
Work-in-progress:			
opening stock			12,000
closing stock			20,000
Direct wages			572,000
Factory overhead:			
variable			290,000
fixed			60,000

Administration – fixed 20,000
Selling expenses:
  variable 100,000
  fixed 40,000
Finished goods:
  opening stock 50,000 100,000
  closing stock 60,000

Production for the period was equivalent to 555,000 units after allowing for increases in work-in-progress. Value the closing stock at the average unit cost of manufacture for the year.

2.5 The production date given below apply without alteration throughout three periods:
Production: 20,000 units

Cost of production:	variable	£3 per unit
	fixed	£40,000
Administration and		
selling expenses:	variable	£1 per unit
	fixed	£5,000

The stock at the start of period 1 was nil.

Ignore work-in-progress.

Selling price throughout, £7

Sales were: period 1, 15,000 units
             period 2, 20,000 units
             period 3, 25,000 units

Prepare profit and loss statements for each of the three periods on a marginal cost basis.

Questions 2.6-2.10 Answers not provided

2.6 Using the information given below, prepare profit statements for the months of March and April 1978 using:
(a) marginal costing;
(b) absorption costing

Per unit: £
  Sales price   50
  Direct material cost   18
  Direct wages   4
  Variable production overhead   3
Per month:
  Fixed production overhead   99,000
  Fixed selling expenses   14,000
  Fixed administration expenses   26,000
Variable selling expenses.
  10% of sales value

Normal capacity was 11,000 units per month.

	March units	April units
Sales	10,000	12,000
Production............................	12,000	10,000

ICMA(CA1)

2.7 The managing director of MC Limited, a manufacturing company, has recently attended a short conference on 'Marginal costing for non-accounting executives', and has returned enthusiastic to learn more about marginal costing in operation. One particular idea which was discussed only briefly at the conference was a suggestion that management should be more interested in marginal costing than absorption costing, because profits were affected by relative volumes of production and sales in any one period.

You are required, as management accountant, to prepare a short paper discussing briefly the concepts of marginal costing and absorption costing and explaining what effect different volumes of production and sales have on profit reported under each system. ICMA(CA2)

2.8 (a) 'Fixed costs are really variable: the more you produce the less they become'.

Explain the above statement and state whether or not you agree with it.

(b) You are required to SKETCH a separate graph for each of the items listed below in order to indicate the behaviour of the expense. Graph paper need not be used but your axes must be labelled.

(i) Supervisory labour;

(ii) depreciation of plant on a machine hour basis;

(iii) planned preventive maintenance plus unexpected maintenance;

(iv) monthly pay of a salesman who receives a salary of £3,000 per annum plus a commission of 1% paid on his previous month's sales when they exceed £20,000; assume that his previous month's sales totalled £30,000. ICMA(CA1).

2.9 Summarised profit and loss statements of DC Electrical Company Limited for the two years ended 31st December, 1974 and 1975 are shown below:

	1974 £000's	1975 £000's
Sales	650	720
Marginal cost of sales	390	340
Contribution	260	380
Fixed overhead	240	260
Net profit	20	120

As a result of the poor performance of the company in 1974, management decided to implement a reorganisation of production methods and to increase selling prices by 20% from 1st January, 1975.

You are required to calculate how much increase in net profit in 1975 was due to the change in:

(a) marginal cost;

(b) sales price;

(c) sales volulme;

(d) total fixed overhead.

State any assumptions you may have made in your calculations. ICMA(CA1)

2.10 The figures shown below are all that could be salvaged after a recent fire in the management accounting department of Fireprone Limited. Fireprone manufactures a single product, has no work in progress and allocates all the actual costs of manufacture to its product. It is known that the unit closing stock valuation in 1975 was the same as in 1974. Stock is valued at actual manufacturing cost on a FIFO basis.

	1975	1976
1. Selling price unit	£10.00	£10.00
2. Variable manufacturing costs, per unit produced	£4.50	£4.00
3. Variable selling costs per unit sold	£1.25	?
4. Quantity sold.	100,000	?
5. Quantity produced	105,000	130,000
6. Contribution margin per unit based upon the production and selling costs of the year in question.	?	?
7. Total contribution margin earned on sales	?	£585,000
8. Fixed costs, manufacturing	£105,000	£117,000
9. Fixed costs, other	£155,000	?
10. Operating profit, before interest and taxation	?	£292,500
11. Total interest charges	£70,000	?
12. Opening finished stock quantity	?	?
13. Closing finished stock quantity.	20,000	20,000
14. Taxation at 52% on operating profit less total interest charges.	?	£110,500
15. Profit after taxation	?	?

You are required to prepare manufacturing, trading and profit and loss accounts for management for both years detailed insofar as the available information permits. ICAEW(MA)

Seminar Problem 2

A small manufacturing business is operated as a separate concern with its own financial records by a parent company which has recently acquired a controlling interest in it. At year end its accountant sends in an income statement and a valuation of stock carried forward. An accountant of the parent company is rather perplexed because the figures reported vary considerably from those of another similar business controlled by his company. On enquiry he finds that the subsidiary company uses the variable costing method.

In other businesses controlled by the parent company the full costing system is employed. The full costing system is, however, related to a 'normal' manufacturing capacity to ensure that stock valuations include a standard charge for fixed manufacturing costs. (No administration costs are included in inventory).

The statistics relating to the subsidiary from which that firm's accountant prepared his reports are given below, together with the figure of 'normal' capacity which would be applicable to his firm.

You are required to prepare:

(i) the income statement and stock valuation initially prepared for the subsidiary company.

(ii) a similar report prepared on the basis normally adopted by the parent company and its other businesses.

Statistics		*Units*	*Price per unit*
Raw Materials:	Opening Stock	200	£10
	Purchases:		
	First half year	1,000	£10
	Second half year	1,000	£12
	Closing Stock	None	
Finished Goods:	Produced................	2,200	
	Closing Stock	400	
	Opening Stock	None	

Variable labour processing cost per unit
   processed £3
Fixed processing costs for the year £20,000
Sales .... 1,800 at £40
Variable selling cost per unit sold £4
Fixed costs of selling department.............. £5,000
Fixed costs of administration................. £7,500

Normal manufacturing (processing) capacity = 2,500 units

N.B. All raw materials initially in stock or purchased are fully processed by year end. Use the F.I.F.O. method of stock valuation.

Chapter 3

Accounting for Materials

Management accountants are involved in two major areas where materials are concerned. One area is that of control. The whole system of ordering, handling, storing and protecting materials needs to be well balanced in terms of costs and benefits. This important subject is fully dealt with in chapter 12, which contains sections on simple optimisation models as well as description of the main features of all material control systems.

The second area is concerned with methods of accounting and is the subject of this chapter. The accountant's model of the firm recognises three stock positions for which data are collected and between which transfers are made. These are raw materials, work-in-progress and finished goods. When bought materials are received on the firm's premises, they are held in special stock areas or rooms dependent upon their nature. These are the raw materials of the firm. They may consist of those commodities which are normally thought of when the term raw materials is used, for example copper or sand. In some cases though, the input will consist of goods manufactured by a supplying company and may be fairly or even very sophisticated equipment.

As the material inputs are issued from the stock areas and used in the production process a transfer has to be made between the raw material accounts and the work-in-progress account. The work-in-progress account also records the input of labour and overheads into the manufacturing process.

The finished product of the firm is finally moved into stock or transferred straight to the customer. Transfers to the finished goods warehouse are recorded by a corresponding entry between work-in-progress and the finished goods account. Delivery of goods to customers causes a transfer from finished goods to cost of goods sold.

These three areas are represented by control accounts. Detailed analysis of the different types of raw materials or the various products in process or finished goods are kept in the appropriate supporting accounts. This follows the normal pattern in accounting and is exactly the same in principle as debtors control accounts backed up by the individual account of each of the firm's debtors. In addition the whole transferring process is one of debiting and crediting.

Debits are used to record the cost accumulation and credits the transformation from one form of stock to another. This transformation is clearly not an instantaneous process but a gradual one. Nevertheless an approximation is made and the entry in the double entry system is made at the end of the manufacturing process.

At each stage in the system it is necessary to put a value on the quantities being transferred. This is not an easy matter nor is it one on which there is agreement between accountants as to the method of valuation to be adopted. The succeeding paragraphs deal with the main points of material pricing.

The Receipt of Goods

The fundamental document relating to the receipt of goods is the invoice. This gives the cost of the items supplied and forms the basis of the first entry into the stock accounts. However, there are particular costs which require special consideration. These are such items as discounts, transport and storage. There are two ways of treating these additions or allowances from the unit price of the items included on the invoice.

1) As part of the cost of the material
2) As an indirect cost of the factory

A simple example given in figure 3.1 may be used to illustrate these alternatives:-

A Supplier's Invoice

	£
100 units of commodity – A @ £2 per unit	200
100 units of commodity – B @ £1 per unit	100
Carriage	6
	£306

Figure 3.1

The carriage on this invoice could be treated in either of the following ways:-

1) Materials: Dr.   Cr.
     Commodity A.   £204
     Commodity B.   102
     Creditors   £306

Here the carriage cost has been allocated to the two items on a pro rata basis in the absence of more precise information.

2) Materials: Dr.   Cr.
     Commodity A.   £200
     Commodity B.   £100
   Factory overheads:
     Carriage in: 6
     Creditors   £306

In this treatment the carriage cost has been included as an overhead charge and will be added to the cost of output in the same way as other factory costs.

Items requiring special consideration:

1. *Discounts*

    These are a deduction from the amount shown due on the invoice and arise for three different reasons;

    a) *Trade Discounts*

        These are allowances made between firms when buying in the normal course of trade. For example between a manufacturer and a wholesaler, or a wholesaler and a retailer. The discount is represented as a certain percentage of the invoice price. The procedure for trade discounts is to treat them as deductions from the price and to enter the nett figure into the accounts.

    b) *Quantity Discounts*

        Additional discounts are often given for purchases of large quantities either in terms of large orders or over a given period of time. Again, these are treated as price deductions and nett figures are used.

    c) *Cash Discounts*

        As an inducement to customers to pay their accounts promptly suppliers frequently offer them a deduction from the amount due if the bill is settled within a specific time period. Such discounts can be handled in the accounts in two ways.

One alternative is to record the cost at gross figure and to enter a separate credit for the discount received when it is taken.

	Dr.	Cr.
Materials control	£400	
creditors		£400
Creditors	£400	
discount received		£10
cash		£390

The value of the discount, in this case £10, is classed as a financial item.

The second method is to enter a nett figure for the cost of the goods. If the firm fails to pay the bill by the stipulated day, it is necessary to debit the amount of the lost discounts to a special account.

Materials control	£390	
Creditors		£390
Discount lost	£10	
Creditors		£10
Creditors	£400	
Cash		£400

The first of these two ways of entering discount recognises that it is, in effect, interest on money loaned. Paying earlier than necessary is tantamount to lending. Hence the treatment as a financial item. The second method highlights the cost of failing to take advantage of discounts and acts as a signal for the need for corrective action.

Cost of receiving, inspecting and storing goods

These costs clearly are related to materials, but they are not particularly identified with individual items. The commonest treatment is to class these costs as factory overheads and deal with them in the normal way. Alternatively, they can be added to material costs on a pro-rata bases.

Containers

The cost of materials can be affected by the charges relating to containers such as boxes, bags, drums, reels, etc. If the container is not returnable then the cost of it will simply be included as part of the purchase price even though it may be shown separately on the invoice. Where the container is charged for on a fully refundable system, a separate account is maintained. Any losses will be added to factory overheads. Sometimes a middle course operates with containers funds funded on return but at a lower rate than the original charge. The difference represents a material cost and can usually be associated with specific items.

Costing Material Issued to Production

When materials are issued from stock to work-in-progress a corresponding entry is made in the control account:

debit work-in-progress
credit materials control

The question that arises at this point is the value to be placed on this transfer. There are a number of reasons why this problem arises. Prices paid for goods change over a period of time either because of general price level changes or because of specific price changes in a commodity resulting from a change in the supply and demand for that particular item. Buying tactics of the firm's purchasing officer may succeed in obtaining some reductions. The fact that prices are changing for whatever reason or combination of reasons, gives rise to a number of possibilities when it comes to valuing the goods issued to production. Why is it important to look closely at these various possibilities? Mainly because the method chosen has a specific bearing on the stock values and on the profit or loss being reported for a period. Again the available methods can be analysed under broad headings:

1) Using an identifiable market price
2) Averaging
3) Having a fixed price for a period.

Identifiable market price

This can be taken in the most direct sense in that a good used in production is priced at the specific amount paid for it. This requires an identification process, such as tagging the item when it is received into stock and using that tag as the trigger for the accounting entry when it is used in production. A procedure like this could operate for particular bought parts used in a cost plus contract for say a government department. More usually, stock merges in bins or tanks and loses its particular identity. This does not preclude the use of a form of identifying each issue to production with a particular market price. The market price may be the one existing when the oldest item in stock was bought, in which case the system being used is F.I.F.O. — First In, First Out. The second possibility is to use the market price pertaining when the most recent physical purchase was made, the analogous name for this is L.I.F.O. — Last In, First Out. Thirdly the transfers could be made at the current cost of purchasing them, the name given to this is replacement cost.

F.I.F.O

This means that the unit costs of issues is equal to the cost of the earliest acquisitions in stock. The system is illustrated in figure 3.2. Throughout each example the following figures will be used:

Goods received:

		units	units price	cost value
19.1	J.1	10	5	50
	J.7	15	10	150
	J.21	20	15	300

Goods issued:

	J.14	5	?	?
	J.28	30	?	?

	Receipts				Issues			Stock		
Date	Units	Unit Price	£	Units	Unit Price	£	Units	Unit Price	£
J.1	10	5	50				10	5	50
J.7	15	10	150				10	5	50)
							15	10	150)
J.14				5	5	25	5	5	25)
							15	10	150)
J.21	20	15	300				5	5	25)
							15	10	150)
							20	15	300)
J.28				5	5	25			
				15	10	150			
				10	15	150	10	15	150

Figure 3.2
Stock account according to F.I.F.O.

The entries in figure 2 are fairly self evident. The first issue of raw material, made on Jan 14th is priced at £5 per unit, because this is the cost price of the oldest unit in stock. The issue of 30 units on January 28th is priced in three portions. The first group of 5 units takes the price of £5 and so exhausts the quantity originally bought at that rate. The second group is priced at the next remaining oldest price of £10 and finally the last price of £15 is used for the third issue.

L.I.F.O.

The unit costs of issues is equal to the acquisition cost of most recent items taken into stock. It should be pointed out particularly that this is an assumed flow and is not to be taken as meaning that old items of stock are left lying around unused in order to satisfy the whims of accountants. The illustration for this is figure 3.3.

	Receipts				Issues			Stock		
Date	Units	Unit Price	£	Units	Unit Price	£	Units	Unit Price	£
J.1	10	5	50				10	5	50
J.7	15	10	150				(10	5	50
							(15	10	150
J.14				5	10	50	(10	5	50
							(10	10	100
J.21	20	15	300				(10	5	50
							(10	10	100
							(20	15	300
J.28				(20	15	300			
				(10	10	100	10	5	50

Figure 3.3
Stock account according to L.I.F.O.

In this example the first issue of 5 units is priced at the latest transaction cost of £10. This leaves 10 units of the receipts of January 7th and all the receipts of January 3rd 1st. The issue of 30 units is similarly costed at £15 up to the limit of 20 set by the last receipt and the remaining at £10 from the January 7th receipt. All the stock at the month end is at the price of the purchases made at the beginning of the month.

Replacement Cost

Here the unit cost of the transfer is equal to the current cost of acquisitions. That is to say the cost of buying in the market. Extra information is needed in the form of replacement costs at the date of issue. Let these be:

January 14	£12
January 28	16

Figure 3.4 illustrates the method.

	Receipts				Issues			Stock	
Date	Units	Unit Price	£	Units	Unit Price	£	Units	Unit Price	£
J.1	10	5	50				10	5	50
J.7	15	10	150						
	10	5	50(1)				25	10	250
J.14	25	2	50(2)	5	12	60	20	12	240
J.21	20	15	300						
	20	3	60(3)				40	15	600
J.28	40	1	40(4)	30	16	480	10	16	160

Figure 3.4

Stock account with replacement costs

Note (1) 10 units revalued to £10 each.
　　(2) 25 units revalued to　12 each.
　　(3) 20 units revalued to　15 each.
　　(4) 40 units revalued to　16 each.

On January 7th, 15 units are bought for £10 each and this necessitates an adjustment to the existing stock of 10 at £5 each. These 10 units are revalued up to £10 each, requiring a $10 \times 5 = £50$ debit to the stock account. On January 14th the 25 units in stock have to be revalued again, this time upwards to £12 each. The next purchase of 20 units January 21 causes another revaluation, as does the issue on January 30th.

The total of the revaluation during January is found by adding the figures for the periodic revaluations, namely £50 + £50 + £60 + £40 = £200. The corresponding credit would be to Stock Revaluation Reserve Account.

	Dr.	Cr.
Material account	£200	
Stock revaluation reserve account		£200

Adjustment to material account to allow for price changes in the period.

Average cost

A typical way of averaging costs is to calculate the average price for all units held of any new deliveries. See figure 3.5.

Receipts				Issues				Stock			
Date	Units	Unit Price	£	Units	Unit Price	£	Units	Unit Price	£		
J.1	10	5	50				10	5	50		
J.7	15	10	150				25	10	150		
(£200/25 = £8 average.							25	8	200		
J.14				5	8	40	20	8	160		
J.21	20	15	300				20	15	300		
(£460/40 = £11.5 average							40	11.5	460		
J.28				30	11.5	345	10	11.5	115		

Figure 3.5

Stock account according to average cost

When an issue is made on January 14th there are 25 units in stock and these have cost £200 in total. The average therefore is £200/25 = £8 and this is the price used for the issue. On January 28th there are 20 units at £8 plus the purchases of January 21st, 20 units at £15. The average is $(20 \times 8 + 20 \times 15)/40 = £11.5$.

Standard Cost

Standard costing is fully dealt with in chapters 8 to 10. If a price can be established that the material should be available at, then it can be used throughout the period. Differences between this standard cost and the actual figures have to be collected and these form the basis of reports requiring some explanation and corrective action. See figure 3.6.

Receipts				Issues				Stock			
Date	Units	Unit Price	£	Units	Unit Price	£	Units	Unit Price	£		
J.1	10	12	120				10	12	120		
J.7	15	12	180				25	12	300		
J.14				5	12	60	20	12	240		
J.21	20	12	240				40	12	480		
J.28				30	12	360	10	12	120		

Figure 3.6

Stock account according to standard costs.

There would be three related entries in the material price variance account. These amounts are the difference between the historic cost figures and the standard price of £12.

Material price variance account

Debit		Credit
J.1		$10 \times 7 = 70$
J.7		$15 \times 2 = 30$
J.21	$20 \times 3 = 60$	

Significance of Stock Pricing Methods

The results of using different pricing methods can be put together in order to make a comparison. See figure 3.7.

	Charge to Production £	Closing stock value £
F.I.F.O.	350	150
L.I.F.O.	450	50
Replacement	540	160
Average	385	115
Standard	420	120

Figure 3.7

On the example used for illustrating the different methods, prices have been rising. This is the prevailing state of the world and is causing considerable agitation for many reasons. One important reason is apparent from figure 3.7. The charge to production varies according to the material costing method used and this in turn affects profit. The lower the charge to production, the higher the profit and vice versa. Use of F.I.F.O. provides the smallest production charge and hence the largest profit. Unfortunately, an element of this profit is entirely identifiable with the change in prices rather than from operating expertise. Replacement cost figures take out this element of holding gain and match sales and costs at current prices.

The choice of method has been largely dominated by taxation rules existing and these vary through time and from country to country. In the United States L.I.F.O. has become acceptable to the Inland Revenue and similar trends towards accepting lower profit reporting methods in periods of rising prices are gradually being accepted in other parts of the world. In particular replacement cost methods are increasingly being advocated.

Valuation of work-in-progress and finished goods

Much of what has been said so far may appear to have been related to purchased items of stock. However, the same ideas should be used when dealing with Work-in-Progress and Finished Goods.

The value of Work-in-Progress is made up of labour and overheads as well as material. Usually on a monthly basis a figure of completed work-in-progress is transferred to Finished Goods. The amount to be transferred is collected through basic cost records. As with purchased stocks the pricing out can be on a F.I.F.O., average, L.I.F.O. standard or replacement cost basis. Similarly for the transfer from Finished Goods to Cost of Goods Sold.

Balance Sheet Values

Stock values on balance sheets are normally based on the costing method used, with an adjustment for items which are not going to cover their costs when sold. In formal terms, this is the 'lower of cost or market value' rule. This procedure is adopted in order to take immediate account of anticipated losses, whereas anticipated profits are ignored until they have been realised. This is in accordance with the conservative principle which accountants employ in their measurement processes.

The term market value used here can mean the cost of replacing the item, either by buying or manufacturing; alternatively it can mean the net realisable value, which is the amount for which it can be sold less the specific costs of disposal. In the case of the use of buying costs as the market value, the emphasis is being placed on the usefulness of the stock item as an income generator. Net realisable value concentrates on the recoverable value of the stock.

Accountants throughout the world use one or other of these methods, or a combination of the two. The most likely combination is to use the net realisable figure for finished goods and replacement cost for raw materials. Whatever method is used, it should be applied consistently and with full disclosure.

Chapter Summary

The cost of transfers between stock accounts is not simply one of recording it at acquisition cost. Prices change because of specific changes in supply and demand for a product and also because of general price level changes. The use of costing methods such as F.I.F.O. tends to report a profit which contains an element of gain through holding stock throughout a period of price rises. There is a strong movement towards using replacement costs, so that the profit reported is in terms of operating gains and holding gains. This provides a better assessment of managerial performance and discourages the distribution of cash dividends which are too high. Too high in the sense that they are eroding the productive capacity of the firm.

Exercise 3

Questions 1-5. (Answers provided)

3.1 Use data set out below to prepare the January entries for the relevant stock account. Prepare these entries using the F.I.F.O. method. Show values for receipts, issues and balance.

January	Receipt = R Issue = I	No. of Units	Unit Price £
1	R	50	3.00
7	R	50	3.02
10	I	40	?
14	R	50	3.02
17	I	70	?
21	R	50	3.03
24	I	80	?
28	R	50	3.04

3.2 Use the data contained in question 1 and repeat the exercise using the L.I.F.O. method.

3.3 Repeat again, this time using the weighted average cost method.

3.4 With this additional information of replacement costs, prepare the account on the replacement cost method.

January	£
10	3.02
17	3.03
24	3.04

3.5 The data for January and February operations of the Fabric department are set out below. Opening stock at 1 January was nil.

	January	February
Selling price/unit	£5	£5
Variable costs/unit	£1	£1
Fixed costs	£40,000	£40,000
Units sold	9,000	8,000
Units manufactured	10,000	8,000

Required: profit calculation for February assuming stock are valued at:
i) variable cost
ii) full cost using F.I.F.O.
iii) full cost using L.I.F.O.
iv) full cost using weighted average of the period.

Questions 3.6-3.10 Answers not provided

3.6 For six months ended 31st October, an importer and distributor of one type of washing machine has the following transactions in his records. There was an opening balance of 100 units which had a value of £3,900.

Date	Bought Quantity in units	Cost per unit £
May	100	41
June	200	50
August	400	51.875

The price of £51.875 each for the August receipt was £6.125 per unit less than the normal price because of the large quantity ordered.

Date	Sold Quantity in units	Price each £
July	250	64
September	350	70
October	100	74

From the information given above and using weighted average, FIFO and LIFO methods for pricing issues, you are required for each method to:

(a) show the stores ledger records including the closing stock balance and stock valuation;

(b) prepare in columnar format, trading accounts for the period to show the gross profit using each of the three methods of pricing issues;

(c) comment on which method, in the situation depicted, is regarded as the best measure of profit, and why.

ICMA(CA1).

3.7 From the information shown below which relates to component ABC, prepare statements using each of the following methods of stock accounting, viz.

(i) weighted average cost

(ii) standard cost

(iii) replacement cost

to show the following

(a) the amount to be charged to cost of production

(b) the value of the closing stock

(c) the difference, if any, between purchase cost and the aggregate of (a) and (b),

indicating how (c) would be dealt with in the accounts.

	Receipts into Stores units	Unit Cost	Issues to production units	Market unit price
		£		£
May 1	100	41		41
10	75	42		42
15			50	43
20			65	44
23	40	45		45
30			50	46

You may assume the company had no opening stock of component ABC and that in the case of method (ii) it is the company's practice to account for component ABC in terms of a standard unit cost of £40. CA(AC2).

3.8 Your company's purchasing officer is about to negotiate some long-term supply contracts for raw materials. He has asked for your advice on the rationale of quantity discounts and how quantitative techniques may be used in this connection.

You are required to prepare detailed notes for him in response to his request under the following headings:

(a) the buyer's costs incidental to purchasing;

(b) the supplier's cost incidental to selling;

(c) the basis for quantity discounts.

ICMA(MA2)

3.9 'With a few exceptions, the differences between inventory methods are merely ones of timing cost releases in relation to income determination' (from *Cost Accounting — a Managerial Emphasis* by C.T. Horngren).

Required:

A critical discussion of the main methods of transferring out the cost of stock.

CA(MA)

3.10 For the purpose of measuring business income it has been suggested that 'the use of LIFO and replacement cost depreciation will almost completely adjust for the misleading result obtained by applying the historical cost convention.'

You are required to:

(a) explain what is meant by 'the misleading result obtained by applying the historical cost convention';

(b) provide definitions of

(i) LIFO

(ii) replacement cost depreciation;

(c) explain how the use of the principles referred to will 'almost completely adjust for the misleading result obtained by applying the historical cost convention'.

CA(AC2)

Seminar Problem 3

The Grampian Co. Ltd. is planning to change its system of stock accounting from F.I.F.O. to an adaptation of replacement cost.

Stock items will be classified with groups and for each group an index of price changes will be maintained.

During 19X5 the original stock account for an item from group X, entered on F.I.F.O. principles was as shown in exhibit A. The index for group X for the year, prepared on a trial basis, was as follows:-

1	January	100
31	January	103
28	February	105
31	March	107
30	April	110
31	May	114
30	June	116
31	July	117
31	August	117
30	September	119
31	October	122
30	November	125
31	December	125

At the end of each month the stock on hand will be revalued at the replacement cost given by the index. During the month issues will be made at the index figure as it stood at the beginning of the month.

Required:

a) Calculate the entries as they would have been in 19X5 if the replacement method had been used in the way described.

b) Discuss the effect of using different stock accounting methods on
   i) production cost
   ii) final stock values
   in
   iii) a period of rising prices
   iv) a period of falling prices

Exhibit A
Stock Account — Item 1 — Group X
(Extract only)

	Receipts		Issues
Date	Qty.	Price	Qty.
		£	
Jan. 1	100	1.00	
Jan. 15			50
Feb. 1	80	1.03	
Feb. 15			60
Mar. 1	70	1.05	
Mar. 15			80
Apr. 1	70	1.07	
Apr. 15			70
May 1	70	1.10	
May 15			80
June 1	70	1.14	
June 16			70
July 1	60	1.16	
July 15			80
Aug. 1	70	1.17	
Aug. 15			80
Sep. 1	70	1.17	
Sept. 15			60
Oct. 1	50	1.19	
Oct. 15			60
Nov. 1	60	1.22	
Nov. 15			70
Dec. 1	70	1.25	
Dec. 15			60

Chapter 4

Labour and Direct Expense

Labour costs

The cost of labour is a significant factor in most unit costs and is of great concern to the management accountant. He needs to be knowledgeable about three aspects of these costs. First, there is the question of the way in which wages are calculated, that is the relationship between the gross wage and the work done. Second, what constitutes labour cost, in terms of gross pay, social security costs and other payments and deductions? Third, how are these elements handled in the accountant's record, in effect, what are the appropriate accounting entries?

Wage Systems

The large majority of people are paid in accordance with rules which are a combination of two main alternative systems. These two alternatives are payment by results and payment for time spent at work.

Payment by results

In its starkest form this consists of paying according to the quantity of good output achieved and can be expressed graphically as in figure 4.1.

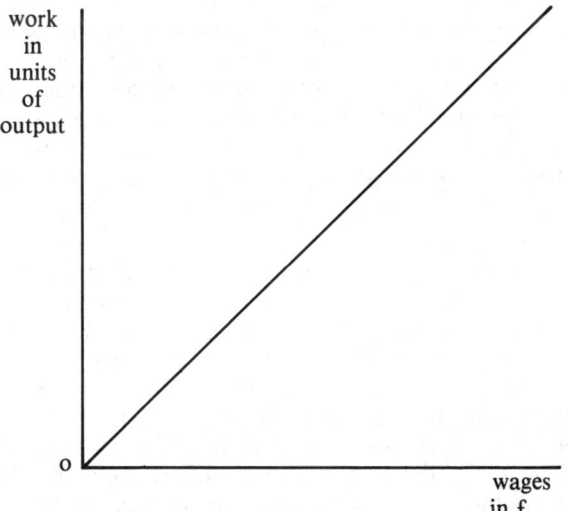

Figure 4.1 Payment at piece-work rates.

For each unit of work produced the same amount of money is added to the employee's wages. At its lowest point, this means no pay. As work is done the wages increase proportionately at a steady rate and the result is depicted on the graph as a straight line. In practice the disadvantages of such a system are so great that it is virtually non-existent in industry today. It is restricted to special cases such as work sub-contracted to individuals working at home. The most obvious objection concern the fairness of such a method of calculation and the effect on the quality of work done.

The question of fairness arises because frequently the cause of employees' idle time is purely an external one. Thus, for example, nil output can be the result of a break in the supply of components. Under such circumstances it would not be fair to withold pay and clearly unacceptable to the trade unions. It is usual to find that piecework is underpinned by a guaranteed minimum wage for an agreed period. The length of the period varies according to the strength of the parties to the agreement.

As for the quality of work done under piecework agreements, this is always going to be a problem when people are encouraged to work at fast rates. Inspection and quality control can be emphasized, but even at its best, this cannot resolve all the difficulties.

Adapted piece-work systems

The great advantage which piecework systems attempt to gain is to motivate the operators to high levels of achievement. It is a matter of personal experience with most people that payment by results does urge them on from relatively low to higher levels of achievement. According to the type of production and factory organisation involved, it is frequently useful to introduce some variant of pure piecework. Differential rates per unit dependent upon the level of working can sometimes be introduced. These are useful when the work is highly repetitive and easily measured in terms of a standard time. In these circumstances the individual is always motivated by possibilities of higher pay and from the management's point of view the advantage is in reducing labour cost per unit. Such systems do not work without limits, as people involved set their own levels of pay requirements versus work effort and seldom go beyond these self-imposed boundaries.

Standards

The basis of control over labour costs is in knowing what a cost *ought* to be. Another way of saying this, is that work done needs to be expressed in standard terms. This is the job of Work Study Engineers. They perform two related functions. First, they study the nature of the work and the methods employed and attempt to improve on the work flow and layout of equipment. This is termed a method study. Second, they measure the time required to perform a task. The final result of this measurement is the standard time allowed. If the standard time allowed for a specified task is one hour, then the quantity of work done in completing the task is one standard hour. Somebody working at twice the standard rate and completing the task twice within one hour, would have done two standard hours of work. A standard hour of work is a measure of work done and not a measure of time. A standard hour may be defined as the amount of which should be performed in one hour by a normal operator working in reasonable conditions. Since these are not closely defined terms, it follows that there is some degree of averaging and estimating in setting standard times. The usual method employed for setting standards is to average a large number of readings involving different work study engineers, operators and times of day and week. In this way, personal factors are smoothed out. In addition to this averaging process, allowances are included the time for personal requirements, fatigue and unavoidable delays.

Perhaps it should be emphasized that the average referred to above is one of measurement adjusted for the time-study engineers experienced opinion of the operators work rate. It is not a simple measurement of how long the job took. If that were the case, then there would be no defence against operators performing slowly when under observation.

Adapted piece work systems

In any system which is designed to increase productivity, the benefit to the employer comes from spreading the fixed overheads over a greater number of units produced. In straight piece work the increase in production results in higher wages to employees and a smaller share of overhead per unit. In time-rate systems, if production is increased the labour cost remains unaltered in total and the employer benefits from lower wage cost per unit as well as from lower overhead cost per unit. There are two variants in piece work which are designed to share the benefits in a way which falls between the two extremes outlined above. They are named after their developers, Halsey and Rowan.

The Halsey systems

Given a standard time for a unit of work done, it is possible to calculate how much time has been saved when the job is completed. It is this time saved, valued at the time-rate which is shared between employee and employer, according to some agreed proportion.

Example

Allowed time/unit:	1 hour
Rate/hour:	£2
Actual time taken:	45 mins.
Proportion:	50%

The rate of pay per unit is then calculated as:

$$\text{Time rate } £2 \times \tfrac{3}{4} = \qquad £1.50$$
$$\text{Bonus } (1-\tfrac{3}{4}) \times £2 \times 50\% = \qquad \underline{25}$$
$$\underline{£1.75}$$

The bonus formula is:

(time allowed — time taken) $\times$ time-rate $\times$ $\times$ %

In this example the rate/unit of output is £1.75 for labour, rather than £2 in piece work.

The Rowan system

Here the system is designed to dampen down the bonus at higher levels of output and appeals to employers in situations where there are severe reservations about the accuracy of the standards. As in the Halsey system as bonus is calculated, but this time the percentage used is given by the rate of time taken to time allowed.

Example

Using the same data as given for the Halsey example, the rate of pay is now calculated as:

Rate/unit,

$$\text{Time rate } £2 \times \tfrac{3}{4} = \qquad £1.500$$
$$\text{Bonus } (1 - \tfrac{3}{4}) \times £2 \times \tfrac{45}{60} = \qquad \underline{.375}$$
$$\underline{£1.875}$$

As the time saved increases, the bonus also increases until the job is being performed at twice the standard rate. After which any further saving in time would actually reduce the bonus. This can be demonstrated easily:

Let X be the time taken.

Let Y be the time allowed.

Bonus, $B = (Y - X) \times \tfrac{X}{Y} \times £R$.

$B = (X - \tfrac{X^2}{Y}) \times R$ where Y and R are constant.

Differentiating:

$\frac{dB}{dX} = (1 - \tfrac{2X}{Y}) \times R$ and $\frac{dB}{dX} = 0$ when $X = \tfrac{1}{2} Y$.

At this point the bonus is a maximum. Note that $\dfrac{d^2B}{dX^2} = - \dfrac{2R}{Y}$ which is negative, as it must be if the point $X = \dfrac{Y}{2}$ is to be a maximum.

Group Bonus Schemes

Not all workers can be associated with individual piecework schemes, either because their work is not easily measured in terms of production or because they work in teams and individual effort cannot be measured. In such cases a gang or team or larger group can be associated and share a group bonus between them. Such bonuses are calculated according to output achieved. Clearly the output must be definitively associated with the group, to avoid the confusion that could result from overlap.

These group bonus schemes can be extended to include the associated indirect workers, such as supervisors and store-keepers. Without these extensions, unfortunate anomalies can occur which are certain to cause considerable labour problems. It is a central feature of incentive schemes that they inevitably have a ripple effect throughout the firm's labour force.

Profit Sharing and Co-Partnership Schemes

In the simplest version of profit sharing the firm issues a bonus to all its employess based on a formula involving profits and wages. The bonus usually takes the form of a percentage of the annual wage, paid in a lump sum. Such schemes are popular at pay-out time and create goodwill amongst employees, but they are remote from day to day working and are felt to have little influence on productivity.

Some schemes go further towards involving employees in the success of the company by encouraging the employees to become shareholders. This can be done either by issuing shares as a bonus or by offering shares at some discount rate. Again these schemes tend to be remote from the daily problems of the workforce. The size of an individual's shareholding is likely to be so small that it will not significantly alter his attitude to his firm as his employer. His theoretical position as shareholder and therefore part-owner is so weak in practice as to have no significance.

Trade Unions are fairly lukewarm about these share-owning schemes and prefer to concentrate on negotiated wages, manning levels and working conditions. It is possible that their attitude would change if there were a significant alteration in size of bonus share issues, but then existing shareholders would offer total resistance since they would be losing control of the company.

Measured Day Work

Despite the adaptations introduced in such systems as Rowan and Halsey, there is a steady present day movement towards paying a fixed wage based on time, with augmentation from group productivity schemes. There are two main sources of pressure, acting in this direction. Opposition to piecework schemes from Trade Unions, who traditionally are opposed to concentrating work into few hands whilst there is unemployment in the general economy. Trade Unions also resist the tendency to put their members into situation of risk of industrial injury. There is always the fear that people anxious to increase their wages are prone to take unnecessary risks and can become impatient with safety regulations and precautions.

Firms, too, find difficulties about piece rate systems. Their main objection is one of cost, since these schemes are costly to run, entailing as they do considerable requirements with regard to maintaining records of individual performance.

Measured Day Work is the result of these pressures. In essence the management and labour representatives agree that for specified wage rates and manning levels, the labour force will achieve a certain level of output. Incentives are built in by agreeing bonuses for achievement over and above the agreed level of output.

Graphical Illustration

A summary of the different systems is presented in graphical form in figure 4.2. This shows the way in which weekly wages vary as productivity increases, according to the wage system used.

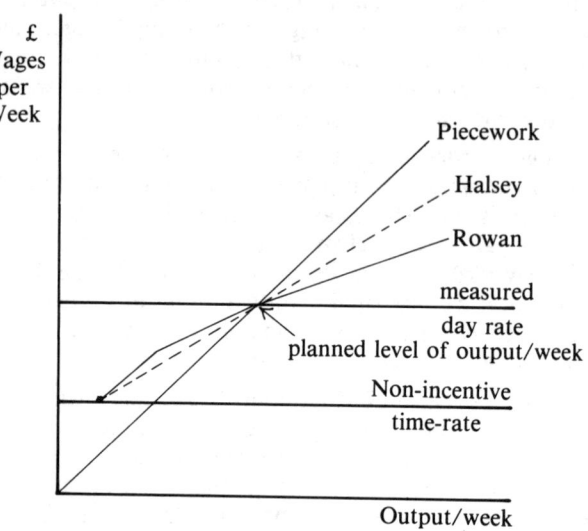

Figure 4.2

Whatever method of wage calculation is used, the management have a plan, usually in the form of an attainable target. Whichever incentive wage method is employed it will tend to give the same results around this planned level and will only deviate markedly when productivity is widely away from.

The Constituents of Labour Cost

Employee's regard their monetary reward as consisting of gross pay less deductions, employers' contribution to social security and pension funds and holiday pay. Furthermore, the gross pay will include overtime premiums and bonuses. Deductions will consist of income tax, pension contributions and social security payments.

The employer has to account for these costs according to very stringent requirements of accuracy, because of the necessity to make correct and timely payment to the labour force on a regular weekly to monthly basis. In addition, the handling of income tax deductions and pension contributions also requires strictly accurate accounting. Failure to calculate wages correctly and to pay them promptly would ruin a firm immediately. It follows then that strict payroll procedures are required.

Time Recording

The first essential is a record of time to be paid for. This is usually obtained by requiring employees to use time clocks. These are clocks which print the time on cards when they are inserted. Employees when reporting for work, take their own clock card, insert them in the machine and place them in the rack on the factory side of the clock. On leaving, the process is reversed and the cards are left on the other side, awaiting the next time of use.

The time clock card gives the total time for payment. In addition, the manner in which time was spent is often required. The time spent on different jobs or processes, plus the time spent on other activities and how much time may have been idle. This analysis is usually recorded on time tickets or time sheets.

The clock cards for wage payment and the time tickets for cost analysis should be reconciled before being sent to the appropriate section for processing.

Payroll Accounting Entries

For each pay period, the wages department would produce the following data:

Gross employee pay.
Employers contribution to Social Security.
Employers contributions to Pension Funds.

This amounts to the total labour cost and is balanced by the sum of deductions and cash payments.

Assume that a firm's payroll for a particular week is as follows:

Gross Pay	£55,459
Employers Social Security	2,964
Employers Pension Fund	3,919
Employee Social Security	2,616
Employee Pension Fund	3,014
Employee Income Tax	10,140
Employee Union dues	406
Cash payment	39,283

To record this payroll must show amounts due to third parties for later settlement. The appropriate ledger accounts would be:

Wages Payable

Cash and deductions	55,459	Analysed and debited to work-in progress and overhead accounts

Social Security (Employer) Expense

Department of Social Security a/c	2,964	As for wages payable

Pension Fund (Employer) Contribution

Pension Fund Ltd.,	3,919	As for wages payable.

Department of Social Security

| Account settled with department, periodically | Wages (employee contribution) | 2,616 |
| | Employer contribution | 2,964 |

Trade Union

As above	Wages	406

Pension Fund Ltd.

| As above | Wages (employee contribution) | 3,014 |
| | Employer contribution | 3,919 |

Inland Revenue (PAYE)

As above	Wages	10,140

Cash (extract)

	Wages	39,283

The balances on the Pension Fund Limited account, the Social Security, Inland Revenue and Trade Unions each represents amounts due to those bodies. Insofar as they are not paid they are included as part of the firm's creditors.

Payroll Analysis

The total debits on wages payable and the employer contributions to Social Security and Pension Funds are the firm's labour cost and must be analysed. Here it is only necessary to distinguish between direct labour cost of the product and indirect labour cost. The way in which these are accumulated and added to product costs will be dealt with in later chapters.

The cost of time spent by labour on production is the direct labour cost. This means that cost which can be attributed to some job or process with reasonable accuracy and not after undue expense of tracing. The main part of gross pay of the factory operatives comes into this category. Ancilliary workers such as storekeepers and clerks are usually equally clearly classed as indirect labour.

Some elements of pay are capable of being treated on either category and it is worthwhile considering a selection of these to illustrate the points of principle.

Overtime Premiums

There is no doubt about this being a manufacturing cost, but should it apply specifically to the jobs or process on which it was incurred, or should it be shared over a wider range? The answer is usually provided by the particular set of circumstances. When the overtime is required to meet a specific deadline on a job for which the customer has agreed to pay a premium, then the job should be charged with the overtime pay. In other cases the work done in the overtime period appears randomly, that is it is next in line for completion, in which case all the jobs performed in the wider accounting period should bear some of the cost of overtime.

Holiday Pay for Direct Labour

This is a seasonal cost which needs special treatment in order to avoid a degree of distortion in reports which include substantial holiday periods. The normal situation is for a firm to have at least one plant shut down during the year and, increasingly, it is becoming two. Suppose then, that the workforce operates in work for around 80% of the available week-days of the year and receives its pay in regular weekly payments for the fifty-two weeks in the year. This would require the debit for gross wages to be increased by 25% with a corresponding credit to Holiday Pay Account. In the accounting period containing holiday payments the appropriate amount would be debited to this account. In this way, the debits to work-in-progress from Wages Account would include the holiday pay.

Social Security and Pension Fund Contributions

The employers contribution to social security and pension funds are usually treated as overheads, appropriate to the classification of labour. The manufacturing labour, both direct and indirect to the product, having their employers contributions added to manufacturing overhead. Similarly with selling, distribution etc.

For more precise costing it would be necessary to charge the contribution directly to work-in-progress and, thus, to jobs and processes. This would incur additional expense which is not normally thought to be justified.

Idle Time

It is impossible to organise a factory so tightly that the direct labour force does not spend some of its time without work to do. This time should be accounted for at the labour cost and debited to idle time accounts. It is usually possible to designate some of this as normal, the rest, therefore, being abnormal. The normal idle time is an acceptable allowance requiring no explanation, anything above that is abnormal and needs to be explained. The two categories are usually treated as factory overheads and included as product costs. It is reasonable, though, to identify the abnormal costs as period costs and not to include them as part of the cost of manufacture.

The appropriate accounting entry is:

	Dr.	Cr.
Idle time — normal	4,000	
Idle time — abnormal	1,000	
Wages payable		5,000

The abnormal idle time would then be explained in terms of causes through machine failure, failure in component flow and such like.

Direct Expense

Expenses are the cost of services including a notional cost for the use of owned assets and, in the usual way, if they are traced to a product, then they are classed as direct. In most cases the expenses are indirect and even when they are direct, no special principle is involved. A good example of a direct expense is the hire of plant for a specific job or contract. Clearly the whole expense of hire is to be charged against the contract.

The idea of notional charges for assets owned is probably not new to the student. It is a measure of the cost consumed or the benefit received during the period. The commonest example is depreciation of fixed assets, a subject which will already have been studied in an introductory financial accounting course. In the case of factory buildings which are owned, the opportunity cost of renting out should be charged against production. This amount should be net of building depreciation and maintenance. Failure to charge for the use of owned buildings will give misleadingly low production costs. Whether these notional charges are direct or indirect depends on the individual circumstances and decisions will be made according to criteria previously discussed.

Chapter Summary

Strong pressure from the workforce ensures that wage calculations are accurate and that payment is prompt. Wage systems are forced to cope with these requirements and, as a consequence, can be easily extended to give an analysis of the work that has been performed.

An important feature of labour control is the ability to assess the value of work in terms of standards. Comparisons of actual work performed against standards is a valuable form of control. This is mainly dealt with in later chapters, but the groundwork is laid in this chapter with the description of work study techniques.

Payment systems play an important part in encouraging high productivity and the general principles involved have been put forward.

Exercises 4

Questions 1-5. (Answers provided)

4.1 The Swallow Company pays its direct labour force a guaranteed minimum wage of £60 a week. In addition it is paid a bonus of £1 for each hour of production time saved. What amount would each of the following employees earn?

Employee	Hours worked	Standard output/hour	Actual output
R	40	60	3000
S	42	60	3300
T	40	60	2350

4.2 The Swift Company operates a Halsey type pay system with the time saved element divided 60%/40% between the employee/employer. The hourly rate is £2. Calculate payments to each of the following:

Employee	Hours worked	Standard and time/unit	Units produced
U	40	1 hour	80
V	40	1 hour	60
W	36	1 hour	48

4.3 In the Martin Company pay is calculated according to the Rowan system. Use the data given in 4.2 to calculate pay.

4.4 A team of workmen in the company are paid a group bonus as well as an hourly rate. The bonus is calculated by establishing the amount by which the group exceeds its standard, expressed as a percentage. Seventy-five percent of this calculated figure is then applied to the basic hourly rate to give the bonus rate. The group record for a week is given below. Calculate the total wages of X, Y and Z whose details of work are also given.

Group:	Hours worked	Units produced	Standard output/hour
	420	28,000	60
		basic rate per hour	
Individual X	42	1.50	
Y	44	1.70	
Z	40	1.40	

4.5 Time allowed   1 hour
Rate/hour   £2

Graph time taken against bonus earned for intervals of 10 minutes between thirty and sixty minutes. The firm operates the Rowan system.

Questions (4.6-4.10) Answers not provided

4.6 Due to recession in its industry, which has caused a reduction in its sales, a manufacturing company is proposing to reduce by one-fifth its productive capacity, as measured in terms of the number of direct labour hours of its operators.

It is considering doing this by either:

(a) putting some of its operators on short time; or

(b) making a number of its operators redundant through dismissal.

You are required to compare and contrast in tabular form the effects that each course of action is likely to have on the composition and level of the company's total annual:

(i) direct materials cost;

(ii) direct wages;

(iii) production overhead;

(iv) other (non-production) overhead.

ICMA(CA2).

4.7 (a) In the context of the output from a factory or group of workers, define and distinguish 'production' and 'productivity'.

(b) X Y and Z are the members of a team making metal brackets. The expected output of the team is 6,000 brackets per week, each member working a 40 hour week and being paid a basic rate of £1.75 for each hour worked. A bonus of 50% of the team's productivity index in excess of 100 is added as a percentage to the basic hourly rate.

During week No. 50, X worked 40 hours, Y 39 hours and Z 38 hours and the output for the week was 6,786 brackets.

You are required to calculate for week No. 50:

(i) the team's productivity index

(ii) the effective hourly rate paid to the operatives

(iii) the wages rate and efficiency variances of the team

(c) Name the type of bonus scheme under which the members of the team are remunerated and demonstrate your understanding of the characteristics of that scheme by reference to your answer to (b). CA(AC2).

4.8 (a) Recent regulations affecting pay policies are causing many businesses to re-examine the use of incentive schemes as a method of remunerating employees. Discuss the general principles which should be applied to incentive schemes.

(b) Certain organisations, for example car manufacturers, have abandoned premium bonus schemes and piece work schemes and substituted a 'high day rate' system. List the advantages and disadvantages expected from following such a policy.

ICMA(CA1).

4.9 A company selling chemicals direct to farmers remunerates its field sales force on a commission and year end bonus basis. The commission is 20% of standard gross margin (planned selling price less the standard cost of goods sold on a full absorption cost basis), contingent only on the collection of the account. A customer's credit is approved by the company's credit department. Price concessions are granted on occasion by the top sales management, but sales commission is not reduced by the granting of such discounts. A year end bonus of 15% of commissions earned is paid to salesmen who equal or exceed their annual sales target or quota. The annual sales target is usually established by applying approximately a 5% increase to the previous year's sales.

You are required to state with reasons:

(a) what features of this remuneration plan are likely to be effective in motivating the salesmen to help meet the company's goals of higher profits and return on investment, and

(b) what features are likely to be counter effective.

ICAEW(MA)

4.10 A company has decided to install semi-automatic machines to replace its existing manually controlled ones now producing long runs of identical products.

From the information given below you are required to state:

(a) the unit cost for both the existing and the replacement machines with one operator to each machine;

(b) the maximum number of the semi-automatic machines each operator should control to minimise the units cost of production;

(c) the hourly bonus that could be offered to the operators to undertake the multi-machine control operations on the basis that they would receive one quarter of the saving obtained against existing units costs.

The following data are given: Standard times, for one operator to handle on machine to produce one unit: Operation:	Existing manual machine, minutes	New semi- automatic machine, minutes
Loading unit on machine	8.5	2.5
Machining	25.0	17.0
Unloading finished unit from machine	2.5	1.5
Inspecting unit	2.5	2.5
Greasing and placing unit into storage box	1.5	1.5
Rates per hour:	£	£
Machine hour rate, overhead	1.68	4.50
Wage of operator	1.50	1.50

The new machines will be so located that the walking time between machines can be ignored.

ICMA(MA2)

Seminar Problem 4

The Migrants company produces a single item. In the year ended 31st December 19X5 it made a net profit of £60,000 as shown.

	£
Sales	500,000
Cost of Goods Sold	260,000
	240,000
Less: selling and administration expenses:	
Variable	60,000
Fixed	120,000
Net profit	60,000

In July 19X6 the company is engaged in wage negotiations with union representatives. The company accountant has prepared the following brief for the company negotiators:

Cost data for 19X5 show that unit cost of direct labour was £0.60. The full details are shown in the table.

	Total costs £	Unit costs £
Materials	100,000	1.00
Direct labour	60,000	0.60
Variable manufacturing overhead	30,000	.30
Fixed manufacturing overhead	100,000	1.00
	290,000	2.90

The average hourly direct labour cost was £2.00.

The company has offered the union negotiators a new wage structure based on piece-work with a rate of 50p per unit. The original union claim is for 10% on the hourly wage rate. Consultant engineers have advised the company that the piece-work plan would give a 10% increase in labour productivity.

Selling prices and other costs will remain as for 19X5, as will sales and production volumes.

Required

Advise the company negotiators on the relative profitability of the two schemes outlined above. If the union negotiators show an interest in the piece-work scheme, how high should the company be prepared to go in raising the rate/unit, assuming that the 10% productivity increase will persist over a relatively wide band and that profits must be at least £50,000.

Chapter 5

Manufacturing Overheads

The nature of manufacturing overheads was discussed in chapter 1. Many firms operate absorption or full costing systems in order to include all such overhead in the stock values and, thus, in their reports on production costs.

Ideally indirect costs of manufacture should never occur. All the factory costs should be traced directly to the appropriate job or process. There are two identifiable reasons why this ideal state does not exist in practice. Some costs are just impossible to trace to a product. An example of this is the factory general manager. Other costs are capable of being traced, but at such high processing costs as to make it not a worthwhile proposition. Small and frequently used materials such as glue or screws could be given as examples.

Accepting then, that indirect costs of manufacturer are to be included as production cost, how is this to be done? The objective is to find some equitable way of attaching to each unit of output a proportion of these overheads. Each unit is to bear its fair share of manufacturing overhead cost. It follows that if the process is to be one of sharing out in some reasonable way, that the resultant cost is going to be an average and not a precise figure. By its very nature, such an averaging process does not give information which can be used in specific instances of decision making and control. The main purpose of spreading these overheads onto products is to provide stock values for periodic income reporting and long-term guides to pricing and company profitability.

Cost Centres

These have been defined as a "location, person or item of equipment (or group of these) for which costs may be ascertained and used for the purposes of cost control". For the moment these cost centres will be considered within the framework of cost accumulation. The organisation needs to divide into these first centres in such a way that there is neither overlap nor gap between any two of them. Cost centres form the base of the accumulation system. Later the idea of control will be emphasized and responsibility centres will be introduced. For the moment though, the consideration is of cost collection. There are two types of cost centres: product and service.

Product Cost Centre

These are the producing or operating departments. The firm's products pass through these and are processed in them.

Service Cost Centres

Simply the rest of the firm. They help the production departments by providing services such as maintenance, data processing, canteen facilities and many more. Most firms include a number of umbrella type centres to include the general overhead factory costs, a sort of miscellaneous cost centre. In this way there is an initial and unique home for every cost.

Apportionment and Allocation of Overheads

The process of including an equitable share of overheads in production costs is divided into two stages. Stage 1 is to divide the costs between the cost centres and then to further share the service cost centres between the product cost centres. In this way all the manufacturing overhead is associated with products. This is done according to some formula which tries to share the cost according to benefits received and is called apportionment.

The next step is to attach a share of these product cost centre totals to the periods production and this is called allocation.

The Apportionment of Overheads

The factory overheads consist of a fairly wide variety of types and, as a consequence of this variety, there are a number of different bases for dividing them between cost centres. Some may relate entirely to one department, for example a departmental supervisor. Others may cover every centre in the factory, an obvious example of this would be the rent. In between these clear out examples there are all shades of mix between the two.

For some of these it may be worthwhile performing a direct measurement. Perhaps a supervisor shares his time between centres and can keep a reasonably accurate record of how his time is divided. This type of overhead is called direct to the cost centre. Alternatively, the word 'traced' can be used, giving it the term 'a traced cost'.

The expenses which cannot reasonably be traced in a direct manner to the centres have to be apportioned. This process of apportionment involves finding some method of equitably dividing the cost as opposed to a more exact form of measurement. Further examples of this class of expenditure are heating, power, depreciation of buildings, general management of the factory etc.

The general principle of the technique involved is to connect the item of expense with some associated thing which can be measured. One item of expense is rent and an obvious thing to associate this with is floor space or alternatively cubic capacity. There are a wide variety of methods used in practice, but a much smaller number of general categories can be identified.

Space

Rent and rates can be associated with the area occupied by cost centres. Sometimes volume could be more appropriate, as with heating costs.

Personnel

These can be either the number of people or the total wages paid. Canteen costs could be related to numbers, whilst pension contributions would be a percentage of wages.

Materials

The quantity or value of materials issued could be used to apportion store-keeping costs and other material related costs.

Activity

Many costs vary in some way with activity levels measured by machine capacity and running time. This could apply to power costs which have not been measured directly by the use of separate metres for each using centre.

Taking the number of people employed as a base as an example, the process can be illustrated with these figures:—

The factory employs 200 people. Certain personal services, e.g. dentistry, are provided free of charge. The figures for a quarter year are as follows—

$$\text{cost centre 1} - 50 \text{ employees}$$
$$\text{cost centre 2} - 100 \text{ employees}$$
$$\text{cost centre 3} - 25 \text{ employees}$$
$$\text{cost centre 4} - 25 \text{ employees}$$

Total cost of the service = £1,000.

The results of the apportionment are easily obtained by simple arithmetic

$$\text{For cost centre 1} - £(50/200 \times 1,000) = 250$$
$$\text{For cost centre 2} - (100/200 \times 1,000) = 500$$
$$\text{For cost centre 3} - (25/200 \times 1,000) = 125$$
$$\text{For cost centre 4} - (25/200 \times 1,000) = 125$$
$$£1,000$$

Figure 5.1 shows the stages that have been described so far.

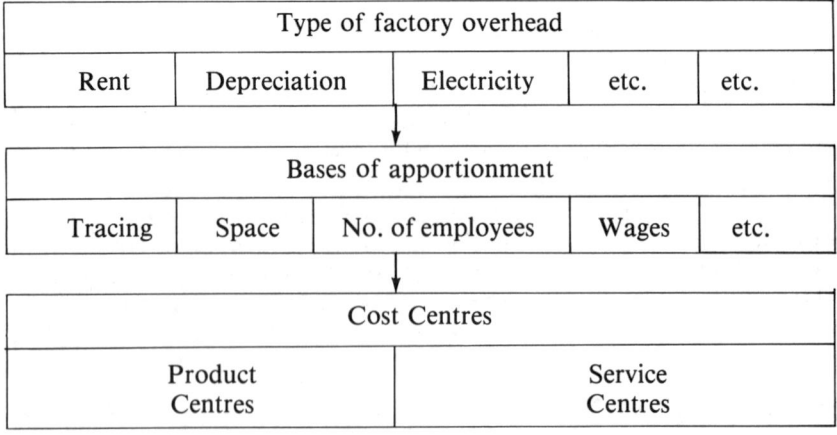

Figure 5.1 Apportionment of factory overheads to cost centres

Continuing towards the objective of arriving at an average historic cost for each unit for production, the next stage is to re-apportion the service centres between the product centres. There are no new ideas involved here and an illustration should be sufficient to make the process clear.

A firm has four production departments and a canteen. Statistics for the four production departments are:-

	no. of employees	Average earnings £	Total earnings £
cutting	10	1,800	18,000
dressmaking	90	967	87,000
coatmaking	90	967	87,000
packing	10	800	8,000

and the cost of the canteen is £5,500.

If the number of employees is chosen as the basis, the apportionment is a simple arithmetic exercise of dividing the £5,500 between the production departments in preportion to the number of employees. The result would be as follows:-

		£
cutting	$10/200 \times 5,500 =$	275
dressmaking	$90/200 \times 5,500 =$	2,475
coatmaking	$90/200 \times 5,500 =$	2,475
packing	$10/200 \times 5,500 =$	275
		5,500

The basis of division could have been relative total earnings instead of the number of employees.

In the example just given the problem was simplified by having only one service department. What happens if there is more than one? Figure 5.2 illustrates the situation.

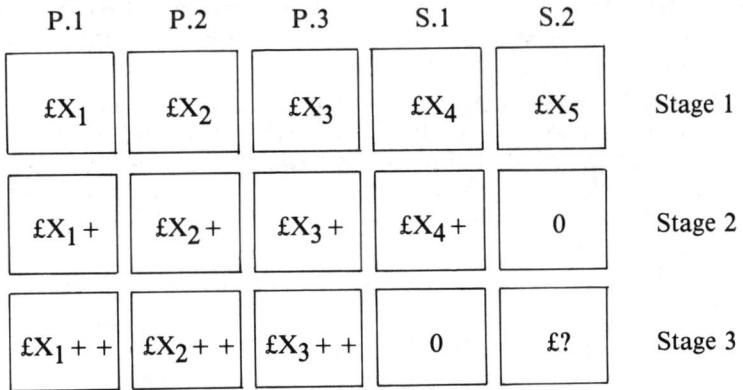

Figure 5.2 Apportionment with more than one service centre

At stage 1 the five cost centres are shown. Three are product centres and the problem is to share the costs of the two service centres between these three product centres.

At stage 2 the second service centre has been reduced to nil.

At stage 3 the first service centre is transferred in turn to the other departments. Unfortunately, since service departments usually operate on behalf of the other service departments (witness the data processors use the canteen), some of the second transfer goes into service centre 2.

This process could go on indefinitely, although with ever reducing amounts being involved.

There are four approaches to dealing with this situation. The first has already been described above, but as soon as the figures are judged to be insignificant a cut off is applied.

The step-down method is a first approximation to this, closing service departments in turn without allowing any form of 'echo back'. Once a service department has been closed, it is treated as being no longer in existence. The least significant cost centres are dealt with first.

The third method involves a cruder approximation, in which the service departments are regarded as providing useful service to product centres only. This means that the total for each service department is divided in some way between product centres and other service centres are ignored.

The fourth and final way is to set up the equations relating the departments to each other, that is using the proportions involved in apportioning. These may be solved in the usual algebraic way, or by use of matrix algebra in the more general case. It is questionable as to whether this procedure is justified in view of the somewhat arbitrary basis on which the original sharing has been conducted.

Allocation of Factory Overheads to Jobs

The apportionment routine has collected all the factory overheads within the product cost centres. The final task is to allocate these to the jobs as they pass through the firms' operations.

This is done by calculating an overhead rate and applying this to the jobs. The need is to establish a relationship between something which has been measured directly to a unit of production and the indirect costs which have been apportioned to product centres. For instance there is close measurement of direct labour hours, direct material consumed, machine hours utilised. Each of these will do according to circumstances. Additionally, derived measures such as direct labour cost fulfil the requirements.

Suppose that a specified period has these results:-

	Department	
	A	B
Total overhead	£39,000	£36,000
Machine hours	20,000	1,000
Direct labour hours	9,500	36,000
Direct labour cost	£19,500	£72,000

Department A is machine dominated and for each machine hour used on the job £1.950 should be allocated. In department B, labour predominates and overheads are allocated at the rate of 50% of direct labour cost. This rate can alternatively be stated as £1.00 per direct labour hour.

Predetermined Overheads

The normal procedure is to calculate these absorption rates in advance and then to use them throughout the ensuing year. If the information used is entirely historic then the allocation to jobs is the analysis of the total overhead apportioned to the product centre. However, this has the disadvantage of being affected by seasonal variations. If costs of production are to be used to help in long run decisions, then it would be helpful to iron out the seasonal differences. This is done by taking estimates of factory overheads over a complete season and dividing this by estimated directed labour hours or whatever is to be used. This provides a predetermined absorption rate.

The use of a rate known in advance of a month end also speeds up the reporting process. This is a useful bonus, even though the value of information about average unit costs is strictly limited for control and decision making purposes.

Additionally, the use of one rate saves the work of recalculating a rate for every month.

Under-over absorption

It is not likely to happen that estimates will be exactly right, either more overheads will be charged to production (over absorption) or the converse of under-absorption will occur.

All that remains to be considered now is the treatment of the under/over absorbed figure. There are three possibilities:-

1) transfer the over/under absorption to the profit and loss account for the period
2) divide the amount proportionately to raw material stock, work-in-progress, finished goods and cost of goods sold. Base the proportions on period end balances
3) carry the difference forward to the next period.

The first method is applicable at the year end if the difference is regarded as being due to failure or success in achievement. In the second case the original application rates are regarded as being wrong. The third way is for interim profit reports (i.e. monthly or quarterly) where it is expected that the normal seasonal variations will cancel out in future periods.

Illustration

The process of apportionment and allocation can now be drawn together into a single illustration. The amounts given in figure 5.3 are estimates for the coming year, based on expectations of future costs, but naturally heavily influenced by the experience of past costs.

Cost	Total	Production Centres				Service Centres	
		P1	P2	P3	P4	S1	S2
Indirect Material	£ 3,000	500	500	500	900	200	300
Indirect Labour	5,000	600	700	700	1,000	1,500	500
Indirect Expenses	4,000	500	500	600	400	1,000	1,000
	12,000	1,600	1,700	1,900	2,300	2,700	1,800
S.2	—	300	400	300	400	400	(1,800)
S.1	—	700	800	800	800	(3,100)	—
	12,000	2,600	2,900	3,000	3,500	—	—
Direct labour cost	£5,700	£1,500	£1,500	£1,700	£2,000		
Overhead rate as %age of direct labour cost		173%	193%	176%	175%		

Figure 5.3 Illustration of overhead rate.

Since these departmental absorption rates are usually calculated in advance there is obviously a problem in choosing an appropriate level of activity or volume of business. There are three possible levels to choose from:

The actual anticipated level — using this figure, the amount added to direct units costs could fluctuate widely from year to year. In a period of low activity, the fixed part of overhead costs would be loaded more heavily onto unit costs, probably at a time when prices were depressed.

The normal volume — the average volume over a period of years and which the management would be prepared to regard as satisfactory.

The ideal volume — a target volume not expected to be attained.

The most useful of these concepts is the normal volume. By using this the charge to production for fixed overheads assumes the nature of a standard and eliminates the affect of fluctuations in activity. The difference between the amount absorbed and the actual fixed overheads is then shown as a volume variance.

Chapter Summary

In the absorption or full cost system, all manufacturing overheads are included as part of the cost of the goods produced and are included in their value for profit calculating purposes. Unfortunately, not all costs can be directly associated with products and some have to be averaged out. The steps in this process are as follows:

1) Trace as many costs as is feasible to the products — these are direct.

2) Divide the firm into cost centres.

3) Apportion all the remaining, that is the indirect, costs between all the cost centres.

4) Re-apportion the service centres amongst the product centres.

5) Apply a measure of activity to the totals in order to obtain an absorption rate.

This can be performed on a historic cost basis, but there are three major disadvantages to doing this. The process has to be repealed monthly, it is slow to produce reports and it does not cope automatically with seasonal fluctuations. The more usual process is to estimate the figure in advance and use a predetermined rate throughout the year. Of course, the amount absorbed using this rate will never equal the amount actually spent and it is necessary to handle amounts under/over absorbed.

The information produced about unit costs is of limited value. It is only an average for the period and should not be used on making decisions about prices or levels of production. The information relevant for this will be discussed in later chapters. Nor can average costs of a product be of much use in control. Again they are averages of historic costs with some element of estimation in them. They lack information about standards and are divorced from such concepts of managerial responsibility and controllability, which, again, is something to be looked at later.

In conclusion, the information gained from fixed overhead absorption is of limited value only. Therefore, the cost of these procedures should always be related to the benefits gained. Refinements of method are not likely to be justified, since they almost invariably cost money and bring in a spurious accuracy in results.

Exercises 5
Questions 1-5. (Answers provided)

5.1 The Thames Company has three product cost centres and two service cost centres. The company factory overheads budgeted for a period are as follows:

	£
Rent and rates	6,000
Heating	3,000
Power	10,000
Depreciation of machinery	10,000
Indirect labour cost	18,000
Miscellaneous	3,000

The following information is available for help in apportionment:

	P_1	P_2	P_3	S_1	S_2	Total
Floor space	2,000	2,000	2,000	1,000	1,000	8,000
Cubic capacity	20,000	20,000	15,000	5,000	5,000	65,000
Machine H.P.	150	60	30	50	10	300
Machine values (£)	50,000	20,000	20,000	30,000	130,000	250,000
Direct labour hours	2,000	2,000	3,000	1,000	1,000	9,000

Required: apportion the overheads to these five departments.

5.2 Use the information given below and the apportionment of 5.1 to re-apportion the service centres to the cost centres.

The expense of S_1 and S_2 are apportioned as follows:

	P_1	P_2	P_3	S_1	S_2
S_1	40	20	20	—	20
S_2	30	30	30	30	—

5.3 Given that the direct material cost of the finished product of the Thames company is £60 and the direct labour cost is £100, what is the total cost? (Use the information from 5.1 and 5.2 to calculate the overhead cost).

5.4 The Mersey Company has prepared the following budget for 19X5:

	£
Sales	100,000
Variable factory expenses	25,000
Fixed factory expenses	80,000
Stock change	NIL
	units
Production	50,000

During the year the actual expenditure of factory overheads was £110,000 and the over-absorption was £5,500. How many units were produced? Ignore work-in-progress.

5.5 The Severn Company reported the following data for the month of January 19X5.

	£
Sales	50,000
Cost of goods sold	40,000
Factory overhead spent	10,000
Factory overhead absorbed	9,700
Selling and administration expenses	4,000
Work-in-progress	1,000
Finished goods stock	10,000

Prepare the profit and loss for January:

a) assuming the under-absorbed overhead is carried forward to later periods.

b) it is immediately charged to the period.

Questions 5.6-5.10 Answers not provided

5.6 The chairman of your company has been studying the budgets for the next accounting period and has shown particular interest in the production cost budget. In this the production overhead will increase from the current absorption rate of 200% of direct wages cost to 300%. The production manager protests that this increase is unacceptable.

As company cost accountant prepare a brief report for the chairman explaining:

(a) how the overhead absorption rate is calculated and used;

(b) which factors may have contributed to the increase in the rate;

(c) the circumstances in which such an increase can be acceptable.

ICMA(CA1).

5.7 AC Engineering Company Limited manufactures a wide variety of products. You have recently been appointed management accountant of the company and are concerned with the current method of absorbing production overhead.

You are required to prepare for the next board meeting of the company a report in which you should discuss briefly five methods of overhead absorption, and in respect of each, you should suggest, with reasons, why you would or would not advocate its possible adoption by the company.

ICMA(CA1).

5.8 The ABC Company has two production departments, viz. Machining and Finishing, and two service departments, viz. Maintenance and Materials Handling.

The overhead budgets per four week period are £9,000 for the Machining Department, and £7,500 for the Finishing Department. The Machining Department overhead is absorbed on a machine hour basis (300 per period) and Finishing Department overhead is absorbed on the basis of direct labour hours (3,000 per period).

In establishing the overhead budgets of the production departments, service department costs have been dealt with as follows:

Maintenance Dept.   60% to Machining Dept.,
                           30% to Finishing Dept., and
                           10% to Materials Handling.

Materials Handling: 30% to Machining Dept.,
                                       50% to Finishing Dept., and
                                       20% to Maintenance Dept.

During Period VI, the Machining Dept. was in operation for 292 hours
and the number of direct labour hours worked by Finishing Dept.
personnel was 3,100. Overhead incurred during Period VI was as
follows:

	Machining	Finishing	Maintenance	Materials Handling
Materials	£2,000	£3,000	£1,000	£200
Labour	3,000	900	2,000	3,000
Other allocated costs	600	400	800	300

You are required to

(a) write up the overhead accounts for each of the production
departments for Period VI showing the disposition of any
under/over absorption,

(b) state the factors which gave rise to the under/over absorption, and

(c) analyse the under/over absorption under the headings you have
stated in your answer to (b).

CA(AC2)

5.9 The following overhead costs were both budgeted and incurred in a
manufacturing company during October:

		Indirect wages £	Indirect materials £	Indirect expenses £
Allocated to:				
Production department:	1	15,000	3,000	—
	2	10,000	6,000	—
	3	20,000	4,000	—
Service department:	A	5,000	2,000	—
	B	10,000	3,000	—
Not allocated		22,000	3,000	55,000

Costs are apportioned to departments on the following bases:

	Production			Service		Total
	1 %	2 %	3 %	A %	B %	%
Overhead costs, not allocated	35	20	30	5	10	100
Service department costs:						
A........................	25	20	40	—	15	100
B........................	15	35	30	20	—	100

Service department costs are apportioned to production and service
departments on the 'repeated distribution' or 'continued allotment'
method.

The company uses predetermined departmental direct labour hour rates for absorption of overhead into its product costs.

Direct labour hours for October were:

	Production department		
	1	2	3
Budgeted......................	20,000	40,000	30,000
Actual	21,200	38,600	28,100

You are required to prepare for October:

(a) an overhead distribution sheet for the production departments;

(b) a production overhead control account for the whole company;

(c) an overhead account for each production department.

ICMA(CA2).

5.10 A manufacturing confectioner has prepared the following budget for the year ending 31st December 1975:

		Fudge £	Gums £	Rock £	Total £
Sales		200,000	160,000	40,000	400,000
Factory costs—					
Direct materials	(a)	40,000	32,000	8,000	80,000
Fixed overhead	(b)	60,000	48,000	12,000	120,000
Service departments—					
Personnel	(c)	4,000	3,000	1,000	8,000
Maintenance	(d)	6,000	4,000	2,000	12,000
Administration	(e)	40,000	30,000	10,000	80,000
Selling	(f)	30,000	24,000	6,000	60,000
		180,000	141,000	39,000	360,000
Net operating income		20,000	19,000	1,000	40,000

Notes (a) sugar comprises over 80% of direct materials
(b) fixed overhead includes operating wages
(c) allocated in terms of the number of factory employees engaged in making each product
(d) allocated in terms of factory square footage used for making each product
(e) allocated on the same basis as the costs of the personnel department
(f) allocated in terms of product sales

The company has 82 employees and occupies 21,000 square feet.

Details are as follows:

	Employees	Occupancy (sq. ft.)
Factory—		
Fudge	20	6,000
Gums	15	4,000
Rock	5	2,000
Offices—		
Personnel	2	500
Maintenance	4	500
Administration	20	5,000
Selling	16	3,000
	82	21,000

For most of 1975 actual activity and costs have closely approximated to budget. In late autumn, however, the managing director hears a rumour that sugar prices may increase and he suggests to the Board that since rock is the least profitable product, its manufacture should be discontinued and the sugar used in its manufacture switched to the other products. The finance director demurs. "All our products make much the same contribution to overheads and profits", he says, "I think that we should review our overheads. The allocation bases are sound, but we should take account, for example, of the fact that Administration does a lot of work for Selling, and Personnel does work for all our departments, not just those engaged in production".

You are required, without giving calculations, to:

(a) give a concise statement of the apparent managerial objective in allocating costs and your views on the validity of such allocations, and

(b) describe two other systematic approaches to overhead allocation and to discuss their relevance to the problem before the Board in the light of your answer to (a).

ICAEW(MA).

Seminar Problem 5

John and Peter Brooks are brothers and jointly own and manage a clothes manufacturing business. John designs ladies rainwear and Peter designs dresses and similar light garments.

The factory is jointly managed by the brothers, who tend to be keen designers and salesmen and rather poor factory managers. Their strengths lie in design and selling with production and accounting as the weak points.

Their accountant has produced the following accounts for the year ended 31st December 19X5.

	Rainwear	Dresses etc.	Total
Materials	75,000	40,000	115,000
Labour	18,000	15,000	33,000
Departmental expenses	7,000	5,000	12,000
	100,000	60,000	160,000
Factory overheads	10,000	6,000	16,000
Total factory cost	110,000	66,000	176,000
Increase in stocks	2,000	1,000	3,000
Cost of Goods Sold	108,000	65,000	173,000
Selling and administration expenses	13,000	8,000	21,000
Profit (loss)	(3,000)	6,000	3,000
Sales	118,000	79,000	197,000

John was despondent with these results and Peter was naturally delighted. The latter proposed that the rainwear section should be reduced in size to the minimum necessary as a complementary product. John was not going to be defeated so easily and enquired further into the accounts. He found that factory overheads had been apportioned as a percentage of the direct material, labour and departmental expenses. The selling and administration expenses had been apportioned as a percentage of the cost of goods sold.

According to John this was very unfair since the two product lines occupied and used almost identical facilities in the factory and in the case of selling and administration costs, these too, could be shared equally.

Required:

(a) Accounts prepared on the basis suggested by John

(b) How would you present the accounts with the available information? Discuss this problem of apportionment.

Chapter 6

Cost Accumulation Systems — 1

Job Costing

Cost accounting systems differ from one firm to another as far as detail is concerned. In general though, it is possible to distinguish between two types of cost accumulation. The individual firm in practice may operate a system which is wholly identifiable with one of these types, but it could just as well employ a mixture of the systems in different parts of the plant, depending upon the nature of the manufacturing process.

This chapter brings together the information set out previously, within the framework of job costing. The next chapter deals with the alternative general heading of process costing. The systems will be examined in terms of actual achievement and will not deal with standards or measures of what ought to have been achieved. This development comes in part II.

Job costing is a system of collecting costs which is the most convenient to use in situations where the product being made can be identified with a particular customer at any stage. Alternatively it may be appopriate when products are manufactured in lots which can also be identified throughout the process. In job costing a customer orders some specific good and receives a quoted price for it. Some examples of job costing are a book being printed, a garment being tailored or a telephone exchange being manufactured and assembled. A particular job may consist of one unit e.g. a telephone exchange, or a number of units, e.g. a particular model of shoe. The size of job unit can be very small, ranging from a small printing job to a major civil engineering contract. Derivatives of job costing are batch and contract costing.

Whatever the size of job it will be assigned a distinguishing job number and a record card or its equivalent will be set up. (see figure 6.1). The signal for this is usually a copy of the production order.

JOB COST SHEET

Job No. . . . . 621 . . . .   Date started   3/5/X6

Customer . . . . . . XYZ . . . . . .   Date Completed   6/5/X6

MATERIAL			LABOUR			
Date	Requisition No.	Amount £	Date	Ticket No.	Hrs.	Amount £
3/5	3176	5.70	3/5	3136	3.00	2.70
			6/5	4016	2.00	1.40
Total		5.70				4.10

Overheads—(on labour cost)	£	Summary—	£
depts 1 – 3 100%	2.70	material	5.70
depts 4 150%	2.10	labour	4.10
	4.80	overhead	4.80
			14.60

Figure 6.1 A specimen job cost sheet.

Materials

The sub-procedure for material, labour and overhead are straight-forward. As material is required it is drawn from stores with a material requisition or stores issue note. An example is given in figure 6.2.

	MATERIAL REQUISITION		Serial No. 1001		
Job No. 621		Dept 3	Req. No. 3176		
Date	Qty.	Item	Code	Unit Cost	Amount £
3/5	10	Model 24	107436	0.57	5.70
Prepared by . . . . Stores received by					

Figure 6.2 A specimen material requisition note.

All these issue notes would be analysed for a period to give the figures for the necessary accounting entry. Suppose that for May the listing of the requisition or issue notes was as follows—

Issue Note	Commodity Code	Job No.	£
1001	107 436	621	5.70
1002	107 436	625	3.30
1003	258 510	622	3.80
	704 326	623	4.20
1004	etc.	etc.	etc.
etc.	etc.	etc.	etc.
etc.	etc.	etc.	etc.
	Total		1,026.20

These would be analysed in two ways to give sub-totals according to commodity code and according to job. The analysis by commodity code would show:

Commodity Code	Issue Note	Amount £	Total £
107 436	1001	5.70	
	1002	3.30	9.00
247 437	1002	4.60	4.60
258 510	1003	3.80	3.80
704 326	1003	4.20	4.20
etc.	etc.	etc.	etc.
etc.	etc.	etc.	etc.
		1,026.20	1,026.20

The analysis by job would be similar and, of course, would agree in total.

Job No.	Issue Note	Amount £	Total £
621	1001	5.70	5.70
622	1002	4.60	
	1003	3.80	8.40
623	1003	4.20	4.20
625	1004	3.30	3.30
etc.	etc.	etc.	etc.
etc.	etc.	etc.	etc.
		1,026.20	1,026.20

This figure of £1,026.50 is entered in the control accounts as a debit to work-in-progress and a credit to raw material control.

| Work-in-progress control | Dr. | £1,026.20 | |
| Raw material control | Cr. | | £1,026.20 |

Each of these controls would have supporting detailed accounts. The work-in-progress is standing in place of individual job cost accounts. Raw material control is for individual commodity accounts.

Wages

In a similar manner the wages section will analyse all wages paid according to the work performed. Here emphasis is on labour whose wages are directly attributable to a specific job. An analysis of work sheets or piece work tickets shows—

job no.	dept. no.	Dept. amount £	Total £
621	3	2.70	
	4	1.40	4.10
622	3	2.60	2.60
etc.	etc.	etc.	etc.
			1,620.00

This total of £1,620 would be debited to work-in-progress and credited to wages control

| Work-in-progress | Dr. £1,620.00 | |
| Wages control | Cr. | £1,620.00 |

Direct Expense

In some cases, expense items are directly related to a specific job and can be attributed to the cost of that job in the same manner as direct material and direct labour. A hiring charge for a special tool or service, for example.

Overheads

These are shared between jobs in some reasonable way. The apportionment of overheads to cost centres and then the allocation to products has been dealt with in detail in chapter 5. Assume that all overheads charged to jobs amount to £1,550.00. The corresponding accounting entry would be:-

| Work-in-progress | Dr. £1,550.00 | |
| Manufacturing overhead control | Cr. | £1,550.00 |

Job costs as an average

The final cost shown on the job cost sheet for job number 621 was £14.60. This cost is arrived at as the result of measuring the elements of direct-material, direct labour, direct expense and all indirect expense or overhead.

The measurement of the direct material labour and expense used on the job are reasonably accurate given good recording procedures. The overheads are arrived at as the result of quite a different process. The £4.80 charged as overhead to this job represents an average figure.

Job Costs Illustration

The Ashton Machine Tool Company manufactures in accordance with specific customer orders.

On June 1st, 19X5 the following balance appeared in the work-in-progress and overheads under-over absorbed accounts.

Work-in-progress control:

Job No.	73475	£20,000	
	73593	25,000	
	74126	30,000	£75,000
Overhead under-over absorbed			£1,000 (credit)

Transactions in June were as follows:

1. Three new production orders were issued for jobs 74261, 74362, 74463.
2. Raw materials were requisitioned as follows:

Job No.	73475	£4,000
	73593	9,000
	74126	15,000
	74261	14,000
	74362	10,000
	74463	9,000
Overhead control		1,000
		£62,000

3. Direct labour costs were incurred as follows:

Job No.	73475	6,000 hours at £1.5 /hr.	£9,000
	73593	8,000 hours at £1.25/hr.	10,000
	74126	10,000 hours at £1.25/hr.	12,500
	74261	12,000 hours at £1.5 /hr.	18,000
	74362	10,000 hours at £1.25/hr.	12,500
	74463	8,000 hours at £1.5 /hr.	12,000
			£74,000

4. Indirect labour costs were £41,000.
5. Other overhead costs (including depreciation) were £50,000.
6. Overhead costs are charged to jobs at the rate of £1.67 per direct labour hour.
7. The following jobs were completed and despatched to customers:

Job No.	73475	Invoiced at £50,000
	73593	Invoiced at 70,000
	74126	Invoiced at 90,000

What are the costs of each of the completed jobs and how are the accounts written up?

Solution

Job Summary — June 1975

Job. No.	b/f £	Material £	Labour £	Overhead £	Total £
73475	20,000	4,000	9,000	10,000	43,000
73593	25,000	9,000	10,000	13,333	57,333
74126	30,000	15,000	12,500	16,667	74,167
74261		14,000	18,000	20,000	52,000
74362		10,000	12,500	16,667	39,167
74463		9,000	12,000	13,333	34,333
Overhead		1,000			1,000
	75,000	62,000	74,000	90,000	301,000

Work-in-progress control				Finished goods control	
	£		£	£	
bal. b/d	75,000	Finished goods			
Material	61,000		174,500	W.I.P. 174,500	
Labour	74,000	bal. c/d	125,500		
Overhead	90,000				
	300,000		300,000		

Overhead control				Over-under absorbed			
	£		£				
Labour	41,000	W.I.P.	90,000	Overhead		bal. c/d	1,000
Other	50,000	Under		control 2,000		bal. c/d	1,000
Material	1,000	absorbed	2,000				
	92,000		92,000				

The cost of each of the completed jobs is shown as the first three items on the June job summary sheet. The remaining jobs are still incomplete and their cost so far is represented by the balance of the work-in-progress account.

Contract Costing

Contracts are large scale jobs and costing for them is similar to job costing. The main point of difference which deserves some discussion concerns period profits. A feature of many contracts is that they extend over long periods and it is necessary to make some decision on what profit should be taken out on accounting data which falls within the contract period.

The contract account

The work-in-progress of contracts is recorded by having a separate account for each contract. These accounts are debited with the direct costs of the contract. In most cases the direct costs cover a wider range than for jobs. This is because most of the work is carried out on site and can easily be identified with a wide variety of costs which relate to services and benefits exclusive to the contract. Treatment of direct material, labour and expense is typically straight-forward and needs no further comment. The depreciation of machinery used at the contract site is usually arrived at by valuing it at the start and finish of the contract.

Overheads to be shared between contracts are treated in the usual way, some equitable basis of sharing being used. Very often it is in the proportion of prime cost, but the other regular bases are also employed.

Certificates of progress

Contractors very rarely finance the whole of the contract themselves or with money borrowed from third parties. The usual procedure is to obtain an architect's certificate at a number of stages and receive payment for the work done. Even with this method a substantial quantity of the finance is put forward by the contractor, in that he finances the whole of each stage's cost and, in addition, has the usual waiting time between obtaining the architect's certificate and the date of payment.

Retentions

Part of the money due from the client to the contractor is witheld for a period of time, in order to give the client the means of ensuring that faults are corrected. Once all the faults have been put right and the time period is up, the retention money falls due.

Period profits

Many contracts are carried on over a long period of time and frequently overlap at least one financial reporting period end. This presents a problem in terms of profit reporting. The conservative approach is to wait until the contract is complete before taking account of the profit earned. In many cases such treatment would lead to large fluctuations in profit because the incidence of contract endings may not follow a regular pattern. It is not considered right that companies which are following a normal pattern of activity, presumably profitably, should report very small profits or even losses in those years when few of the contracts are completed.

Some means of calculating profits needs to be developed to cover these circumstances. These will differ according to whether the contract is in the early stages before the issue of an architect's certificate or at a later stage. In many cases the treatment recognises a further sub-division between contracts in the final stage and others.

Contracts at an early stage

No profit is calculated for these.

Contracts at an intermediate stage

The starting point is the profit represented by the difference between the value of the work certified and its cost. From that point onwards caution takes over and moves towards a more conservative and subjective approach. This is done by applying a reducing formula to the profit calculated, typically on the following lines:

$$\frac{x\% \text{ of profit} \times \text{cash received}}{\text{value of work certified.}}$$

The motivation behind such reductions are clear, since a conservative policy is normally regarded as prudent. It protects the reporting management from the inevitable criticism that follows when predicted profits are replaced by eventual losses. It can be argued, though, that the best policy is one of limited conservatism with clear disclosure of method.

Example

Total cost of contract so far £120,000
Cost of work not certified 10,000
Value of work certified 180,000
Cash received 170,000

$$2/3 \times 70,000 \times \frac{170,000}{180,000}$$

A proportion of 2/3rds is frequently used in practice.

Contracts in the final stages

Such contracts would have just one final certificate to be issued and would be nearer completion than the point at which the penultimate certificate was issued. This time the starting point of the profit calculation would be the difference between the contract price and the estimated total cost. The latter figure would consist of known costs plus estimates of future expenditure. The estimates would be relatively small in relation to total costs and would be compiled cautiously. As with contracts at the intermediate stage, this estimated profit is then scaled down according to some formula.

Example

Using the same figures as for the previous example, plus estimated additional expenditure to complete the contract £15,000 and a contract price of £210,000.

Estimated profit: £
contract price 210,000
expenditure:
recorded 120,000
estimated 15,000 135,000
75,000

$$£75,000 \times \frac{180,000}{210,000}$$

where the scaling factor is the value of work certified/contract price.

Contract Losses

Where a loss is expected on a contract immediate recognition should be made. This is the usual accounting practice and is in line with cautious estimates of profits. In effect, recognising and accounting for full estimated losses simultaneously, reduces the value of the contract work from the cost to its net realisable value.

Work-in-progress

The amounts shown as representing the work-on-progress value of contracts should be the cost plus the attributable profit or less the foreseeable loss.

Illustration of contract costing

Contract Account

Jan/Dec	£	Jan/Dec	£
Materials	75,610	Materials c/d	5,415
Labour	70,206	Machinery c/d	31,000
Direct expense	10,110	Work-in-progress c/d	193,111
Machinery-valued 1 Jan.	35,000		
Shared overhead costs	5,000		
Profit	33,600		
	229,526		229,526

The profit calculation is made on the basis of work certified and its cost, with adjustments designed to cover adverse contingencies.

			£
Value of work certified:			200,000
Cost of work certified			
Materials	75,610		
less	5,415	70,195	
Labour		70,206	
Expense		10,110	
Depreciation	35,000		
	31,000	4,000	
Overheads		5,000	
		159,511	
Less: estimated cost of work			
not certified		15,111	144,000
			56,000

Proportion of profit assumed:

$$2/3 \times \frac{\text{cash received (180,000)}}{\text{value of work certified (200,000)}} \times 56,000$$
$$= £33,600$$

The work-in-progress is the balancing figure and represents all costs to date plus the assumed profit.

Client (Contractee) Account

Amount certified less		Cash	180,000
retention	180,000		

Batch Costing

Another special version of job costing applies when a significant number of items are made under one production order. Thus it applies to certain types of finished goods which are manufactured under one production order and put into the warehouse until they are bought. Similarly, components used in substantial quantities can be made in a batch and held in stock until needed. Thus, in effect, a batch is a job and is costed accordingly.

Economic Batch Size

One feature which is additional to batch costing concerns the size of the batch. It is usual to find that there is an optimal size, due to the fact that some costs are best spread over large numbers, whereas others increase with batch size. Setting up the machines for each batch is a cost best shared between large runs. Unfortunately, long runs mean large quantities to store and this increases warehousing costs.

The problem is similar to one concerning the size of the amount of material to be ordered and these will be dealt with in chapter 13.

Chapter Summary

It is difficult to talk in terms of this industry employing that type of costing system, simply because cost accounting is tailor made to an organisation's needs. Fortunately, it is possible to isolate certain features which go to make-up most hybrid cost schemes. These are job costing and process costing and a chapter has been devoted to each of these.

Job costing applies when the product can be identified as a separate item from an early stage in its manufacture, very often for a particular customer, or is closely related in that a number of units can be directly associated by a production order number. The direct cost of material and labour can be measured very closely to the finished article, by means of material requisition notes and time records. Thus, the work-in-progress control account has a set of job cost accounts as its subsidiary ledger.

The manufacturing overhead costs have to be shared between jobs and so the job cost contains some figures which are averages.

Costs which are both historic and average are not a good basis for control or decision making. They can be used to some extent, to check that price estimates are in line with costs in the long run. Apart from that, job costs provide stock values on a perpetual inventory basis, so allowing valuable periodic reports.

Where jobs are very large and a firm's activity consists in operating on a few of these, job costing gives way to contract costing. There is very little difference in principle, with the exception of the time span of the contract. A job which is not complete at the end of a financial year is included in work-in-progress at its cost, it does not include any anticipated profit in its value, although anticipated losses would be included. This is not feasible for a firm which is engaged on relatively few jobs, i.e. contracts and some assessment of profit has to be made. This anticipated profit is shown on the profit and loss account and included as part of the value of the work-in-progress.

Exercises 6

Questions 6.1-6.5 answers provided.

6.1 The London Shop Fittings Company specialises in custom made work and maintains a job costing system. In the month of February 19X5 work was started and completed on an order for which the details are given below:

Job No. 2-104

	Costs £
Materials:	
300 m. of type A shelving at £1.00/m.	300
200 m. of edging at £0.10/m.	20
Labour:	
30 hours at £2.50/hr.	75
Overhead	
30 d.l.h. at £2.00/hr.	60
Total cost	455

Prepare journal entries to record this information.

6.2 The Edinburgh Special Products Company had the following balances in their accounts at the start of April 19X5.

Raw material control	£50,000
Work-in-progress control	£75,000
Overhead under absorbed	£10,000

During April the following figures were recorded:

	£
Raw materials purchased	60,000
Direct labour costs	72,000
Raw materials issued:	
to production	65,000
to maintenance	5,000
Indirect labour costs	40,000
Factory overhead costs	50,000
Transfers to finished goods	220,000

Finished jobs having a production cost of £200,000 were delivered to customers at an invoiced total of £300,000.

Factory overhead costs are charged to work-in-progress at the rate of 125% of direct labour.

Required: journal entries to record this information.

6.3 The Cardiff Printing Company recorded the following information for June 19X5:

1. Materials used:

	£
Job 100	1,200
Job 101	1,600
Job 102	2,100
Job 103	2,500
Job 104	1,000

2. Direct labour hours and costs:

Job No.	Hours.	Costs £
100	200	400
101	250	500
102	270	540
103	290	580
104	210	420

3. Factory overheads are absorbed at the rate of £3.00 per direct labour hour.

4. Jobs 100, 101, 102 and 103 were completed and of these, 100 and 101 were delivered to customers at invoiced prices of £3,000 and £4,000 respectively.

Actual factory overheads for June were £3,750.

All these jobs were started in June 19X5.

Required: T accounts to record this data.

6.4 The Douglas Construction Company has the following accounts for one of its contracts, which started in January 19X5.

Contract Account

Jan/Dec.
Materials	103,600
Labour	141,200
Direct expense	70,300
Machinery	130,000

The accountant has the following additional information:

1) Stocks of materials at 31 December were £3,400

2) The machinery is shown at cost on 1st January. At the year end it is valued at £70,000

3) The share of company overheads attributable to the contract is £15,000.

4) The value of work certified at 15th December is £500,000

5) The estimated cost of work not certified is £15,000.

Required: The profit on this contract for 19X5.

6.5 The St. Helier Building Company assumed a period profit for each contract according to the formula:

$$\frac{75\% \text{ of cash received}}{\text{value of work certified}} \times \text{calculated profit.}$$

Information for one of their contracts is given in account form below:

Contract Account 0 19X5

Jan. 1		Dec. 31	
balances b/d		balances c/d:	
Material	5,000	Material	6,000
Machinery	30,000	Machinery	20,000
Work-in-			
progress	100,000		
Jan/Dec.			
Material	75,000		
Labour	100,000		
Expenses	65,000		

The cash received in the period was £350,000 and the value of work certified was £430,000. The estimate for work done but not yet certified was £20,000.

Required: calculate the profit for 19X5 and work-in-progress at the year end.

Questions 6.6-6.10 answers not provided.

6.6 A factory with three departments uses a single production overhead absorption rate expressed as a percentage of direct wages cost. It has been suggested that departmental overhead absorption rates would result in more accurate job costs. Set out below are the budgeted and actual data for the previous period, together with information relating to job No. 657.

		Direct wages £000's	Hours in thousands Direct labour	Machine	Production overhead £000's
Budget:					
Department:	A	25	10	40	120
	B	100	50	10	30
	C	25	25	—	75
Total:		150	85	50	225
Actual:					
Department:	A	30	12	45	130
	B	80	45	14	28
	C	30	30	—	80
Total:		140	87	59	238

During this period job No. 657 incurred the actual costs and actual times in the departments as shown below:

		Direct material £	Direct wages £	Direct labour hours	Machine hours
Department:	A	120	100	20	40
	B	60	60	40	10
	C	10	10	10	—

After adding production overhead to prime cost, one third is added to production cost for gross profit. This assumes that a reasonable profit is earned after deducting administration, selling and distribution costs.

You are required to:

(a) calculate the current overhead absorption rate;

(b) using the rate obtained in (a) above, calculate the production overhead charged to job No. 657 and state the production cost and expected gross profit on this job;

(c) (i) comment on the suggestion that departmental overhead absorption rates would result in more accurate job costs; and

(ii) compute such rates, briefly explaining your reason for each rate;

(d) using the rates calculated in (c) (ii) above, show the overhead, by department and in total, that would apply to job No. 657;

(e) show the over/under absorption, by department and in total, for the period using:

(i) the current rate in your answer to (a) above, and

(ii) your suggested rates in your answer to (c) (ii) above.

ICMA(CA1).

6.7 On 3rd January 1978, B Construction Limited started work on the construction of an office block for a contracted price of £750,000 with completion promised by 31st March 1979. Budgeted cost of the contract was £600,000. The construction company's financial year end was 31st October 1978 and on that date the accounts appropriate to the contract contained the following balances:

	£000
Materials issued to site	161
Materials returned from site	14
Wages paid	68
Own plant in use on site, at cost	96
Hire of plant and scaffolding	72
Suerpvisory staff: direct	11
indirect	12
Head office charges	63
Value of work certified to 31st October 1978	400
Cost of work completed but not yet certified	40
Cash received related to work certified	330

Depreciation on own plant is to be provided at the rate of 12½% per annum on cost.

£2,000 is owing for wages.

Estimated value of materials on site is £24,000.

No difficulties are envisaged during the remaining time to complete the contract.

You are required to:

(a) prepare the contract account for the period ended 31st October 1978 showing the amount to be included in the construction company's profit and loss account;

(b) explain the reason(s) for including the amount of profit to be shown in the profit and loss account;

(c) show extracts from the construction company's balance sheet at 31st October 1978 so far as the information provided will allow.

ICMA(CA1).

6.8 B. Idler commenced business on 1 May, 1976 having obtained three orders for house extensions, the costs of which during his first month's trading were as follows:

	Job 1	Job 2	Job 3
	£	£	£
Direct wages	528	451	308
Materials issued from stores	2,752	2,341	1,473
Special materials bought in	215	—	46
Materials returned to stores	71	—	—

Ilder has estimated his overhead for the year ending 30 April, 1977 at £10,500 and the direct labour hours at 17,500. Under a trade union agreement dated 1 May all direct workers were paid 110p per hour from that date. For costing purposes overhead is absorbed on a direct labour hour basis; the overhead incurred in May was £800.

Job No. 1 was completed on 31 May and invoiced to the customer at the contracted amount of £4,500.

You are required to:

(a) Prepare

(i) cost accounts for each of the three jobs;

(ii) control accounts for overhead and work in progress for May;

(iii) Profit and Loss Account for May.

(b) Given that the cost estimate for Job No. 1 was as follows:

	£
Materials	2,850
Direct wages (500 hours)	525
Overhead	300

prepare a reconciliation of estimated and actual costs and comment briefly on the possible causes of any differences.

CA(AC2).

6.9 A manufacturing company has two production cost centres, A and B, and one general services cost centre, GS, to which all common costs are charged.

The following data concerning the standard costs of its four products and its annual budgets are available:

		W	X	Y	Z
Per unit:		£	£	£	£
Prime cost		40	70	50	60
Selling price:					
first quality products		148	218	117	148
second quality products		30	36	35	30
Direct labour:		hours	hours	hours	hours
Production cost centre:	A	12	14	6	8
	B	16	24	8	8
Sales and production, per annum		units	units	units	units
		300	200	600	400

Fixed overhead, per annum:		£
Production cost centre:	A	26,400
	B	52,800
General services cost centre	GS	15,400*

*excludes any loss from second quality products.

Overhead of cost centre GS is apportioned to production cost centres according to their direct labour hours. Overhead is absorbed into product costs by a direct labour hour rate.

The company budgets for 10% of its production as second quality products, which are sold at the prices shown above.

You are required:

(a) on the assumption that there were no second quality products, to calculate:

(i) the cost per unit of each product;

(ii) the total profit budgeted to be earned in the year;

(b) on the assumption that second quality products are as budgeted and that loss on these is charged entirely to cost centre GS, to calculate:

(i) the cost per unit of each product;

(ii) the total profit budgeted to be earned in the year;

(c) on the assumption that second quality products are as budgeted but that the income from these is treated entirely as an addition to sales income, to calculate

the total profit budgeted to be earned in the year;

(d) on the assumption that second quality products were as budgeted but that sales were only 85% of production in the year, to state whether you would charge against sales for the year the cost of:

(i) all second quality products manufactured in the year; or

(ii) only those second quality products that had been sold in the year;

and to give very briefly reasons for your choice.

ICMA(CA2).

6.10 The Anglia Company undertakes civil engineering contracts in East Anglia. Based upon Norwich, the basis of the organisation's operations is to send a project manager and plant to the site of contracts. The manager recruits any labour required locally and arranges for Head Office to supply materials used in the contract.

Some time ago the company tendered successfully for two contracts which have now become mutually exclusive. It is currently considering which of these to accept. Both jobs would last for twelve months and there appears to be no possibility of any other suitable projects arising in the area.

The following information about the contracts is available:

Job	Gt. Yarmouth £000's	Lowestoft £000's
Contract price	85	90
Penalty payment (this is a condition of the tender, if offered the contract and not accepting it)	8	4
Materials required		
In store (at cost)	10	12
Contracted for	—	18
To be ordered (at current cost)	20	17
Labour required		
Project manager: Salary	5	5
Travel, lodgings, etc.	2	2
Local recruitment	35	28
Head Office		
Plant depreciation	3	4
Interest on plant	1	1
General administration	4	4

Notes on this information are as follows:

(1) The materials that would be used on the Great Yarmouth job have increased in money value from their purchase cost by 50%. Although the Anglia Company does not expect to be able to use these materials if they are not required for the Great Yarmouth contract, they are in common use in the industry and thus they could be resold. However, transportation and other selling costs would reduce the cash inflow from the sale of these materials by 20%.

The materials required for the Lowestoft job are fairly specific to the Anglia Company's uses. They have no resale value apart from scrap, which is 5% of their cost, costs of transport etc. being paid by the scrap merchant. However, it is probable that these materials could be used by the organisation next year in substitution for a different material normally costing the company 10% less than the cost of materials to be used on the Lowestoft contract.

(2) Local labour can be hired as and when required.

(3) Plant is depreciated by Head Office on a straight line basis. The item of depreciation expense on plant used by the Great Yarmouth job is lower than on the Lowestoft contract as less plant would be used. Head Office would be able to sub-contract out the plant not required on the Great Yarmouth job for £1,000 per annum. The interest charged on the plant has been notionally calculated for bookkeeping purposes.

(4) Head Office expenses are expected to be fixed at £10,000 during the year whatever number of contracts are undertaken. These expenses do not include the cost of the organisation's project managers who were given five year contracts last year.

Required:

(a) Present the data to management in a form which will assist them in their decision as to which job to undertake. Provide notes to show the principles which you have used in the selection of your data and support any calculations made.

(b) Comment on the appropriateness of the approach used in your analysis.

CA(MA)

Seminar Problem 6

The Kirkwell Company had the following balances in its accounts at the 31st December 19X5:

			£	£
Materials control		Dr.	40,000	
Work-in-Progress		Dr.	30,000	

The work-in-progress subsidiary job accounts had balances of:

job no.	100	15,000
job no.	101	10,000
job no.	102	4,000
job no.	103	1,000

January events were:

1) Materials:
   purchased   65,000
   issued:

job no.	100		3,000
job no.	101		7,000
job no.	102		12,000
job no.	103		15,000
job no.	104		10,000
job no.	105		7,000
job no.	106		2,000
product centre P1			4,000
product centre P2			5,000
service centre S1			2,000

2) Wages analysis:

	P1	P2	S1	S2
Direct labour	£20,000	£16,000	£—	£—
Indirect labour	5,000	2,000	3,000	1,000
	25,000	18,000	3,000	1,000

Labour time records apportioned the direct labour to jobs as follows:

	£
job no. 100	4,000
job no. 101	6,000
job no. 102	7,000
job no. 103	9,000
job no. 104	6,000
job no. 105	4,000
job no. 106	2,000

3) Other expenses:

	£
product centre P1	5,000
product centre P2	3,000
service centre S1	2,000
service centre S2	1,000
	11,000

Service centre S2 is a non-factory cost.

Both product centres apply an overhead rate of 75% of direct labour cost.

4) Job numbers 100, 101, 102 were completed and delivered at invoiced prices of £30,000, £30,000 and £32,000 respectively whilst job no. 103 was completed but not delivered. The agreed price for it was £35,000.

Required:

(a) Accounts to record the January events and a profit statement for the month.

(b) How useful to management are reports made up from records such as these?

Chapter 7

Cost Accumulation Systems — 2

Process Costing

Chapter 6 examined the costing procedures for a jobbing firm. Now attention is turned to process costing. Much that was said about product and service cost centres, apportionment and allocation, will apply in this chapter. The essential difference is that process costing is relevant in a firm whose product during manufacture is not identifiable with the eventual customer.

The steps in process costing are the same as in job costing and are set out again:-

1. Trace the direct material and the direct labour to cost centres.
2. Accumulate the factory overheads to cost centres according to the following methods:
   a) by tracing them directly, or
   b) apportioning them according to a basis which seems to be the least arbitrary, then
   c) redistribute the service centres so that all manufacturing overheads are finally apportioned to product cost centres and
   d) apply these costs to products on an average basis, by dividing the number of units produced into total cost, thus obtaining a cost per unit.

An imaginary factory set-up will help to illustrate the flow. The organisation of the factory is shown in figure 7.1

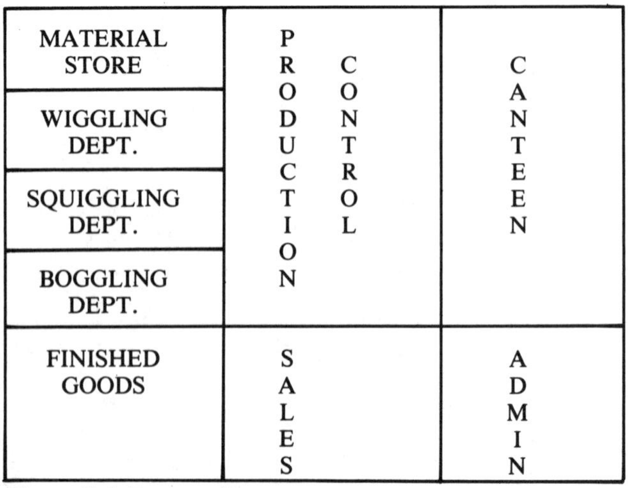

Figure 7.1 Factory Layout

The factory makes Puddles as a finished product. The accounting system would be in accordance with the scheme shown in figure 7.2.

Wiggling Production Account

Traced Directly { Direct material Direct Labour Electricity Depreciation Share of plant overhead (apportioned)	Output to Squiggling

Squiggling Production Account

Traced Directly { Input from Wiggling Direct Material Direct Labour Electricity Depreciation Share of plant Overhead (apportioned)	Output to Boggling

Boggling Production Account

Traced Directly { Input from Boggling Direct Material Direct Labour Electricity Depreciation Share of plant Overhead (apportioned)	Output to finished stock

Figure 7.2

Examples of traced costs are the materials used in production and the direct labour. In addition electricity could be measured to each department using meters. Depreciation of machinery, too could serve as an example of a cost being measured direct to cost centres. The apportioned costs would include such items as rent and rates, which could be spread about according to space occupied. The stages that follow are concerned with absorbing all the factory overheads to production to arrive at a full factory cost valuation of the finished product. Of the nine cost centres, six are service centres and three are product centres. Out of the service centres only the canteen provides its services for the production, admin. etc. as well as the three main factory departments.

After transferring the service department costs to the product centres, the account for a period would be as shown in figure 7.3.

110

Wiggling Department

	£		units	£
Starting W-in-P	0			
Direct Material	1,000	Transferred to Squiggling	1,000	2,800
Direct Labour	1,000			
Electricity	100	Closing W-in-P		-0-
Depreciation	200			
Plant overhead — share	500			
	2,800		1,000	2,800

Figure 7.3 Wiggling department-Work-in-progress

Output amounted to 1,000 units which are completed as far as the wiggling process is concerned. Averaging the departmental costs over the production is a simple arithmetic process here, because opening and closing stocks of work-in-progress have been excluded.

The 1,000 units are transferred to squiggling at a value of £2.80/unit given by £2,800/1,000 per unit.

Work-in-progress

This simple procedure is almost always made more complicated by the existence of period end quantities of partially completed units. The usual process is to identify the average state of completeness in terms of material and of conversion costs. These conversion costs consist of labour and overhead.

If the example is continued by putting wiggled units through the squiggling process, the point can be illustrated. In the squiggling department, additional material is added to the wiggled units at the onset of the process and then processed into squiggled units. Figure 7.4 shows the account. This time there is closing work-in-progress, but none at the start. This closing stock is 100% complete for material and 50% for conversion.

Squiggling Production Account

	Units	Material £	Conversion £	Total £		Units	Material £	Conversion £	Total £
Opening work-in-progress	—	—	—	—	Transfer to Boggling	800	3,040	1,600	4,640
Transfer from Wiggling	1,000	2,800	—	2,800	$(4/5 \times 3,800 + 8/9 \times 1,800)$				
Direct Material	—	1,000	—	1,000	Work-in-progress:	200	760	200	960
Conversion costs:					$(1/5 \times 3,800 + 1/9 \times 1,800)$				
Direct labour			1,000	1,000					
Electricity			100	100					
Depreciation			200	200					
Plant over-head share			500	500					
	1,000	3,800	1,800	5,600		1,000	3,800	1,800	5,600

Figure 7.4 Production accounting with closing work-in-progress

Here the account is considered as two parts, material and conversion. The monthly output is 100% complete for material both as regards the transferred units and the work-in-progress. Therefore, the material cost of £(2,800 + 1,000) is divided proportionately between the finished and the unfinished stock.

The conversion costs amount to £1,800. Of course the finished stock is complete as far as conversion costs are concerned just as in the case of material. The work-in-progress is not. In this case it is judged to be half converted, on average. So there are 800 completely converted units and 200 half completed or converted units. These latter are termed 100 equivalent units. Now the arithmetical process is to share the £1,800 between 800 finished units and 100 equivalent of finished units.

Work-in-progress at start and finish

The output from Squiggling goes to the Boggling department. Imagine that in this final process the material is added evenly throughout the process. A unit transferred from Squiggling and halfway through the Boggling process would have had half the blodgets or Boggling material added. Assume that conversion costs accrue in the same even manner. The account for the Boggling centre is given in figure 7.5.

The point of this section of the illustration is the treatment of opening as well as closing stock. This time there will be both opening and closing work-in-progress. Furthermore the material to be added in this stage will be used evenly throughout the process as will the conversion costs. Both opening and closing work-in-progress are 50% complete as to material and conversion. Input from the previous process is complete, of course.

Boggling Production Account

	£		£
Opening work-in-progress		Finished	
100 units		700 units	6,020
100% squiggled	580		
50% complete — material	50	Work-in-progress	
50% complete — conversion	90	200 units (50% complete as	
		to material from this	1,440
Units started in the period—	800	process and conversion)	
Transfer from squiggling	4,640		
Direct material	750		
Direct Labour			
Electricity	1,350		
Depreciation			
Plant overhead-share			
	7,460		7,460

Figure 7.5

Calculation of the closing work-in-progress and value of finished units is as follows:-

	£
Finished — 700 units	
$7/9 \times$ transfer in from Squiggling $(580 + 4,640)$	4,060
$7/8 \times$ material added in process $(50 + 750)$	700
$7/8 \times$ conversion costs of process $(90 + 1,350)$	1,260
	6,020

	£
Work-in-progress — 200 units	
100% complete from Squiggling	
50% complete material	
50% complete conversion	
$2/9 \times$ transfer in $(580 + 4,640)$	1,160
$1/8 \times$ material added $(50 + 750)$	100
$1/8 \times$ conversion cost $(90 + 1,350)$	180
	1,440

These process accounts are simply amalgamations of separate accounts for the different classes of input. This can be illustrated by representing it in columnar form. This is done in figure 7.6.

Boggling

	Transfer in		Material		Conversion		Total
	units	£	units	£	units	£	£
Work in progress at start	100	580	50	50	50	90	720
Completion of this w.i.p.	—	—	50	50	50	90	140
Started and completed in the period	600	3,480	600	600	600	1,080	5,160
Completed in the period	700	4,060	700	700	700	1,260	6,020
Started and half completed at the period end	200	1,160	100	100	100	180	1,440
	900	5,220	800	800	800	1,440	7,460

Figure 7.6

This analysis of the figures is another way of showing the results. For example, the added direct material shows—

		£50
used in the opening w.i.p.		
added during the period—		
to complete the w.i.p.	50	
to start & complete 600 units	600	
to start & ½ complete 200 units	100	750
		800

Wastage

There is usually some measureable loss of volume during production due to wastage or spoilage. This can be accounted for by one of two methods or a combination of these.

1) The loss can be accounted for and shown as a separate figure.

2) The total cost is divided over the output without regard to lost units.

These can easily be illustrated using the data in figure 7.7.

Process 1

Work-in-progress	NIL	Output	
Direct material		45,000 units	?
50,000 units at £1	£50,000	Loss 5,000	?
Conversion cost	50,000	Work-in-progress	NIL
	100,000		100,000

Figure 7.7

Using the first method the output would be valued at £90,000 and the loss transferred to a loss account of £10,000. The second method would give a unit cost of £100,000/45,000 = £2.2 to the output. The treatment chosen would depend on the nature of the loss in terms of it being normal or abnormal. Normal losses are ones that are unavoidable and expected as a result of production techniques and conditions. These losses could be reasonably treated as a product cost. Abnormal losses due to some form of inefficiency should be separated from the normal production costs.

Joint Costs

A special case of process costing is provided in instances where there are two or more products resulting from a raw material or process. To be classed as joint products, each would need to be judged as significant in relation to total revenue. If one of the products is judged to be comparatively insignificant it is referred to as a by-product (see later).

The joint cost situations most commonly arise in manufacturing processes which are concerned with breaking materials down and or refining them. Well known examples are concerned with the meat trade and oil refining. In meat packing an animinal carcase produces various cuts of meat, offal and the hide. In the petroleum refining process the crude oil produces petrol, lubricating and the various fuel oils.

The special problem of joint costing is one of allocation. First there is a pool of common costs for the common process. Then there is further processing specific to each product. The problem is to allocate the common or joint costs to each product in order to provide a unit cost for income determination and balance sheet purposes.

There are several methods of allocating joint costs to products and the more commonly used ones will be illustrated here. Since there is no clear theoretical base for making a choice it is impossible to say where and when each type should be used. The most popular method is the one based on selling values, presumably because of the general expectation that all costs are eventually recovered by a process of marking up for profit. In every case the method chosen should be clearly understood and communicated to the users of the information provided.

These methods fall into two categories. Those which are based on selling values and those which allocate according to some physical measure of output from the common process.

Market Price Method

Assume that there is a market value available for all the products at the split off point. If there is not an additional step is required.

In figure 7.8 the first column gives the physical quantities of the joint products at the cut off point. Column 2 shows the market value per unit at the same point. Column 3 is simply the extension of columns 1×2. Column 4 is the result of the simple arithmetic process of allocating the £42,500 of joint costs in accordance with the relative market values.

Joint Products	Col. 1	Col. 2	Col. 3	Col. 4
	No. of units produced	Market Value/ Unit	Total Market Value	Allocation of Joint Costs
		£	£	£
1	30,000	1.00	30,000	?
11	10,000	1.50	15,000	?
111	20,000	2.00	40,000	?
			85,000	42,500

Figure 7.8

The joint manufacturing cost is £42,500. The allocation is shown below:

Product		£
1	$(30,000/85,000) \times 42,500 =$	15,000
11	$(15,000/85,000) \times 42,500 =$	7,500
111	$(40,000/85,000) \times 42,500 =$	20,000
		£42,500

If there is no market value at the split off point, a hypothetical one can be given by subtracting subsequent unique costs from the eventual market value. The unique costs here are the costs between the split off point and the point at which the product is in a marketable state. See figure 7.9 for a set of figures which can be used to illustrate.

Product	Units Produced	Final Market Value/Unit £	Unique Costs £
1	30,000	2.00	30,000
11	10,000	3.00	10,000
111	20,000	2.50	15,000

Figure 7.9

The joint production costs equal £42,500. The second stage of the calculation is shown in figure 7.10.

Joint Product	Market Value Col. 1 £	Unique Costs Col. 2 £	Hypoth. Market Value £ (1) − (2)	Allocation of Joint Cost
1	60,000	30,000	30,000	15,000
11	30,000	10,000	20,000	10,000
111	50,000	15,000	35,000	17,500
			85,000	42,500

Figure 7.10

The figures in column 4 are calculated in the same way as the previous example. Thus for product 1 it is $30,000/85,000 \times 42,500 = 15,000$.

Physical Quantities Method

Using the figures given in 7.9 the number of units produced for each product can be totalled to give 60,000 units in all. The joint cost is £42,500 and by division the average cost per unit is £0.7083. Applying this to each product,

Product	1	is allocated $30,000 \times £0.7083 =$	£21,250
	11	is allocated $10,000 \times £0.7083 =$	£7,083
	111	is allocated $20,000 \times £0.7083 =$	£14,167
			£42,500

The same basic figures have been used in these illustrations and, yet, the results in terms of period end stock values are different. This illustrates the point that the choice between methods is mainly arbitrary. The allocation of joint costs is used for obtaining stock values and hence for income reporting. The results cannot be used for specific decision making. See chapter 17 for a discussion on the relevant costs. The arbitrary nature of this cost spreading is recognised by some firms who value their stocks at the eventual selling value less the estimated separate costs of completing and selling. This is the net realizable value. Since this contains a profit element it is usual to make a further deduction to remove the equivalent of the normal profit margin.

By-products

By-products are a special class of joint-products and are treated differently. They exist in cases where some of the firms products are relatively unimportant in terms of sales. One way is to ignore them in the cost accounts and record net revenue as other income. Net revenue equals sales minus selling and distribution cost. The other product(s) absorb all the joint costs. This method treats the income as a simple bonus. It will not do if the amount involved is sufficient to require some decision making, since it records net revenue only and ignores any unique processing costs. This method treates the product rather as scrap or salvage.

A second way is to assign a value to the by-product at the split off point and deduct this from the joint costs. These latter can then be divided between the main products. Suppose we have two main products and a secondary one in terms of importance. Joint costs of the process are £50,000. The by-product is given a value of £1,000 leaving £49,000 joint costs to be shared between the two main products. The £1,000 is either

a) a net realizable value — that is an ultimate market value minus unique costs or

b) the acquisition value, that is the cost to the firm of acquiring the product in the same state from another firm.

Illustration

Joint products with a by-product

Process Cost Account

Opening work-in-progress	-o-	Product X — 30,000 units	24,000
Total process costs	45,000	Product Y — 20,000 units	16,000
		Product Z — 500 units	5,000
		Closing work-in-progress	-o-
	45,000		45,000

Product Z is the by-product and is valued at £5,000, using one of the bases given above. This reduces the processing costs to be shared between products X and Y from £45,000 to £40,000. This amount is then shared between them using one of the methods described in the course of this chapter. In the illustration the physical quantities method has been used.

Chapter Summary

Process costing operates in circumstances where the products are not separately identifiable during their manufacture. The same basic costing ideas apply as in job costing, but rather more averaging takes place, as this applies to all the costs and not just the indirect. This is not to say that the direct material and labour are apportioned to cost centres, because they are not. The direct tracing takes place in the usual way, but costs for the period are then averaged over the units produced.

In the illustrations of this chapter, only average cost methods have been used in calculating stocks. It should be understood that all the stock accounting methods described in chapter 3 (F.I.F.O., L.I.F.O. etc.) are applicable and could be used.

The special case of joint-product costing was illustrated, using figures prepared in such a way as to demonstrate the arbitrary nature of the allocating process. The figures obtained are a guide to product pricing and profit reporting, but cannot be used in decision making. The special case of by-product costing is shown as a version of product costing in which the relative sales of the output concerned is considered.

Exercises

Questions 7.1-7.5 (Answers provided)

7.1 The Sefton Processing Company had the following data for January 19X5.

	£
Opening stock	4,500
January costs:	
Materials (added continuously)	27,600
Labour and overheads	35,750
Production:	Units
Opening stock	1,500 (50% complete)
Units transferred to net process	9,000
Units still in process	2,000 (40% complete)

Required: costs assigned to the transferred product and the closing stock using the F.I.F.O. method of valuing inventory.

7.2 The Knotty Ash Detergent Company had the following production record and costs in July 19X5:

Production:	Gallons
Work-in-progress 1 July	140,000
Work started in July	620,000
Finished quantities	59,400
Work-in-progress 31 July	166,000

Costs:	£
Opening work-in-progress,	
materials conversion	42,000
July costs:	
materials	186,000
conversion	70,000

All materials are added at the beginning of the process. The work-in-progress at July 31 was 50% complete as to conversion costs. Value on an average cost basis.

Required: The unit cost per gallon.

7.3 The Wavertree Company operates a two process system of manufacture. Production information and costs are set out below:

	Process 1	Process 2
	£	£
Starting work-in-progress	4,500	6,000
Transfer from 1		– ? –
Costs for September 19X5		
Materials	25,000	19,000
Conversion	30,000	28,000
	Units	Units
Starting work-in-progress	1,500	2,500
	(50% complete)	(10% complete)
Units transferred	8,000	9,000
Closing work-in-progress	2,000	2,500
	(40% complete)	(60% complete)

Units are transferred from process 1 to process 2. The material for process 1 is added at the beginning and for process 2 at the end. Use F.I.F.O. for stock valuations. Percentages refer to conversion costs.

Required: Cost of units transferred and closing work-in-progress values.

7.4 Add to the information given above the following details on spoilt units

	Process 1	Process 2
Units spoiled		
Normal	70	50
Abnormal	40	20

Required: Revised cost of units transferred and closing work-in-progress values.

7.5 Complete the accounts shown below:

Process 1				Process 2			
£		£		£			£
Materials 4,000	Transfer to			Input from 1 ?	Transfer to		
Labour 1,000	process 2	?		Materials 900	finished stock ?		
Overheads 1,000	process 3	?		Labour 1,000	Closing w.i.p. ?		
				Overheads 800			

```
              Process 3                £
Work-in-          £
  progress    100
Input from 1    ?
Materials     300   Transfer to
Labour        500   finished goods?
Overheads     800
             ─────        ─────
```

Notes for the period:

1) 12,000 units were started and completed in the period, of which 9,000 went to process 2 and 3,000 to process 3.

2) 6,000 of the 9,000 units transferred to process 2 were completed, with the remaining units being 100% completed as to material and 80% as to conversion costs.

3) The opening work-in-progress of process 3 was 100% complete as to material and 50% as to conversion costs.

Questions 7.6-7.10 answers not provided

7.6 (a) MA Chemicals Limited process a range of products including a detergent 'Washo', which passes through three processes before completion and transfer to the finished goods warehouse. During April, data relating to this product were as shown:

		Process		
	1	2	3	Total
	£	£	£	£
Basic raw material (10,000 units)	6,000	—	—	6,000
Direct materials added in process	8,500	9,500	5,500	23,500
Direct wages	4,000	6,000	12,000	22,000
Direct expenses	1,200	930	1,340	3,470
Production overhead				16,500
(Production overhead is absorbed as a percentage of direct wages)				
	units	units	units	
Output	9,200	8,700	7,900	
	%	%	%	
Normal loss in process of input	10	5	10	
	£	£	£	
All loss has a scrap value, per unit of	0.20	0.50	1.00	

There was no stock at start or at end in any process.

You are required to prepare the following accounts:
(i) process 1;
(ii) process 2;
(iii) process 3;
(iv) abnormal loss;
(v) abnormal gain.

(b) Define briefly the following:
(i) normal loss;
(ii) abnormal loss;
(iii) abnormal gain;
(iv) scrap;
(v) waste.

ICMA(CA1).

7.7 (a) Explain the fundamental differences between job costing and process costing and state three industries, other than the food industry, which use process costing.

(b) A company within the food industry mixes powdered ingredients in two different processes to produce one product. The output of process 1 becomes the input of process 2 and the output of process 2 is transferred to the packing department.

From the information given below, you are required to open accounts for process 1, process 2, abnormal scrap and packing department and to records the transactions for the week ended 11th November 1978.

Process 1

Input: Material A   6,000 kilograms at £0.50 per kilogram
       Material B   4,000 kilograms at £1.00 per kilogram
Mixing labour   430 hours at £2 per hour
Normal scrap   5% of weight input
Scrap was sold for   £0.16 per kilogram
Output was   9,200 kilograms

There was no work in process at the beginning or end of the week.

Process 2

Input: Material C   6,600 kilograms at £1.25 per kilogram
       Material D   4,200 kilograms at £0.75 per kilogram
       Flavouring essence £300
Mixing labour   370 hours at £2 per hour
Normal waste   5% of weight input
Output was   18,000 kilograms

There was no work in process at the beginning of the week but 1,000 kilograms were in process at the end of the week and were estimated to be only 50% complete so far as labour and overhead were concerned.

Overhead of £3,200 incurred by the two processes was absorbed on the basis of mixing labour hours.

Within process 1, abnormal scrap arose because some batches failed to pass the quality control check at the end of each mix. However, no loss in weight occurred and all scrap was sold for cash on the last day of the week. Any resultant balance on the abnormal scrap account was transferred to profit and loss account.

ICMA(CA1).

7.8 A company manufactures a variety of liquids which pass through a number of processes. One of these products, P, passes through processes 1, 2 and 4 before being transferred to the finished goods warehouse.

You are required, from the details given below, to prepare accounts for the months of October 1978 for:

(a) process 4;
(b) abnormal loss/gain;
(c) finished goods.

	Cost £
Data for process 4, October 1978:	
Work in process, 1st October 1978: 6,000 units	19,440
degree of completion:	
Direct materials added 60%	
Direct wages and production overhead 40%	
Transferred from process 2:	
48,000 units at £2.30 per unit	
Transferred to finished goods: 46,500 units	
Incurred: Direct materials added	27,180
Direct wages	18,240
Production overhead	36,480

Work in process, 31st October 1978: 4,000 units
degree of completion:
  Direct materials added 50%
  Direct wages and production overhead 30%

Normal loss in process: 6% of units
in opening stock plus transfers from process 2
less closing stock

At a certain stage in the process, it is convenient for the quality control inspector to examine the product and where necessary reject it. Rejected products are then sold for £0.80 per unit. During October 1978 an actual loss of 7% was incurred, with product P having reached the following stage of production:

Direct materials added	80%
Direct wages and production overhead	60%

ICMA(CA2).

7.9 Product P63 is made by three sequential processes, I, II, and III. In process III a by-product arises and after further processing in process BP, at a cost of £2 per unit, by-product BP9 is produced. Selling and distribution expenses of £1 per unit are incurred in marketing BP9 at a selling price of £9 per unit.

	Process I	Process II	Process III
Standards provide for:			
—normal loss in process, of input of	10%	5%	10%
—loss in process, having a scrap value, per unit, of	£1	£3	£5

For the month of April 1978 the following data are given:

	Process I	Process II	Process III	Process BP
Output, in units	8,800	8,400	7,000 of P63	420 of BP9
				Total
Costs:	£	£	£	£
Direct materials introduced (10,000 units)	20,000			20,000
Direct materials added	6,000	12,640	23,200	41,840
Direct wages	5,000	6,000	10,000	21,000
Direct expenses	4,000	6,200	4,080	14,280

Budgeted production overhead for the month was £84,000. Absorption is based on a percentage of direct wages.

There were no stocks at the beginning or end of the month.

You are required, using the information given, to prepare accounts for:
(a) each of processes I, II and III;
(b) process BP;
(c) (i) abnormal losses;
    (ii) abnormal gains:

showing the balances to be transferred to the profit and loss statement.

ICMA(CA2).

7.10 XY Chemical Company Limited has three processing departments: 1, 2 and 3.

In department 1, batches of ingredients P, Q and R are mixed which, after processing produce three products: QA, PA and PB.

QA requires no further processing and can be sold;

PA can either be sold or subjected to further processing in department 3;

PB requires further processing in department 2, having no saleable value in its present form.

In department 2, PB is mixed with ingredient S to produce PX, which is saleable.

In department 3, PA is mixed with ingredient S and, after processing, produces PAS, which can be sold. It also produces a by-product AZ, which can be sold, but needs packing beforehand at a cost of £0.05 per lb.

Standard yields in each department are as follows:

Department 1—a batch of 50 lbs P, 70 lbs Q, and 30 lbs R will yield 30 lbs PA, 20 lbs PB, and 50 lbs QA;

Department 2—a batch of 20 lbs PB and 50 lbs S will yield 50 lbs PX;

Department 3—a batch of 30 lbs PA and 20 lbs S will yield 10 lbs PAS and 40 lbs AZ.

Price and cost data are as follows:

Costs of ingredients:	Ingredient	Cost per lb £
	P	0.8
	Q	0.6
	R	0.2
	S	0.3

Conversion cost per batch

		£
Department:	1	32.00
	2	10.00
	3	24.00
Selling prices (per lb):	PA	2.00
	QA	3.00
	PX	1.10
	PAS	15.00
	AZ	0.40

During period 5, a total of 80 batches was produced in all three departments. At the end of the period, the following proportions of the period's production remained unsold:

QA 10% : PX 15% : AZ 20%

With the above exception, opening and closing stocks were equal.

Fixed overhead of £6,000 per period is incurred; the company's practice is to treat it as a period cost and not to apportion it to departments, or to absorb it into product costs.

You are required:

1. On the assumption that the company apportions costs on the basis of weight at the split-off point, to calculate:

   (a) the costs per batch of PA, PB, QA and PX;

   (b) the costs per lb of PAS on the basis that the net revenue from the sale of AZ is treated as:

   (i) income of the company as a whole;

   (ii) a reduction in the cost of the main product in the department in which it is produced;

   (c) the total profit that the company made during period 5. (Assume for this purpose that closing stocks of by-product AZ have no value.)

2. If the company wished to apportion department 1 costs on the basis of the net sales value at the split-off point, to calculate:

   (a) the net sales value per lb of PB;

   (b) the costs per batch of PA, PB and QA, using the answer to 2 (a) above.

ICMA(CA2).

Seminar Problem 7

The Larkhill Company produces three products which are inter-related in their manufacture. In recent years the proportions of output have been 2 : 1 : 1. The proposal for the coming year is to manufacture the following quantities at the budgeted costs shown:

	A gallons	B gallons	C gallons
Units produced	100,000	50,000	50,000
	£	£	£
Selling prices/unit	2.00	1.60	1.50
Unique process cost/unit	1.00	0.70	0.55
Joint costs/unit	0.30	0.15	0.15

However, other combinations are possible and the marketing manager has proposed that two other feasible plans should be considered. The first plan is to divert manufacture of B entirely to A and the second is to divert half of each of B and C to the manufacture of A.

The conversion would be on a 1 to 1 basis in both cases, so the total units produced would be the same for all three plans. The unit processing costs would stay the same as shown above.

The cost accountant opposes these plans on the grounds that unit profit for A is less than for B and C.

Required: an assessment of the cost accountant's objection.

Chapter 8

Budgeting

Most people will at sometime or other plan ahead in terms of the their activities and their available resources. They do this in order to arrive at their correct standard of living in relation to the income available, to make decisions about savings and to arrange a suitable cash flow. The more complicated the forms of incomings and outgoings, the more essential it is to plan. Firms have this need and should prepare such plans in the form of a budget. As well as being a plan, a budget also acts as a control against which actual performance can be evaluated.

In order to make its decision wisely, the management of a firm must have a vision about its future. Without such a vision, the decision made now may prove to be harmful to the company in the long run. What is needed is a strategy for the foreseeable future, which can be called the long term plan. This should cover such items as growth, development of products, size and location of markets, management succession and so on. Long term planning such as this needs to be flexible and reviewed constantly. In essence it will be a rolling plan, reaching forward into the future and always moving with the years.

Major decisions such as those concerning new plant and product development must be compatible with the company's overall strategy. These decisions are medium term and usually concern the next four to seven years. Within this framework the coming year needs to be planned in detail. It is true that a budget for the forthcoming year can be prepared with little thought for longer term considerations, but in such circumstances the overall management effectiveness must be diminished.

The first decision to be made about a budget is to choose between goals and average expected performance. A budget based on goals which are tight is a device for encouraging improved performance. How this can be successful or otherwise is a matter for consideration at another point in the text. The point made here is that such a budget if used for planning purposes may lead to shortages of one resource or another. Very often it would be cash. This can be avoided in a number of ways. One obvious technique is to relax the goals to the level of their becoming the average expected performance. Another way is to use goals for most parts of the budget but to play safe when implementing the plans for resources, e.g. plan for a cash balance above the minimum based on achievement of the plans. A third approach is to separate the control information and the planning information. This third way give two budgets, one for controlling the operations of the firm and the other to plan its availability of resources.

The conventional system used extensively in industry today is to combine the two functions. At the same time many firms implicitly move towards a system of goals with a safeguard of some slack in the resource budgets.

Budgeting is an iterative process which leads to an acceptable plan for the firm. In it the sales and production activities have to be compatible with each other and have to be possible in terms of the physical resource available to the firm.

Figure 8.1 is a diagram of the main features of a firm's budgeting system.

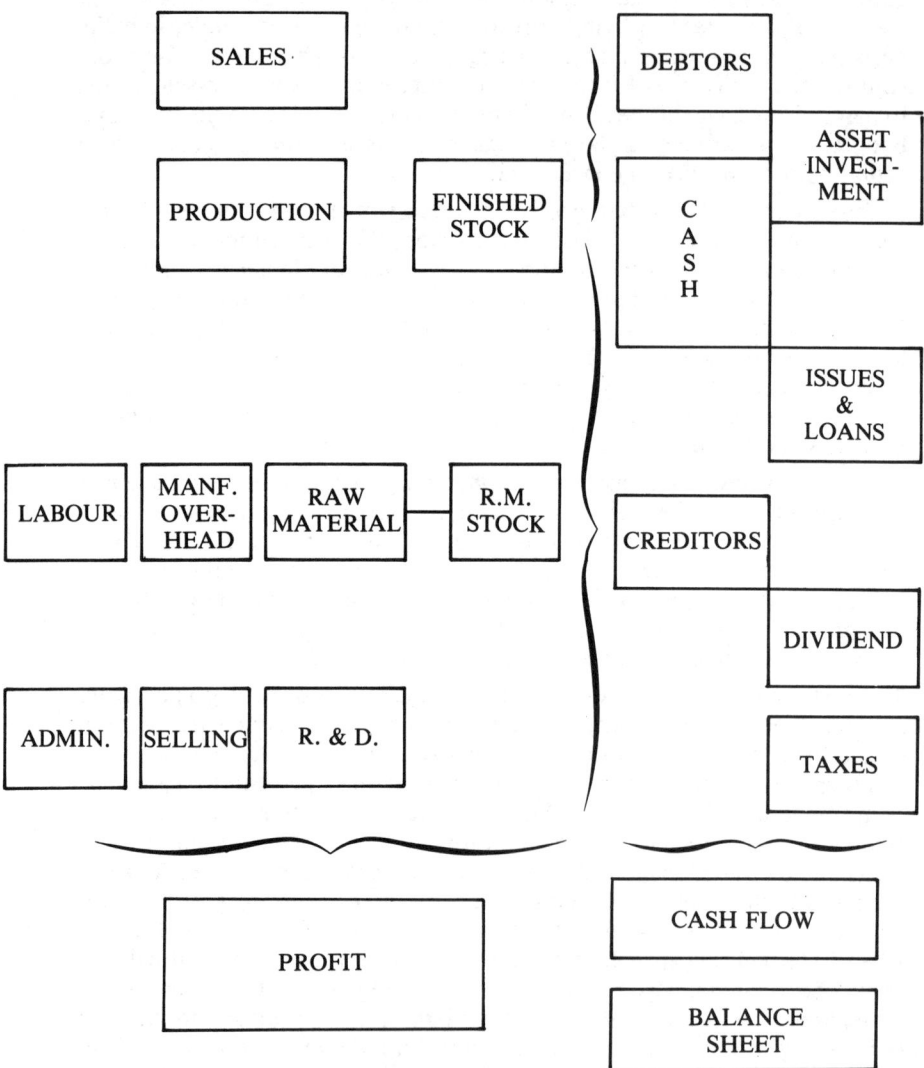

Figure 8.1. A Firm's Budgetary System.

Preparing the Budget

Figure 8.1 indicates that sales quantity equals the units produced plus or minus additions or withdrawals from stock of finished goods. A common starting point is to begin with a sales budget and to build the other budgets to match. These other budgets may reveal problems which call for special management decisions. Sometimes it is necessary to go back and amend previously determined figures. Hence, the statement earlier that budgeting is an iterative process. In practice the number of iterations is usually very limited and the resulting plan can only be regarded at best as a satisfactory one as opposed to the best one possible.

Sales Budget

This is prepared by analysing the available historic information on sales and adjusting the factors which are expected to influence the pattern in the coming period. To some extent the firm can plan alterations by making decisions on matters which are under its direct control. Additional sales can be encouraged by extra marketing effort for example. Other influences will be outside the control of the firm. Some of these may be capable of reasonably accurate predictions, others may be completely uncertain. The whole process of predicting this expected level of sales can be based on a fairly intuitive extrapolation of past figures with adjustments, or relatively sophisticated planning models can be used.

The following sample budgets illustrate the inter-relationship of the individual budgets and the putting together of the final master budget. The figures given relate to a firm which is about to start its first year of operations. For the sales budget the sales team have suggested the following plan—

Territory	1	2	3	4	Total
Sales in units	6,000	7,000	8,000	9,000	30,000
Sales in value	£900,000	£1,050,000	£1,200,000	£1,350,000	£4,500,000
Variable selling expense	£150,000	£175,000	£200,000	£225,000	£750,000
Fixed selling expense					£1,000,000

These are summary figures which would be supported by more detailed schedules.

Production Budget

This is a decision about stock levels after sales have been satisfied. The number of units to be manufactured is the sales quantity minus the amount in stock at the beginning of the period plus the stock level desired at the period end.

In the illustration there was nil stock at the beginning and management have made a decision to finish with 5000 completed units.

Sales	30,000
Opening stock	nil
	30,000
Closing stock	5,000
Make	35,000

Purchases of Direct Material

In a similar way to the production budget the procurement of direct material is a decision based on stock movements as well as on production requirements. The quantity bought will equal the quantity used on production, less the opening stock and plus the closing stock. For this firm, each units produced requires £20 worth of material. As before opening stock was nil, but the management has authorised a closing stock of £20,000.

Production requirements 35,000 × £20 =	£700,000
Planned closing stock	20,000
Buy	£720,000

Direct Labour Budget

The standard quantity of labour required for each unit produced times the expected wage rate gives the labour budget. The way in which these standard allowances are calculated is something that was looked at in chapter 4 and will be referred to again in the chapters on Standard Costing.

Labour hours per unit	12
Wage rate/hour	£1.25
Labour cost/unit	£15
Units of production planned	35,000
Total wages	£525,000

Manufacturing Overhead Budget

This budget contains figures for items such as heat, power, maintenance rent, depreciation of machinery, supervision and insurance. The behaviour of these costs will each have its own characteristics. Some will be variable, other semi-variable, yet others will be step or fixed. For each type of expense it will be necessary to establish its variability with activity. This is not an easy task, but the less an attempt is made to do this, the less value can be attached to the budget for its control aspects.

Variable expense/unit	£15
Planned production	35000
Variable cost 35000 × 15	£525.000
Fixed cost	£500,000

The budget of fixed costs relates to the size of organisation necessary to produce the 35000 units.

Selling and Administration Budgets

Both selling and administration budgets should be prepared in a similar manner to the manufacturing overhead budget. These deal with such items as salesman's salaries and commission, advertising, area office costs and so on under selling. Administration costs consist of residual expenses and include company legal fees, audit fees and donations as examples. A number of selling expenses are variable and semi-variable. In the main this does not apply to administration costs which are usually fixed.

The selling expense budget has already been given, but for convenience it is repeated here, along with the adminstration budget.

Variable selling expenses	£750,000
Fixed selling expenses	£1,000,000
Fixed administration	£500,000

Research and Development Budget

Research and development expenditure can be treated either in one of two extreme ways or in a compromise between these two. At one end of the scale all R & D can be written off against profit in the period to which it is incurred. That is to say, it is dealt with as a period expense. Alternatively, it can be regarded as expenditure with a long term benefit, just as expenditure on fixed assets. In this case the cost is accounted for as a capital payment and periodic charges are made against profit. Clearly, the compromise is to analyse the research and development expenditure and deal with items on their merits. The general principle is simply stated. Research and development expenditure which can be closely associated with identifiable products which are judged to have profitable prospects should be capitalised. Unfortunately, although it is quite easy to set down the principles for analysis, the designation of this area of expenditure is very much a matter of judgement and opinion. Since in most of the important firms in the economy, research and development is a large consumer of funds, it follows that the treatment afforded it has a significant impact on profits.

The firm spends in the illustration relatively little under this heading and writes off against profit as a period expense.

Planned R & D expenditure £40,000.

Cash Budget

So far the details given under the various budget headings have been in accordance with the usual conventions governing profit calculation. Additional information concerning the corresponding movements of cash is needed if a cash budget is to be prepared. Consequently each participant in the budgeting exercise, must provide the cash flow equivalent of the figures provided so far.

Sales would schedule inflows from debtors according to the terms of credit and allowing for some slow payment. For the period of this budget, this may be £3,500,000. The equivalent outgoings of cash for the purchase of direct material, after allowing for credit taken, may be estimated at £640,000. Other items are as shown in the cash flow statement. As well as allowing for the difference in time between the contracting of an obligation and the payment or receipt of money, there is the additional factor of depreciation. This is an expense against profit which does not have a cash flow counterpart. Of course, the payment for new fixed assets does enter the cash flow calculations.

Full details of cash flows from each party in the budget are set out below—

	£
Cash at start of the period	nil
Receipts from debtors	3,500,000
Payments—	
purchases of direct material	640,000
direct labour	525,000
manufacturing overhead—variables	480,000
manufacturing overhead—fixed	400,000
selling expenses — variable	700,000
selling expenses — fixed	820,000
administration	450,000
research and development	35,000
	4,050,000
Net cash outflow from operations	550,000
Expenditure on fixed assets—	200,000
Total cash deficit for the period	750,000
Financed by—	
Ownership interest	400,000
Bank loan	400,000

This cash budget reveals that the combined cash deficit from operations and capital purchases amounts to £750,000. This is to be met by ownership money plus a bank loan. For the purposes of reducing the amount of detail in the illustration, the exact time span has not been specified, but has always been referred to as a "period". If the period had in fact been twelve months then it would be necessary to phase the budgets into at least quarter year periods, if not months. This closer look at anticipated events could reveal some significant peaks or troughs. This is particularly true in the cash budget. The use of phased cash budgets is examined in the chapter on the control of working capital.

Profit and Loss Budget

Bringing all the figures together into a planned profit statement is a relatively simple affair and follows the normal accounting rules. Using the figures set out previously, the following budgeted profit and loss account is obtained.

	£	£
Sales		4,500,000
Opening stock	—	
Variable cost of production:-		
Material	700,000	
Labour	525,000	
Manufacturing overhead	525,000	
	1,750,000	
Closing stock (5000 × £50)	250,000	
	1,500,000	
Variable selling cost	750,000	2,250,000
Contribution to fixed overhead and profit		2,250,000
Fixed cost of		
Manufacturing	500,000	
Selling	1,000,000	
Administration	500,000	
Research and development	40,000	2,040,000
Profit		£210,000

The closing stock is valued as follows:

	£
Material	20
Labour	15
Variable manufacturing overhead	15
	50

The fixed element of manufacturing overhead is being written off as a period expense.

Budgeted Balance Sheet

Here is the balance sheet for the period end resulting from the plan:-

	£	£
Fixed Assets		200,000
Less Provision for Depreciation		20,000
		180,000

Current Assets—
  Stock of finished goods   250,000
  Stock of raw materials   20,000
  Debtors   1,000,000
  Cash   50,000
                                 _____
                                 1,320,000
Current Liabilities—
  Creditors   490,000
                                 _____
Net Current Assets   830,000
                                                    _____
                                                    1,010,000
Ownership—
  Capital Introduced   400,000
  Profit   210,000   610,000
                                 _____
Loan   400,000
                                                    _____
                                                    1,010,000
                                                    =========

Some of these figures may need an explanatory note:

Creditors—

	Expense deducted from Profit £	Depreciation Expense £	Cash Paid £	Amount Owing to Creditors £
Purchase of materials				
for production	700,000			
for stock	20,000			
	720,000	—	640,000	80,000
Labour	525,000	—	525,000	—
Manufacturing Overhead—				
—variable	525,000	—	480,000	45,000
—fixed	500,000	10,000	400,000	90,000
Selling expenses—				
—variable	750,000	—	700,000	50,000
—fixed	1,000,000	10,000	820,000	170,000
Administration	500,000	—	450,000	50,000
Research	40,000	—	35,000	5,000
	4,560,000	20,000	4,050,000	490,000

Debtors— Sales   4,500,000
        Collections   3,500,000
                         _____
                         1,000,000

The Budget as a Model of the Firm

Budgets are used as a planning device in the first instance. Later they are used for control purposes. As a planning device they provide a means of examining a number of alternative sets of proposals and choosing between them. Unfortunately, the number of iterations done in the process is usually very few, because of limitations in terms of time and labour.

This means that the final plan is the most satisfactory one chosen form a limited number of possibilities. Computers are making an impact here and an increasing number of firms are developing computer based models of the firm. In the majority of cases these simulate the firm's activities and enable the management to investigate a wider range of possible alternatives. These methods give the most satisfactory solution from a wider number of possibilities. A longer term approach, but potentially very rewarding, is to develop computer models of the firm which are optimising models. These are more mathematically developed and aim to produce the best solution possible, as opposed to the best of the limited number of solutions considered.

Behavioural Aspects of Budgeting

This chapter has been entirely concerned with putting figures together into a plan. How these figures are arrived at is a connected consideration, to which a great deal of importance is being increasingly attached. The preparation of a budget should be an exercise which enhances the motivation of various levels of people working in the firm. With thought and care it can be made to do this. On the other hand it can swing in the opposite direction and be seen as punitive instrument of management.

Flexible Budgets

One problem associated with the adoption of a single budget is that it is based on an assumption about the coming level of activity. Since the actual level of activity may be significantly different, there can be occasions when it is difficult to interpret variances between the budget and actual. The problem is to analyse between spending variations and volume variations. The technique introduced to handle this is called flexible budgeting. It requires a knowledge of how costs behave under conditions of changing levels of activity. The result is that a budget is available for control purposes, whichever the achieved scheme of activity. Flexible budgets are illustrated in chapter 9.

Zero base budgets

Most managers prepare their departmental budgets on the basis of previous years expenditure, adjusted for new developments, inflation and other anticipated changes. Ideally, they should operate a strict review of their departmental activities and fully justify their budget proposals from scratch. This would involve them in a fundamental re-appraisal of their work. It would mean asking questions that go to the very heart of their existence. Each activity would be tested to see whether it should be continued, modified or discontinued. This would mean answering searching questions about the quality of the output versus the needs of recipient and also questions about justifiable cost levels.

All in all, a zero base review is a powerful tool for management, if used sparingly. A thorough audit of a centre's activities is a big task which would become trivialised if undertaken too frequently. A programme to complete such a review throughout a firm every five years would be reasonable.

Chapter Summary

Ideally a firm should prepare a series of plans, ranging from the long term strategic down through the medium-term to the short-term and of the year ahead.

The budget is a multi-featured process and this needs to be recognised if the best case is to be made of it. Firstly it is a plan and as such it needs to be recognised that plans are arrived at under different basic assumptions. Some managements plan in an optimistic way, setting targets and seeking to obtain motivation from the figures. This can be done quite successfully, given an awareness of what is involved and a subsequential degree of participation down the line. Nevertheless, if the budget is this sort of plan it must be recognised as such and not used as a control device. Investigations into failure to meet desired standards is one thing, investigations with failure to meet targets could have punitive overtones and be counter-production. In any event, the consequence of failing to reach targets must be fully thought out, since this may result in problems in specific areas, usually cash flow.

Budgets are also controlling devices. It was stated in the text that most firms set a plan which is explicitly the level of achievement that they regard as good and possible and as such is a control.

A completed budget is a means of communication throughout the organisation. Properly and widely disseminated it informs all levels of employees of the firms plans and shows them the part that they are called upon to play.

However, the completed budget must not be the first contact that employees have with the budgeting process. They should have performed a considerable amount of work on the budget and for best results should feel committed to it as something which is good in terms of realism, practicability and profitability.

The preparation of budgets is currently undergoing change. It is changing from a largely clerical process to a computerised one, with the computer system including an increasing number of advanced techniques. This speeding up of the process enables the management to investigate a wide number of alternative possibilities and gives them more change of improving the level of satisfaction which their model gives. The type of technique which can be incorporated into these computer based budgets includes sales forecasting techniques and stock control models. As this type of simulation grows more acceptable and widespread in use, it will lead towards computer model building based on optimising techniques.

Exercises

Questions 8.1-8.5 (Answers provided)

8.1 The Lancaster Trading Company has a sales budget of 100,000 completed units for the three months ending 31st December 19X5. The company manufactures a finished article which is an assembly of a dozen units, two of which are the same type X.

At 1st October 19X5 the stock of X was 10,000 and the management wishes to increase this by 5,000 during the quarter year.

The opening stock of finished goods was 7,000 and this is to be increased to 10,000 by 31st December.

Required: the number of units of X that should be purchased during the three months to 31st December?

8.2 The Canterbury (Electronics) Company has a factory which manufacturers a single product. Budget information for the forthcoming year is set out as follows:

Sales, 50,000 units at £20 each.

Production is to be sufficient to meet these sales and fulfil the policy of maintaining finishing stock at 10% of sales for the year. The current year's sales are projected to be 40,000 units.

Raw material is taken in daily and stock can be ignored. The current direct material unit cost of the finished product is £3.00. A 10% price increase is expected mid-year.

Direct labour man hours per unit have been reasonably steady throughout the previous period and are expected to remain at the same level of productivity. A 10% increase in hourly rates is forecast for the mid-point of the year. Each unit required 20 man hours. The hourly rate at the time of budgeting was £2.00.

Factory overheads can be budgeted from the formula:

$$y = ax + b$$

where Y = total factory overhead costs
x = level of production
a = £2
b = fixed costs estimated at £150,000.
Production is evenly spread throughout the year. Value opening stock at £45/unit.
Required: forecast manufacturing and trading account for the year.

8.3 George and Michael York are planning to start a new business and wish to draw up a budget for the first twelve months. They are negotiating to buy a leasehold property with a term of 20 years to run, at a cost of £20,000 and expect to sell one quarter of the property immediately for £6,000. £5,000 will be spent on fixtures and equipment. A loan of £10,000 at 6% per annum can be obtained. Discussion produces the following trading estimates:

Sales: £4,000 per month for six months increasing to £6,000 per month in the second six months and remaining at this figure in the following year.

		Gross Profit
Gross Profit on Sales:	Group A (50% of Sales)	15%
	Group B (30% of Sales)	25%
	Group C (20% of Sales)	30%

Debtors: 1½ month's sales

Creditors: 1 month's purchases of goods
£500 for Expenses

Stock Turnover: 5 times per annum

Selling and Administrative Expenses: £7,500

Bad Debts: Provision to be made amounting to 3% of debtors at the end of the year. Depreciation to be provided on the straight line basis on fixtures and equipment at 10% per annum and on property at 5% per annum.

Partners' drawings will be restricted to £750 per annum each and the partners will introduce sufficient capital to provide a cash balance of £1,000 at the end of the year.

Prepare a Budgeted Profit and Loss Account and Balance Sheet for the first year.

8.4 Durham (Products) Limited accounts for 19X5 are as follows:

Balance Sheet at 31st December

	19X5 £
Share Capital	6000
Reserves...............................	8000
Debentures	2000
Current Liabilities (including tax and dividend)	17000
	33000
Fixed Assets at cost	10100
Less depreciation	2600
	7500
Current Assets:	
Stock	12500
Debtors	11000
Cash.............................	2000
	33000

Profit and Loss Account for the year ended 31st December 19X5

Sales		55000
Expenses (including depreciation 600)		49800
Profit before taxation		5200
Corporation Tax (payable October 19X6)	2200	
Proposed Dividend	1200	
		3400
Transfer to Reserves		1800

Information on planned expansion for 19X6 is set out below:

Additional plant to be bought in January 19X6 at a cost of £1500.

Depreciation on fixed assets to be 10% of the written down value.

Sales for 19X6 expected to be £80,000 on which a gross profit of 50% will be earned. (£50,000 sales expected in the second half of the year).

Fixed overhead expenses for 19X6 other than depreciation will be £24000.

Variable expenses will be 9% of sales.

At 31st December stock will be equivalent to six months purchases, customers will take two months credit and suppliers of goods will allow 3 months credit. Unpaid overhead expenses will be £3,000.

The proposed dividend at 31st December 19X5 will be paid on 31st March 19X6 and an interim dividend of £600 paid on 30th September 19X6.

Taxation on the years profits is expected to be at the rate of 40% (payable in October 19X7).

Required:

(1) A statement showing the expected cash position at 31st Dec. 19X6.

(2) A budgeted balance sheet at that date on historic cost basis.

8.5 Peter Derby retired recently from his employment abroad and returned to this country with the intention of buying a small retail business.

He is currently negotiating for the purchase of a small concern which he considers suitable for a first venture. In order to assess a purchase price he has persuaded the existing owner to show him his bank account for the past twelve months and a petty cash book that had been kept but not shown to anyone else.

Derby has summarised this evidence to show the following:

Bankings from shop	£25,774
Rent for 12 months	2,000
Rates for 12 months	1,500
Electricity	500
Equipment Hire	500
Stock purchases by cheque	16,400
Stock purchases by cash	3,424
Assistant's wages	1,000
Miscellaneous expenses	420
Cash drawings	5,200

Derby is confident that these are true figures and that he can use them to assess current profitability. He is asking you to do this for him.

Required:

a) What other information do you need?

b) Assuming figures as necessary, calculate the business profit for the period.

Questions 8.6-8.10 answers not provided

8.6 The trading results for the year ending 30th June 1978 of D Limited, a face cream manufacturer, are expected to be as follows:

	£000	£000
Sales (100,000 jars)		400
Costs:		
Material	50	
Wages: direct	82	
indirect, fixed	19	
Production expenses:		
variable	25	
fixed	30	
Administration expenses:		
fixed	24	
Selling expenses:		
variable	20	
fixed	22	
Distribution expenses:		
variable	18	
fixed	10	
		300
Profit		100

Forecasts for year ending 30th June 1979 are given below:

1. A sales price reduction to £3 per jar will increase sales volume by 50%.
2. Material prices will remain unchanged except that, because of increased quantities purchased, a 5% quantity discount will be obtained.
3. Direct wage rates will increase by 10%.
4. Variable selling costs will increase proportionately with sales value.
5. Inflation will increase variable production and distribution expenses by 10%.
6. All fixed costs will increase by 20%.
7. There will be no stocks of work-in-progress at the beginning or end of the year.

You are required, using the information, to:

(a) prepare a statement showing the profit forecast for the year ending 30th June 1979 on a marginal costing basis;
(b) comment on the result forecast in your answer to (a) above;
(c) prepare an alternative profit statement for the year ending 30th June 1979 based on a sales price increase of 10% on 1977/78 price and a sales volume of 100,000 jars;
(d) state the price increase per jar (and as a percentage to three decimal places) needed, above the current sales prices, for year ending 30th June 1979 to achieve a profit of £110,000.

ICMA(CA1)

8.7 (a) Explain the main function s of a cash budget and discuss briefly its importance in a system of budgetary control.

(b) From the data given below, prepare a cash budget for each of the first three months of 1978:

—Cash balance on 1st January, 1978 is forecast as £40,000.

—A new computer is to be installed in January 1978 at a cost of £100,000 and will be paid for on 1st March, 1978.

—A sales commission of 2½% on sales is to be paid within one month of the month of sale.

—Taxation of £180,000 is to be paid in February.

—In January a dividends of £40,000 is to be paid to ordinary shareholders (ignore taxation).

—£10,000 per month is payable under a leasing agreement.

—An issue of debentures is expected to be made in February, which will result in £50,000 being received during that month.

—The period of credit allowed by suppliers averages two months.

140

—Delay in payment of overhead averages one month.

—Delay in payment of research and development costs averages half a month.

—Delay in payment of wages averages a quarter of a month.

—To encourage payment of invoices, the company allows a cash discount of 5% if payment is made within one week and of 2½% if payment is made within one month. It is estimated that 25% of the debtors of each month pay within one week, and a further 60% of the debtors of each month pay within one month. The remaining debtors are expected to pay their invoices in full within two months.

A forecast of costs and revenues includes the following:

		1977		
Month:		Oct.	Nov.	Dec.
Direct:		£	£	£
Materials		50,000	45,000	60,000
Wages		40,00	36,000	44,000
Overhead				
Production		15,000	14,000	18,000
Administration		10,000	9,000	12,000
Selling and distribution		6,000	5,000	8,000
Research and development costs		4,000	5,000	5,000
Sales		160,000	200,000	240,000

		1978		
Month:		Jan	Feb	Mar
Direct:		£	£	£
Materials		40,000	30,000	35,000
Wages		32,000	24,000	28,000
Overhead:				
Production		20,000	16,000	18,000
Administration		10,000	11,000	12,000
Selling and distribution		6,000	5,000	7,000
Research and development costs		6,000	6,000	7,000
Sales		200,000	160,000	160,000

ICMA(CA1)

8.8 In the year ended 31st December, 1975 the actual costs, output, and sales of a company manufacturing a range of products were as follows:

	Product			
	A	B	C	D
Per unit:	£	£	£	£
Selling price	20	40	50	30
Variable costs:				
Direct materials	4	9	10	3
Direct wages	3	5	10	4
	units	units	units	units
Manufactured and sold	7,500	5,000	3,000	6,000

Variable overhead was incurred at a rate of 200% of direct wages.

Fixed overhead was £200,000 for the year.

The company's summarized budgeted results for the year ended 31st December were:

	£
Sales	700,000
Variable costs of sales ...	455,000
Contribution	245,000
Fixed overhead.........	190,000
Budgeted profit	£55,000

In preparing its budget for the year ending 31st December, 1976 the company has made the following allowances for inflation over the actual figures for 1975:

(i) an increase in all selling prices of 10%; these increases are not expected to alter the quantities of each product sold, as compared with 1975;

(ii) an increase in unit product costs of:

	%
Direct materials	10
Direct wages........	20
Variable overhead ...	10

(iii) an increase of 2% in fixed overhead.

In addition to those allowances for inflation, the company proposes the following changes in its cost, sales volume, and selling price structure.

Product A increase the price by 10%, yielding a reduction of 5% in volume sold;

Product B use of different direct materials which will reduce direct materials cost by £2 per unit and reduce volume sold by 4%;

Product C (i) incur advertising cost of £10,000 for the year which is expected to increase sales by 20%;

(ii) buy a machine costing £8,000 which would reduce direct labour hours by 20% for the same grades of labour;

Product D reduce the selling price by 10%, giving an increase in sales volume of 15%;

Increase stock held by an average of £40,000 over the whole year; this would be financed by bank overdraft at an interest rate of 12% per annum;

Increase the size of the delivery van fleet at an outlay of £9,000 and an increase in annual fixed costs of £2,000 (excluding depreciation).

The company calculates its depreciation on a straight-line basis with a standard life of five years for production equipment and three years for non-production equipment.

You are required to:

(a) show, in a format helpful to management, a summary statement of the budgeted and actual results for the year ended 31st December, 1975 with an analysis of the difference between the two profits;

(b) compile a budgeted profit and loss account for the company for the year ending 31st December, 1976 after taking account of:

(i) allowances for inflation only;

(ii) allowances for inflation and the additional changes proposed;

(c) calculate (to the nearest £1,000) the separate breakeven points for the actual results of the year ended 31st December, 1975 and the budget for 1976 at (b) (ii) above;

(d) comment very briefly on:

(i) the differences between the results of (b) (i) and (b) (ii) above;

(ii) the implications for the company of the results of (c) above.

ICMA(CA2).

8.9 At the end of April 1978, CD Limited, which supplies a component to leading manufacturers in a segment of the engineering industry, fears that its largest customer EF Limited is likely to be subject to a strike. This strike is expected to last from 1st May to 31st July 1978, during which time EF Limited will be unable to purchase any components from CD Limited.

CD Limited believes, however, that as from 1st August 1978, when the strike will have finished, EF Limited's demand for components will be £100,000 per month for several months compared with its present monthly demand of £75,000.

Demand from other smaller customers for an identical item, however, is expected to continue as at present at £25,000 per month throughout the period May to August, 1978.

CD Limited is considering two possible plans for dealing with this situation:

Plan A: To continue producing at its normal (effectively maximum) level of £100,000 worth per month of the component, putting the unsold production into stock. If this is done, it will have enough stock to enable it to meet the higher demand from EF Limited during August.

Plan B: To produce at the normal level during May, to stop production during June and July, and to re-start at the normal level in August. If this is done, it will be able to meet the higher level of demand from EF Limited during August only.

The following additional information is available:

1. Profit and loss statements for the year to 31st January 1978 and the three months to 30th April 1978. (Appendix 1).

2. Balance sheets as at 31st January 1978 and 30th April 1978. (Appendix 2).

3. Budgeted monthly income statement for period May to August if normal production is maintained. (Appendix 3).

4. It is the company's practice to absorb fixed production costs into finished goods. If, however, no goods are produced, fixed production costs for that month would be charged to profit and loss account. Selling and administration costs can be regarded as fixed and charged to profit and loss account.

5. Direct wages are paid in the months in which they are incurred. Overhead is paid one month after it is incurred.

6. Assume that selling prices remain constant over the period and that tax is chargeable at 50%.

You are required to:

(a) prepare a cash forecast for the total four-month period 1st May 1978 to 31st August 1978 for the company:

  (i) if plan A were adopted;

  (ii) if plan A were adopted;

(b) prepare a balance sheet for the company as at 31st August 1978 assuming that plan B were adopted;

(c) briefly identify the factors that are likely to influence the company's decision in favour of plan A or plan B.

Appendix 1   ICMA(MA1).

Profit and Loss Statements (in £000)

	For year ended 31st January 1978		For 3 months ended 30th April 1978	
Sales		1,058.4		297.1
Cost of sales:				
Direct materials	236.7		66.1	
Direct wages	205.2		61.8	
Other expenses	158.1	600.0	38.0	165.9
Selling and administration expenses		252.4		69.4
Total		852.4		235.3
Profit before tax		206.0		61.8

Appendix 2

Balance Sheets (in £000)

	As at 31st January 1978		As at 30th April 1978	
Fixed assets:				
Plant and machinery	637.3		637.3	
Less: Accumulated depreciation	140.1	497.2	158.1	479.2
Current assets:				
Stocks: Raw materials	19.2		22.0	
Finished goods	19.3		21.4	
	38.5		43.4	
Debtors	92.1		106.2	
Cash	111.2	241.8	99.2	248.8
		739.0		728.0
Issued capital	450.0		450.0	
Profit and loss account	140.6	590.6	158.7	608.7
Current liabilities:				
Trade creditors	62.2		64.4	
Other current liabilities	30.3		30.0	
Tax due	55.9	148.4	24.9	119.3
		739.0		728.0

Appendix 3

Budgeted monthly income statement for period May to August 1978 if normal production is maintained

		£000
Sales		100
Cost of sales:		
Direct materials	22	
Direct wages	20	
Fixed production costs	12	54
Selling and administration costs*		24
Total		78
Profit before tax		22
*includes depreciation		6

8.10 Pickled Cauliflower Ltd. operates two departments to produce its pickled cauliflower. The 'Epicaul' brand is produced in one department and the standard label is produced in the other. The two departments are referred to as E and S respectively.

In recent years demand for the Epicaul brand has been falling and the firm has made the decision to shut down department E. However the timing of the closure has yet to be agreed. A budget for department E for the year ending 30th June, 1976 has been prepared as follows:

Budget for Department E
for the year ending 30th June, 1976

	Total	Per case of output
Direct costs		
Material C	£50,000	£0.50
Material V	10,000	0.10
Packaging material	30,000	0.30
Labour	100,000	1.00
Overheads		
Variable	50,000	0.50
Fixed	40,000	0.40
Total Costs	280,000	2.80
Less		
Sales Revenue (100,000 cases)	250,000	2.50
Budgeted Net Loss for Year	(30,000)	(£0.30)

The managing director of Pickled Cauliflower Ltd. suggests that as this budget indicates that department E will be in a loss-,making position next-year, it should be closed down immediately. The firm's accountant says that he thinks that a flexible budget should be drawn up, showing the contribution of this department to fixed overheads and profit, before a decision is finally made. He arranges for a flexible budget to be prepared based on activities of 80,000, 100,000 and 120,000 cases, the latter quantity being the maximum that the department can produce.

The following information is available in addition to that contained in the original budget:

1. *Direct Materials*
   (a) Each case of the final product requires a bushel of material C and there are 100,000 bushels of C in stock. This material originally cost £50,000 but today has no resale value. Unless it is used to manufacture Epicaul next year it will have to be disposed of at a cost of £1,000 to the firm for every 10,000 bushels which have to be dumped. Additional material C can be obtained by importing it from abroad at a cost of £1 per bushel.
   (b) The stock of material V would be sufficient to produce 120,000 cases of the product. However, this could also be used in the production of the standard product, which requires the same amount of material V to produce one case as the Epicaul brand does. The original cost of the material V in stock was £5,000 and this now has a market cost of £24,000.

(c) Sufficient packaging material to pack 100,000 cases of the Epicaul product is in stock. As this has been overprinted with Epicaul information, only half the value of this could be salvaged for use with the standard product. There have been no price changes associated with packaging materials and scrapping costs would be negligible.

2. *Variable Overheads and Machinery*

The machinery used in department E is ten years old. It originally cost £100,000 and is currently being depreciated by the straight line method over a twenty year period. No scrap value is expected at the end of the life of the machinery. Depreciation is recovered by including it in the variable overheads. The market value of the machinery on the 1st July, 1974 was £60,000. This value would fall during the next year through use only, at a rate of £1 per ten cases produced.

Variable overheads for department E vary in proportion to output.

3. *Fixed Overheads*

The fixed overhead recovery rate includes occupancy costs and general expenses which cannot be reduced in the year ahead, even if department E is closed. It also includes the salary of the departmental manager at £5,000 per annum. He is over retiring age, although he is prepared to continue if department E remains open.

4. *Price Elasticity*

The marketing director estimates that the price which could be obtained for the quantities suggested for the flexible budget would be:

Cases sold	Price obtainable per case (for all cases)
80,000	£3.00
100,000	£2.50
120,000	£2.00

Required:

(a) Prepare the flexible budgets required by the accountant. State clearly any assumptions that you make and show your workings.

(b) Advise the managing direct, at what level of production the department should operate in the year to 30th June, 1976, and what decision criterion he should use if immediate closure is to be considered.

CA(MA).

Seminar Problem 8

The Chester Gadget Company Limited was started some years ago by Vera Chester. Her plan was to assemble and market a novel household gadget. In order to raise the necessary finance she approached a bank for a loan. In support of her application, Vera had carefully prepared forecasts for the first year's acticity. She asked for help in bringing the budgets together.

The budgets were as set out below:-

(a) Sales budget:

Sales — 12000 units per annum occurring evenly throughout the year.

Selling price — £5 per unit.

(b) Production budget:

Planned production to meet sales and provide a stock of finished goods — 13000 units in the year.

(c) Raw materials budget:

X 1 unit of the company's product requires 4 units of X.

X purchase price — £0.25 per unit.

Y 1 unit of the company's product requires 2 units of Y.

Y purchase price — £0.50 per unit.

Minimum Stock of raw material are to be built up immediately to the level of 1000 of X and 500 of Y.

(d) Direct labour budget:

Labour hours per unit of production — 1.00

Wage rate — £1.50 per hour.

(e) Manufacturing overhead budget:

Plant and equipment depreciation	£2900
Other items	£3600
	£6500

(f) Selling and administration budget: £6000

(g) Capital expenditure budget:

Immediate investment required—

Buildings —	£10000
Equipment —	£10000

(h) Finance budget:

Debtors collection — the terms of sale will be one month's credit.

Payments to creditors — these will all be on receipt of goods or services.

The available cash at the start £15000

Assume that finished goods in stock at the year end would have been valued at average full factory cost.

Required:

(a) The bank overdraft forecast for the end of the first year.

(b) The forecast profit and loss account for the first year and balance sheet.

Chapter 9

Standard Costing — 1

Standards and Direct Cost Variances

The idea of standards was touched on in the chapter dealing with labour costs. The purpose of this chapter is to explain standards more fully and to incorporate them into the costing system. Standard costs form the basis of budgets, which are built up by valuing the physical volumes expected at standard. The standards also act as the centre-piece of the control system, since they are the measure of expected performance. A final point about standards in costing is that it reduces the work involved in maintaining the cost records, particularly in the area of stock valuation.

Standards represent a relationship that ought to exist between the inputs and output of a firm. They are an attempt to say in a scientific way, how efficient a firm should be. Not by looking at and criticising past results, say in comparison with others; but by a process of measurement and evaluation related to the nature of the work itself. It is fairly easy to see that from a given input of raw material a given output ought to be maintained. the quantity of metal needed in the manufacture of a dust bin is not a difficult thing to quantify. The same approach can be made to other costs, although not all standards can be laid down with equal certainty. Such standards of achievement form the basis of the control system. This system communicates to the members of the organisation the performance levels that are expected of them in the forthcoming period. It also provides a means of isolating some variance between expected performance and actual; such variance reporting is consistent with management by exceptions in that features requiring attention are highlighted.

Types of Standard

The extent to which standard rates can be determined scientifically varies from one types of expense to another. For the direct material content a considerable degree of exactitude is possible, but some allowance has to be made for waste and spoilage. It is the extent of this allowance that enables subjective variations to enter the standard setting process. If very little allowance is made then 'ideal' standards are being set. Further down the line the standard becomes a 'good attainable' performance. The final level is merely one 'average expected' performance based on past experience.

If the standard is to be a realistic means of communication and measurement of performance, whilst at the same time setting out desirable goals, then the second type of standard is the one to be preferred.

Direct labour is a cost for which some scientific attempt can be made to provide a standard rate. The substance of the following section was dealt with in chapter 4, but is repeated here for students following a different pattern of study. The initial stage is to set out a good work flow and environment through 'method study'. Once the scene is set correctly for efficient working, the job is measured by time study specialists. It is their job to break the task being measured into component parts. Then they measure the time taken to perform each part. It is necessary to take a large number of timings for a number of people at different working periods, in order to iron out the natural variations that occur. Alternatively, the components of the operators work may be expressed as very simple and basic movements for which pre-determined times are available. Either way a result is obtained which expresses the rate that ought to pertain for a normal operator who is working according to his ability. This rate describes the job content in terms of standard hours of work. If a task is worth half a standard hour, then the achievement aimed for is to perform the task twice in the hour. A standard hour of work is a unit of work done, not of time taken. The degree of exactness in the measurement is subject to the skill and experience of the work study engineers (and to the same attributes of the operator, who may be working for slack standards against the engineers judgement). Then again the labour unions have a part to play in arriving at final agreement on the content of a standard hour.

Examples of standard costs are shown in figures 9.1 and 9.2.

	Part No. 16-4321		
	Qty.	Unit Cost £	Total Cost £
Widgets	2	1.00	2.00
Squidgets	3	0.50	1.50
Blodgets	1	0.25	0.25
			3.75

Figure 9.1. Standard Material Cost.

	Part No. 16-4321		
Activity	Hours	Rate/hr. £	Total Cost £
Wiggling	0.250	0.89	0.225
Squiggling	0.125	0.72	0.090
Boggling	0.250	0.80	0.200
			0.515

Figure 9.2. Standard Labour Cost.

Standards for manufacturing overhead are not arrived at by such direct forms of measurement. The first step is to classify the overheads according to cost centres and to budget for different levels of output. Unavoidably, there has to be allowance for different volume levels because, as has already been demonstrated, these overheads will exhibit different behaviour characteristics as activity alters. This process of examining cost behaviour and setting out different budgets for various levels of activity is called 'flexible budgeting'.

Flexible Budgets

Figure 9.3 shows the various overhead expenses relating to a department. Alongside each one is the cost equation. In the columns to the right of the cost equation there are four columns. Each of these is for a specified volume level and contains the quantities arrived at by applying the cost equation.

Output Range 10,000 — 25,000 hours

Volume		10,000	15,000	20,000	25,000
		£	£	£	£
Variable Costs	*Equation*				
Electricity	$TC = £0.12$ d.l.h.	1,200	1,800	2,400	3,000
Semi-variable costs					
Indirect labour	$TC = £1,000 +$ £0.10 d.l.h.	2,000	2,500	3,000	3,500
Indirect material	$TC = £400 +$ £0.05 d.l.h.	900	1,150	1,400	1,650
Miscellaneous	$TC = £100 +$ £0.01 d.l.h.	200	250	300	350
Fixed and Step costs					
Supervision	TC 2,300 for $0 \leqslant$ $X \leqslant 15000$ d.l.h. 3,000 for $15001 \leqslant$ $X \leqslant 25000$	2,000	2,000	3,000	3,000
Rent etc.	$TC = 600$	600	600	600	600
		6,900	8,300	10,700	12,100

Figure 9.3. Flexible budget for department 100.

The actual technique of arriving at these cost equations is dealt with in chapter 15. For control purposes these flexible budgets for individual cost centres are enough to enable management to monitor departmental costs. However, for external reporting, it is necessary to aggregate these departmental summaries to produce overhead standards for units of production. For the department 100 featured in figure 9.3. the costs can be expressed as £0.28 per direct labour hour plus £5,100 fixed. The variable rate is the total for the cost centre, obtained from adding the individual variable items from the equations given.

	per d.l.h.
	£
Electricity	0.12
Indirect labour	0.10
Indirect material	0.05
Miscellaneous	0.01
	0.28

This is the standard variable cost added to production cost for each direct labour hour, assuming that these are producing at the standard rate. The standard for fixed cost is also the departmental total, assuming a volume of at least 20,000 hours. This assumption enables a decision to be made between including £2,000 or £3,000 for supervision.

	£
Indirect labour	1,000
Indirect material	400
Miscellaneous	100
Supervision	3,000
Rent	600
	5,100

The standard for fixed overhead cost is £5,100/20,000 d.l.h. equals £0.255 per d.l.h.

This assumption of 20,000 standard hours of output could have been made on one of three bases —

(1) that this was the amount that the department could produce when operating at an ideally efficient level.

(2) that this was the amount that the firm operated at or about in the long run, disregarding variations for periods of boom and recession.

(3) that this was the amount that the firm expected to be operating at in this particular forthcoming period.

Choice number one is an 'ideal' and would given an unrealistic standard. The third possibility would given fluctuating standards from period to period and hence differing product total standards, which is something of a contradiction in terms. The number two measure of capacity is the usual one chosen. This is usually referred to as 'normal' capacity.

All this information can be brought together to provide a unit standard cost. This is done in figure 9.4.

Part number 16-4321			
	qty. £	unit cost £	total cost £
Material-Widgets	2	1.00	2.00
Squidgets	3	0.50	1.50
Blodgets	1	0.25	0.25
			3.75
Labour and Overhead			

Standard hours per unit	Department	Operation	Std. rate per hour £	Total cost £
0.250	100	Wiggling	1.425	0.356
0.125	101	Squiggling	1.400	0.175
0.250	102	Boggling	1.600	0.400
				0.931
Total standard cost				£4.681

Figure 9.4. A Standard Cost Card.

In figure 9.4 the amounts shown have largely been drawn from the earlier illustrations. The standard rate per hour for labour and overhead in department 100 is made up of three components

	£
Labour	0.890
Variable overhead	0.280
Fixed overhead	0.255
	1.425

The figures for departments 101 and 102 have been assumed and details are not given in the text.

Standard Cost Variances

Given a ratio between input and output that is an acceptable goal, then it is possible to compare the actual performance with the standard and obtain control information. Differences are called variances. These shall be examined under the headings of direct material, direct labour, manufacturing overheads and sales.

Direct Material Variances

The standard cost for the material content of a product is made up of two elements, the quantity and the price. The description of standards has so far concentrated on the technical aspect of assessing material quantities. The price also enters into the control system. If the standard cost is represented by a rectangle, as in figure 9.5 a second rectangle can be superimposed to represent actual results.

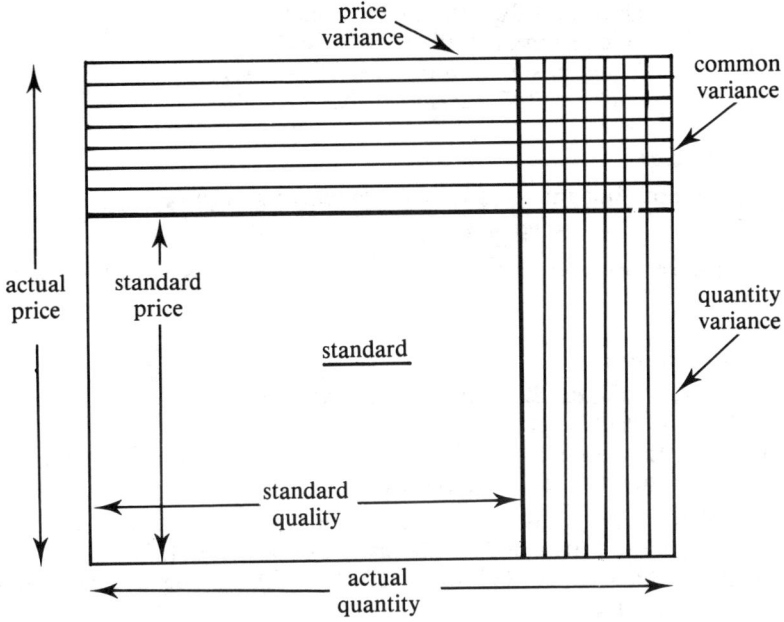

Figure 9.5. Material standard and variances.

In figure 9.5 the standard cost i.e. the standard unit quantity × the standard unit price, is represented by the inner, unshaded, rectangle. Actual results give a higher unit price and a higher quantity used, enlarging the rectangle to include the shaded portions. The new, larger, rectangle represents the actual cost. The difference is given by the shaded areas and these are the variances.

The initial division of the material variance is into price and quantity. The price difference has caused the shaded portion at the top of the diagram and the quantity difference has caused the shaded portion at the right hand side. In the top right corner there is a shaded area common to both. By convention, this is included in the price variance.

Price variance

The price variance, in words, is: actual quantity bought × (actual — standard) unit price.

Quantity variance

In words, this is: (actual — standard) quantity × standard price.

Illustration

Production statistics for department 100 for the January period were as follows:

Purchases, 5100 widgets at £0.99
Output, 2520 units of 16 — 4321
Widgets used, 5100
Material standard cost per 16 — 4321;
2 Widgets at £1.00 = £2.00

Price variance

actual quantity bought $\times$ (actual — standard) unit price

$$5100 \times £(0.99 - 1.00) = £51F.$$

this variance is favourable since the price paid is less than the standard price.

Quantity variance

(actual — standard) quantity $\times$ standard price
$(5100 - 2520 \times 2) \times £1.00 = £60U$
in this case the variance is unfavourable because the actual quantity used was greater than the standard allowance.

The total material variance is given by the difference between the actual cost $(5100 \times £0.99 = £5049)$ and the standard cost of output $(2520 \times 2 \times £1.00 - £5040)$ which equals $£(5049 - 5040) = £9$, giving a check on the individual calculations.

Direct labour variances

In the same way the difference between the actual direct labour cost and the standard allowance, can be analysed. As before there are price and quantity variances. The price variance results from pay rate differences and is often called the rate variance. The quantity of labour, measured in hours, when analysed as a variance is equally referred to as the efficiency variance.

Price or rate variance

Actual labours hours $\times$ (actual — standard) rate per hour.
The formula in words is very similar to the material price variance.

Quantity or efficiency variance

(actual — standard) hours $\times$ standard rate per hour.

Total labour variance

The total labour variance is given by the difference of:
Actual labour hours $\times$ actual rate per hour and standard labour hours $\times$ standard rate per hour.

Illustration

Labour and production statistics for department 100 in January were:

hours of work recorded	625
gross pay	£600
units of 16 − 4321 produced	2520

Each unit passing through the wiggling process of department 100 is measured as 0.25 standard hours of work. The standard pay for the wiggling operators is £0.89/hour. The measured output, therefore, is worth £(2520 × 0.25 × 0.89) equals £561.

Calculation

Actual labour hours × actual rate per hour

625   £0.96   £600

Price variance (£44 u)

Actual labour hours × standard rate per hour

625   £556

Quantity variance (£5F)

Standard labour hours × standard rate per hour

2520 × 0.25   £561
630   £0.890

This way of presenting the variance illustrates the point that the analyses is made of choosing an intermediate point between the actual cost and the standard cost.

Extraction of variances — timing

Figure 9.6 shows the most effective point in the recording process at which direct cost variances are calculated.

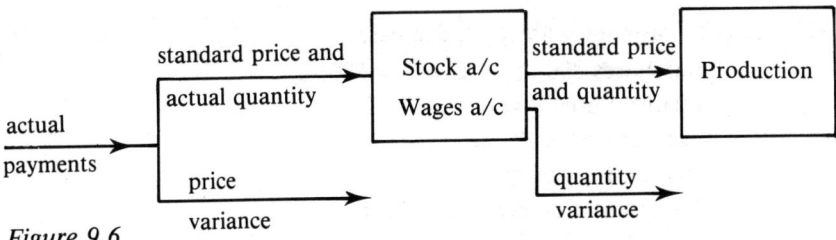

Figure 9.6.

It is possible to time the extraction of variances differently, but that shown above gives the quickest report. This speed of reporting can be offset against the additional cost. The diagram shows the situation whereby the price variance of material, for example, is calculated from invoices. The quantity variance can be isolated by issuing user departments with documentation for standard quantities of material. Extra material, if required, is drawn on special issue notes and these form the quantity variance.

Figure 9.6 also illustrates that stocks of raw material are usually fluctuating daily and this point was circumvented in the illustration showing the calculation of material variances. The following illustration allows for an increase in raw material during the period.

Illustration

(a) Material variance with stock increases.

purchases 1000 lb at £1.01 = £1010

quantity used 900 lb.

standard price £1.00

standard quantity for production achieved 850 lb.

price variance £(1010 — 1000) = £10u

quantity variance (900 — 850) £1.00 = £50u

The total material variance for the period can be analysed as follows:

		£
	actual purchases	1010
	standard use	850
		160

consisting of:

		£
	price variance	10
	increase in stock	
	at standard price	100
	quantity variance	50
		160

(b) Material variance with stock decreases.

purchases 800 lb. at £1.01 = £808

quantity used 900 lb

standard price £1.00

standard quantity

for production achieved 850 lb

Here the total material variance for the period is £(808 — 850) = £42

		£
	price variance £(808 — 800)	8
	decrease in stock at	
	standard price (100 × £1)	(100)
	quantity variance	50
		(42)

Sub-variances
Mix variance

Whenever a product can be manufactured with differing ratios of a set of inputs, an additional mix variance can be calculated. The inputs may be material or labour. In the case of material, two or more ingredients may combined in different proportions to provide an output which is within defined limits of quality. For labour there can be different combinations of skilled semi-skilled and unskilled workpeople. This mix variance is part of the original quantity variance.

The quantity variance has been given, but now the additional possibility of mix changes is incorporated:

actual quantities $\times$ actual mix $\times$ standard rate

---

mix variance

---

actual quantities $\times$ standard mix $\times$ standard rate

---

yield (quantity) variance

---

standard quantities $\times$ standard mix $\times$ standard rate.

Illustration

Production of 1 gallon of Flumenite is from a standard mix of 0.7 gallons of liquid type A and 0.4 gallons of liquid type B.

Standard costs are: £1.00 per gallon for A
£2.00 per gallon for B

Actual production for a period consisted of 770 gallons of Flemenite from 583 gallons of A and 341 gallons of B, costing £1.01 and £2.01 per gallon respectively.

Calculation	A £	B £	Total £
(a) Actual input costs	583 × 1.01 = 588.83	341 × 2.01 = 685.41	1274.24
Price variance	5.83u	3.41u	9.24u
(b) Actual qty × standard rate × actual mix	583 × 1.00 = 583	341 × 2.00 = 682	1265
Mix variance	5F	10u	5u
(c) Actual qty × standard rate × standard mix	588 × 1.00 = 588	336 × 2.00 = 672	1260
Yield variance			105u
(d) Standards qty × standard rate × standard mix	539 × 1.00 = 539	308 × 2 = 616	1155

line (a) gives the actual figures.

line (b) substitutes the standard prices for the actual prices.

line (c) apportions the total inputs $(583 + 341 = 924)$ in accordance with the standard rates of 7:4, giving 588 and 336 which again equal 924.

line (d) is all at standard. The standard quantities of input for 770 gallons of output are A 770×0.7 gallons and B 770×0.4 gallons, which equal 539 and 308 respectively.

Whereas the individual A and B product variances are significant for price and mix, this is not so for the yield. The price variance is self evident and as far as the mix is concerned, using less of A and more of B gives savings on the former which are more than offset by greater expense on the other. The yield variance refers only to the finished product and cannot be applied to the individual components.

Overtime premium and idle time variances

Further sub-divisions of labour variances are also possible. In the example given for labour variances, earlier in this chapter, the rate variance was £44 unfavourable. The original standard was without need of overtime, but in fact some overtime was worked because of the necessity to complete the job earlier than originally planned. This cost £30 in overtime premium, leaving £14 differences due to a slight drift in the basic pay rates.

As for the quantity variance, there was a period of enforced idle time due to external circumstances, amounting to 30 hours. At the standard rate, this equals $30 \times £0.89 = £26.7$. The quantity or efficiency variance therefore becomes:

idle time variance	£26.8u
amended efficiency variance	31.7F
	5F

These two sub-variances illustrate the point that the analyses and explanatory repots of variances can often be quantified.

The Usefulness of Variances

Each variance represents a deviation from the desired goal. As such they are an important aid to reporting only exceptional items to management. By the time the report reaches the higher levels of management, action appropriate to the situation should have been taken at a lower level and a suitable note added to the exception report.

So, for example, the labour efficiency variance may be the result of better supervision, or a better quality of material has been used. Whatever the cause, some report will be required, unless the amount is not regarded as significant.

Significance of variances

Since standards are representative of what should happen, it follows that all variances are undesirable. Clearly though, some are more unacceptable than others, if only on account of their size. Most firms endeavour to limit the number of reports and investigations to the worthwhile ones. Some do this informally, in that all variances are reported, but managers use judgement in calling for special explanations.

A more formal system is to treat a standard as though it were a mean and set control limits above and below. Only results falling outside these controls warrant any special investigation (see figure 9.7).

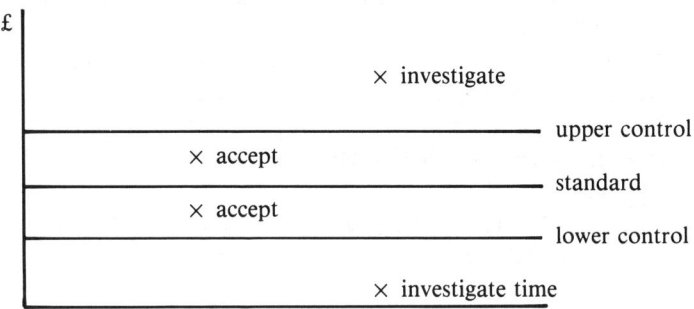

Figure 9.7. Significance of variances.

Chapter Summary

The contents of this and later chapters represent a major step forward in the development of cost accounting systems. The management is no longer the passive recipient of historic cost informtion. A new, normative element has been introduced. Now the cost reports contain comparisons with these standards.

Standard costs are a measure of what ought to be. They are set as objectively as possible, employing knowledge which has gained by much critical observation and experiment. The application of standards as far as direct material and labour are concerned, can be said to be scientific.

Deviations from standards form the basis of standard cost reports. Such reports bring to the attention of management those areas of the company budget which require their attention. Ideally, by the time reports reach senior management, any corrective action required within the organisation will have been taken. It would be wrong to suggest that the costing system is the prime source for revealing problems, because the line management is almost invariably aware of trouble as it occurs. What standard costing does, within the framework of a responsibility accounting system, is to put cost onto the troubles. Even more importantly, it ensures that senior management will be notified of problems without fail. This certainly ensures that the appropriate line management acts promptly to rectify faults.

Specific variances explained were those relating to direct materials and labour. In each case the total variance is the difference between the actual expenditure and the standard amount relating to the level of activity. This was shown as having two components, price and quantity. Some further illustrations were given of sub-analysis in appropriate circumstances. Finally, brief references were made to the timing of the extractions of these variances and to a method of assessing their significance from a managerial point of view.

Exercises 9.1-9.5 (Answers provided)

9.1   Production statistics for cost centre 101 for January 19X5 included the following:

Purchases		Usage	Standards
Units	Actual Cost	Units	
4000 lb	£41,000	3,000	21 lb at £10/lb

Output for the month was 1400 completed units.

Required:
Calculate the material price variance at the time of purchase and the quantity variance.

9.2   Labour statistics for cost centre 100 for January 19X5 were as follows:

	Standard		Actual (totals)	
	Hours/unit	Rate/hour £	Hours	Cost £
Skilled	1.0	2.00	3010	6030
Semi-skilled	2.0	1.50	5990	9010
Unskilled	3.0	1.00	9030	9050

Output for the period was 3000 completed units

Required:
Calculate direct labour rate and efficiency variances for each class.

9.3   Using the data given in 9.2 for skilled labour, draw a diagram to illustrate the variances. Describe the treatment of the joint variance.

9.4   The Standard Foundry Company Limited makes castings. Standard costs are as follows:-

Cronium	70%	at £200 per ton
Draconium	30%	at £100 per ton

Standard loss in production is 10% of input.

Actual results for a costing period were:

Opening stock	Cronium	100 tons
	Draconium	50 tons
Closing stocks	Cronium	105 tons
	Draconium	40 tons

Purchases	Cronium	395 tons at £79,500 cost
	Draconium	100 tons at £9,000 cost

Metal used in production,	500 tons
Weight of output castings,	468 tons

Required:

Calculate material price, mix and yield variances.

9.5 The Standard Exploitation Company Limited had the following cost report for one of its overseas companies:-

Output	930 units	
Actual	Male Employees	Female Employees
hours:		
Good time	980	1860
idle time	70	40
overtime	50	—
	1100	1900
Actual pay	£1170	£1490

Overtime premium is 50% of ordinary time

Standard cost: rates of pay, men £1.00/hr
and women £0.75/hr.
: one complete unit equals 3 standard hours or work, performed in the ratio of one male to two female standard hours.

Required:

Calculate:

(a) direct labour variances in terms of rate, mix and quantity.

(b) sub-divide further to show overtime and idle time variances.

(c) comment on the results.

Questions 9.6-9.10 Answers not provided.

9.6 Explain briefly:

(i) how standards are compiled for material and labour costs for a product;

(ii) the nature and purpose of material and labour variances.

Calculate the material and labour variances from the data set out below and present answers in the form of a statement for presentation to management.

	Standard
Weight to produce one units	12 kilograms
Price, per kilogram	£9
Hours to produce one unit	10
Wage rate, per hour	£2

Actual production and costs for week ended 12th November, 1977:

Units produced	240
Material used	2,640 kilograms
Material cost	£26,400
Hours worked	2,520
Wages paid	£5,544

ICMA (CA1)

9.7   The trading results of Bloggs & Co, manufacturers of the 'Bloggett', for the two years ended 31 May 1976 and 1977 are set out below:

Year ended 31 May

	1976 £'000		1977 £'000	
Sales		880		1,188
Costs of Goods sold				
Direct Material	352		500	
Direct Labour	220		330	
		572		830
Gross profit		308		358
Marketing Costs	66		100	
Administration Costs	42		58	
		108		158
Net Profit		£200		£200

Your enquiries reveal the following:

(a) the unit selling price of the Bloggett was 12½% higher in 1976-77 than in 1975-76;

(b) there were no stocks or work-in-progress at the beginning or end of either year;

(c) Marketing costs vary in relation to quantity sold;

(d) Administration costs are 'fixed' in the sense that they do not vary in relation to activity levels.

Using the 1975-76 figures as a basis, you are required to explain with supporting calculations, why the increased turnover in 1976-77 did not result in an increase in net profit.

CA(AC2).

9.8   Chemico Ltd. manufactures and distributes an industrial cleaning compound known as Splodge, the standard direct costs per cylinder of which are:

Material	100 Kg of A at 20p per Kg
	200 Kg of B at 25p per Kg
Labour	10 hours at 90p per hour

The budgeted monthly production/sales is 500 cylinders and the selling price is £100 per cylinder.

The following details relate to May 1975 when 510 cylinders of Splodge were produced and sold:

Sales	£50,650
Materials used:	
A 51,600 Kg, cost	10,250
B 101,500 Kg, cost	25,880
Labour:	
5,000 hours, cost	4,575

You are required to compute

(a) the price and usage variances for each material

(b) the wages rate and efficiency variances

(c) the sales price and volume variances, and

to comment briefly upon the information revealed by each of the variances you have computed.

CA(AC2).

9.9 (a) Compound XYZ is manufactured in batches of 100 cylinders, the standard input material per batch being 250 gallons of ABC at £1.20 per gallon.

During November, 30 batches of XYZ were produced from an input of 7,450 gallons of ABC which cost £9,076.

You are required to calculate the material price and usage variances and to show the relevant entries in the Work in Process Account, assuming the materials are debited thereto at actual cost price.

(b) Discuss the limitations of material price and usage variances as instruments of management control, making reference, if you wish, to the variances you have calculated in (a).

CA(AC2).

9.10 A chemical company has the following standards for manufacturing a machine lubricant:

	£
5 gallons of material P at £0.70 per gallon —	3.50
5 gallons of material Q at £0.92 per gallon —	4.60
10	8.10*

*Cost of 10 gallons of standard mix which should produce 9 gallons of finished product at a standard cost of £0.90 (£8.10 ÷ 9) a gallon.

No stocks of raw materials are kept. Purchases are made as needed so that all price variances relate to materials used. Actual results showed that 100,000 gallons of material were used during a particular period as follows:

		£
45,000 gallons of material P at an actual cost per gallons used of £0.80 —		36,000
55,000 gallons of material Q at an actual cost per gallons used of £0.97 —		53,350
100,000		89,350

Good output:

92,070 gallons at a standard cost of £0.90 per gallon produced 82,863

Total unfavourable material variance   6,487

You are required to:

(a) analyse
    (i) the total material variance in terms of price and usage variances,
    (ii) the usage variance in terms of mix and yield variances, and
(b) explain the circumstances under which a material mix variance is relevant to managerial control.

ICAEW(MA).

Seminar Problem 9

Standard Part Company Limited

You have just been appointed as managment accountant of the Standard Part Company Limited. Your predecessor was not noted for the clarity of his reports. Figure 1 (giving an extract only) is a fair example of his work:

Immediately you are asked to explain the reasons for an increase in direct costs in the main production department 100, for which the cost figures are shown in figure 1.

	19X5 £	19X6	Difference
Materials	250,000	327,750	77,750
Direct Labour	48,000	62,040	14,040
Overhead: etc			
etc			

Figure 1. Manufacturing Costs Department 100

Since you are unfamiliar with the firm's activities your first step is to visit department 100. The supervisor shows you around and explains the work. This, basically, is an assembly process using one standard metal component. These components are brought together to make three different output units. Other raw material used in the assembly process is treated as indirect material to production. The design of the units require 4, 6 and 8 basic components for each of the small, medium and large sizes respectively. A reasonable allowance for waste is 5% of components issued to work-in-progress.

During 19X5 and 19X6, the Department had produced:

	19X5	19X6
S	16000	16,000
M	14000	17,000
L	10000	12,000

The supervisor was also able to give information about direct labour. The standard, set by a consultant work study engineer is taken as 3 S units per labour hour, 2 M per labour hour and 1 L unit per labour hour. There is no standard mix. All direct labour receive the same hourly rate. Given normal efficiency of working and scheduling, there is not need for overtime.

Your second visit was to the stores department. During 19X5 250,000 units had been issued to department 100 and for 19X6 the corresponding quantity was 285,000.

Next the purchasing department gave you prices. In 19X5 the price per component was £1.00 and for 19X6 it was £1.15.

Wages department were able to analyse wages paid. In 19X5 direct labour hours were paid for at a cost of £48,000, none of which was overtime. In 19X6 there were 2900 direct labour hours, including 400 hours overtime, at a cost of just over £62,000. The overtime premium was 50% of ordinary time.

Required:

Give an explanation of the increase in costs between 19X5 and 19X6 for material and labour.

Chapter 10

Standard Costing — II
Overhead Variance Analysis

The scientific basis for setting overhead standards is much less in evidence than for direct expenses of material and labour. In the case of manufacturing overheads the use of statistical techniques helps in the development of standards which are responsibe to changes in activity. For the non-manufacturing overheads it is more a question of allocating resources to activities, such as selling or research, according to a programme. Control then becomes a matter of ensuring that the expenditure is not exceeded.

Manufacturing Overheads

As with direct expenses, the object is to establish the difference between the actual expenditure and the standard and then to analyse this difference in some useful way. The standard in this case, though, is based on the amount that will be absorbed by production if a predetermined volume is met.

Recapitulating the figures in chapter 9, the standard overheads relating the wiggling process in department 100 are £0.535 per direct labour hour. This is made up of variable cost £0.28 and fixed cost £0.255. The variable amount is the sum of the individual items as shown in figure 9.3. The fixed amount is the result of £5,100/20,000, where the numerator is the total fixed costs and the 20,000 a measure of normal activity in hours.

Spending Variance

Manufacturing overhead variances can be analysed in a number of ways, but the starting point is to separate out the amount which comes from lack of control over spending levels, as opposed to differences caused by fluctuations in volume.

The question asked is this: at the current level of activity how much should have been spent on manufacturing overheads and how does this compare with the amount actually spent? The answer to the first part of the question establishes the standard and the second part gives the spending variance.

Refer again to the wiggling process in department 100 and use the same figures as in Chapter 9. This is the information given in figure 10.1.

Standard hours of work earned (1)	Flexible budget allowance (2)	Actual Expenditure (3)
21,000	10,980	11,000

Figure 10.1. Department 100 overhead summary.

The calculation for column 2 is made as follows:-

	Variable overheads:	£
(earned) $\times$ (variable)		
(output) (rate)		
21,000 0.28	=	5,880
	fixed overheads	5,100
		10,980

The difference between column (2) and (3) is the spending or budget variance. In this example it is £20 unfavourable. For better control over the cost centres spending it would be necessary to break this total figure down according to individual expenses. An example of this is shown later.

Volume Variance

As the value of the standard labour is added to the work-in-progress, an added value is made for manufacturing overheads in the usual way under absorption costing. This overhead absorption rate includes an element for fixed overhead, based on expected fixed costs and normal activity. In fact, the volume of activity will not be exactly at the normal level, except by chance. So there will be a difference between the manufacturing overheads absorbed and the amount budgeted. This difference is the volume variance.

The flexible budget allowance calculated above is the starting point. The earned output of the department times the absorption rate for overheads is the finishing point.

	£
Flexible budget (as above)	10,980
Earned output (21000) $\times$ absorption rate (0.535)	11,235
Volume variance	£255

Two and three-way analysis

In this examination of manufacturing overhead performance, three points have been used to give a two-way analysis. The three points were:

i)   actual expenditure

ii) the budget (flexible) relevant to the level of activity achieved, when this is measured in terms of completed output (standard hours)

iii) the overheads absorbed using the standard rate developed.

The intermediate point of these assumes that the expenses involved are variable with the quantity of successful work done. This is not obviously so in all cases. For examples such as lighting it would seem likely that the variability is more directly related to actual hours worked. This gives another possibility as an intermediate point. Using this, as well as the one above, three variances are obtained, hence the terms three way analysis. Now, it would appear as follows:-

	£
Actual expenditure	11,000
Spending or budget variance (amended)	120F
Flexible budget allowance (actual hours worked)	11,120
Efficiency variance	140 u
Flexible budget allowance (earned output)	10,980
Volume variance	255F
Total overheads absorbed	11,235

There are a number of points to make here. The calculation of flexible budget based on actual hours is:-

$$£$$

variable
actual hrs. × variable rate
21500	0.28	=	6020
fixed			5100
			11,120

The spending variance in the three way analysis is often referred to as 'amended spending'. This distinguishes it in the literature from the figure of spending variance in the two way analysis. Clearly, in the situation of a firm deciding to use the three-way basis, then there is no need to make this distinction and the adjective is unnecessary. The new variance is labelled as an efficiency variance. However, it is entirely based on the difference between direct labour hours worked and standards hours of work achieved. It revises the spending variance to take account of good or otherwise use of production facilities.

Even so, both the flexible budget points used are making assumptions which relate to all the individual items of the manufacturing overhead class. In fact, some of these will be more influenced by hours worked than by output achieved. It could be vice-versa for the others.

An improved answer would be obtained by using a flexible budget allowance which was specifically related to hours worked for some expenses and hours achieved for others. In the absence of this refinement, the additional effort involved in obtaining the three variances as opposed to two, would need to be balanced against the value of the extra information gained.

The volume variance (or capacity) puts a value on to the extent to which the actual output is different from the normal capacity used when calculating the fixed overhead absorption rate. It is in fact the (normal output — earned output) × the fixed overhead rate. The usefulness of this figure is at least doubtful, since the assessment of producing amounts different from normal capacity is not relevant to the current situation. What is relevant, is the quantity of output compared to the budget amount and an assessment of the gain or loss on profit margins resulting from the difference. It is possible to have a favourable volume variance in a situation where the additional units of production are unsaleable.

Certainly, the volume variance is necessary for the completeness and neatness of the accountants' double-entry system. However, it could just as well be referred to as a 'balancing difference'.

Reference was made earlier to the use of a tailor made flexible budget figure. This is now illustrated in figure 10.2

Dept 100 — Flexible Budget

Hours worked 21,500		Standard hours output 21,000		
Item	Basis	Budget £	Actual £	Spending Variance
Electricity	Input	2580	2480	100 F
Indirect labour	Input	3150	3050	100 F
Indirect material	Input	1475	1450	25 F
Miscellaneous	Output	310	320	10 u
Supervision	Fixed	3000	3100	100 u
Rent etc.	Fixed	600	600	—
		11,115	11,000	115 F

Figure 10.2. Flexible budget refined.

The individual calculations use the cost equations already given and either 21,500 hours worked (input) or 21,000 standard hours achieved (output).

		£
Electricity	$0.12 \times 21,500$	2,580
Indirect labour	$1000 + 0.10 \times 21,500 =$	3,150
Indirect material	$400 + 0.05 \times 21,500 =$	1,475
Miscellaneous	$100 + 0.01 \times 21,000 =$	310

The result of this refinement is to give the three variances as:-

	£
spending	115 F
efficiency	135 u
volume	255 F

Sales Variances

The difference between the budget for sales and the actual performance can be analysed in a similar manner. However, it is more helpful to analyse the variances relating to margins between sales price and unit cost of sales. This is because the main concern is the difference between these, rather than with each item individually and because a change in selling volume affects net income according to the margin being obtained.

The usual components of the margin variance are selling price, volume and mix.

The selling price variance reflects the difference between the actual unit selling price and the budgeted figure.

Volume variance arises out of the increase or decrease between actual and budgeted quantities.

Finally, the mix variance isolate the change resulting from the fact that the proportion of product lines is different in actual fact than was budgeted for. The process is illustrated using the information given in figure 10.3.

Computation of Sales Variances

Product	Budget				Actual			
	%	Units	Unit margin £	Total margin £	%	Units	Unit margin £	Total margin £
X	25	100	10	1,000	20	100	11	1,100
Y	50	200	15	3,000	55	275	14	3,850
Z	25	100	10	1,000	25	125	11	1,375
	100	400		5,000	100	500		6,325

Figure 10.3

The total difference to be analysed is £(6325 — 5000) = £1325F. This is labelled favourable clearly because the actual being greater than budget is increasing the income.

Price Variance

	$\begin{bmatrix}\text{(Actual)}\\\text{(margin)}\end{bmatrix}$	$-\begin{bmatrix}\text{(Budgeted)}\\\text{(margin)}\end{bmatrix} \times$	Actual volume	=	Price Variance
X	11	10	100		100 F
Y	14	15	275		275 U
Z	11	10	125		125 F
			500		50 U

Mix Variance

	$\begin{bmatrix}\text{(Actual)}\\\text{(mix)}\end{bmatrix}$	$-\begin{bmatrix}\text{(Budgeted)*}\\\text{(mix)}\end{bmatrix} \times$	Budgeted Margin	=	Mix Variance
X	100	125	10		250 U
Y	275	250	15		375 F
Z	125	125	10		—
	500	500			125 F

*The actual total of 500 reallocated in the budgeted proportion of 1:2:1.

Volume Variance

	$\begin{bmatrix}\text{(Actual)}\\\text{(volume)}\\\text{(at)}\\\text{(budget)}\\\text{(mix)}\end{bmatrix}$	$-\begin{bmatrix}\text{(Budgeted)}\\\text{(volume)}\\\text{(at)}\\\text{(budget)}\\\text{(mix)}\end{bmatrix} \times$	Budgeted margin	=	Volume variance
X	125	100	10		250 F
Y	250	200	15		750 F
Z	125	100	10		250 F
	500	400			1250.0 F

Summarizing these variances:

	£
price variance	50 u
mix variance	125 F
volume variance	1250 F
	1325 F

The nature of these calculations is worth some explanation. Figure 10.3 shows the total difference of £1325, which is to be analysed. The first comparison is made between the actual volume × actual margin and the actual volume × budget margin. This gives the effect of price differences since the margins are given by price − standard costs.

The second comparison is made by rearranging the actual volume of 500 units into the same proportion as the original budget, that is 1:2:1 in this case. This is the mix variance which compares the standards of the actual mix and the budgeted mix.

Finally, the actual volume in total, but arranged according to the budget volume. This last variance can be presented in a different way, viz

actual	budget	budget	volume
volume	volume	margin	variance
500	400	£12.50	£1250

The budget of margin of £12.50 is the weighted average of the margins in the original budget. It is calculated as follows

$$£ \frac{100 \times 10 + 200 \times 15 + 100 \times 10}{400} \quad £12.50$$

As with the original demonstration of variances for the direct material, the order of calculation is conventional and determines the treatment of common figures.

Chapter Summary

This chapter is a continuation of the examination of various analyses. The concept of flexible budgeting was utilised for manufacturing overhead to obtain standards for spending. The flexible budget could be based on output alone, or on both input and output to give an additional source of variance. It was suggested that the best practice is to provide the additional intermediate point by examining the individual items of expense within the cost centre and establishing a 'custom' made figure.

To complete the process of reconciling budgets based on standards and actual results, sales variances were analysed. These variances were based on margins rather than selling prices, mainly on the grounds that this most reflects management interest. The most common analysis is between price and volume change. Additionally, mix variance can be useful and an example of these was given.

Exercises

Questions 10.1-10.5 (Answers provided)

10.1 The Manx Canning Company had the following flexible budget for one of its departments:

Activity in machine hours	900	1000	1100
Cost:			
indirect materials	585	650	715
indirect labour	480	500	520
power	1000	1100	1200
repairs	330	350	370
supervision	500	500	500
rent	400	400	400
depreciation	600	600	600
	3895	4100	4305

Calculate the flexible budget at the level of 1050 machine hours. How much would be absorbed into work-in-progress at this level of activity? Normal output = 1000 machine hours.

10.2 The Orkney Cooperative operates a flexible budgeting system. The activity used is direct labour hours and the company absorption rates are £3.1/hour variable and £2.1/hour hour fixed. Normal level of activity is taken as 3000 hours. During the period under review 3050 hours were worked and the good output achieved was equivalent to 3010 hours. The actual expenditure was £15,585.

Required: spending, efficiency and volume variances.

10.3 The Wight (Novelty Manufacturers) Company have developed the following cost equations for factory overheads:

indirect materials	$y = 0.5x$
indirect labour	$y = 1.3x + 100$
indirect expenses:	
power	$y = 2.3x + 200$
repairs	$y = 1.4x + 150$
supervision	$y = 300$
other fixed expenses	$y = 700$

These fixed elements are for a monthly period. In the equations x represent the appropriate activity, in this case machine hours.

Normal machine activity for a month is 1000.

Actual factory overheads incurred were £7800 in the month.

Hours worked totalled 1100 and the earned output was 1050 hours.

Required: Overhead variance analysis for the month.

10.4 The Scilly (Artificial Flowers) Company had the following results for their last period:

	budget	actual
Sales (in units)	50,000	60,000
Sales value	£50,000	£57,000

The standard cost of manufacture of a unit was £0.6.

Required: the price and volume variances of sales.

10.5

Product	Budget				Actual			
	% mix	units	unit margin	total margin	% mix	units	unit margin	total margin
X	25	200	1.00	200	30	210	0.90	189
Y	50	400	1.50	600	60	420	1.40	588
Z	25	200	1.20	240	10	70	1.20	84
		600		1040		700		861

Required: analysed sales variances.

Questions 10.6-10.10 Answers not provided.

10.6 A company manufactures one product which passes through two processes before transfer to finished goods stock. Standard cost data for each process are as follows:

		Process A £	Process B £
		£		
Direct materials	20 units at 0.30	6.00	
	14 units at 0.50		7.00
Direct wages	2 hours at 1.50	3.00	
	3 hours at 2.00		6.00
Production overhead	2 hours at 3.00	6.00	
	3 hours at 4.00		12.00
		£15.00	£25.00

Budgeted output for October was 5,000 products.

Actual costs incurred in October were:

	£	£
Direct material	30,720	31,740
Direct wages	15,840	25,650
Production overhead	31,680	58,425

An analysis of the production variances which had been calculated for October was as follows:

Note:

Adverse variances are indicated by (A), and favourable variances by (F).

		£	£
Direct materials:	price	1,920(A)	2,760(F)
	usage	300(F)	550(A)
Direct wages:	rate	990(A)	2,850(F)
	efficiency	300(A)	600(F)
Production overhead:	expenditure	1,680(A)	1,575(F)
	capacity	300(A)	3,000(A)
	productivity	600(A)	1,200(F)

From each of the Questions 1 to 8 below, you are required to select the appropriate answer. You must support each answer with a reasoned explanation or calculation.

1. What was the actual output of products for the month?
   (a) 5,000
   (b) 5,120
   (c) 4,800
   (d) 5,440
   (e) None of the above. It is not possible to obtain an answer from data provided.
   (f) None of the above. In my opinion the output was ..... units.

2. What was the actual price per unit of direct material used in Process A?
   (a) £0.28
   (b) £0.30
   (c) £0.32
   (d) £0.34
   (e) None of the above. It is not possible to obtain an answer from data provided.
   (f) None of the above. In my opinion the price per unit was £....

3. What was the total standard cost of direct materials in Process B?
   (a) £34,500
   (b) £33,950
   (c) £28,980
   (d) £29,530
   (e) None of the above. It is not possible to obtain an answer from data provided.
   (f) None of the above. In my opinion the standard cost was £...

4. What was the actual cost per labour hour in Process B?
   (a) £2.00
   (b) £1.90
   (c) £1.80
   (d) £2.25
   (e) None of the above. It is not possible to obtain an answer from data provided.
   (f) None of the above. In my opinion the actual cost was £....

5. What was the total standard cost of direct wages in Process A?
   (a) £14,550
   (b) £14,850
   (c) £15,830
   (d) £16,130
   (e) None of the above. It is not possible to obtain an answer from data provided.
   (f) None of the above. In my opinion the standard cost was £...

6. What was the cause of the overhead productivity variance in Process B?
   (a) The actual overhead incurred being less than the amount budgeted.
   (b) The actual hours worked differing from those budgeted.
   (c) The actual hours worked being greater than the standard hours.
   (d) The actual capacity utilised being greater than budgeted.
   (e) None of the above. It is not possible to obtain an answer from data provided.
   (f) None of the above. In my opinion the variance was caused by ......

7. What was the amount of the production overhead absorbed in both processes during the month?
   (a) £87,300
   (b) £90,000
   (c) £90,105
   (d) £89,895
   (e) None of the above. It is not possible to obtain an answer from data provided.
   (f) None of the above. In my opinion the amount absorbed was £....

8. What was the actual profit realised in Process B?
   (a) £50,000
   (b) £60,000
   (c) £121,250
   (d) £58,200
   (e) None of the above. It is not possible to obtain an answer from data provided.
   (f) None of the above. In my opinion the profit was £.....

ICMA(CA1)

10.7 K Limited uses standard costs and flexible budgets for control purposes. The following information is given:

Standard and budgeted data:

— The standard material allowed per unit is 4 kilograms at a standard price of £0.75 per kilogram.

— Budgeted direct labour hours for a four-week period were 80,000 hours at a budgeted cost of £152,000.
— Budgeted variable production overhead for 80,000 hours was £96,000.

Details for four-week period ended 29th April 1978 were:

— Incurred: £
    Direct wages   163,800
— Variances:
    Direct wages rate, £0.20 per hour adverse.
    Direct materials price (calculated on purchases
    at time of receipt at £0.05 per kilogram) 9,000 favourable
    Direct materials usage   1,500 adverse
    Variable production overhead   2,200 favourable
    Variable production overhead efficiency 2,400 adverse
— Production, 28,000 units.

There were no stock at beginning of period, but there were 26,000 kilograms of direct materials in stock at 29th April 1978.

You are required to state for the period:

(a) the number of kilograms of direct material purchased;
(b) the number of kilograms of direct material used above the standard allowed;
(c) the variable production overhead expenditure variance;
(d) the actual hours worked;
(e) the number of standard hours allowed for the production achieved.

ICMA(CA1).

10.8   On the basis of a production/sales level of 10,000 units a month, the standard unit cost of a carton of Gimmet which sells for £12 is:

	£
Material	
12 Kg at 50p	6.00
Labour	
1½ hours at £1.60	2.40
Fixed Overhead	0.60

The Operating Statement for November 1977 was as follows:

	£	£	£
Budgeted Profit			30,000
Add favourable variances			
Sales volume margin	1,500		
Materials price	1,268		
Wages efficiency	240		
Fixed Overhead volume	300		
		3,308	
Less adverse variances			
Sales price	1,000		
Material usage	400		
Wages rates	780		
Fixed Overhead expenditure	200		
		2,380	
Net favourable variance			928
Actual Profit			£30,928

You are required to:

(a) Produce an operating statement in conventional accounting form.

(b) Explain what is meant by 'interdependence' of variances, illustrating your answer by references to the above statement.

CA(AC2).

10.9 A company with two cost centres, 1 and 2, manufactures two products, A and B, whose standard variable costs per article are as follows:

Cost Centre	Element	Quantity	Price/rate £	Amount £
	Product A	units	per unit	
1	Direct material: X	6	2.50	15.00
2	Y	2	7.50	15.00
		hours	per hour	
	Direct wages,			
1	grade: I	5	1.70	8.50
1	II	3	1.20	3.60
2	III	8	0.90	7.20
1	Variable overhead	8	0.30	2.40
2	Variable overhead	8	0.25	2.00
				£53.70
	Product B	units	per unit	
1	Direct material: X	8	2.50	20.00
2	Z	3	2.00	6.00
		hours	per hour	
	Direct wages,			
1	grade: II	7	1.20	8.40
2	III	6	0.90	5.40
1	Variable overhead	7	0.30	2.10
2	Variable overhead	6	0.25	1.50
				£43.40

Budgeted data for a period of 4 weeks each of 40 hours are:

	Product A	Product B
Standard selling prices per article	£105	£90
Budgeted output of articles on which standard costs are based	165	285
Budgeted sales for period No. 7	160	310
	Cost centre 1	Cost centre 2
Fixed production overhead	£6,630	£4,545

Selling and distribution, and administration expenses total £4,500 per period; they are treated as fixed and as a cost of the period.

Actual data for period No. 7 were as follows:

Opening and closing stocks of raw materials and work-in-progress were the same.

		Product A	Product B
		articles	articles
	Actual output	150	300
	Actual sales:		
	at standard selling prices	145	250
	at £120 each	25	—
	at £85 each	—	30
Cost centre	Costs:		Price per unit
		units	£
1	Direct materials: X	3,900	2.30
2	Y	280	7.50
2	Z	1,040	2.10
			Rate per hour
		hours	£
1	Direct wages, grade: I	720	1.85
1	II	2,750	1.10
2	III	3,180	0.90
		Cost centre 1	Cost centre 2
		£	£
	Overhead: Variable	960	920
	Fixed	7,050	4,250

The company absorbs its fixed production overhead into products by means of cost centre labour hour rates. All variances are transferred to the profit and loss account.

You are required to:

1. calculate for the period No. 7 the following variances for each cost centre:

   (a) (i)   direct materials price;
       (ii) direct materials usage;
   (b) (i)   direct wages rate;
       (ii) direct labour efficiency;
   (c) variable production overhead;
   (d) (i)   fixed production overhead expenditure;
       (ii) capacity;
       (iii) fixed cost productivity;

2. present a profit statement of the company for period No. 7;

3. comment on the relative performance of the two cost centres.

ICMA(MA1).

10.10 A furniture manufacturer has established standard costs in the joinery department, in which one size of a particularly styled kitchen cabinet is produced. The standard costs of producing one of these cabinets are shown below:

Kitchen Cabinet Style 1200/01

		£
Materials:	Timber 50 ft. of board at 10p per ft.	5.00
Direct Labour:	3 hours at £3 per hour	9.00
Indirect costs:		
	Variable charges—3 hours at 50p	1.50
	Fixed charges —3 hours at 25p	.75
		16.25

The cost of operations to produce 400 of these cabinets during October are stated below. There were no opening stocks.

		£
Materials purchased:	25,000 ft. of board at 11p	2,750
Materials used:	19,000 ft. of board	
Direct labour:	1,100 hours at £2.95	3,245
Indirect costs:		
	Variable charges	650
	Fixed charges	355

The flexible budget for this department called for 1,400 direct labour hours of operation at the monthly activity level used to set the fixed overhead rate.

You are required to compute the following variances from standard cost, identifying them as favourable (F) or unfavourable (U):

(a) material purchase price

(b) material usage

(c) (i) direct labour rate
    (ii) direct labour efficiency variance

(d) (i) variable overhead total variance
    (ii) fixed overhead budget variance
    (iii) fixed overhead volume variance

(e) (i) variable overhead expenditure variance
    (ii) variable overhead efficiency variance.

ICAEW(MA).

Seminar Problem 10

Skye Light Industry Limited manufactures a detergent for the disposal of oil slicks. The budgeted profit and loss account for the month of September 19X5 is set out below:

	£	£
Sales: (20,000 gallons)		30,000
Manufacturing cost of goods sold (standard)		
Materials	10,000	
Labour	5,000	
Variable overhead	2,000	
Fixed overhead	3,000	20,000
Administration expenses		3,000
Selling expenses		4,000
		27,000
Net profit		3,000

The standard cost per gallon is given as:

	£
Material: 2 lb of X at £0.25/lb.	0.50
Labour: 10 minutes at £1.50/hour	0.25
Variable overhead: £0.60 per labour hour	0.10
Fixed overhead £3000/20,000	0.15
	1.00

Actual figures for the month were:

Sales and production 21,000 gallons	£32,700
Materials bought and used 43,000 lbs for	£11,000
Wages paid to direct labour for 3550 hours	£5,550
Manufacturing overheads	£5,200
Administration expenses	£3,050
Selling expenses	£3,900

Required:

Profit report with variance analysis for September 19X5.

Chapter 11

Standard Costs — Accounting Entries

A comprehensive example of standard costing procedures will help to bring together all the information set out in the previous two chapters. As well as calculating variances, this example incorporates the double entries in the cost accounting model.

Example

The company manufacturers and sells Flumenite for the restoration of polluted rivers.

The manufacturing process is a simple one and is carried on in a single cost centre.

Normal volume of production in a given period is 10,000 gallons.

Standard Cost per Gallon

	£
Direct material (1 lb)	0.2
Direct labour (0.125 hrs)	0.2
Variable overhead	0.1
Fixed overhead*	0.1
	0.6

*Budget £1,000 ÷ normal volume

For the period under review the following budgeted and actual results are provided:-

Budgeted Sales — 10,000 gallons at £1.0/gallon =   £10,000
Actual sales — 11,000 gallons at £1.1/gallon   £12,100
Production 11,500 gallons.
Purchases of raw material — 12000 lb for   £2,520
Quantity of raw material used 11600 lbs.
Wages paid for direct labour £2,505
Direct labour hours recorded 1500
Variable overheads spent £1,100
Fixed overheads spent £1,100
Selling expenses budget £400
Actual selling expenses £350
Administration expenses budget £500
Actual administration expenses £550

The stock or work-in-progress at the beginning and end of the month is nil.
The budgeted and actual results for the period are given in figure 1.1

	Budget gall. 10,000	Actual gall. 12,100	Variance £
	£	£	
Sales	10,000	12,100	
Standard Cost of Goods Sold (£0.6)	6,000	6,600	
Standard margin	4,000	5,500	1500 F
Manufacturing variances	—	245 U	245 U
Gross profit	4,000	5,255	1255 F
Selling	400	350	50 F
Administration	500	550	50 u
Profit before tax	3,100	4,355	1255 F

Figure 11.1. Accounting report.

The report in figure 11.1 is the end product of the accounting entries which are to be illustrated in this chapter. The detail of it should be accepted for the moment.

The design of the report summarises the difference between the budget and actual results with three variances. The first is the sales variance, the second is for the manufacturing process. The third is the area of selling and administration expenses for which standards as such are not available. Instead an amount of resources is allocated for an agreed programme of activity.

The sales and manufacturing variances are total figures and can be analysed into price and volume or use components. This analysis follows, using the formulae established in earlier chapters. In addition, the double-entry accounting will be illustrated.

Selling price variance:-

$$£ \left[\begin{array}{c}\text{Actual} \\ \text{Margin}\end{array}\right] - \left[\begin{array}{c}\text{Budget} \\ \text{Margin}\end{array}\right] \times \begin{array}{c}\text{Actual} = \\ \text{volume}\end{array} \quad \text{Variance}$$

$$£ \quad (0.50 \quad - \quad 0.40) \quad \times \quad 11,000 = \quad £1100\ F$$

Volume variance:-

$$\left[\begin{array}{c}\text{Actual} \\ \text{Volume}\end{array}\right] - \left[\begin{array}{c}\text{Budget} \\ \text{Volume}\end{array}\right] \times \begin{array}{c}\text{Budgeted} \\ \text{margin}\end{array}$$

$$(11,000 \quad - \quad 10,000) \quad \times \quad £0.40 = \quad £400\ F$$

$$£1500\ F$$

The double-entry for sales can be adapted to include these variances. More usually the figures are entered at their actual values and the variances incorporated into the reports.

| A. | Debtors | Dr. | 12,100 | |
| | Sales | | | 12,100 |

Material price variance:-

Actual × (Actual standard) = Variance
$-$

quantity   (price price)
12000   ×   (0.21p − 0.20p)   =   £120 u

Accounting entry —

B.	Material control	Dr.	£2,400	
	Material price variance		£120	
	Creditors			£2,520

In this way the raw material control account and its subsidiaries, are kept at standard prices.

Material use variance:-

(Actual − Standard)   Standard   variance
(quantity quantity) ×   price   =
(11,600 − £11,500) ×   £0.20   =   £20 u

Accounting entry:-

C.	Work-in-progress	Dr.	£2,300	
	Material use variance		£20	
	Material control			£2,320

There is a difference in the period between the quantity of raw material bought and consumed. This amounted to 400 lb at the standard price of £0.20 = £80 increase in raw material stock.

Labour rate (price) variance:-

Actual   × (actual − standard) =   variance
hours   (rate   rate)
worked
1500   ×   (£1.67 − £1.60)   =   £105 u

The accounting entry for this will be dealt with when the labour efficiency variance has been calculated.

Labour efficiency (use) variance:-

Actual   −   Standard   × Standard = variance
Hours Worked   Hours achieved   rate
(1500   −   1437.5)   × £1.60 = £100 u

Accounting entry:-

D.	Work-in-progress	Dr.	£2,300	
	Labour rate variance		£105	
	Labour efficiency variance		£100	
	Wages control			£2,505

As with material, the work-in-progress account is debited with the standard cost of the work performed and the variances are hived off.

Some explanation may be necessary for individual figures. The actual rate of pay is £2505/1500. The standard rate of pay is shown on the standard cost per gallon, i.e. 0.125 hours $\times$ £1.6 = £0.2 per gallon. The standard hours achieved are the output of 11,500 gallons $\times$ 0.125 hours per gallon = 1437.5 standard hours of work.

Manufacturing overhead variances.

Spending variance:-

Actual Expenditure	−	Flexible Budget Allowance	=	Spending Variance
£(1100 + 1100)	−	(1150 + 1000)*	=	£50 u

	£
*earned output $\times$ variable rate (11500 $\times$ 0.1)	1150
budgeted fixed overheads	1000
	2150

Volume variance:-

Flexible Budget Allowance	−	Manufacturing Overheads Absorbed	=	Volume Variance
£2,150 (see above) − 11500 $\times$ 0.2** =				150

**earned output $\times$ overhead absorption rate.

Accounting Entry:

		£	
E.	Work-in-progress control	2,300	
	Spending variance	50	
	Volume variance		150
	Manufacturing overhead control		220

This entry clears the manufacturing overhead control of the amount spent and debits the work-in-progress with the amount absorbed accoridng to the predetermined standards and budgets. The differences resulting from effective or ineffective control of spending and volume fluctuations are separated into variance accounts.

Work-in-progress transferred to Finished Goods.

The total work completed was 11500 gallons. The standard cost is £0.6 per gallon. The debit to finished goods account is, therefore, 11500 $\times$ £0.6 = £6900

| F. | Finished stock | £6,900 | |
| | Work-in-progress | | £6,900 |

Actual sales were 11,000 gallons and the standard cost of this is to be transferred from finished goods to cost of goods sold. This is $11,000 \times £0.6 = £6,600$.

| G. | Cost of goods sold | £6,600 | |
| | Finished goods | | £6,600 |

The selling and administration expenses are entered directly as they are incurred. The variances from the original programmed amounts are not included in the double-entry records.

		£	£
H.	Selling expenses	350	
	Administration expenses	550	
	Creditors/cash		900

The main accounts in T form are shown below:-

Sales
  | A £12100

Creditors
  | B £2520

Raw Material Control
B £2400 | C £2320

Material Price Variance
B £120 |

Work-in-Progress
C £2300 | F £6900
D £2300
E £2300

Material Use Variance
C £20 |

Labour Rate Variance
D £105 |

Labour Efficiency Variance
D £100 |

Overhead Volume Variance
  | E £150

Overhead Spending Variance
E £50 |

Finished Stocks
F £6900 | G £6600

Cost of Goods Sold
G £6600 |

Selling Expenses
H £350 |

Administration Expenses
H £550 |

When put into a profit report these give:-

	£
Sales	12,100
Cost of Goods Sold	6,600
	5,500

Variance:-

	U	F	
	£	£	£
Material price	120		
Material use	20		
Labour rate	105		
Labour efficiency	100		
Overhead spending	50		
Overhead volume		150	245
	395	150	5255
Selling expenses			350
Administration expenses			550
			£4355

Chapter Summary

This simple numerical example illustrates the basic recording which is utilised in a budgeting and standard cost control system. Standards and corresponding variances which relate to the manufacturing costs are incorporated into the double-entry model. For sales and non-manufacturing expenses the budget figures can be set against actual in the report itself, so that the double-entry need only contain the actual results.

The standard cost report and a report cased solely on the historic cost figures would give slightly different results. This is because in the first case stocks are at standard, whereas in the second case they would be on historic costs based on F.I.F.O. or L.I.F.O. etc.

Exercises

Questions 11.1-11.5 (Answers provided)

11.1 The Keele Company had these direct material figures for October 19X5:

2000 bought at £1.00/unit	£2000
Material price variance	£200 u
Issued to production 1700	
at the standard of £0.9	£1530
Material use variance	100 u

Required: journal entries to record the material element of procurement and production.

11.2 The Open Company had these labour results for October 19X5:

actual — 3200 hours for £6530

standards— rate equals £2.00/hour

— earned output equals 3000 hours

Required: journal entries to record labour cost and variances.

11.3 The Independent Company had the following overhead costs and variances for November 19X5:

	£
Actual spending	12,500
Flexible budget allowance	13,010
Standard overhead absorption	14,000

Required: the journal entries to record the overhead cost and variances.

11.4 The Bath Manufacturing Company had the following journal entries for March 19X5:

Work-in-progress (? hours × £?)	Dr ?
Labour rate variance (? hours × £0.20)	Dr 200
Labour efficiency variance (? hours × £1.00)	Dr 100
Wages payable (? hours × £?)	?

Required: complete the entries.

11.5 The City Trading Company had the following direct material report for January 19X5:

Material bought,	1000 at £?/lb.
Price variance	? lbs at £0.01/lb.
Material used	? lbs at £?
Use variance	50 lbs at £?
Increase in material stock	100 lbs at £2.00

Required: complete the entries.

Questions 11.6-11.10. Answers not provided.

11.6 B Limited operates an integrated accounting system and the following details given relate to one year.

You are required from the details given to:

(a) enter in the appropriate ledger accounts the transactions for the year;

(b) prepare a profit and loss account for the year; and

(c) prepare a balance sheet as at the end of the year.

Trial balance at beginning of the year:

	£000's	£000's
Capital	—	1,000
Reserves	—	200
Creditors	—	150
Expense creditors	—	20
Freehold buildings, at cost	500	—
Plant and machinery, at cost	300	—
Provision for depreciation of plant and machinery	—	100
Stock of: raw materials	220	—
work-in-progress	40	—
finished goods	60	—
Debtors	200	—
Bank	150	—
	1,470	1,470

The following data for the year are given:

	£000's
Materials: purchased on credit	990
returned to suppliers	40
issued to production	850
Production: wages incurred	250
salaries	60
expenses incurred	320
Carriage inwards	45
Provision for depreciation of plant and machinery	50
Production: overhead absorbed	425
Production, at standard cost	1,600
Administration: salaries	100
expenses incurred	260
overhead absorbed in finished goods	380
Selling and distribution: salaries	80
expenses incurred	120
absorbed in cost of sales	210
Finished goods sold	2,000
Sales on credit	2,500
Sales returns	60
Variance: direct material: price (adverse)	35
usage (favourable)	20
direct wages rate (favourable)	15
direct labour efficiency (favourable)	30
production overhead: expenditure (adverse)	25
efficiency (favourable)	40
Abnormal loss of raw material stock, insurance claim agreed and cash received	60
New machinery purchased, paid by cheque	50
Paid: creditors	895
expense creditors	730
Cash discount received from trade creditors	25
Paid wages and salaries	425
Deduction from wages and salaries	50
Received cheques from debtors	2,350
Cash discount allowed	35
Bad debts written off	25

All 'price' variances (i.e. direct material price, direct wages rate, production overhead expenditure) are recorded in the relevant expenditure accounts; 'quantity' variances (i.e. direct material usage, direct labour efficiency, production overhead efficiency) are recorded in the work-in-progress account.

ICMA(CA2).

11.7 A manufacturing company has two production departments, viz. Machining and Assembly, and two service departments, viz. Tooling and Maintenance.

The budgeted monthly activity level of the Machining Department is 400 machine hours and the budgeted overhead cost £16,000. The Assembly Department's overhead budget is £9,600 per month during which 2,400 direct labour hours are expected to be worked.

In determining the overhead budgets of the production departments, the expenses of the service departments were dealt with as follows:

Tooling 70% to Machining
     20% to Assembly
     10% to Maintenance

Maintenance 50% to Machining
     30% to Assembly
     20% to Tooling

During May 1978, the Machining Department booked 415 hours of machine time to production, and the Assembly Department booked 2,350 labour hours.

Overhead incurred during the month was as follows:

	Machining £	Assembly £	Tooling £	Maintenance £
Material	4,600	5,200	1,800	600
Labour	6,100	1,200	2,700	1,600
Miscellaneous	700	900	500	300

You are required to:

(a) prepare the overhead account for each production department showing the amount of any over/under absorption and its disposition;

(b) identify the causes which gave rise to the over/under absorption in each departmant, and state the amount attributable to each cause.

CA(AC2).

11.8 (a) The standard processing loss in refining certain basic materials into an industrial cleaning compound is 15%, this scrap being sold for 50p per kg.

At the beginning of Period 6, 8,000 kg of basic material was put into a process, the output of which was 7,000 kg of cleaning compound. The basic material cost 80p per kg, wages of process operators amounted to £1,200 and overhead applied to the process was £480.

Prepare the necessary account to show the results of the process.

(b) The production of a product known as a Tojo requires the treatment of input units through three distinct processes at each of which refining material is added and labour and overhead costs are incurred.

Work in progress at the beginning of Period 9 consisted of 8,000 input units which had passed through the first process, the cost to that point being £96,000. During Period 9, refining material which cost £31,594 was added and labour costs amounted to £23,940. Process Overhead is applied at the rate of 40% of process labour.

7,200 units were completed during the Period and transferred to Process 3. Of the remainder, the firm's Chief Chemist estimated that in respect of refining material, labour and overhead, half were 75% complete at the end of Period 9, and the other half, 40% complete.

You are required to write up Process 2 Account for Period 9 showing clearly the cost to be transferred to Process 3, and the value of the work in progress at the end of the period.

CA(AC2).

11.9 Seeka Limited manufacturers and markets a single product. As the newly appointed management accountant, you have been asked to review the basis of the system which is currently in operation. One of the reports of this system, the results of the four-weekly period which has recently ended, is shown below:

Seeka Ltd.

Operating Statement for Period 6
(Weeks 21-24)

	£
Standard profit for the period	60,000
Variances (brackets indicates unfavourable)	
Sales margin quantity	6,000
Material price	5,000
Material usage	(8,000)
Factory overhead:	
Expenditure	(3,000)
Volume—capacity	15,000
Selling overhead:	
Volume	4,000
Expenditure—fixed	(1,000)
Expenditure—variable	(500)
Total variances	17,500
ACTUAL PROFIT FOR THE PERIOD	£77,500

The budgeted levels of activity and unit standards for each four-week period in the current financial year are:

Budgeted production and sales	20,000 units
	£
Standards per unit	
Materials—6 lbs at 50p	3.00
Labour—4 hours at £1.50	6.00
Recovery of fixed overheads:	
Factory	5.00
Selling	2.00
Selling expenses—variable	1.00
	17.00
Selling price	20.00
Standard profit per unit	£3.00

It is company practice to value all stocks at standard cost, writing-off variances in the period in which they occur. Stocks of raw material and work in progress were unchanged between the beginning and end of Period 6.

Required:

(a) The re-presentation of the operating statement for Period 6 in 'contribution' form, using marginal costing principles. Stock are to continue to be valued at standard cost and variances written-off.

(b) A reconciliation and explanation of the difference between the profit shown in the original statement and that which you prepared in (a).

(c) State with reasons, which of the two forms of presentation you would recommend for management control purposes. In your statement indicate any areas of weakness which remain in your preferred form of presentation. CA(MA).

11.10 Stafford Limited, a member of the Terrier Group, manufacturers and markets a single product. The company operates a standard costing system and prepares its operating statements on a four-week period basis.

The results of weeks 9—12, referred to as period 3, of the current financial year for Stafford Limited are shown below:

	Budget		Actual	
	£	£	£	£
Sales		80,000		60,000
Manufacturing costs				
Direct materials	32,000		26,000	
Direct labour	16,000		12,600	
Overheads	20,000		19,500	
		68,000		58,100

Manufacturing profit	12,000	1,900
Selling and distribution expenses	4,000	4,300
Net profit/(loss)	£8,000	£(2,400)

The following additional information is available:

(1) Group policy is that no stocks of finished goods should be maintained, a requirement to which Stafford Ltd always conforms. Stock of materials and work in progress were also unchanged over the period.

(2) The budget was prepared on the basis of producing 1000 units each week. All production produced in any week is also sold during that week. Unit standards, for selling price were £20 to show a net profit of £2.

(3) All sales and purchases were made at the standard prices used in the preparation of the budget.

(4) The standard labour time for each unit is 4 hours. The direct labour hours worked, and paid, in period 3 were 12,000.

(5) Following an industrial dispute, all direct labour employees were on strike for the whole of week 12. The dispute was settled in time for work to be resumed at the commencement of the following week. The employees who participated in the strike were not paid for this time. However, it was agreed that overtime should be worked in the next period, to be paid at time-and-a-half, to make up for the time lost. Previous experience of overtime working is that labour efficiency has been 90% of standard and therefore management does not consider it will be possible to fully recover the production which has been lost during the period of dispute.

(6) All manufacturing overheads are fixed. Selling expenses are also fixed. Distribution costs amount to 3% of sales revenue.

Required:

The preparation of an operating statement for Period 3. This is to be presented to show the financial effects of the events of that period. Your statement should be in the form which you consider to be most informative to management and should include a narrative in which you state the principles which have guided your analysis and presentation.

CA(MA).

Seminar Problem 11

The Oxbridge (Elite Cleaners) Ltd., manufacturers a superior form of car cleaning and protection polish, which is sold in 1 litre containers.

The budget for the quarter ended 31st March 19X5 is given below:

		£
Sales (30,000 litres)		120,000
Cost of goods sold (at standard)	£	
Materials	45,000	
Labour (6000 hours)	9,000	
Manufacturing overheads:		
variable	9,000	
fixed	15,000	78,000
		42,000
Selling expenses (fixed)	15,000	
Administration expenses (fixed)	10,000	25,000
Net profit		17,000

The actual results for the period were:

		£
Sales (33,000 litres)		125,000
Production (33,000 litres)		—
Opening stock	nil	
Materials (bought and used)		
at standard prices		52,000
at actual prices		50,000
Wages – 6500 hours worked		
– payment		10,100
Manufacturing overheads		35,000
Selling expenses		15,600
Administration expenses		9,200

The variable manufacturing overheads are taken as being linearly variable with the quality of output.

Required: a reconciliation of the original budget and actual standard cost report with variances.

Chapter 12

Responsibility Accounting

This chapter in the section on control will contain much that has already been included, either explicitly or implicitly, in earlier chapters. However, the emphasis in the text so far has been technical, in the sense that it has dealt largely with the procedures of cost accounting. These technical aspects need an additional dimension, which is given by operating them within the framework of a well developed control system.

Control systems

A schematic view of control system is given in figure 12.1.

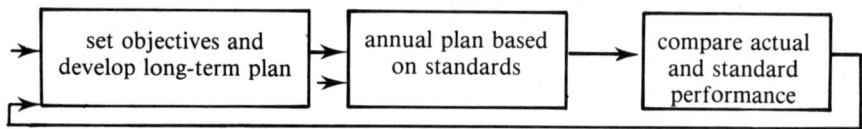

Figure 12.1. Control System.

The main features of a control system consist of the following sequential steps:

1. Set the goals of the organisation and develop the long-term plan. This will be constrained by external factors as well as feed back from the internal reporting system.

2. Develop an annual plan which is consistent with the long-term plan and which is based on standards.

3. Perform the operations and measure the actual results against the standard allowances.

4. Feed the results of these comparisons back into the early stages of the cycle and as output to other control systems.

Within a firm there will be a hierarchy of such control systems, monitoring the activities of segments which vary in size from department to dvisions. An important aspect, contained in 4 above, is that of effective communications. This calls for clear reporting, but even more fundamentally it can only be truly effective if it is clearly related to good organisation.

Cost Centres

A well organised firm has a clearly defined set of cost centres. These have been fully introduced in chapter 5, but the essential features are worth repeating here. They consist of units of the firm with which costs can be associated. Taken together they must provide the means whereby all costs are collected. Consequently, they must include all areas of expenditure, leaving no gaps and providing no overlap. Every cost must be traceable to a cost centre and there should be no ambiguity about the process. The array of cost centres covers the base of a hierarchical information system.

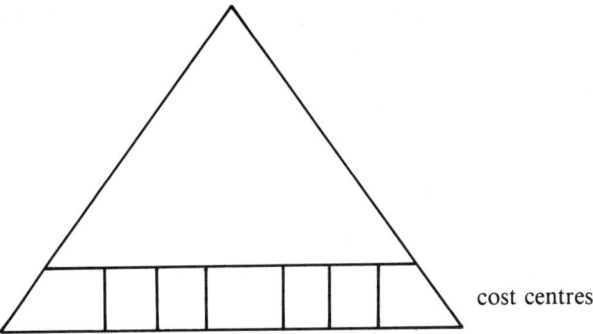

cost centres

Figure 12.2.

Figure 12.2 indicates that all events recorded in the cost accounting system are reported as belonging to a cost centre. Frequently, they are re-allocated to product cost centres for the purposes of product costing, but control is exercised over the basic centre. Reporting for control of these centres needs to be appropriately adapted to the circumstances. These circumstances are determined by assessing controllability of and responsibility for costs. In a good cost control system, responsibility is clear cut and the reporting reflects this fact.

Responsibility Centres

Figure 12.3 is an adapted version of 12.2 and introduces responsibility centres. These are groups of one or more cost centres, or in turn are groups of responsibility centres. Each centre should have a head who is clearly and uniquely responsible for it. As is so often the case, it is harder to achieve this in practice than in theory. Responsibility centres form ascending platforms in the hierarchy. See figure 12.3.

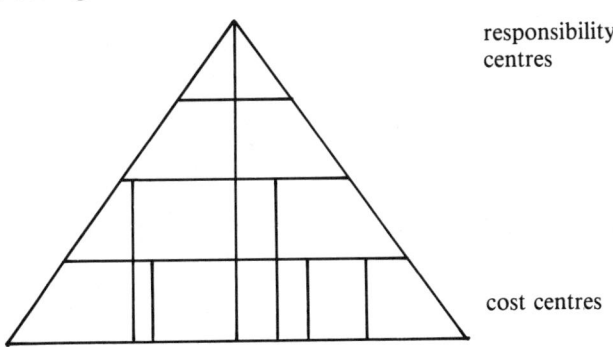

responsibility centres

cost centres

Figure 12.3. Cost and responsibility centres.

196

The top centre is the whole company, immediately below this could be divisions, then factory locations and so on down to the level of cost centres. Cost reports are made up for each of these units and the essential point to be stressed here, is that each report must be designed specifically to enhance the overall effectiveness of the system. By design, each centre is the responsibility of a named person and the purpose of the report is to give information about his centre's performance, with particular stress on factors over which he has control.

Controllable/non-controllable costs

Yet another dichotomy is introduced here. Again the idea is a simple one, but there are difficulties in its practical application. Reports about a centre should as far as possible, be confined to the presentation of information about revenues and costs, which are within control of the responsible manager. The outline of a set of such reports is shown in figure 12.4. In practice, the elements of cost which are referred to as controllable, are more likely to be costs over which the manager has considerable influence, but which stops short of complete control. In figure 12.4 the foreman is shown as being responsible for a budget of £6000 over which he has a significant measure of influence. Other costs are shown as non-controllable and consist of such expenses as departmental heating. These may be added to give the foreman an idea of the costs of supporting his department. Alternatively, the company may take the view that this information will do more harm than good and omit it from the foreman's report.

Foreman level
Department 100
period ....

	Budget	Actual	Variance
Material	xx	xx	xx
Labour	xx	xx	xx
Overhead:			
Utilities	xx	xx	xx
Supplies	xx	xx	xx
Total controllable costs	6000	6500	500
Non-controllable costs:			
Heating	xxx	xxx	xxx
Rent etc.	xxx	xxx	xxx
	£7000	£7500	£500

Plant Manager level
Factory X
period ....

	Budget	Actual	Variance
Controllable costs of:			
Dept. 100	6000	6500	500
Dept. 101	XXX	XXX	XX
Dept. 102	XXX	XXX	XX
	19000	21000	2000
Other controllable costs:			
Factory heating	XX	XX	XX
etc.	XX	XX	XX
	24000	27000	3000
Non-controllable costs:			
Rent	XXX	XXX	XXX
etc.	XXX	XXX	XXX
	£30000	£33000	£3000

Divisional Manager level
Alpha Division
period ....

	Budget	Actual	Variance
Controllable costs of:			
Factory X	30000	33000	3000
Factory Y	XXX	XXX	XXX
Factory Z	XXX	XXX	XXX
	80000	84000	4000
Non-controllable costs:			
Share of central			
administration costs	XXX	XXX	XXX
etc.	XXX	XXX	XXX
	90000	94000	4000

Figure 12.4. Responsibility accounting cost reports.

Expense and profit centres

Cost centres are normally associated with the expenditure side of their activities only and, as such, can be referred to as expense centres. It is sometimes feasible to expand them by introducing revenue and, thus, developing profit centres. Associating with revenue means valuing output with an element for profit, or charging for services rendered. The use of this approach is intended to motivate the department to give its best efforts and contribute to the overall good of the firm.

In practice, there are a number of difficulties. Not the least of these is valuing output. Sometimes there is a readily available market value which could be used, but this is seldom the case. This is most likely to occur when the centre is transferring out some finished product, which is available from other sources. Problems about the assessment of these transfer price is dealt with later. Service departments, such as maintenance, data processing and legal, could easily charge for their services. This would encourage the service department concerned to achieve an efficient level of service for the fee charged. Against this, some user departmental heads may underspend on the service in a short-sighted way and act detrimentally to the firm's interest.

Whereas the difficulties are often very great in terms of turning cost centres into profit centres, this is not so when dealing with the highest levels of responsibility centres, or at least they are not so great at first sight. At the top, the firm has to be a profit reporting unit. But further down the pyramid the difficulties soon manifest themselves, so that even for such large centres as divisions, the calculation of segment profit is quite difficult. This is very often because of the problem of fixing a fair price of the output, which is frequently being transferred to another division as input.

Investment centres

Profit centres can in turn be re-designed as investment centres. In these the management is held responsible not just for the profit, but also for the investment involved. Investment centres are almost always responsibility centres at the higher levels of the hierarchical structure, usually in the form of divisions which may take a number of forms in practice. The objective when organising a firm into a set of smaller investment centres is to combine within the one organisation, the economies of scale associated with largeness and the scope to manage effectively associated with smallness.

Measures of Performance

The evaluation of managerial performance at the top level of the company is usually done on the basis of profit and return on capital employed or investment. The same considerations can be applied when looking for a measure of the performance of managers at lower levels in the scale, for example divisional managers and plant managers. Students should already be aware of the general problems associated with profit measurement and asset valuation. It is suffice to say here that such matters as changing price-levels and different accounting policies are major difficulties in the way of a satisfactory assessment of the profit of a firm. These and other difficulties are currently being tackled with new urgency, but it will be many years before fully satisfactory solutions are found. Such difficulties are compounded by further snags when dealing with the profitability of lower segments of the firm. A variant on the profit measure will be introduced and this is called the residual profit. It is designed to improve the assessment of investment centres.

Profit

The profit of a segment of the firm can be used to assess the managers performance, but there are considerable difficulties and care must be exercised.

The first difficulty relates to the revenue. How is the output of the centre to be valued? This is the problem of transfer pricing referred to above and dealt with in a later paragraph.

On the expenses side a distinction can be made between controllable and non-controllable. This calls for a decision to be made as to the responsibility of the manager for each class of expense. Is he responsible for it or not? In some cases it is not too easy to decide. For example, how much of the firms legal department costs should be charged to a division? Can the divisional manager assume full responsibility for calling on the services of the legal department and pay simply for services received? Can he go further and employ an independent firm of solicitors? These courses give him freedom of action and control over legal costs. The cost of failing to use the legal department may be substantial and the top management may decide that level costs should be pro-rated between divisions and that the services can be called upon free of particular charge. Many services fall into this category.

Residual profit

This is a measure of performance based on the difference between profit as arrived at above and the cost of the capital employed in earning that profit. It is a concept which is finding increasing favour in large firms with clear divisional organisation. First of all an example to clarify the idea:

Alpha Division

Reported profit	£20,000
Net capital invested	£100,000
Cost of capital	12%
Excess of profit over cost of capital	£20,000 − £12,000
	= £8,000

The requirement of managers is to maximise their residual profit or residual income as it is more usually called. In accordance with the concept of controllable costs, it is possible to interpret residual income to mean the excess of revenue over controllable costs and the cost of capital, thus arriving at a form of contribution to company profit. It is more likely though that the divisional or other segment profit report will contain controllable and non-controllable items suitably described.

The question of reporting on segments in order to achieve the highest motivation of that segments management, within a framework of overall company good is a major study. Maximising residual income is considered by many to be the most satisfactory form of such appraisals. An example of a divisional profit report is given in figure 12.5. A study of this example indicates the variety of possibilities open to those people who are designing the control system.

Alpha division

Profit for the period ....

Sales: External customers	xxx	
Internal transfers	xxx	xxx
Less: Variable manufacturing cost of goods sold	xxx	
Other variable costs (e.g. selling)	xxx	xxx
Contribution to overheads etc.		xxx
Less: Controllable divisional overheads (itemised)		xxx
Controllable profit		xxx
Less: Interest on controllable investment		xxx
Controllable residual income etc.		xxx

Figure 12.5.

The section of the report following on from the controllable residual income would, if developed, show the non-controllable costs of the divisional, separated between wholly divisional items and apportioned common costs, plus taxes.

Return on Investment

This is common and popular measure of performance used by many companies. It is an expression of profit to capital employed. As a measure of performance it is considered to be inferior to the residual income concept considered above. However, some of the difficulties in applying residual income are associated with establishing the investment figure and then distinguishing between controllable and non-controllable elements. It is convenient, therefore, to look at these problems here.

For a start, it is possible to view assets employed according to a number of valuation concepts, including historic costs and replacements costs. This then calls for a first decision. Then again, the asset figure may mean fixed plus current assets, fixed plus net current assets, or total assets minus total liabilities.

Other decisions relate to the treatment of commonly shared assets and this usually includes cash, since most companies organise their cash holdings on a central basis. Finally, should values be taken at the beginning of the year, at the end of the year or at some average value? These are questions without an attempt at answers. To some extent they way in which a firm formulates its answers can be influenced by its particular circumstances. In general though, the usual answers to the questions posed are to use total assets suitably indexed to current values; not to allocate shared assets; to use average investment figures for the period. This simple question and answer treatment has been given in this abrupt form as an indicator of the problems involved. It is a major study in its own right and students are likely to want to study it in some depth as their careers advance.

Transfer Pricing

The application of profit centre concepts to a firm bring the problem of transfer pricing right into the spotlight. Where a company has a relatively small portion of its sales as transactions between divisions, then the formula adopted for the transfer price is an adaptation of the market price. The usual forms of adaptation make allowances for the absence of selling and debt collection expenses.

As the level of dependence of one division on another increases, so that much higher proportions of output are being transferred, the availability of a clear market price may diminish to the extent that another rule has to be found. In such cases the transfer price is at the level of production for which the marginal cost of the transferring division equals the net marginal revenue of the receiving division. This is in accordance with the viewpoint of seeing the firm as a whole, ignoring divisional boundaries and increasing production to the point where the marginal cost of output equals the marginal revenue to be obtained.

In practice there are many variants of transfer pricing formulae, including free negotiations. A useful device used in many companies is to set up a staff department at headquarters, charged with the task of mediating between divisions in cases of conflict and overseeing the interests of the company as a whole.

Control and People

An important element of all the systems involved in control, is the way in which people behave within them. It is just not possible to operate control systems in a purely technical way, ruling by decree as it were.

It is not too difficult to envisage the sort of end result that top management would like to achieve in their organisations. They want good results from achieving budgets that represent good attainment. In other words they want budgets which are at the very top end of the attainable level. They want these budgets to be met and studies so far, indicate that the chance of this happening are greatest where the individual accepts standards as his goal.

Participation in budgeting and standard setting

An increasing amount of research and experimentation has taken place in recent years in the area of employee participation in preparing budgets and setting standards. The general hypothesis is that a higher level of performance can be obtained if the aforementioned participation is introduced. However, success is not assumed and wrong implementation of the idea can indeed result in a lower performance level. The approach is to foster a team spirit among the management group and to couple this with incentives. If the introduction is lacking in some elements, possibly in terms of half-heartedness on the part of some of the higher management level, it can turn out to be a failure. Substituting pseudo participation methods for more direct styles of standard setting only leads to lowering of standards, since neither one nor the other style is being pursued.

Setting standards according to individual characteristics

A second area of research has led to suggestions that the personality of individuals should be considered when setting standards. People react differently to standards set before them. The same standards set before different people can produce, it is thought, quite different reactions. Thus, what encourages one supervisor to reach a level may be regarded by another as discrediting the budget.

Chapter Summary

Management accounting systems are more than the sum of the collection of inter-locking techniques. Whilst it is essential for cost accountants to understand fully the workings of the accounting model that they employ, they are of limited value to the management team if they do not recognise the wider considerations.

The end products of the working model must be reports which are relevant to the situation and which are sensitive to the fact that the organisation is made up of human beings. Reports must relate to the level and extent of the true responsibility of individuals. Inadequate thinking in this respect often results in a downgrading of an individual's performance. Either by inducing a sense of not being associated with the figures, or by distorting his performance since he is being measured against the wrong activity. Reports have to measure accurately a responsible manager's freedom of action and capture his performance in those terms. This is not an easy task. Especially when it may be necessary to incorporate personal characteristics into the picture in order to obtain optimal results.

It is also true that some inputs to the model require sensitive handling. This applies to the budgeting process, where behavioural considerations can make an impact on the quality of the figures produced, particularly with regard to the attitude adopted towards the budgets when performance is underway.

Exercises

Questions 12.1-12.5 (Answers provided)

12.1　Explain the idea of a cost centre. Give five examples of service and product cost centres.

12.2　Explain the relationships between cost centres and responsibility centres.

12.3　Distinguish between expense centres, profit centres and investment centres.

12.4 What are the main difficulties involved in operating profit and investment centres?

12.5 Develop the idea of controllable costs and their use in cost reports.

Questions 12.6-12.10 Answers not provided.

12.6 BUE is a group consisting of four subsidiary operating companies: British Angles, British Bards, British Circles and British Dies.

British Dies proposes to place a contract for a sub-assembly to be used in one of its new products and, in accordance with BUE policy, has to obtain quotations form any suitable company within the group and at least one outside company.

Within the group, British Angles is approached as the most suitable company and submits a quotation of £2,400 per 1,000 sub-assemblies. In order to do the job, however, British Angles will need to sub-contract some of the work to British Bards and some to British Circles.

The arrangements between the companies for this sub-contract (per batch of completed 1,000 sub-assemblies) are as follows:

British Angles will buy from British Bars special parts at a price of £200.

British Angles will buy from British Circles components at a price of £1,500.

To make up its components, however, British Circles must buy from British Bars standard parts at a price of £380.

From companies outside the group, British Dies obtains the following quotations batch of 1,000 completed sub-assemblies:

—Italmet quotes £1,650 including all carriage and import duties for sub-assemblies manufactured in Italy.

—Deutschmet quotes £1,800 for sub-assemblies manufactured in its U.K. plant, but will buy certain components from British Angles for this job at £550. In order to make these components, British Angles will have to buy parts from British Circles at a price of £350.

The following information is also given:

1. British Circles' prices include a 25% profit margin on its total cost (including, where appropriate, any special parts bought in).

2. British Bars' price of £380 is the current market price for these parts. They are in heavy demand by buyers outside the BUE group, and their supply from British Bars is severely limited.

3. The out-of-pocket costs of each group company relating to the work for which it has quoted are:

As a proportion of the total cost of the work it does itself (i.e. excluding parts or components bought from other group companies):

British Angles	60%
British Circles	80%

As a proportion of selling price:

British Bars	75%

4. British Angles' total costs (including purchases from British Bars and British Circles) for the British Dies contract are £2,200, and it assesses that it could make a profit of $33\frac{1}{3}\%$ on the cost of its own work on the Deutschmet contract.

As management accountant of British Dies you are required to:

(a) Recommend whether, from the BUE group point of view, it is more advantageous for the contract to be placed with British Angles, Italment, or Deutschmet.

Show figures to support your recommendations.

(b) List any assumptions you have made in deciding on your recommendations.

ICMA(MA1).

12.7 Pinkun Limited has three manufacturing divisions. Eastern Division manufacturers Product E which is then sold to Southern Division as a component of Product S is then sold to Western Division which uses it as a component in Product W. Product W, the final assembly, is sold by Western Division to Pinkun's outside customers for £28 each. Products E and S have no outside market. A unit of product W uses one unit of product E and one unit of product S. Current standard costs and other data relating to the three products for 1977 are shown below:

Standard cost per unit	Product E	Product S	Product W
Material purchased from outside	£2.00	£3.00	£1.00
Direct labour (variable)	£1.00	£1.00	£2.00
Variable overhead	£1.00	£1.00	£2.00
Fixed overhead per unit	£3.00	£4.00	£1.00
Standard volume (units)	10,000	10,000	10,000
Stocks and work in progress (average)	£70,000	£15,000	£30,000
Fixed assets (net)	£30,000	£45,000	£16,000

You are required, as general manager of Western Division trying to maximise your reported divisional profits, to:

(a) prepare a profit and loss forecast for the Western Division for 1977 on the basis of 90% of standard volume under each of the following alternative rules for the inter divisional transfer pricing of Products E and S:

 (i) standard cost per unit, plus an additional charge per unit based on a 10% per annum return on average stocks and work in progress and on fixed assets,

 (ii) standard cost per unit, plus a fixed monthly charge invoiced by Eastern and Southern Divisions to Western Division equal to their total fixed overhead costs together with a 10% per annum return on the current average stocks, work in progress and fixed assets, and

(b) give your views, with reasons, as to which of the two transfer pricing rules is likely to be preferred by the managing director of Pinkun Limited.

ICAEW(MA).

12.8 A company operates four factories. Each makes components which are incorporated into the products sold by one or more of the other factories. To encourage a competitive environment the directors have decided that each factory should becomes a separate profit centre. This will neccessitate the use of transfer prices for the inter-factory components.

You are required:

(a) describe three different methods of establishing the transfer prices;

(b) state which method you would recommend for the company described, giving reasons for your choice; and

(c) prepare for the one method chosen a policy statement outlining how the pricing system would be operated among the different factories.

ICMA(MA1).

12.9 AB Limited manufactures two products, P and Q, which are normally made in a standard grade of material.

On some occasions AB Limited receives orders for its products to be made in a much more expensive material, whilst on others customers place orders for the two products, but require special material to be used that the customer provides as a free issue. Neither of these variations from the normal procedure alters the conversion cost of the products manufactured.

Data on AB Limited's products are as follows:

Products:	P	Q
Per units of product:		
Direct materials, in yards	5	10
Direct labour, in man-hours	4	6
Selling price:	£	£
using standard material	28	47
using expensive material	68	127
using free issue material	18	27

Cost of material, per yard:	£
standard	2
expensive	10

Rate of pay for direct labour, £1 per hour

Variable overhead is 50% of direct wages

Fixed overhead is absorbed at a rate of £2 per man-hour

Budgeted man-hours per period are 4,400

For each of three successive periods Nos 7, 8 and 9, AB Limited's total output in numbers of each product was identical, but the proportions of each produced in standard material, expensive material, and free issue material varied as shown below. Opening and closing stocks were same for each period.

Number of units of product: Made in:	Period 7		Period 8		Period 9	
	P	Q	P	Q	P	Q
standard material	300	300	200	100	250	100
expensive material	100	50	300	250	50	50
free issue material	100	50	—	50	200	250
Total	500	400	500	400	500	400

AB Limited prepares periodic accounts, and the managing direct views with special interest the ratio of profit as a percentage of sales.

You are required to:

(a) calculate the percentage of profit to sales for each of periods 7, 8 and 9.

(b) state whether or not you consider the ratio of profit to sales to be a satisfactory index or periodic performance for AB Limited: explain very briefly your views;

(c) state what other indices of profit performance (that can be drawn from the data available in this question) the managing director of AB Limited could advantageously use. List their advantages over the percentage of profit to sales.

ICMA(CA2).

Seminar Problem 12

Electronic Systems Limited is a decentralized company with each division judged independently on the basis of its profit and return on investment. Each divisional manager has full authority on all decisions regarding sales to internal or external customers, subject to an informal arbitration system conducted by a full-time executive director.

Recently, E division has asked for bids for 200 units of a sub-assembly, which in the past has been supplied almost entirely by C division. C division quoted £24 a unit, in competition with £22 form the lowest bidding outside firm. Quality was the same in both samples provided.

When asked to justify his quotation the manager of C division made the following points. Profit margins of companies in the same line of business were being squeezed at the present time. His strategy, however, was to carry on giving full cost quotations, because he believed that the market situation would soon improve. Thus he would benefit from the fact that this rivals would be operating on order books with very low profit margins. In addition, C division had just bought some specialized equipment for making this component and a high depreciation charge was increasing the price. This new equipment could not be used in any other process.

C division accountant computed variable costs as £18 and fixed out of pocket costs as £3 per unit. If C division receives the order 50% of the variable costs will be for sub units normally bought from M division of the same firm. M divisions out of pocket costs for the sub units would be about 50% of their selling price.

If the outside supplier received the contract, it would probably buy 25% of its requirements of this particular sub unit from M division. M division sold to C division at the currently ruling market price.

The manager of C division appeals to the director concerned (see first paragraph) to instruct E division to buy at the price of £24 a unit.

Required:

(a) Examine the effects of the alternatives on company profits.

(b) Explain how you would respond to this request from C's manager, if you were the director responsible for arbitration. Give full reasons.

(c) Why should it be necessary to have a system of arbitration in a decentralized firm?

Chapter 13

Control of Working Capital

This section of the book has dealt with control, mainly on the basis of setting standards and operating budgets. For the most part this means a concentration of the efficient use of material labour and expense, plus control over the prices paid for these cost elements. So far little has been said about the stock of materials available, or the rate of collection of debtors, or the cash flow. This is the area of working capital management. Failure to control the working capital can only result in a firm having serious problems of survial. Interest in this section of a firm's assets has been growing fast in recent years and an analysis of fund changes has been featured more and more prominently in management and published reports.

Working capital consists of the current assets of the firm less the creditors. Expanding these terms, it is the stocks of raw material, work-in-progress and finished goods, the debtors and the cash including easily liquidated short-term securities. These are to differing extents finance by short-term borrowings, e.g. bank overdrafts and by creditors.

These, then, are the elements of working capital and they need to be controlled since they are high cost items and are associated with high risk also. The cost of maintaining too high a level of inventory can be offset against the risk of running out of essential stocks. Too much cash has an opportunity cost, but against this too little cash and there is a danger of not being able to pay creditors and obtain supplies. Alternatively, slow payment of creditors can mean lost discounts and higher prices, since a slow payer can find himself at the mercy of his supplier. Working capital management is a process of setting these benefits and risks against each other and seeking an optimum result.

Stock Control

Chapter 3 contained an explanation of the way in which material accounts are maintained in cost accounting records. However, the cost accountant needs to know more than this if he is to influence some degree of control over stock levels. Such control comes in two ways. One by having good systems of buying, receiving, inspecting, storing and issuing. The second by developing models of stock-holding and applying quantitative techniques. Each of these approaches will be examined.

Materials
Materials Classification

The term 'material' is used in a general sense to include all the substances needed by a firm in its operations. These may be 'direct' or 'indirect' according to products or cost centres, as has been explained in the early chapters. More specifically the term includes substances which form part of the finished product and substance which do not. The latter are frequently called supplies. Ultimately they for part of the firm's overheads and, as such, will be analysed between product and period costs. To increase control it is normal to treat all these materials in a similar manner. That is to say they are accepted into stores pending issue. It is only when they are issued that they are classified as to purpose.

Objectives of Material Control

To put it rather tritely, material control is about providing the right material, at the right place, at the right time and at the right cost. Material control than is concerned with quality; with the requirements of the production plan; and with maintaining a proper balance between security and expense.

The materials held by a firm in its stock-holding areas tie up a significant proportion of its working capital. Because of this fact there is pressure working to reduce stock to a minimum size. On the other hand if the supply of material fails at any point the results can be far reaching in terms of loss of production, especially in a business where work flows from one point to another in a continuous fashion. Consequently, fear of such a loss acts as pressure to main unnecessarily high stock levels. A material control system recognises the legitimacy of these influences and works to satisfy all parties, by demonstrating that the needs of all concerned have been built into the system.

Material and Production Control Systems

It is impossible to avoid linking material control with production control, except at the very elementary level. The systems are shown diagrammatically in figure 13.1 and should be referred to both before and whilst reading the following description.

The systems are triggered into operation by the receipt of a customer's order. If this requires manufacture it is analysed in terms of materials needed and demands on labour and machine time, that is to say, on capacity. To ascertain the position concerning materials enquiries are made from stores records. At this stage it is possible to decide whether or not the order can be accepted without alteration to the delivery date specified by the customer. If it can, the order is included in the master planning schedules and detailed works orders are prepared.

The detailed works orders include documents authorising the issue of necessary materials from stores to production. An advance copy of the

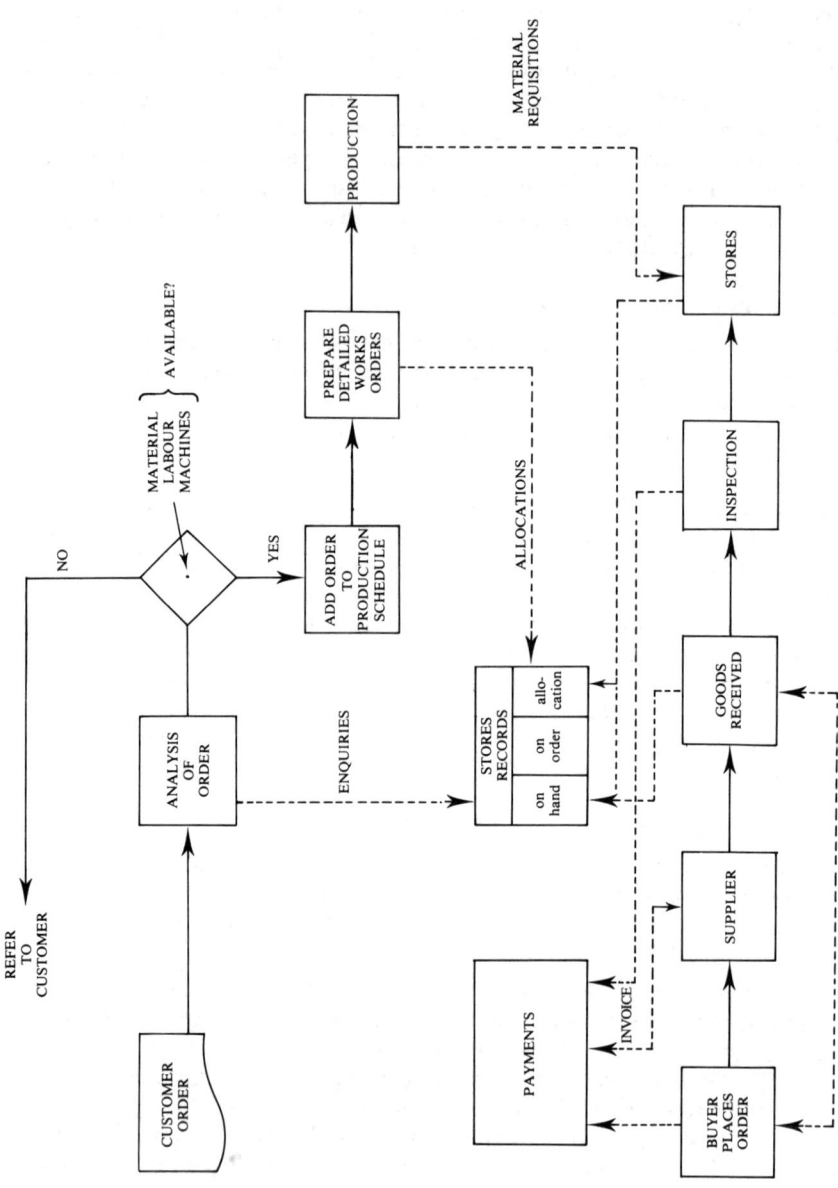

Figure 13.1. Material and Production Control Systems.

material requisitions will go to stores records, so that part of the available stock can be earmarked for future issue. This process of allocation is an important feature of a material control system. When the manufacturing process begins, material requisitions will be used progressively to authorize issues from stores. These requisitions will act as posting documents to record issues.

The advance copies of material requisitions, referred to as allocations, will set up a testing routine within stores records to see if replenishment orders are required for any specific items. In such cases a purchase requisition will be made out and set to the Buying department. The Buying department will make out orders, copies which are sent to the supplier, to the goods received section and to the payments section.

When the goods are received they are checked against the details of the order. If the delivery is satisfactory the goods are taken into store. Stores records are updated and the payments section is sent details of the goods received.

Eventually the supplier's invoice is received in the payments section. It is checked against the original order and the notification from the Inspection section. If everything is correct it is passed for payment, usually at the month end, but possibly sooner if a special cash discount is available.

Purchasing

The Buyer or Purchasing Officer of a firm has two major responsibilities. Firstly he has to obtain materials at the lowest price consistent with the quality of goods required. Secondly, he has to ensure that the goods ordered are properly progressed, so that material shortages will not upset production plans.

Notification of items required comes from stores or a user department. In the case of a user department it may be part of the production function, but equally well it could come from administration or sales. The point is that all buying should be channelled through the one department. The notification is called a Purchase Requisition. It will contain details of quantity, date required and possible suppliers. The requisition must be signed by a person who has power to authorise the particular type of transaction.

The Buyer fulfils his first major function, as set out above, by obtaining tenders. He chooses between these on the basis of quality, delivery times, price and possibly special relationships. Normally there are special agreements to cover items which are continuously being bought.

The order on the suppliers is made out on a multi-copy document known as a Purchase Order. A typical distribution of copies would be as follows:

1) To the supplier.
2) To the goods section to authorize acceptance of delivery.
3) To the accountants for comparison with the invoice which will eventually be received.

4) To stores records for inclusion in the balance for quantity on order.
5) Retained in the office to progress the order.

Receipt of Goods

In general terms a firm will have two sections dealing with inward deliveries, before the goods are taken into store. One section accepts the delivery onto the premises and the other inspects them. The inspection process covers these essential points:

1) checks correctness of goods against the description.
2) checks against damage in transit.
3) checks quanity.

As a result of these checks, inspection reports are made and sent out as follows:

1) To stores with the goods.
2) To the accountants as a check against the suppliers invoice, particularly with regard to the amount.
3) To the buying department to record progress.

Where it is necessary to return goods to a supplier the accountants will be notified of the details. A debit note will be made out and set to the supplier, who will confirm his agreement by issuing a corresponding credit note.

Stores

The maintenance of stores on the premises is relatively expensive and, consequently, much effort is devoted to reducing them to a minimum but safe level. A parallel approach to cutting costs of storage is to study the elements of this cost and to minimise these as far as possible. Natural wastage through evaporation, shrinking etc. should be controlled but only at a reasonable cost. Theft should be guarded against both from internal and external sources.

Handling costs can be reduced in a number of ways. Mechanical equipment can play a big part in reducing these costs. Also siting of the stores in relation to goods received and production departments affects handling costs.

The stores building itself should be efficient. It needs to be well lit, the right size and well equipped with storing aids. That is, suitable bins, vertical racks and specialist storage furniture.

Centralised and Decentralised Stores

The factors which determine the choice between maintaining stores in a centralised or decentralised manner are very similar to other areas of activity in which the same choice is offered. By having everything at a central point these are fairly obvious advantages to be gained. The avoidance of duplicating stock better buying deals are made, reduction of building overheads makes a more efficient central store possible, a higher quality store-keeper can be employed, stock checking can be more efficient. All of these advantages stem from the greater control that can be exercised over a single central store.

However, the disadvantages are also fairly apparent. Particularly for a production controller in a unit some distance from the proposed central store. The distance between the control store and the user department will increase handling costs. The aim will be to reduce these by giving advance notification of requirements so that deliveries can be planned to be as efficient as possible.

To choose between the two possibilities is to take sides in an argument which is fundamental to much reorganisation. On the one hand there are advantages of cost saving with the possible dangers resulting from the setting up of a centralised bureaucracy. On the other hand the manager on the spot feels exposed to danger through the inefficiency of others. He prefers to be his own master as far as fulfilling his own responsibilities are concerned, even though there is a cost involved.

Very often a compromise solution is put into practice. A main store is set up centrally, with on the spot subsidiary stores meeting local needs. The subsidiary stores meet local requirement quickly and efficiently. The stocks in these subsidiary stores are replenished from the central store and this process is also efficient, since the loads involved will be sufficient to reduce the unit transport cost. Usually the basis for replenishing local stocks will be an imprest system, similar to that employed for petty cash.

Types of Stores

Separate stores or sections of stores are very often maintained for different categories of material.

Raw Materials. These are the primary materials purchased by the firm. One firm's raw material is another firm's finished product. Some types of raw material are particularly bulky and are maintained in stock yards. These are usually controlled in terms of weight or volume.

Work-in-Progress. Sometimes work-in-progress is only notionally held in store. However, where components and sub-assemblies are made these are usually taken into a store and issued as required. In this way they come under the stock control producers outlined later in the chapter.

Finished Goods. When the product is completed it is physically transferred from work-in-progress into finished goods stock awaiting despatch.

Indirect Materials. Many items of material are held by a firm which well constitute an indirect expense when they are consumed. For example, packing materials, stationery, tools, fuel oil etc. These too are maintained in stores and are subject to stock control procedures.

Stores Records

As well as taking good care of stores physically, it is necessary to maintain accurate records concerning consumption and quantities on hand. The basic information required concerns quantities received and issued which by deduction gives balances. Additional the use to which a material has been put must also be recorded.

The movement of receipts, issues, transfers and return to store are used to post up material accounts. Ideally, only one set of material accounts need to be maintained. However, many sections of an organisation refer to these records and their requirements do not coincide. In particular three main parties can be named. The storekeeper wants an on-the spot record, quickly and easily updated and dealing with quantities which are free or earmarked for specific purposes. Between these two there is a conflict because the storekeeper wants his individual record sheets to be physically near the relevant stock items, whereas the production controller wants his information held in a compact filing system. The third party is the accountant, who is concerned with values as well as quantities.

Very often the result is three sets of records. However, the problem has always been recognised and now the solution is available. The advances in accounting machinery and computers are enabling the organisation and methods personnel to amalgamate the records without detriment to the needs of the individuals concerned.

Bin Cards

On the spot records maintained by the storekeeper are referred to as bin cards. Their prime purpose is to enable the store-keeper to ensure that goods under his control are maintained in the correct quantities. That is, within maximum and minimum limits. Since there is a time-lag between the placing of an order and the receipt of goods, it is also necessary to indicate the level at which the order should be made out. This is usually referred to as the re-order level.

	Bin Card.		Location ....
Description			Code no. ....
Minimum level			Re-order level ....

Date	Receipts		Issues		Balance
	Ref.	Qty.	Ref.	Qty.	

In some cases it is possible to dispense with bin cards and substitute a system of control by inspection of physical quantities. To do this, stocks of a particular commodity are separated into three piles. The first pile constitutes the minimum stock level; the second pile is the difference between the re-order level and the minimum level; the third pile is the balance in excess of the re-order level.

Description............ Code............. Maximum Stock 1000 Order Level 600
Minimum 400 Order Quantity 600

	Date	Reference	Goods Received	Goods Issued	Balance on Hand	Goods Ordered	Received	Goods Allocated	Used	Free Balance
line 1	1 Jan.	b/f			800					800
line 2	2 Jan.	MR 200		300	500					500
line 3	3 Jan.	PR 100				600				1100
line 4	4 Jan.	12345						400		700
line 5	7 Jan.	MR 250		200	300				200	700
line 6	10 Jan.	GR 300	600		900		600			

Figure 13.3. Stock Record Card.

Stock Record Cards

These cards are likely to be kept in a production control department. They are usually updated from the same transactions documents that have been used to update bin cards. So here is a source of danger. All too often these records have their usefulness undermined because of slow posting. Their distinguishing features are columns showing quantities on order and quantities earmarked for specific purposes, in addition to the normal ins and outs and balances on hand. Refer to figure 13.2 and study and study the transactions and explanations given below in relation to it.

Line 1: The quantity of stock on hand, none of which has been allocated to production

Line 2: 300 units are issued on Material Requisition

Line 3: 600 units are ordered on Purchase Requisition. This quantity is added to the free balance since it will be available before the minimum stock level is exhausted.

Line 4: 400 units are specifically earmarked for job number 12345.

Line 5: 200 are issued, which had previously been allocated, thus affecting stock on hand, but not free stock.

Line 6: 600 units are received. The balance on is increased to 900 but free stock remains unaltered, as this figure already includes the 600 units.

Stock Ledger Accounts

The information given to the production controler is also required by the accountant. In addition the accountant expresses the movements and balance on hand in terms of money values. This information may be kept in the cost office. Alternatively some centralised, machine based system may reduce the number of stores records from three to one.

Transaction Documents

These will vary from firm to firm, but essentially there will be documents to record the following movements.

1) Receipt of goods into store.
2) Issues to work-in-progress.
3) Transfers from one store to another.
4) Goods returned to supplier after having been taken into store.
5) Returns from work-in-progress in the case of excess issues.
6) Transfers between two sections of work-in-progress, for example where goods have been transferred from specific job to another without being returned to store in the interim.
7) Losses due to evaporation, cut offs, pilfering etc.

Stock Control

Maintaining stocks is an expensive operation and one of the accountants functions is to help to minimise this expense. There are two basic approaches.

Firstly, good storekeeping procedures. These will take care of unnecessary losses. Perishable goods will be maintained in suitable temperatures, humidities etc. Losses through pilferage and careless handling will be cut down.

Secondly, a systematic analysis of stock levels will indicate which particular items of stock should be investigated. This is an application of the principle of management by exception. This systematic analysis takes place as a regular part of stock record updating procedures. In broad terms, stock levels are compared with figures representing maximum and minimum stock levels. In additional a point is established at which a replenishment order should be initiated. The best size of order can also be established. Finally, a periodic review of frequency of movement is undertaken to determine which stocks are no longer required as a result of changes in product specifications.

Stock Turnover Rates v. Optimum Stock Levels

One approach to reducing the cost of stock carrying is to express the combined quantities of stock on hand and on order as so many months supply on hand. For example, a particular item of stock at a month end has £400 on hand and £300 on order and an annual usage amount to £2800. This gives $\frac{700}{2800} \times 12$ months' supply on hand, equalling 3 months in this case. Alternatively, the same figures can be used to calculate a turnover rate of 4.0.

The firm's management would set standards against which these figures would be compared. Apart from the difficulty on arriving at definitive standards, this system suffers from a fundamental theoretical weakness. It ignores entirely all consideration of costs connected with ordering, receiving and storing. Each order placed requires an ordering routine involving purchasing clerks, typists etc. Each delivery has to be received, inspected and carried to stores. The size of the order affects unit costs since special discounts can often be obtained on large orders. Storage costs are affected by the size of stock levels.

Optimum Stock Levels

The individual costs listed above have conflicting affects on stock levels. On the one hand some cut down the number of times the ordering routine is set in motion and order large quantities. On the other hand, some avoid unnecessarily large levels of stock. Clearly there is opposition here. The solution is to seek the best combination of opposing forces to given an optimum or best result. Before examining some simple approaches to this, a schematic representation of the stock usage cycle is set out in figure 12.3.

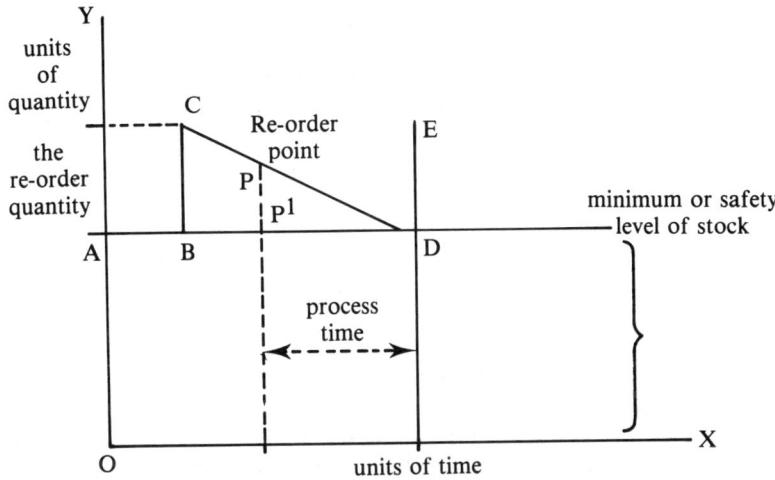

The X axis represents time and the Y axis some unit of quantity. The amount O A is the lowest level of stock planned for, that is to say it is a safety level. It this part of the stock is being used then the 'alarm bells' of the system should be ringing, loud and clear. The diagram shows the level of stock at different times. Starting at B the level is at the minimum. The quantity on order is received, sending the level up to C. In the course of the following period the stock is used until it is at the level P. The time period $D'D$ represents the time required to obtain the replenishing order, it is also the time span over which the remaining stock above the safety level would be used. The point P represents the re-order point. The quantity BC represents the quantity to be ordered when the replenishment point is reached. It is referred to as the economic order quantity (EOQ) or re-order quantity (ROQ). The size of the EOQ is arrived at by developing stock control models.

Stock control models.

Such models, using mathematical techniques are a useful aid in stock control. In this section an example of such a model is given, but it does represent a simple introduction only. First of all consider in more detail than has been done before, the components of the cost of stock control.

Costs of stock control

As has been continually stressed throughout this course of study and will be, even more, in later sections; all areas of decision making have associated costs which are relevant to the problem solving situation on hand. Costs for decision-taking in terms of stock holding are no exception. There are three sub-divisions into which these relevant costs can be analysed.

a) Costs of acquisition

Frequently referred to as procurement costs. They arise because no order for materials can be made without incurring two forms of expense. The costs of the goods themselves and the cost of setting up the order either to a supplier or a production order when internally manufactured goods are under consideration. The reason for including the cost of the goods may not appear obvious at first sight, since they will not vary in terms of units ordered and therefore should not affect the decision of how many to buy at a particular point in time. However they are relevant because the size of a new order comes into the calculation of money used in the maintenance of stock.

The set up costs of the order consists largely of the clerical costs of placing and progressing the order, receiving and checking the invoice and arranging payment. Such costs are of course the incremental ones that is to say they are additional to each order. The same remarks apply in the case of internal production orders. A particular difficulty here is that such clerical costs are common to a number of activities. The relevant cost to take is the appropriate hourly rate of pay since this represents the opportunity cost of employing the clerk on some other operation. Emphasis has been on the clerical costs because they represent the most substantial element, but of course there are material elements in the form of paper and service elements from equipment.

b) Carrying costs

These relate directly to the funds tied up in the stock, to the provision of a place of storage and to servicing.

The cost of funds is the opportunity cost of using the funds elsewhere if the levels were reduced. The use of the funds may be to reduce borrowing. The two factors in the calculation are the acquisition cost of adding to stock and the interest charge. The first of these is the cost of buying and is therefore the replacement cost. The second would depend upon the opportunities available. As an example if funds released were used to reduce borrowing then the charge relating to this borrowing would be appropriate.

The storage costs consists of the running expenses of the warehouse which would typically consist of wages, insurance, lighting, heating and rent. These are relevant in so far as they vary as a function of the investment in stocks. In cases where the warehousing is owned by the firm the correct treatment is to ignore depreciation, but to substitute any opportunity cost obtained from the best alternative use available for the space in question.

Deterioration is a generic term for such items as spoilage, evaporation etc. A charge for this can usually be included on the basis that deterioration is something that takes place fairly evenly over time, that is to say it has an approximately linear relationship to the time for which items are held in stock.

Obsolescence is often catered for as a carrying cost on the same basis as deterioration. In fact this unjustifiably assumes that the two are similar in terms of having a linear relationship with time. In fact obsolescence is a factor of uncertain incidence and should not be treated in this way.

c) Stockout Cost

These occur when a firm is unable to meet an order resulting in customer dissatisfaction and loss of goodwill; this, clearly is a very difficult cost to quantify.

Alternatively when this stock condition arises it may be remedied by processing a special order, commonly referred to as a back-order. Most firms have special routines for these which give rise to additional clerical, handling and delivery costs. These would fluctuate from order to order since differing sets of circumstances would pertain, so that it would be necessary to consider an average unit cost.

The Model

The statements of the separate costs of holding stock revealed that there are conflicting pressures at work. The firm that never runs out of any stock item must have considerably over invested in that area. The firm that correspondingly sails close to the wind and suffers from frequent stock-outs is going to pay a heavy price in terms of lost custom. There is a need for some way to balance the conflicts. A solution is required that can be regarded as the best balanced of all, taking into accounts the needs that have to be met.

A technique to give such an answer is to be found in the differential calculus. Using branches of mathematics in this way to study a problem and to formulate solutions is referred to as model building. Something is constructed to stand in the place of the real thing and so to be examined according to some known techniques and rules. In this case it is to set up an equation to represent the variable cost of holding stock for a period expressed in terms of the quantity to be ordered. The task then is to find a minimum value for this quantity.

When calculus is used to provide solutions to this kind of problem is assumed that one basic requirement is met, namely that events are taking place in a continuous way without intervening breaks. That is to say in this case that sales are continuous and not being made at discrete intervals. To some extent this is not a valid assumption, but in most situations it is sufficiently near to being so as to make no difference. First of all specify the terms to be used and given them a suitable notation:

q = the amount to be ordered on each occasion
d = total demand for stock in a year
c = the cost of putting out an order
I = the annual cost of holding the item in stock expressed as a percentage of the average stock value, i.e. the holding cost per unit per annum.

The second step is to specify the assumptions that are to be made with regard to the conditions under which the model is operating. An examination of these assumptions will reveal a great deal of information about the worthwhileness of the model, and hence the usefulness of the results. If the assumptions are too far from reality to be justified then the model will have to be amended in some way.

The following example is of a simple set of equations based on the assumptions given below:

1) The time between placing an order and receiving the goods is known with certainty and is always the same. This time is referred to as the lead time.

2) The prices and costs to be included are known with certainty and are unchanging, thus cutting out speculation as a reason for holding stock.

3) Demand is a constant and must be satisfied from stock. This assumption cuts out the possibility of meeting demand by holding back delivery whilst the goods are obtained through quick ordering routines.

4) There is no end to the cycle within the foreseeable future.

The cirumstances determined by this set of assumptions are shown graphically in figure 13.4

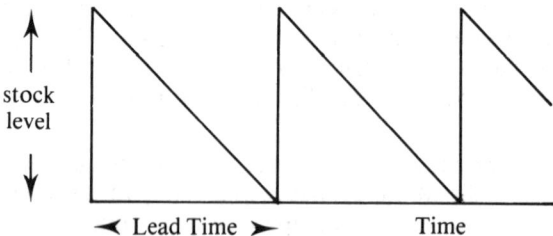

Figure 13.4. Derivation of Economic Ordering Quantity.

Total Cost = Carrying costs for the period + cost of purchasing × number of orders in the period.

Let Total cost = TC

Carrying cost = average stock × cost of storage per unit per period.

A glance at figure 13.4 shows that stock moves steadily down to nil level and is replenished at this point by the quantity of the optimum order quantity. Therefore average stock $= q/2$

The cost of storage is I

giving $q/2 \times I$ for the carrying cost/annum

The number of orders in a period $=$ demand in the period/the constant amount ordered

giving d/q for the order placing cost/annum

$$\therefore TC = \frac{q}{2} \cdot I + \frac{d}{q} \cdot C$$

The minimum value of the total cost can be found by differentiating with respect to q, assuming that q can be treated as a continuous variable.

$$\frac{d(TC)}{dp} = \frac{I}{2} - \frac{C.d}{q^2}$$

at the stationary value $\frac{I}{2} = \frac{C.d}{q^2}$

and $q^2 = \frac{2Cd}{I}$

giving $q^* = \sqrt{\frac{2Cd}{I}}$

where q^* is the economic or optimum ordering quantity. The point is a minimum since the second derivative is $2C.d/q^3$ which is positive thus satisfying the necessary and sufficient conditions.

It will be useful to examine this formula by putting up a set of figures and arriving at the optimal situation by setting out the whole range or possibilities and verifying the result from the formula.

Stock-holding cost is 20% per annum of the stock value on £1 per annum/unit

Cost per item is £5

Annual demand is 1200 units

The cost of placing each order is £5

No. of orders per yr.	size of order	average stock in units	£	stock holding cost per annum	order placing cost per annum	Total costs
30	40	20	100	20	150	170
25	48	24	120	24	125	149
20	60	30	150	30	100	130
15	80	40	200	40	75	115
10	120	60	300	60	50	110
5	240	120	600	120	25	145

By inspection it can be seen that the total costs are at their minimum somewhere in the region of ten orders per year giving a quantity of 120 to be ordered on each occasion.

A closer look at this region is shown below:

8	150	75	375	75	40	115
10	120	60	300	60	50	110
12	100	50	250	50	60	110
11	109	54.5	272.5	54.5	55	109.5

From the table the E.O.Q. is approximately 109 and is clearly in the region of 100 to 120.

Using the same information in the formula that has been developed then the result is obtained as follows:

$$(109,5)$$

$$q^* = \sqrt{\frac{2.5.\ 1200}{20\%.5}}$$

$$\sqrt{12000} = 109.5$$

Extensions of the model

The relationships developed for the simple deterministic model developed above were based on a set of assumptions which because of their simplicity detract from the value of the results. In a number of important cases it is possible to bring in extra factors and by complicating the manipulation to obtain more satisfactory results.

The following extensions can be incorporated:

i) the incorporation of back-ordering. This is a recognition that as a matter of policy some customers may be made to wait until the next delivery of goods to the firm or the next batch to be manufactured. The benefit to be obtained from this is usually in terms of obtaining a smooth product schedule. The cost of the policy comes at the least in the loss of goodwill and other costs are possible.

ii) the inclusion of safety stocks. These are necessary according as to the unreliability of lead times and uncertainties of the demand schedule.

Such models as these and other developments in terms of simulation are increasingly being incorporated in the systems of management. Nevertheless, they are not universal and many firms apply less rigorous approaches to determining re-order points and minimum stocks.

Re-order Point

Two factors are considered in the process of determining the point at which new orders are placed. One is the time period which elapses between placing the order and receiving the goods. This information is after referred to as the 'buying lead time'. The purchasing officer is responsible for supplying this. The second factor is the rate at which the item of stock is consumed. For example, if the lead time is given as four weeks and the average consumption is 100 units per week, then the re-order point would be 100×4 units.

This basis for establishing the R.O.P. gives no room for margins of error. Lead times fluctuate and actual rates of consumption will sometimes vary considerably from the average quoted. A simple way of ensuring safety from a stock turn-out is to uplift the R.O.P. by the quantity of the minimum stock.

The re-order point is then given by the formula:

R.O.P. = Average consumption × lead time + minimum stock.

Where periodic usage fluctuates widely about an average it will be necessary to alter the R.O.P. in line with the seasonal changes.

Minimum Stock

The minimum stock is a safety level. It covers such eventualities as extensions to normal lead times or a rapid increase in consumption. Additionally, stock updating routines themselves may be performed as a weekly operation; in which case there could be a margin of four days usage before the necessary order routine could be triggered into action. Since the object of the minimum stock level is to provide a safety measure, it should be as small as possible. Excessive safety levels are an unjustifiably drain on resources. Once the minimum stock is being used, the purchasing officer will go all out to obtain the replenishment in the minimum period. The production manager, on the other hand will be tending towards minimum usage of the stock item in short supply. Therefore one approach to determining minimum stock figures is to take it as being minimum usage for the minimum lead time.

Sometimes figures are quoted for maximum levels of stock. Given adherence to ordering economic quantities at the re-order point, talk of maximum figures becomes irrelevent. Except, that is, as a control figure to check against errors in the system. In which case it is more a validity check than anything else.

Classification of stock by value

It is not usually practicable for management to consider applying sophisticated techniques of stock control to all of the firm's stocks. Fortunately, it usually happens that a relatively small proportion of the items accounts for a high proportion of the value. Thus, by classifying into three or four categories, it is possible for the advanced techniques to be applied in the most effective places, leaving the rest to less sophisticated controls.

Slow Moving Dormant and Obsolete Stocks

Inevitably some items of stock are called upon less than others. Sometimes there is no particular significance in this. On other occasions it is the beginning of a trend. As production methods are constantly scrutinised in cost reduction exercises, then so do stock requirements change. Any item which has few transactions attached to it should be the object of a periodic management report. Whether action should be taken in the form of disposal then becomes a management decision.

Stock-Taking

The physical act of counting the stocks on hand can be done according to one of two methods. Where the firm maintains a set of records which give book figures for the stock at any time, the physical checking can be done on a continuous basis throughout the year. This is the system of perpetual inventory when all stock movement are recorded in a set of stores records. The continuous checking will probably be done by full time stock audit clerks.

When there is a system of continuous stock-taking in conjunction with a perpetual inventory, certain good practices should be observed. The stock auditor should be independent of stock recording staff and stock handling staff. This is an elementary precaution which should be automatically included in the internal check system. The routine should be to check all stock items within a specified period at least once.

Differences between the book figure and the physical count will have to be reconciled. Generally speaking these differences are either clerical errors in the records or the result of some stores handling deficiency including theft. The recording errors can be traced by auditing the entries. Deficiences in stores handling techniques may be traced to some particular trouble or fault. It may be some error in calculation or conversion of units; or loss through evaporation as a result of bad storage. There is usually some satisfactory explanation for the difference and this in turn usually leads to a remedy.

The advantage of the continuous stock taking is that it enables periodic accounts to be prepared without a full scale physical count. Furthermore, it pinpoints losses earlier which helps in their overall reduction. With such a system it should not be necessary to count stock at the year end.

However, not all firms maintain perpetual inventories. In these cases it is necessary to take a physical stock-take at any point in time up to which an income report is to be made. The main points of a stock taking programme can be set down as follows—

1) The stores clerks will determine quantities and enter these on tickets which are kept with the appropriate stocks.

2) Non-stores personnel will check the quantities and initial the tickets.

3) The tickets will be collected and passed for pricing.

4) The bulk of the countring work should be done at the week-end, since the movement of stocks has to be frozen and additional labour is required.

5) A special routine must be followed to ensure that goods recently received have all been invoiced by suppliers. Alternatively, some invoices may have been received in advance of the goods. If finished goods are being counted the same care must be taken to see that the paper work of invoicing is in line with the physical movement of goods.

6) Work-in-progress merits some special consideration. This involves identifying work on the shop floor and assessing the extent to which the work is complete. For example, each job can be classed as 25%, 50%, 75% or 100% complete with regard to material or labour and overheads. The assumption is that the result will be about correct through an automatic averaging process.

Debtors control

This is mainly a question of establishing a good system, but some model building can be introduced. To organise a good debtors control system, it is necessary to establish its main features. These are: selection of credit customers, customers' credit limits, credit periods, cash discounts and collection costs.

Granting credit

The principle involved in granting credit is clear. The expected value of the sale to the customer should be greater than the expected amount of the bad debt. In other words, the probability of successfully gaining the profit on the sale should be worth more than the loss associated with parting with a product and receiving no cash.

Let x = profit

m = profit margin for each unit sold

p = probability of customer's debt proving good.

Then

$E(x) = m p - (1 - m)(1 - p)$

where $(1 - m)$ = cost of the goods per unit and $(1 - p)$ probability of customers debt proving bad.

In practice firms make their decisions by use of credit agencies and references, plus sets of accounts where these are available. Some firms codify these sources and give numerical scores to credit applicants according to some scale and establish a hurdle figure. Applicants rated below this are bad risks and those above are accepted.

Customers credit limits

As a corrollary to granting credit to a customer, a definite limit should be fixed. This will be decided from the same sources. Setting such limits is a device for limiting the consequences for wrong decisions.

Credit periods

Extended credit periods attract extra custom and, thus, given a profit margin on the units sold contributes to a greater profit. These greater profits have to be set against the additional costs of:

1) interest in funds tied up in debtors

2) increased collection expenses

3) increased bad debts which may arise because the extension of the customer range may result in weaker customers being granted credit facilities.

Collection costs

Increased effort in debt collection must involve greater costs, but should result in savings from bad debt losses and interest costs. The balance of this cost and saving can best be achieved by recording results from specific programmes of debt collection, possibly in restricted areas and for types of debtors.

Cash discount

Firm's can induce their customers to pay promptly by allowing them to deduct a discount from the amount due, provided payment is made within a specified period of time. For example, normally accepted trade terms may be a month's credit, with $1\frac{1}{2}\%$ discount if the bill is paid within 7 days. The rate of discount when expressed in annual terms is usually very high, in which case the price is really being reduced as well. Failure to take trade discounts is expensive.

The cost of the discounts has to be set against a number of benefits:

i) interest saving on funds tied up in debtors

ii) collection expense reduction

iii) a decrease in bad debts. Poor payers often concentrate on selective payments and in making these, discounts are a big factor.

iv) since the large discounts are to some extent price reductions, it follows that there should be an increase in sales volume. Although it does not necessarily follow that an increase in volume at a lower profit margin will give an increase in profit.

Debtors

The development of debt collecting facilities has led to specialisation in this area. It is now possible to factor debts for a charge. This means transferring the ownership of the debts to the agency in return for their face value less a fee. In this way the firm is relieved of a number of costs and can make a saving. The debt collecting firms make profits because of the developed skills and facilities and because they can amalgamate the sets of debts they are collecting into one group.

Reporting on debtors

A typical report on debtors is shown in figure 13.5. The main feature is that it schedules the debts according to the age and enables the reader to improve his awareness with regard to the worth of the total debtors figure.

Schedule of Debtors
As at 31st December 19X5

Transaction period	Total	Analysis by customer type		Comment
		I	II	
previous year	350	350		
Jan/Mar	250	250		
April/June	500		500	
July	200	100	100	
August	400	300	100	
September	800	500	300	
October	900	600	300	
November	1100	900	200	
December	2500	2000	500	
	7000	5000	2000	

Figure 13.5.

The schedule gives an expanded description of the year and debts of £7000. The analysis by customer would be specific to the trade. The comment column would inform on the action taken and an assessment of the eventual outcome. As a result of the credit controllers recommendation a part of the debts would be written off as bad, even though there has to be an element of subjective anticipation in this.

Cash

Cash here means cash in hand, cash in the bank and securities which can quickly be turned to cash if needed. As with materials, it is wasteful to have more cash available at any time than is necessary for the business operations. What is required is enough for daily transactions and some cushion against unforeseen demands.

The handling of cash is very flexible within limits and most firms aim to maintain minimum balances for transaction purposes and provide for their precautionary balances by means of secondary sources. These secondary sources either provide some return of interest or are costless until called upon. A firm with surplus cash requirements can put the money into short-term investments and receive interest payments. In time this invested surplus can be used against unforeseen demands or may be needed to meet an expected upsurge in transactional needs. Other ways of providing funds on an 'if needed' basis, is to establish overdraft facilities with the bank. If needs are relatively modest and short-term, some rephasing of payments to creditors will suffice but such action can damage relationships with suppliers and be expensive in the long term. As mentioned above, factoring debts can provide another source of cash at times.

Cash budgeting

These are a standard part of the budget. However, because a short-fall in cash can be serious, it is advisable to look in detail at movements in cash balances over short intervals of time.

An example of a cash budget is given in figure 13.6.

Month	1 £	2 £	3 £	etc
Receipts:				
cash sales	1000	1200	1300	etc.
debt collections	3000	4000	7000	etc.
	4000	5200	8300	etc.
Payments:				
creditors	2500	3500	5000	etc.
wages and other				
cash expenses	3000	3000	3000	etc.
machinery	—	1000	—	
	5500	7500	8000	etc.
Net cash flow	(1500)	(2300)	300	etc.
Balance b/f	3500	2000	(300)	etc.
Balance c/f	2000	(300)	—	etc.

Figure 13.6. A cash budget.

The preparation of these detailed budgets highlights the problems that can sometimes arise because of an irregularity of the cash flows, or a strain in cash resources resulting from asset purchases or dividend payments. They are a simple reporting device which can be of considerable value, whilst being easy to prepare. However, they report likely cash flows, they do not give guides to the optimum balances to be held.

Cash models

Holding cash is in many ways similar to holding stocks of materials and it should come as no surprise to learn that mathematical optimising models can be developed. At the simplest level it shows:

$$C^* = \sqrt{\frac{2\,r\,t}{i}}$$

where t = the total demand for a period
r = the cost of obtaining the amount C
i = interest rate on borrowed funds
C = the amount paid into cash balance at equal intervals in the period.

This is a very simple relationship drawn up on the assumption that the cash flows are constant through the year. The model can be developed to cater for much more realistic situations, involving probability distributions of cash outflows. The conflict to be solved is between the loss foregone on excess cash balances and the cost of inadequate cash periods. Clearly, this represents the most challenge when the cash flows are of a random nature.

Chapter Summary

The stress in this chapter has been laid on the control of working capital through two approaches. An introduction has been given to the idea of mathematical models being developed. Simultaneously, these models form part only of an overall system and it is the strength of these systems that counts largely in overall success. A similar theme will be developed with regard to the selection and control of investment projects.

Exercises

Questions 13.1-13.5 (Answers provided)

13.1 T. Rose operates a small manufacturing business. Material costs are dominated by one item, which he wishes to control. The planned usage during the coming year amounts to 100,000 units. The incremental cost of placing an order is £3 and the cost of storing one unit for one year is £1.00. The lead time of an order is 5 days and it is usual to keep a reserve supply of three days.

Required:
a) the reorder point
b) the economic order quantity.

13.2 Given:

Opening stock	100 Kg.
Usage 1st 10 days :	12 Kg. per day
2nd 10 days :	9 Kg. per day
3rd 10 days :	15 Kg. per day
Reorder level 60 Kg.	
Order quantity 100 Kg.	
Lead time: 3 days	

Required: calculate a reorder point and minimum stock level for this commodity.

13.3 An electrical goods retailer has the following information concerning his supply of bulbs. Maximum sales 10 per day, average 8 per day and minimum 6 per day. The average stock during the year has been 100 bulbs and the buying lead time is 10 days.

Required: calculate the minimum stock and the reorder point.

13.4. Prepare a cash budget for Mary Gold showing clearly the balance at the end of each month for the six months to December:

(a) Cash at 1 July £3,000

(b) Sales at £10 per unit

April	May	June	July	August	September	October	November	December
220	240	280	320	360	300	260	160	140

Cash is received from Debtors two months after sale.

(c) Production in units.

April	May	June	July	August	September	October	November	December
300	340	360	400	260	220	200	180	140

(d) Raw material costs £3 per unit and is paid for 1 month after its use in production.

(e) Labour costs are £2 per unit and are paid in the same month as production.

(f) A machine costing £2,000 will be paid for in September.

13.5 Draw up a cash budget for William Sweet showing clearly the balance at the end of each month, from the following information for the six months ended 30 June, 19X5:

(a) Opening cash and bank balance £1,000

(b) Production in units:

	19X4				19X5				
Oct.	Nov.	Dec.	Jan.	Feb.	March	April	May	June	July
300	400	460	540	700	640	560	500	420	380

(c) Raw materials used in production cost £4 per unit. Of this one quarter is paid one month before production and three quarters in the same month as production.

(d) Direct labour costs of £6 per unit are payable in the same month as production.

(e) Variable expenses at £6 per unit, payable three-quarters in the same month as production and one-quarter in the month following production.

(f) Sales at £20 per unit

	19X4				19X5			
Oct.	Nov.	Dec.	Jan.	Feb.	Mar.	April	May	June
240	360	480	580	620	720	680	520	360

Debtors pay their accounts in the month following delivery.

(g) Fixed expenses are £400 per month payable each month.

(h) Extensions to the premises costing £6,000 are to be paid for in February 19X2.

(i) An income tax payment of £5,000 is due in June 19X5.

Questions 13.6-13.10. Answers not provided.

13.6 X Limited, a manufacturing company with several stores, has a materials control system which includes perpetual inventory records, re-order levels and continuous stocktaking.

You are required for X Limited to:

(a) draw a diagram or flow chart to show how materials would be issued, replenished and paid for. The cycle should indicate the departments involved, the procedures used and documents raised.

(b) (i) draft a form for use by the stock checkers andinclude on it the following information of stockchecks made in store Z on 15th May 1978.

Item	Balances, in units		Physical stock, in units	Cost per unit £
	Stock card	Stores ledger		
A	200	200	180	20.00
B	170	170	172	5.00
C	740	760	700	0.60

(ii) state action to be taken and documents to be raised to adjust discrepancies recorded in (b) (i) above;

(iii) state a possible reason for the shortages and recommend a possible course of action by management to prevent future losses.

ICMA(CA1).

13.7 From the following information which relates to The ACA Magic Lantern Co. Ltd. you are required to prepare a month by month cash budget for the second half of 1975 and to append such brief comments as you consider might be helpful to management.

(a) The Magic Lantern sells at £40 and has a variable cost of £26 made up as follows:

Material £20; Labour £4; Overhead £2

(b) Fixed costs amount to £6,000 per month and are paid on the 25th of each month.

(c) Quantities sold/to be sold on credit are

May	June	July	Aug.	Sept.	Oct.	Nov.	Dec.
1,000	1,200	1,400	1,600	1,800	2,000	2,200	2,600

(d) Production quantities:

May	June	July	Aug.	Sept.	Oct.	Nov.	Dec.
1,200	1,400	1,600	2,000	2,400	2,600	2,400	2,200

(e) Cash sales, at a discount of 5%, are expected to average 100 a month.

(f) Customers are expected to settle their accounts by the end of the second month following sale.

(g) Suppliers of material are paid two months after the material is used in production.

(h) Wages are paid in the same month as the Magic Lanterns are produced.

(i) 70% of the variable overhead is paid in the month of production , the remainder in the following months.

(j) Corporation Tax of £18,000 is to be paid in October.

(k) A new delivery vehicle was bought in June, the cost of which, £8,000, is to be paid in August. The old vehicle was sold for £600, the buyer undertaking to pay in July.

(l) The company is expected to be £3,000 overdrawn at the bank at 30th June, 1975.

CA(AC2).

13.8 (a) Explain what is meant by the term 'economic order quantity'. Your explanation should be supported by a sketch or graph, which need not be on graph paper.

(b) Using the information stated below, you are required to prepare a schedule showing the associated costs if 1, 2, 3, 4, 5 or 6 orders were placed during a year for a single product.

From you schedule, state the number of orders to be placed each year and the economic order quantity.

Annual usage of product	600 units
Unit cost of product	£2.4
Cost of placing an order	£6.0
Stock holding cost as a percentage of average stock value	20%

(c) Comment briefly on three problems met in determining the economic order quantity.

ICMA(CA1)

13.9 A wholesale company ends its financial year on 30th June. You have been requested, in early July 1975, to assist in the preparation of a cash forecast. The following information is available regarding the company's operations:

(1) Management believes the 1974/75 sales level and pattern is a reasonable estimate of 1975/76 sales. Sales in 1974/75 were as follows:

		£
1975	July	360,000
	August	420,000
	September	600,000
	October	540,000
	November	480,000
	December	400,000

1975	January	350,000
	February	550,000
	March	500,000
	April	400,000
	May	600,000
	June	800,000
	Total	6,000,000

(2) The accounts receivable at 30th June 1975 total £380,000. Sales collections are generally made as follows:

During month of sale	60%
In first subsequent month	30%
In second subsequent month	9%
Uncollectable	1%

(3) The purchase cost of goods averages 60 per cent of selling price. The cost of the stock on hand at 30th June 1975 is £840,000, of which £30,000 is obsolete. Arrangements have been made to sell the obsolete stock in July at half the normal selling price on a 'cash on delivery' basis.

The company wishes to maintain the stock, as of the first of each month, at a level of three months' sales as determined by the sales forecast for the next three months. All purchases are paid for on the tenth of the following month. Accounts payable for purchases at 30th June 1975 total £370,000.

(4) Payments in respect of fixed and variable expenses are forecast for the first three months of 1975/76 as follows:

July	August	September
£	£	£
160,620	118,800	158,400

(5) It is anticipated that cash dividends of £40,000 will be paid each half-year, on the fifteenth day of September and March.

(6) During the year, unusual advertising costs will be incurred that will required can payments of £10,000 in August and £15,000 in September. The advertising costs are in addition to the expeses in item (4) above.

(7) Equipment replacements are made at a rate which requires a cash outlay of £3,000 per month. The equipment has an average estimated life of six years.

(8) A £60,000 payments for corporation tax is to be made on 15th September 1975.

(9) At 30th June 1975 the company had a bank loan with an unpaid balance of £280,000. The entire balance is due on 30th September 1975 together with accumulated interest from 1st July 1975 at the rate of 12% per annum.

(10) The cash balance at 30th June 1975 is £100,000.

You are required to prepare a cash forecast statement by months for the first three months of the 1975/76 financial year. The statement should show the amount of cash on hand (or deficiency of cash) at the end of each month. All computations and supporting schedules should be presented in clear and readable form.

ICAEW(MA).

13.10 As management accountant you have the task of co-ordinating your company's budgets. The sales forecast for the six months ending 31st December 1977 is given in section A below. During this period it is planned to reduce the inventory of finished goods from 9,000 units at 1st July to 5,000 units at the end of December.

The production manager would like to spread the manufacturing requirements evenly over the six months. This is opposed by the warehouse manager who insists on the inventory reduction being achieved as soon as possible after 1st July and held at that level throughout the period.

The estimated costs of the operations involved are given in section B below.

You are required to:

(a) (i) provide for each manager's plan a graphical representation showing monthly sales, production and inventory levels;

(ii) calculate the total cost each plan would incur;

(iii) list the most significant disadvantages of each plan; and

(b) recommend your solution for overcoming the conflict between the two views.

Section A

1977	Sales forecast units
July	16,000
August	12,000
September	16,000
October	12,000
November	17,000
December	15,000

Section B

Production costs:	£
Fixed per month	
up to and including 14,000 units	210,000
up to and including 15,000 units	225,000
up to and including 16,000 units	250,000
over 16,000 units	300,000

	£
Variable per unit	
first 14,000 per month	7
next 1,000 per month	9
next 1,000 per month	10
over 16,000 per month	11
Inventory costs:	£
Fixed per month	
up to and including 5,000 units (average)	5,000
up to and including 7,500 units (average)	8,000
up to and including 10,000 units (average)	14,000
Variable per unit	
first 5,000 units (average/month)	1
next 2,500 units (average/month)	2
over 7,500 units (average/month)	3

ICMA(MA2).

Seminar Problem 13

The directors of Arges Ltd are concerned at a recent increase in the Company's working capital requirements. The have initiated a special study of the levels of stock of each product in an attempt to effect economies. One of the main products is the Cyclops. It is manufactured in batches and sold at £25 per unit. At this price, sales are expected to be 5,000 units per annum, spread evenly through the year.

The Cyclops requires the following resources:

Materials   Cost £7 per unit.

Labour hours   One grade is employed for machining and assembly. Preparation and machine set-up time require 16 hours at the start of production of each batch. Subsequently each unit of output requires 2 labour hours. The wage rate is £0.99 per hour. Labour is currently subject to a substantial amount of idle time because of a recession is the industry. The directors have decided not to dismiss any employees not to reduce the number of hours for which employees are paid.

Machine hours One standard type of machine is used. Set-up time for a batch is 9 hours and each unit of output requires one machine hour. Machine costs amount to £4 per hour.

Stocks are kept in a warehouse which was rented on a long lease ten years ago for £2 per square foot per annum. Warehouse space available exceeds current requirements and spare capacity is sub-let on annual contracts at £3 per square foot per annum. Each unit of Cyclops requires 3 square feet of space. Other costs of holding Cyclops in stock are estimated at £7 per unit per annum.

You are required to:

(a) calculate the optimal batch size and the associated maximum and average stock levels; (you may use the formula given below or work from first principles);

(b) explain shortly the rationale of the formula given below; and,

(c) explain for the benefit of the managing director (who is not familiar with accounting) the reasons for your treatment of the cost of labour and warehouse space.

Formula for optimal batch size:

$$x = \sqrt{\frac{2fs}{h}}$$

where x is the optimal batch size
f is fixed costs per batch
s is expected sales volume per annum
and h is the cost of holding a unit in stock for one year.

(I.C.A.E.W.)

Chapter 14

Control of Capital Expenditure and other Programmed Costs

Not all expenditure can be controlled by means of establishing standards, measuring variances and taking corrective action. In major areas of programmed cost the magnitude of spending is such that, lacking standards, management look for other means of exercising control.

Programmed costs are those costs which are authorised by management on criteria which are not set by notions of volume and standards. Notable examples are capital investment, research and development and marketing. Such proposals are authorised because a case has been made in their favour which is sufficiently convincing to persuage the senior management to accept them. Such a case can contain assessments of a quantifiable nature, as in D.C.F. calculations as well as more subjective assessments of benefits accruing. Inevitably, the proposals contain forecast cost figures and it is these which the cost accountant should use as his measure.

However, there is a fundamental difference between these programmed costs and other forms of expense. This difference can be easily illustrated by considering capital expenditure. Once a project has begun there are strong pressures pushing it towards completion. Sub-item of expenditure are once only costs in many cases. Failure to accomplish this sub-task within the forecast limit does not trigger off correcting devices, as in standard costing, nor is it likely to cause the project to be abandoned. There can be exceptions, of course. Sometimes repetitive expenditure does figure strongly and sometimes past failure to control expenditure causes a revision of expectations about costs still to come and this revision could cause cancellation.

All this leads to the conclusion that with programmed costs it is essential to lay down systems which are geared towards the importance of having things right at the first attempt, because very often there are no second tries. This need has led to the development of network analysis as a planning device for these programmes and this technique will be explained in the succeeding paragraphs.

Network Analysis

This is a process of analysis which is particularly useful in cases of inter-related sub-project which require to be co-ordinated. These activities may be either capable of parallel completion or needing to be done consecutively. Each activity has to be identified and also has to be related to the other activities in terms of time and sequence. The result of this analysis is put down as a network, from which some important conclusions can be drawn. Network methods will be introduced by an explanation of Critical Past Analysis, which uses single time estimates. The technique will be extended to incorporate some considerations of uncertainty.

Critical Path Analysis

Some definitions first of all:

1) A *project* has a clearly defined beginning, end and objective; it is made up a number of *activities*

2) An activity is a significant task to be completed in marking the projects objective.

Each activity begins and ends at an event node. Thus:

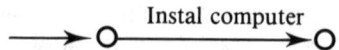

The activity is represented by an arrow, with the tail signifying the start and the head signifying the completion. The length and direction of the arrow are not significant. Each activity starts and finishes at an event node, so:

3) An *event node* occurs at the point of inter-connection of activities and is represented by a circle.

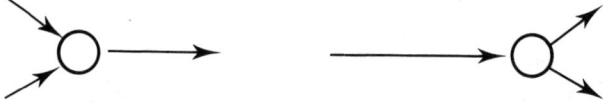

The two illustrations above demonstrate that an event node can mark the completion of a number of activities and the start of more than one activity. Each of these event nodes is given a number. Therefore, since activities start and finish at these nodes, they are identified by the two relevant node numbers.

Conventionally, networks flow from left to right, using ascending nodal numbers, but not necessarily without gaps. No two events can have the same number.

Here is a simple illustration drawn from everyday life.

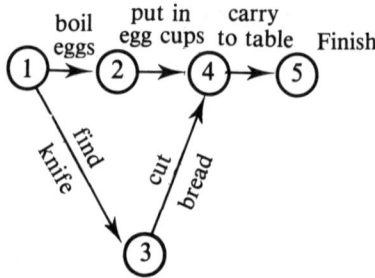

The responsibility for completion of each activity should be clearly given to individuals or units of organisation.

4) *Dummy Activities* — Sometimes the network cannot be so unambiguously presented and it is necessary to introduce a dummy activity. An example of such a situation is given in figure 14.1.

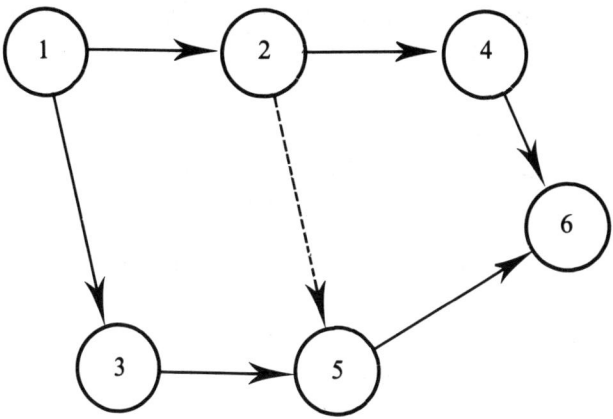

Figure 14.1

Dummy variables are used when two parallel activities must be completed before a third can be started. In the diagram the dummy activity is shown by the dotted line between the event nodes 2 and 5. This represents the fact that activity 5-6 cannot be started until both activities 1-2 and 3-5 are finished. The activity 2-5 itself does not require any physical resources or allocations of time.

5) *Duration of activities* — The information given by the network is increased by adding the estimated time necessary to complete the activity under normal circumstances. Naturally the time units should be consistently applied. With major capital projects one would expect the limit to be weeks and certainly not less than days. The normal circumstances will vary between activities. It would frequently refer to single shift working, but two and three shift working can rank as the norm.

6) *Event Dates* — At this stage the network shows the sequence of activities and the associated time. Each event can be given an *early event date* by working forward and adding together the times of the chain of activities leading to that event date.

It is also possible to work backward through the network and give to each event the appropriate *late event date*. Again this is given by taking the longest chain to the event. The significance of the late event date is that it gives the latest data by which an event must be completed if the project is not to be adversely affected.

Both these dates are attached to the nodes, sometimes in special symbols, but always with the early date on the left of the pair.

7) *Float* — The measure of excess time available for an activity is referred to as the *float*. The *total float* is the slack time for an activity which can be used with delaying the project's completion. It is given by:

$$\left[\begin{array}{l} \text{Late event date of completion } - \text{ early event date of} \\ \text{starting } - \text{ duration of activity.} \end{array} \right]$$

8) *The Critical Path*

The various paths that can be followed in travelling along the network from start to finish have different total time requirements. The longest time gives the *Critical Path*. Each activity along this path is known as a critical activity.

There are three features of the critical path which should be emphasised:

a) delays to critical activities will delay the project.

b) a project may have more than one critical path.

c) critical activities have no excess time available to them, i.e. they have zero float.

Reducing activity times is only worthwhile if the activity is critical. There is no points in reducing the time of an activity which is not on the critical path. Such a reduction will have no effect on overall project completion time. When activity times are reduced it is necessary to check on the whole network, since the planned reduction may result in a new critical path.

Network illustration

A problem in moving house. A firm's senior executive has to sell his present house and buy a new one in a different part of the country. He is already heavily indebted to his bank and cannot obtain a bridging loan. Consequently, he must complete the sale of his present house before he can do the same for his new one.

The first step is to detail the activities or tasks to be performed and to give each a time. These are given below, with no particular regard to sequence.

Tasks	Time (Days)
Appoint estate agent	3
Investigate possible new houses	10
Choose removal firm	5
Move furniture etc.	20
Choose a new house	25
Make offer for new house	5
Investigate mortgage possibilities	5
Obtain fresh mortgage	5
Reach agreement on new house	1
Repair roof on old house	7
Paint outside of old house	10
Partial decoration of old house	5

Final clean up of old house	5
Display old house to prospective buyers	15
Agree sales of old house	10
Repairs to new house	5
Clean new house — fit curtain (before removal)	5
Move to new house	1

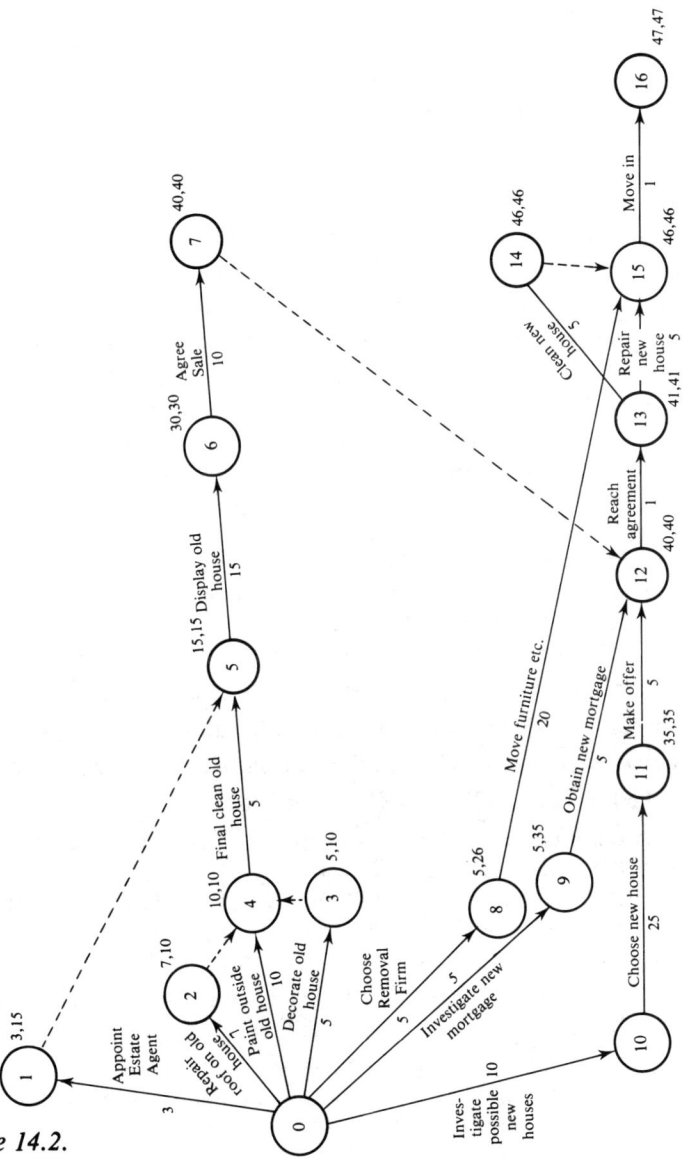

Figure 14.2.

Detailing all the jobs to be done is of immediate benefit in planning. In simple situations, as here, the various tasks could be carried in the head and the necessary co-ordination of activities could also be achieved informally. In more complex systems, it would be essential to write everything down in some form of planning document. A network drawing can form the basis of such a plan.

This solution illustrates the various features of network analysis that have previously been defined.

Each activity starts and finishes at an event node. These nodes are numbered in such a way that an activity is defined by giving these numbers, e.g. $\overset{6}{\bigcirc} \xrightarrow[\text{sale}]{\text{Agree}} \overset{7}{\bigcirc}$ Note that the node on the left at the beginning of the event must always have the smaller number.

At every node there are a pair of numbers. These are the early event data and the late event date. The former is obtained by working forward from left to right and the latter by working backwards from the end.

Some nodes have a pair of numbers which are different. An example, is given by $\overset{10}{\bigcirc}$ which has 5, 35. This means that the earliest date at which this point can be reached is 5 days from the start. That is 5 days to contact building societies etc. with a view to obtaining the necessary finance. However, other activities can be undertaken in parallel and no harm is done provided the initial promise of finance is obtained within 35 days of the start. This activity clearly has slack time associated with it.

There are five dummy activities shown in the network. Two of them occur prior to the final cleaning of the old house. There are three activities to perform before this can be done, namely, repairing the roof (7 days), outside painting (10 days) and some decorating (5 days). These can be done in parallel, but the earliest at which they can be finished is 10 days, the time taken to paint the exterior $\overset{0}{\bigcirc} \rightarrow \overset{2}{\bigcirc}$ and $\overset{0}{\bigcirc} \rightarrow \overset{3}{\bigcirc}$ have to be finished before $\overset{4}{\bigcirc} \rightarrow \overset{5}{\bigcirc}$ can begin. In the absence of a bridging loan, the old house has to be sold before the new one can be bought. Node 7 has to be reached before $\overset{12}{\bigcirc} \rightarrow \overset{13}{\bigcirc}$ can start.

There are two critical paths in this example. The first is given by $0 - 4 - 5 - 6 - 7 - 12 - 13 - 15 - 16$. The second by $0 - 10 - 11 - 12 - 13 - 15 - 16$. There is a common section from $\overset{12}{\bigcirc} \rightarrow \overset{13}{\bigcirc}$ onwards, with two paths leading up to it. Note that the critical activities along these paths have no slack time. If an attempt is to be made on the critical path. Here it could be a day saved on $\overset{13}{\bigcirc} \xrightarrow{\text{cleaning}} \overset{15}{\bigcirc}$ together with a day saved on $\overset{13}{\bigcirc} \xrightarrow{\text{repairs}} \overset{14}{\bigcirc}$ Saving a day on $\overset{13}{\bigcirc} \rightarrow \overset{15}{\bigcirc}$ alone would not achieve an overall reduction. The same would be true of saving time on one of the critical paths leading up to $\overset{12}{\bigcirc}$, without a corresponding saving on the other path. It is also clear that shortening the time of activities away from the critical path achieves nothing. Repairing the roof of the old house in 3 days instead of 7 would not help, since cleaning cannot be done until the painters have gone.

Reductions to the critical path can result in the path itself being changed. Suppose for example, that painting could be done in 5 days and the choosing of the new house could be done in 20 days. Thus 5 days would be saved along each parallel section of the critical path. The overall saving would only be 3 days since the critical parth has moved to incorporate $\underset{\text{roof}}{(0) \xrightarrow{\text{repair}} (2)}$. In fact, it would only be necessary to reduce the number of days for choosing the new home by 3 days.

Advantages of network analysis.

It is possible to discern a number of features of this technique which amount to plus points in its favour

1) It demands systematic thought about the component tasks of the project.

2) It goes further in that it requires the individual relationships existing between these tasks to be stated.

3) It reveals the critical activities which have to be reduced in time if the overall period of the project is to be reduced.

4) It enables alternative strategies to be considered.

5) Finally, it forms a basis for the control of the actual operations.

Limitations

The basic limitation of the network technique considered so far is that it assumes certainty of knowledge about the time required for each activity.

It also ignores cost estimates for these activities.

Programme evaluation and review technique

The network analysis described above is incorporated into P.E.R.T. form the initial letters of the sub-heading above. P.E.R.T. is a much developed range of methods now available for modern management to use. Two developments in particular can be introduced here to indicate the ways in which the two limitations can be overcome.

P.E.R.T./Time introduces three limits instead of one. These are for the most optimistc time t_a, the most likely time t_m and the most pessimistic time t_b.

The optimistic forecast assumes that there are no snags and the pessimistic one anticipates difficulties but does not go so far as to allow for catastrophe. These time estimates are then incorporated into this formula

$$t_a = \frac{t_a + 4t_m + t_b}{6}$$

to give the expected time t_e. The formulat used cannot be justified here, but has been developed by P.E.R.T. researchers as the one likely to give best results:

Here is a simple P.E.R.T. network with which to demonstrate the idea and to extend it a little further:

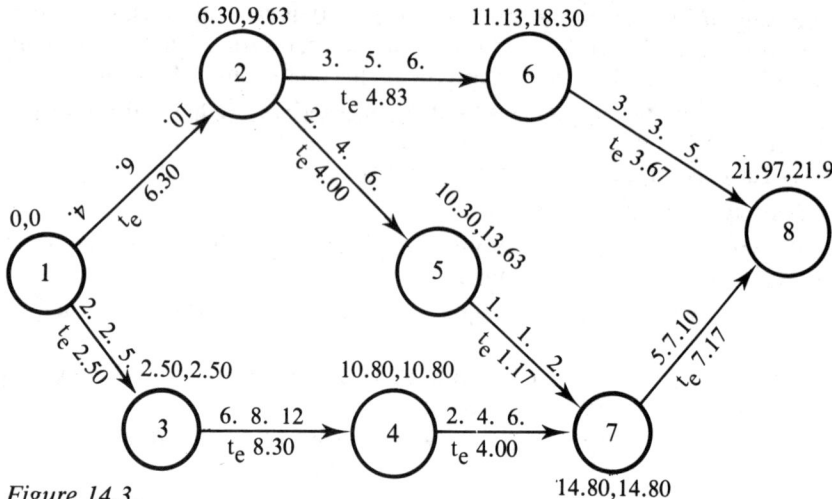

Figure 14.3.

The critical path appears as the one having no slack time for any activity, namely $1 - 3 - 4 - 7 - 8$. The completion time for the project as a whole will be given by obtaining the standard deviation from this formula:

$$= \sqrt{\sum_{i=1}^{n} \frac{(b-a)^2}{36}}$$

and using normal distribution tables to ascertain the probability of meeting the target date. The i symbolises the activity. For this formula to be valid it is necessary to have a large number of activities preceding the one in question, in this case the last one. The illustration really contains too few such activities.

P.E.R.T./Cost — this further extension of P.E.R.T. brings in cost estimates for the expected time. Whenever a project needs to be completed in less time than given by the original estimates, or when targets are not being met, it becomes necessary to introduce the idea of costing crash programmes. Additional crash times and crash costs have to be introduced into the review.

In the simplest situation, the cost of saving one unit of time is given as:

$$\text{Cost of one unit of time} = \frac{\text{crash cost} - \text{normal cost}}{\text{normal time} - \text{crash time}}$$

For example, the engineer and cost accountant gives the following estimates:

	time (weeks)	Cost (£)
normal	10	1000
crash	5	2000

$$\text{Cost of one week} = £\frac{(2000-1000)}{10-5} = £200$$

Reducing the activity time from ten weeks to six weeks would cost $4 \times 200 = £800$. This is dependent on the validity of the assumption that there is a straight line relationship between the costs and time.

Illustration

An extract from a network gives the critical path only

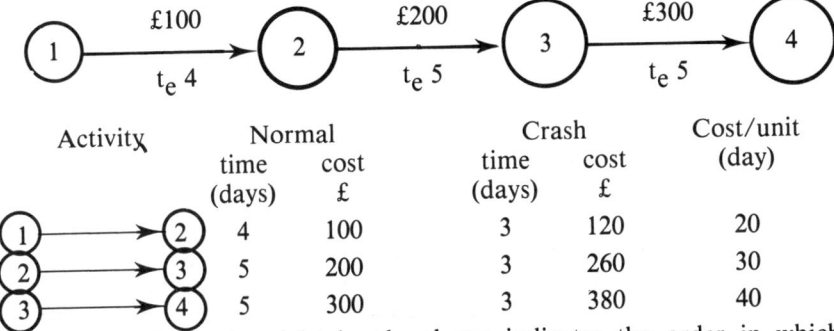

Activity	Normal time (days)	cost £	Crash time (days)	cost £	Cost/unit (day)
1→2	4	100	3	120	20
2→3	5	200	3	260	30
3→4	5	300	3	380	40

The cost/unit in the right hand column indicates the order in which activities should be reduced in time, in order to achieve an overall reduction in project time at least cost.

To summarise, P.E.R.T. is a useful management tool, subject to a number of caveats. It is most useful when the assumptions concerning the nature of the distribution of the figures is correct, but this will not always be so.

Progress control of capital expenditure

The basic budget figures used to set up the network can form the 'standards' for a current review of progress of the project. As was stated earlier this seldom leads to corrective action, since the activities are usually single rather than repetitive. The examination can still be useful though, since it reveals projects which are running into trouble for one reason or another and which demand more managerial attention. A simple review is illustrated:

Activity	Actual Cost to date	Estimated Completion cost	Estimated Total cost	Budget Cost	Variance
(1)	(2) £	(3) £	(4)=(2)+(3) £	(5) £	(6)=(5)–(4) £
1→2	890	210	1100	1000	100 u

Auditing Capital Programmes

Checking on completion costs after the event may seem to be on a par with shutting the stable door after the horse has bolted, but many firms find it a valuable procedure. Their main objectives are to establish weaknesses in control which can be eradicated in the future and to discourage wild forecasting by interested parties.

The second of these objectives is aimed at discouraging over enthusiastic advocacy of particular projects by highly involved managers. Given the certainty of an eventual audit, they should be discouraged, at least in part, from being unreasonably optimistic in their costings.

As well as auditing the cost of the programme a review should also be made of other figures, usually revenues, included in the original justification. In practice, it is often difficult to assign benefits between a new system and other claimants, but it is worthwhile making some attempt, at least for major projects.

Research and Development

R & D and control of expenditure do not relate to each other naturally. The one requires flair and imagination as well as other qualities of hard work and patience, whereas control suggests rules and routines which could stifle the research effort. However, the extent of R & D expenditure is frequently too greater to allow it to go unconsidered within the overall framework of the firm's resource allocation.

It is impossible to lay down a precise set of rules for the control of this sector, but some guidlines can be put forward.

1) Separate fundamental from applied research and in turn from the development. This enables differing types of situations to be catered for more individualistically.

2) Since the main concern is to control in the sense of obtaining value for money, then the whole system of generating ideas should be reviewed. Fundamentally, are they coming through? When this receives an affirmative answer, then thought can be given to their screening. Generally, this is a successive filtering process allowing only the most promising proposals to progress through each stage.

3) Proposals should be formally presented with clear aims and costs. Other interested parties within the firm should be firmly involved.

4) Regular reporting on projects, on lines similar to the ones outlined under the heading of capital expenditure.

5) Major functional reviews of the whole research and development programme should be conducted regularly. In this way the section is examined in depth, both in terms of current work, but in terms of successful contributions to current profits of past research effort.

Marketing

In many ways the marketing programme resembles that of research and development. Certainly it is becoming an ever increasing factor in many firms overall costs. The marketing costs cover those activities which are related to obtaining orders, fulfilling them and providing an after sales service. The usual questions asked about the marketing effort relate to their impact upon individual products or product groups and on territorial or distribution type considerations. In other words, they need to be classified in a variety of ways in order to provide all the answers to the varied types of questions put by management.

The key to this is flexibility and, in particular, a flexible coding system should be installed. With this as the base of the system, modern data processing equipment can soon perform the necessary analysis. The items of marketing expense are usually analysed in terms of their nature, their function and product or territorial groupings.

An example of analysis by territories is given in figure 14.4.

Profit analysis by territories				
	Territory			
	1	2	4	Total
Sales	396,000	445,000	545,000	
Costs direct to territories:				
Cost of Goods Sold	97,000	136,000	156,000	
Transport & depot costs	11,000	15,000	16,000	
Salesmans' salaries & commission	80,000	111,000	120,000	
Salesmens' expenses	15,000	12,000	11,000	
Regional advertising	45,000	48,000	60,000	
Regional sales office rent and expenses	18,000	15,000	17,000	
Total direct territory cost	266,000	337,000	380,000	
Contribution to central costs and profit	130,000	108,000	165,000	
Indirect cost of territories				
Advertising	30,000	30,000	30,000	
General distribution costs	25,000	30,000	33,000	
General administration costs	40,000	50,000	60,000	
	95,000	110,000	123,000	
Net operating profit (loss)	35,000	(3,000)	42,000	

Figure 14.4.

The statement is divided into two segments. The first set of items are closely associated with the regions and have been directly traced to them. Many of these items are largely controllable by the regional management. Items coming after the contribution figure are central and far from under regional control. They are added so as to complete the picture for the firm as a whole. Whether the final results show swollen head office costs or lack of contribution from regions can be a matter for further investigation.

The general advertising, distribution and administration costs are divided between the territories on some apportionment basis felt to be suitable.

It would be possible to analyse the contributions made on other bases, say by product or by type of customer. The latter could be divided between wholesalers and retailers or one major industry and another. Such statements are less common than the one illustrated and generally less useful. This is because it is usually difficult to trace many items directly to products and so apportionment of costs are much more general.

Summary

There are considerable quantities of firms' resources applied to areas of expenditure which are difficult to control, since it is difficult to establish cost levels appropriate to the aims of the programme. The approach to control lies in three areas:

1) The programme of costs of the new project should be well screened. In cases of capital expenditure, the expected revenues and costs should be clearly set out and applied in a discounting model. Programmes to do with research, marketing, administration etc., should be justified, not in terms of comparison with last year, but from basic considerations. In other words, last year's level of expenditure should not be accepted as the norm, but a genuinely fresh justification should be made on each occasion.

2) Techniques such as P.E.R.T. should be applied where appropriate. That is in cases where the analysis would prove cost effective.

3) Regular reviews and audits should be maintained.

Exercises

Questions 14.1-14.5 (Answers provided)

14.1 Design a network to illustrate any everyday activity you care to choose. It should consist of about seven to ten events.

14.2

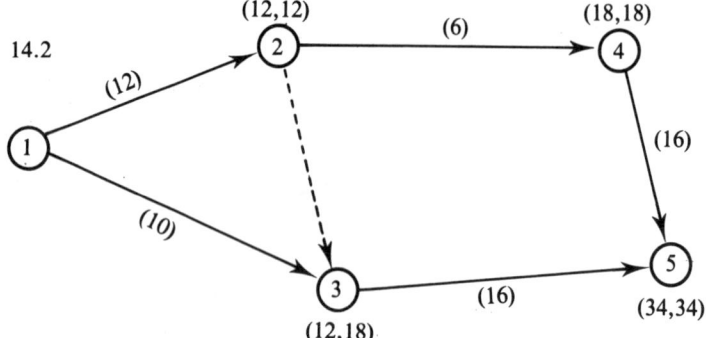

Required:
a) why is the early event date at node 3 not equal to 10?
b) if the project starts on January 1st and you are responsible for ① ⟶ ③ , by what date must you complete the task?
c) if you are in charge of both ① ⟶ ③ and ③ ⟶ ⑤ what is the earliest data that you could arrive at the finish?
d) which is the critical path?

14.3

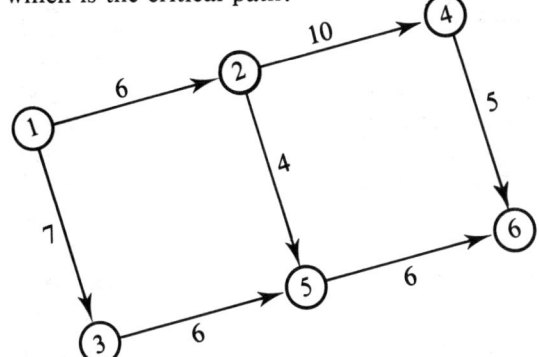

Required:
a) the critical path?
b) if it were possible to reduce ③ ⟶ ⑤ by 2 days how much time would be saved?
c) if it were possible to reduced ② ⟶ ④ by 3 days how much time would be saved?

14.4. Draw a network from the following specification:

Activity	Previous Activities	Time in days
A	—	10
B	—	7
C	—	9
D	B	0
E	A, D	6
F	B	8
G	B	4
H	C	3
I	C	8
J	E, F	5
K	G, H	4

What is the critical path? If activity A is reduced to 8 days, which path becomes critical?

14.5 The Ayrshire Company had the following profit statement for the year ended 31st December 19X5.

	£
Sales	1,500,000
Cost of Goods sold (full)	800,000
Gross profit	700,000
Delivery costs:	
Transport	50,000
Packing	40,000
	90,000
Salesmen's salaries	70,000
Salesmen's commissions	60,000
Other salaries	50,000
Advertising — local	80,000
— national	60,000
	410,000
Administrative expenses	150,000
Total costs	560,000
Opering profit	140,000

Required: Your managing director has asked you to report on the feasibility of the report in future being based on the contribution approach. He also wants an analysis by sales area. Explain what would be involved in doing this.

Questions 14.6-14.10. Answers not provided.

14.6 Edward Ltd. is preparing plans for carrying out the work on a new contract which it has just been awarded. The following table gives estimates of the time and cost according to standard procedures for activities involved in the contract.

Activity	Previous activities	Time required days	Cost £
A	—	8 — 12	7,000 — 9,000
B	—	11 — 13	6,000 — 7,000
C	A, B	7 — 9	4,000 — 4,500
D	—	12 — 16	12,000 — 15,000
E	—	13 — 15	9,000 — 9,500
F	E	7 — 9	5,000 — 6,000
G	C, D, F	5 — 7	6,000 — 6,500

"Previous activities" must be completed before the activity in question can be started. Information on time required and cost for each activity is given in the form of a 95 per cent confidence interval. The probability distributions for time and cost are symmetrical about the mean values.

Alternative methods of operation could be applied to some of the activities:

(1) activity D could be completed in 11-13 days at a cost of £11,000—13,000 (alternative (i)) or in 8-12 days at a cost of £12,000—16,000 (alternative (ii));

(2) activity E could be completed in 9-11 days at a cost of £14,000—15,000;

(3) activity B could be completed in 10-12 days at a cost of £8,000—9,000.

Edward's customer is willing to increase the contract price by £2,500 for each day saved on the contract below 30 days. It is not possible to use a combination of standard procedures and alternative procedures on one activity.

You are required to:

(a) calculate the minimum expected value of the time required to complete the contract and the expected value of the cost given the use of standard procedures;

(b) evaluate the worthwhileness of using each of the alternative methods of operation in terms of expected values; and

(c) comment on the limitations of expected values as bases for decision processes.

ICAEW(EFD).

14.7 Slick Sales Ltd have a sales force structure based upon a national sales manager situated in Birmingham, and 15 representatives who cover the kingdom. The sales force, including the sales manager, are all provided with the same sort of car. This costs £3,200 when new and there is a replacement programme when it is traded in after two years for a guaranteed £1,200. The salesman covering the lowest mileage, which is 18,000 miles annually, operates in the London area. The one with the highest mileage travels 40,000 miles throughout the Scottish Highlands. The sales manager has averaged an annual 25,100 miles over the last three years. The annual average mileage of the complete sales team works out at 30,000 miles per vehicle.

Members of the sales force are allowed to use their cars for local private journeys at no cost to them. However, it they wish to use their company car for a long holiday journey, they are expected to make a contribution towards the annual running costs of the vehicle, based upon the mileage that they cover whilst on holiday.

The average annual cost of operating a salesmen's vehicle is:

	£
Petrol and oil	1,200
Road tax	40
Insurance	160
Repairs (*see note* (i))	240
Miscellaneous (see note (ii))	100
	£1,740

Notes

(i) Annual repairs include £80 for regular maintenance. Tyre life is around 30,000 miles and replacement sets cost £120. No additional repair costs are incurred during the first year of a vehicle's life because a special warranty agreement exists with the supplying garage to cover these. However, on average £200 is paid for repairs in the second year. Repair costs are averaged over the two years with regular maintenance and repairs being variables to mileage rather than time.

(ii) This includes such things as subscriptions to motoring organisations, cleaning vehicles, parking fees, allowances for garaging, etc.

Required:

It is important that you clearly state any assumptions that you make when answering the various parts of this question.

(a) Computations showing the cost of operating the organisation's highest and lowest mileage vehicles each year.

(b) The salesman based at London wishes to take his car on a holilday tour of Wales and the Lake District. He expects to cover 1,800 miles. Suggest ways in which the contribution that he should pay to Slick Sales Ltd for the use of the car during this tour could be calculated.

(c) The sales manager has to make a special journey to Ireland to carry out negotiations with a potential large new customer. If he takes his car he will have to cover an additional mileage to that normally incurred in a year. This will be 151 miles to the ferry, where he will have to pay £35 for the return ferry fare for himself and his car, and then travel for another 100 miles on the other side to his ultimate destination. He could fly directly to the potential customer's office for £60 return. Which method of transportation would you advise him to use?

Note that the cost of capital, taxation considerations and inflation can all be ignored in answers to this question.

CA(MA)

14.8 (a) The works manager has proposed that new equipment be installed to improve a manufacturing process. This equipment will reduce operating and maintenance costs and increase output. A sales forecast, however, indicates that no extra demand is anticipated until after 1978.

You are required to prepare notes to assist in evaluating this project listing the advantages and disadvantages of delaying investment in the circumstances given.

(b) If the project is implemented a post-completion audit will be required. Explain the purposes of this and indicate some of the problems likely to be encountered.

ICMA(MA2).

14.9 (a) Why can the methods of control of research and development expenditure in an industrial company be expected to differ from the control of expenditure of other functions such as manufacturing, selling or administration?

(b) What are the main features that you would expect to find in a system for control of research and development expenditure in a large industrial company?

ICMA(MA1).

14.10 One of the most important decisions which concerns financial management is the decision to incur capital expenditure. Discuss the information which is required in a system for the planning and control of such expenditure.

CA(FM).

Seminar Problem 14

Stereopes Ltd undertakes special contracts. The following table gives estimates of the time and cost for activities involved in completing one contract which has just been offered to the firm:

Activity	Previous Activities	Normal time	Normal cost	Minimum time	Cost for Minimum time
		days	£	days	£
A	—	12	10,000	8	14,000
B	—	10	5,000	10	5,000
C	A	0	0	0	0
D	A	6	4,000	4	5,000
E	B,C	16	9,000	14	12,000
F	D	16	3,200	8	8,000
		60	31,200	44	44,000

"Previous activities" must be completed before the activity in question can be started. The minimum time represents the shortest time in which the activity can be completed given the use of especially costly methods of operation. Assume that it is possible to reduce the normal time to the minimum time in small steps and that the extra cost incurred will be proportional to the time saved.

You are required to:

(a) draw a network diagram for the contract and identify the critical path assuming that normal procedures are adopted,

(b) recommend what programme should be followed if the job must be completed in 30 days, and calculate the total cost for that programme, and

(c) explain how you would modify your analysis if the estimates were subject to uncertainty. Illustrate your answer by assuming that estimates of the time required for E are uncertain. Normal time is expected to be in the range 12 days to 20 days, but 2 days could still be saved by spending an extra £3,000. You remain confident about the estimates for other activities. Target time for the contract is 30 days and there would be penalty of £5,000 for later completion.

(I.C.A.E.W.)

Chapter 15

Estimating Cost Equations

There have been many references throughout this book to the ways in which costs vary in differing circumstances. Chapter 2 dealt with this idea of cost variability and throughout the book, the idea of variable costing has always been at the forefront. Marginal costing and flexible budgeting presupposes knowledge of cost behaviour. In this section, dealing with decisions, emphasis will be placed on establishing the costs which are relevant to the decision and this usually means establishing the differential costs. Those are the ones which are dependent upon the course of action taken. They are the subject of chapter 17.

Management decisions and procedures require estimates of future costs, since decisions are about future courses of action. The preparation of operating budgets or embarking on capital expenditure programmes require such estimates. Because of their importance, the reliability of these estimates is vital to the validity of the decisions.

In order to make these estimates it is usually necessary to establish a relationship between the costs and some measure of activity. The question being asked of the accountant is this — given a volume of production (say) what will be the associated costs?

For some costs this is not too difficult a question to answer. The technical department in a firm can give figures for material use and direct labour hours required for the projected production. Purchasing costs and labour ratre agreements when applied to these engineering estimates, give the estimated cost. The same considerations apply to machine usage.

Unfortunately, once away from this area of directly traceable costs, such engineering methods can no longer apply. The difficulties are too great for their application. For indirect costs, such as supervision, other methods need to be developed.

The accountant attempts to divide these indirect costs into their component fixed and variable parts. This establishes a cost equation which can then be used in the estimating process.

A hypothetic equation is illustrated in figure 15.1.

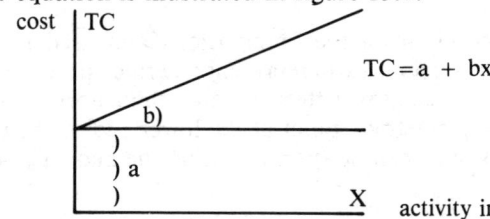

Figure 15.1.

This straight line equation has TC (total cost) for the dependent variable and x (a measure of activity) as the independent variable. The parameters are 'a' for the fixed cost element and 'b' the lines gradient or amount by which x increases the variable contribution to total cost. Given a knowledge of this and other equations, the accountant can put together a flexible budget, or a decision model concerning production. The problem to be discussed here, is how are such equations constructed?

Before considering ways, there ought to be an examination of the assumptions that have been made in order to conclude that such equations exist.

The first assumption is that there is onlyone factor which causes the cost to vary. This would normally be a measure of activity. Second, it is assumed that the relationship between the cost and the activity measure is a linear one.

To increase familiarity with the idea of these equations, study these three simple methods which provide approximations, before going on to look at a more sophisticated approach.

Visual Curve Fitting

Simply plot readings of activity versus cost on graph paper. See figure 15.2.

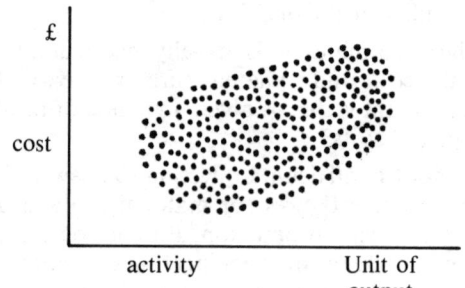

Figure 15.2.

The technique is to draw a line through the dotted area which most represents the underlying relationship between cost and activity. Clearly, it is not an easy thing to do and different people would probably interpret the line through the group of dots quite differently.

High-low Method

Two points are chosen from the observations and used to provide the straight line. One of the points will represent a defined position at the upper end of the output range, say fifteen greater than normal activity. The second would be a symmetrical point at the lower end of the range. Given two points a straight line can be specified using the known co-ordinates of the two points.

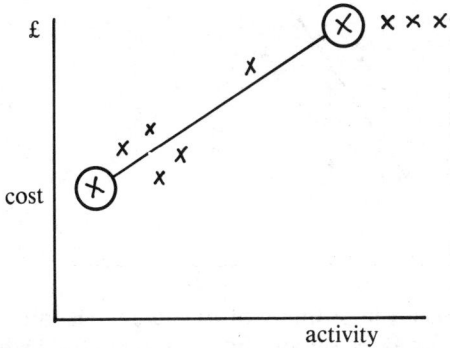

Figure 15.3.

activity

Accounts Method

This is an arbitrary assessment by the accountant of the fixed and variable elements of a cost, which are then used to provide the cost equation. The method is illustrated in figure 15.4.

Account Classification

Account	Amount £	Variable £	Fixed £	Output
Electricity	1320	1100	220	4000

Figure 15.4.

This equation is formed from two points as with the high-low method. In this case one of the points is at zero activity, when the fixed costs apply. The high point is at 4000 units when the total cost of £1320 applies. The equation is:-

$$TC = 220 + \frac{1100}{4000} \times$$
$$TC = 0.275x + 220.$$

Statistical Methods

All the methods described above are easy to apply and are quick and cheap. The results are correspondingly approximate and can be used only when the model is not sensitive to the information. An improvement in results comes from using statistical techniques. The problem has previously been stated, as one of looking for a relationship between two things, here cost and activity. In statistics such relationships are established by regression analysis.

Regression analysis takes two sets of data and finds the line which fits them best, according to a specific application of rules. Here the rule will be to find the line for which the sum of the squared distances between itself and the plotted points is minimised. This is the method of least squares.

Figure 15.5 illustrates the idea, each point shown is an actual cost and the straight-line is the result that is sought.

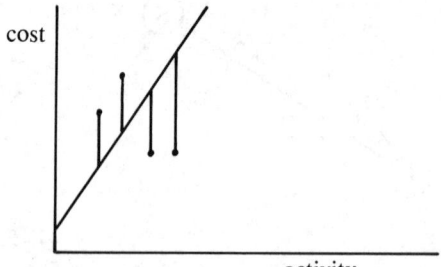

cost

Figure 15.5.

activity

The difference between the ordinate of the actual cost and the ordinate of the straight line vertically below or above, is given by the expression:

$$TC (actual) - (a + bx)$$

which simply expresses mathematically the difference between the actual cost recorded for a level of activity and the corresponding point on the line $y = a + bx$.

This expression applies to all the observations, each of which is squared and then the squares summed to give

$$E^2 = \sum_{i=1}^{n} (TC_{act} - (a + bx)^2$$

The method of least squares requires this to be a minimum. Differentiating in turn for 'a' and 'b' and setting the derivative to zero gives two equations. These can be solved to find the values for 'a' and 'b' which give the straight-line with the minimum values of 'least squares'.

$$\frac{d(E)^2}{da} = \Sigma - 2TC_{act} + \Sigma 2a + \Sigma 2bx$$

$$= o \text{ when } \quad \Sigma TC_{act} = \Sigma a + \Sigma bx$$

$$\text{that is} \quad \Sigma TC_{act} = na + b\Sigma x$$

where n is the number of readings and x the measure activity.

$$\frac{d(E)^2}{db} = \Sigma - 2TC.x_{act} \Sigma 2a.x + \Sigma 2bx^2$$

$$= o \text{ when } \Sigma TC.x_{act} = a \Sigma x + b \Sigma x^2$$

reverting to y for TC we have

$$\Sigma y = na + b \Sigma x \qquad 1)$$

and $\quad \Sigma x.y = a \Sigma x + b \Sigma x^2 \qquad 2)$

The equations are referred to as normal equations. Their use can be illustrated with a small set of observations.

Production in units (x)	Total Cost (y)	x^2	xy	y^2
12	140	144	1680	19600
20	230	400	4600	52900
17	190	289	3230	36100
25	300	625	7500	90000
9	110	81	990	12100
18	240	324	4320	57600
15	180	225	2700	32400
12	160	144	1920	26500
22	270	484	5940	72900
30	320	900	9600	102400
180	2140	3616	42480	501600

$\Sigma y = na + b \Sigma x$ gives $2140 = 10a + 180b$

and $\quad \Sigma xy = a \Sigma x + b \Sigma x^2$ gives $42480 = 280a + 3616b$

$$a = £24.46$$
$$b = £10.53 \text{ per unit}$$

This technique has the added facility of the correlation coefficient. This coefficient provides a measure of the extent to which the least squares estimate of the cost function actually succeeds in minimising the distances between the actual observations and the derived line.

It is given by the formula:

$$r = \frac{n \Sigma xy - (\Sigma x)(\Sigma y)}{\sqrt{n \Sigma x^2 - (\Sigma x)^2}\sqrt{n \Sigma y^2 - (\Sigma y)^2}}$$

in this example $r = 0.99$

Correlation coefficients lie between $+1$ and -1. An r of ± 1 indicates a perfect fit of an upward $(+)$ or downward slope $(-)$ and o means there is not relationship between x and y.

Problems associated with staistical methods

In order to obtain an acceptable degree of statistical significance, there must be a substantial number of observations. Collection may take the form of cross series or time series. In the former, data is collected from a number of points at the same time. The latter consists of readings made at the same point through time. It is in the nature of most accounting exercises that usually times series data are used.

Collecting the data is subject to special problems of which the accountant should be aware. These are apart from the basic fact that most accounting records do not record the requisite facts in readily available form. These special problems have additional techniques for solution, such techniques being the tools of the specialist statistician.

For time series data a stable process is required, otherwise the validity of the results is undermined by the changing environment. The almost universal existence of technological change ensures that such stability is only a reasonable assumption for short periods of time.

The individual time periods too, must be considered with a view to choosing some length between a long and short boundary. Too long and the costs become averages whereas one is seeking a pattern of behaviour which is not obscured by the averaging process. Too short and the recording itself becomes inaccurate.

It may be that the use of a single independent variable is inadequate for the analysis. Cost behaviour may relate to more than one such variable, in which case multi-regression analysis is required. The use of such a technique gives a result in the form:-

$$y = f(x_1, x_2......x_k)$$
$$= b_0 + b_1 x_1 + b_2 x_2 + b_k x_k + u$$

where u is a random variable.

Within the framework of multi-regression analysis, it is possible to meet the case of the independent variables moving together. The word for this is multi-collinearity and the solution is to deal in packs or groups of such variables.

The 'u' term in the expression above is the random variable. Strictly, such a term should have been included in the single regression equation. The usual assumption is that this random variation has a normal distribution and a zero mean. It can happen that it does not, say where we have a steadily increasing level of output.

Or, it may be that there is a lack of serial independence of the random variable. The events of a previous period can be having an influence. A clear example is the reduction of costs as output falls. There must always be a time lag or stickiness about matching reductions in costs to decreased activity. Some costs, such as labour, are highly resistant to such changes.

Seasonal variations can influence results and require special consideration in the application of statistical techniques.

All of these statistical problems, with the long titles of multi-collinearity, heteroscedasticity, auto-correlation are catered for by the statisticians in their development of computer programs to perform regression analyses.

Despite this catalogue of pitfalls, the statistical methods does give advantages of greater consistency and objectivity. Remember though, that the observations are made within a range of activities and that extrapolation beyond that range is a leap in the dark.

Exercises
Questions 15.1-15.5. (Answers provided)

15.1

Production in Units	Total Cost in £'s
12	143
10	121
15	168
28	299
25	250
20	211
18	207
22	237
15	168
16	183
181	1987

Required: the cost equation derived by visual curve fitting.

15.2 Use the data in question 1 and calculate the variable and fixed elements of cost using the high-low method. Take observations 25% above and 25% below the normal production level of 20 units.

15.3 Use the data in question 1 and find the line of best fit using regression. Calculate the correlation coefficient and comment.

15.4

Production (units)	Costs (£)
8000	1610
10400	1820
11300	1950
11100	1870
9900	1790
9100	1710
7400	1520
8200	1670
6100	1510
9600	1750

The planned production for the coming period is 10,000 units. Give an estimate of total costs. (Use least squares).

15.5 Use the analysis of accounts technique to calculate fixed and variable costs from the accounts and additional information given.

	£
raw materials	10,000
direct labour	9,000
depreciation on equipment	1,000
electricity	3,000
heating	1,000
rent	500
supplies	400
miscellaneous	200

The centre performs a very simple finishing process prior to assembly. Parts are coated with chemicals and dried in a kiln. The work is seasonal, but the work force is kept together throughout the year. When the season is slack essential maintenance is carried out by the same people. It is estimated that an average 75% of the time is spent productively. The kiln is electric and accounts for 90% of the electricity costs. The supplies are for such items as protective clothing. During the peiod in question there were 500 machine hours worked.

Questions 15.6-15.10. Answers not provided.

15.6 The results of the Mercia division of Offa Ltd over the last five years are summarised as follows:

	£'000				
Year	1	2	3	4	5
Sales	70	93	119	118	152
Costs—Materials	20	28	42	37	48
—Labour	27	36	39	48	54
—Overheads	24	24	28	33	32
	71	88	109	118	134
Net Profit	(1)	5	10	0	18
Sales units	2,100	2,800	3,400	3,100	4,000

The Mercia Division manufactures a single product. Stocks have been negligible at all relevant times. Price changes have been rare in Offa's business. During the last five years, the only changes in the prices of resources used have been an increase in the price of materials of 25 per cent three years ago (at the end of year 2), and an increase in wage rates of 33⅓ per cent 2 years ago (at the end of year 3); overhead costs have not bee affected by price changes.

Plans for the coming year (year 6) are now being prepared. No further increases in the prices of resources are expected. The sales manager has provided the following estimates of the sales price-volume relationship for the coming year:

volume	price
4,500	£37
4,000	£40
3,400	£42

You are required to:

(a) estimate the optimal selling price from amongst the three possible prices £37, £40 or £42 using linear regression analysis to estimate the cost-volume relationship, and

(b) discuss the advantages and limitations of linear regression analysis for the estimation of cost-volume relationships.

ICAEW(EFD).

15.7 The sales forecast is frequently a critical factor in the budgeting process. Sometimes the periodic sales of an organisation are found to be serially correlated. When this happens the method of extrapolating past sales information may be helpful in the provision of a sales forecast. Refinements to extrapolation include: use moving averages; the weighting of these averages by a constant which acts as a surrogate to combine the effects of most of the other variables which influence the organisation's sales. In the process of weighting moving averages, the sales for the future period, $S_{(t+1)}$, are assumed to be related to the average sales for a past number of stated years, $(n + 1)$, multiplied by some constant, K. i.e.

$$S_{(t+1)} = \frac{K(S_{(t)} + S_{(t-1)} \dots + S_{(t-n)})}{(n + 1)} \qquad \dots(1)$$

One of the disadvantages of this method is that it gives equal weighting to each item in the average. To overcome this disadvantage the technique of moving weighted averages with decreasing weightings may be used. This technique provides greater weightings to the more recent items in the series.

Better Results Ltd has been using formula (1) to make its sale forecast, with $K = 1.5.$, and $n = 2$. However, the firm is considering a refinement of this approach. Two suggestions have been made as to how this could be done. Both would still use $K = 1.5$ and $n = 2$.

The first proposal is that the sales of the year preceding the forecast should be weighted by 2, to provide the following formula:

$$S_{(t+1)} = \frac{K(2S_{(t)} + S_{(t-1)} + S_{(t-2)})}{4} \qquad \dots(2)$$

The second suggestion is that the sales of the year preceding the forecast should be weighted by 3, and the year before this by 2, to provide the formula:

$$S_{(t-1)} = \frac{K(3S_{(t)} + 2S_{(t-1)} + S_{(t-2)})}{6} \qquad \dots(3)$$

Sales for the company over the past 8 years have been as follows: 65; 78; 101; 129; 164; 208; 269 and 343 in the most recent year.

Required:

(a) Calculations showing the forecasts for Better Results Ltd's sales for years 4 to 8, using each of the *three* formulae shown above. Present your results in tabular form.

(b) A report to Better Results Ltd to indicate which of the above formulae you would recommend them to use. Give the reasons clearly for your recommendation, stating any assumptions that you have made. In your report provide details of any other sources of information about demand that you think the firm should consider before their final forecast of sales for use in the next period's budget is made.

CA(MA).

15.8 A division of Barwa Ltd. processes a single type of chemical. Processing costs and output for the last thirteen accounting periods (of four weeks each) have been as follows:

Period	1	2	3	4	5	6	7	8	9	10	11	12	13
Costs	£	£	£	£	£	£	£	£	£	£	£	£	£
Materials	1260	1480	1610	1740	1990	1930	2160	2140	2010	1780	1570	1660	1590
Direct Labour	1870	2140	2160	2260	2540	2340	2520	2550	2400	2690	2500	2560	2480
Overheads	770	820	810	830	960	900	940	950	940	870	800	820	790
Total costs	3900	4440	4580	4830	5490	5170	5620	5640	5350	5340	4870	5040	4860
Output (in tons)	120	150	160	170	200	170	200	200	180	160	140	150	140

The price of materials was increased by 10 per cent at the end of period 5; a wage increase of 20 per cent was given to all employees classified as "direct" at the end of period 9. There have been no other increases in processing costs during the past year.

You have been requested, as divisional accountant, to prepare a flexible budget for the coming year.

You are required to:

(a) describe what calculations you would undertake, using the above information, as a basis for your budget; give your description in sufficient detail for the examiner to carry out the proposed calculations but do *not* carry out the calculations yourself,

(b) explain how you would establish the reliability of the budgetary estimates derived from the calculations, and

(c) discuss the limitations of your method of calculation.

ICAEW(EFD).

15.9 A manufacturing company is introducing a system of flexible budgetary control and wishes to establish a suitable index of activity for its personnel function. Two possible indices have been suggested for this purpose; these and total personnel function costs for last year are shown below:

4-week period No.	Personnel function total costs £	Index No. 1 Total number of employees in the company	Index No. 2 Number of employees engaged and discharged
1	20,785	6,070	251
2	20,038	6,056	224
3	19,844	5,985	213
4	19,714	5,900	204
5	19,250	5,810	186
6	18,664	5,742	165
7	18,508	5,725	156
8	19,656	5,730	182
9	20,142	5,861	190
10	21,015	5,842	208
11	21,709	5,930	221
12	22,527	6,125	237
13	23,632	6,081	260

An index of the change in total costs of the personnel function due to inflation last year was as follows:

4-week period	Index
No. 1	100
2	101
3	102

... and so on to period No. 13 when the index was 112.

You are required to:

(a) (i) advise which of the two indices would be the better as a measure of the activity of the personnel function;

(ii) support your advice with appropriate calculations or other relevant data;

(b) recommend, on the basis of last year's figures, what should be the basis of the flexible budget allowance for the personnel function;

(c) assuming that the personnel function is also a cost centre, explain very briefly the process by which the costs of the personnel function would be absorbed into the cost of the company's products.

ICMA(CA2).

15.10 In cases where sales is the principle budgeting factor the sales forecast is a crucial part of the budgeting process. Frequently firms base their forecast of future sales on some relationship of past sales, which at the simplest level is mere extrapolation. However attempts are often made to refine any such extrapolation by considering the factors which affect the sales of an organisation.

The marketing director of the Four Casts Fishing Tackle Company has found that the sales of his firm can be predicted with some accuracy from:

$$S_{(t+1)} = K (S_t + S_{(t-1)} + S_{(t-2)})$$

where S is the sales figure for a period; t the period just completed; (t − 1) etc. the previous period; and (t + 1) the next period, the one for which the forecast is required. K is some constant which is used to combine the effect of the major variables which affect the company's sales and is itself a function of five variables (v), i.e.:

$$K = f (v_1, v_2, v_3, v_4, v_5)$$

Thus, in simple terms, the next year's sales forecast for the Four Casts Fishing Tackle Company is found from the sum of the last three years sales multiplied by some constant.

The only disadvantage found from this approach is that the constant has to be revised every 3 or 4 years.

Sales for the company over the past 10 years have been increasing as follows: 24; 25; 27; 33; 40; 52; 65; 81; 116; 150.

Required:

(a) Calculate three values for K (working to one decimal place), each of which gives a reasonable forecast of the company's sales for a period during years 4 to 10.

Use these values of K to prepare three sets of sales forecasts for years 4 to 10.

(b) Draw a graph which shows for the last seven years the company's actual sales and the sales forecasts that you obtained in part (a). Comment upon the results.

(c) What sort of factors do you think would go to make up the five variables (v) in the functional relationship which provides the company with its constant K?

(d) Briefly comment upon this method of sales forecasting.

Seminar Problem 15

Lambert Ltd. manufactures and sells a single product. The product is highly perishable and the company keeps virtually no stocks of either the product or raw materials. The company's results during the past 4 years have been as follows:

	1975	1976	1977	1978 (estimated)
Output and sales (units)	18,100	17,500	18,800	19,600
	£	£	£	£
Sales revenue	72,400	78,750	84,600	98,000
Labour	(27,200)	(29,600)	(31,100)	(39,800)
Materials	(13,800)	(14,700)	(16,900)	(20,600)
Overheads	(18,500)	(21,400)	(25,300)	(29,500)
Net profit	12,900	13,050	11,300	8,100

During the last four years material costs have increased steadily at a compound annual rate of 10%, and overhead costs at a compound annual rate of 15%. Wage rates were increased by 10% on 1st January, 1976, and by 20% on 1st January, 1978. During 1979 both material and overhead costs are expected to increase by a further 10%. The company intends to increase wage rates by 15% on 1st January, 1979.

The company is now considering its selling price and output level policy for 1979. Some members of the board of directors believe that the existing selling price of £5 per unit should be maintained. Others favour an increase to £6 per unit, and one member believes that a reduction to £4 per unit would be beneficial. Recent market research information suggests that the likely quantity of the company's product to be demanded during 1979, at each of the three prices mentioned, would be as follows:

Unit selling price	Quantity demanded
£4	34,000
£5	25,000
£6	15,000

You are required to:

(a) use linear regression analysis to estimate the cost-volume relationship of Lambert Ltd for 1979,

(b) advise the directors which of the three selling prices, £4, £5 or £6, they should adopt for 1979, and

(c) discuss briefly the advantages and limitations of linear regression analysis for the estimation of cost-volumes relationships.

Ignore taxation.

ICAEW(EFD).

Chapter 16

Cost-volume-profit analysis

The analysis is used to examine the effect of changes in the variables contained in this profit equation.

Profit = revenue − costs

= sales volume × unit price − (variable and fixed) costs.

It suggests answers to the question − what happens if the price is changed with a corresponding volume change? The analysis can be performed algebraically, but the technique is usually associated with graphical methods and frequently used in presentations to management. Chapter 2 introduced the concept of variable cost and chapter 15 explored ways of estimating cost equations.

The cost-volume-profit relationships will be developed in algebraic terms, first of all.

If V = sales volume in units

and P = selling price per unit

then R = revenue = $V.P.$

If a = estimated fixed costs

and b = estimated variable cost per unit

then C = total cost = $a + b.v.$

Note the assumption that v = volume both of sales and production. This means that nothing has been added to or taken from stock. Other assumptions are also implicitly included in these relationships and these will be referred to later.

Profit = P = $v.p. − (a + b.v.)$

= $(p−b). v − a.$

The expression $(p−b). v$ is the contribution margin of sales less variable costs. $(p−b)$ is the unit contribution margin. Revenue and costs are equal when $P = 0$, that is:

$0 = (p−b). v^1 − a$

$v^1 = a/(p−b)$

v^1 is the break-even volume of sales and production. This reads as the fixed cost divided by the unit contribution margin. In other words, each unit produced and sold is contributing to fixed costs and the break-even point is found by dividing these fixed costs by the contribution each unit is making. The break-even revenue point is obtained by $v^1 p$, which substituting on the right hand side of the equation above, gives:

a. $p/(p-b)$

which can also be shown as:

$$\frac{a}{(p-b)/p}$$

Illustration

A company accountant provides the following relevant details:

Unit selling price   =   £4.50
Unit variable cost   =   £2.00
Fixed cost   =   £5000

The following can be derived from these figures:

unit contribution $(p-b)$ =   £2.50
break-even volume   = $\dfrac{5000}{2.5}$ =   2000
break-even revenue   =   2000 $\times$ £4.50 = £9000.

In this example the missing variable or the unknown, was the volume. Given the linear equation being used, any other variable could have been presented as missing instead of the volume. So, given the volume but missing the selling price per unit, at what price is the break-even point reached:

v = 2000
b = £2.00
a = £5000
v = $a/(p-b)$

rearranging $p = b + a/v$
         = 2.00 + 5000/2000
         = £4.50

Or again, given all the variables except fixed costs, at what level of these would the firm just break-even?

v = $a/(p-b)$
a = $v\,(p-b)$
      = 2000 (4.50 − 2.00)
      = 5000

These algebraic examples demonstrate that under certain assumptions, it is possible to use forecast information to arrive at projected break-even points. These points are valuable landmarks in incremental analysis.

The solutions to the problems posed above can be arrived at graphically and it is graphical representation which is most common in this form of analysis. Certainly, this is a valuable way of communicating the results to decision taking groups.

Figure 16.1 shows two straight line graphs, one of revenue and the other of total costs. The point interraction of these two lines is the break-even point.

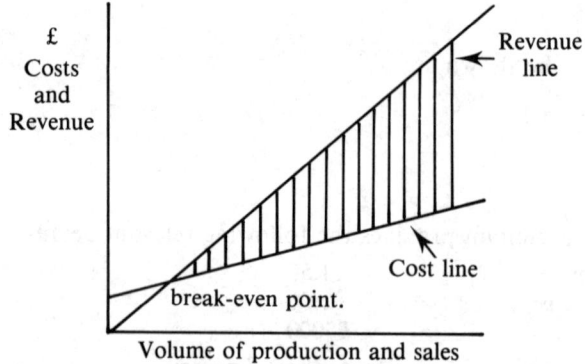

Volume of production and sales

The shaded area to the right of the break-even point represents the profit and the corresponding, unshaded, area to the left represents loss. The amount of profit at any volume of sales and production is given by the distance between the two lines.

As an example of the graphical technique see figure 16.2. The quantities used in plotting the lines are given in the table below and are the same as the ones used in the algebraic solution.

No. of Units	Fixed Cost £	Variable Costs £	Total Cost £	Sales Revenue £
0	5,000	0	5,000	0
1,000	5,000	2,000	7,000	4,500
2,000	5,000	4,000	9,000	9,000
3,000	5,000	6,000	11,000	13,500
4,000	5,000	8,000	13,000	18,000
5,000	5,000	10,000	15,000	22,500

Figure 16.2. Break-even graph.

When other questions are being asked of this simple model slight changes are necessary, but really there is no change in principle. As an example, figure 16.3 shows the effect of changing the selling price to £5 a unit. Apart from this price change, the quantities are the same as for figure 16.2. Reading from 16.2, the new break-even volume of sales and production is 1667.

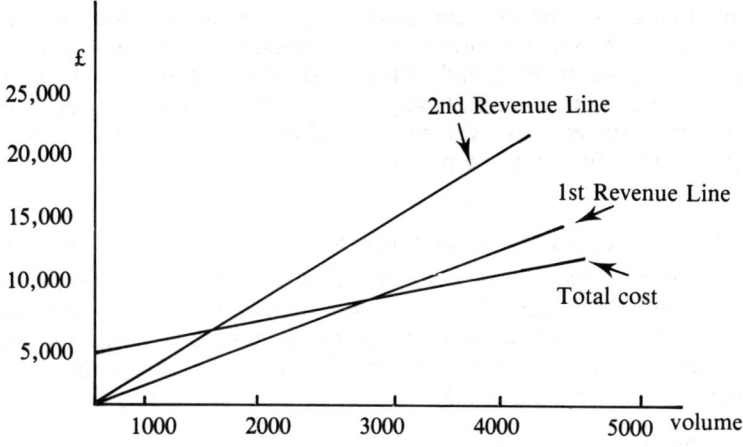

Figure 16.3. Break-even graph with alternative revenue line.

In the same way a graph could be drawn showing alternative cost patterns illustrating the resultant profit changes.

Sometimes it is helpful in arriving at decisions about output to present the figures in a different graph form. The same ones are used again, but this time it shows the average cost curve. See figure 16.4.

No. of Units	Total Cost £	Unit Avg. Cost £	Unit Selling Price £
0	5,000	—	4.50
1,000	7,000	7.00	4.50
2,000	9,000	4.50	4.50
3,000	11,000	3.67	4.50
4,000	13,000	3.25	4.50
5,000	15,000	3.00	4.50

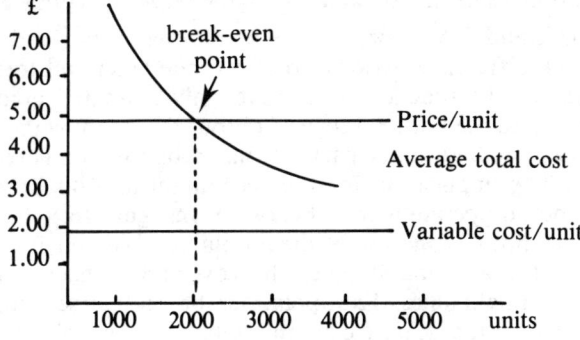

Figure 16.4. Alternative form of break-even graph.

Figure 16.4 shows the same break-even point, as it must since it has been plotted from the same information. As the number of units increases the average total cost will fall and so the curve representing this will approach the variable cost line asymptotically. That is, the average total cost/unit will fall as output increase, but will never equal variable cost/unit since the fixed costs element will always be present.

Break-even Graph and the Economic Model

The break-even graph represented by the accountant can be compared with the economists' model. The differences lie in the nature of the cost and revenue functions. The accountant has taken these to be linear, whereas the economist takes a more realistic curvilinear view. The usual economic model is shown in figure 16.5.

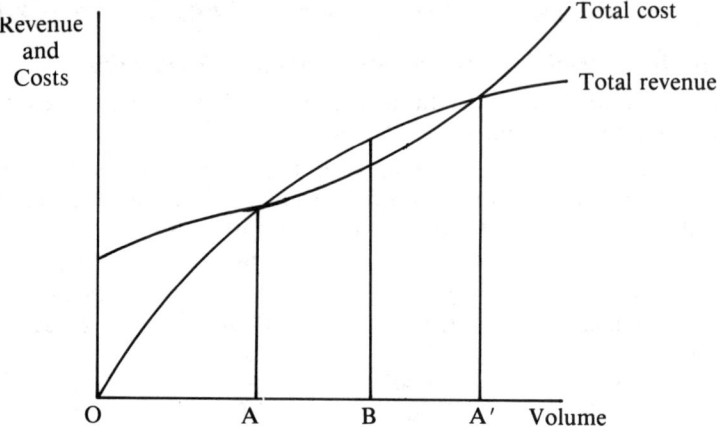

Figure 16.5. The economists' break-even model.

The cost curve shows that over the whole range of production the units cost is dropping until a level of activity is reached, which is sufficiently restrictive as to cause the unit cost to start increasing. The revenue curve reflects that additional sales are obtained at higher levels by reducing prices.

In figure 16.5, OA and OA′ represent the break-even points and OB the point at which the difference between total revenue (TR) and total costs (TC) is a maximum. In practice firms have only a limited amount of information relating to the normal range of output for a firm with its given facilities and it is within these limits that the firms accounting system contains detailed records. The implication for the accountant and his break-even chart is that he should operate within this range. In figure 16.6 the graphs are bounded by the bottom and top of the normal level of activity. Within these boundaries, the accountant takes the cost and revenue curves as approximately to straight lines. Extrapolations beyond these boundaries should be treated with the utmost caution. A break-even point found in such a way may be a best estimate, but it should be treated with little confidence.

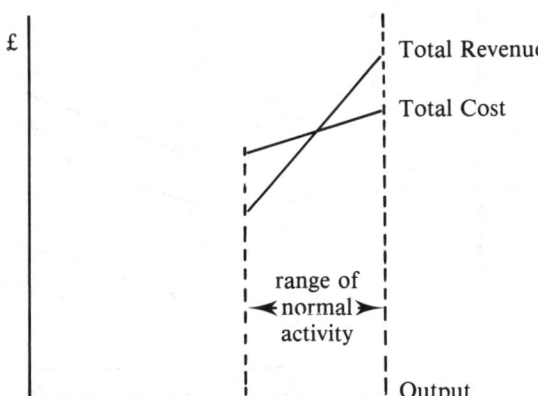

Figure 16.6.

The straight-line representations of the total revenue and total cost curves are approximations of the probably non-linear functions.

Assumptions

The presentation of the information in the manner outlined so far in this chapter, is only valid if certain assumptions are made.

The first of these is that the firm produces one product only or a constant mix of products. This can be relaxed to some extent and this will be done later. Production equals sales, which means either nil or unchanging stock levels. Without this, the analysis is complicated by the graph showing the cost of goods sold based on full average cost.

The graphs show straight lines only, which implies linear relationships. This ignores the fact that price changes are very likely to occur as a direct results of changes in the volume of sales. Similarly, no allowances is being included for changes in the prices of input factors, such as raw materials and wages. Again, the efficiency of the use of these factors may change.

The costs are shown as consisting of variable and fixed types, whereas other, such as step costs, may be present.

Step costs

A further adjustment to the model can be made by recognising that the cost functions may include step costs. As a remainder of what a step cost is, take supervisory salaries is an example. As the number of distinct operators is increased so must the extent of supervision. For more workers there is a need for more supervisors. Within the normal range of activity the need may be for six supervisors (say) at the bottom to ten (say) at the top. Such a situation of the fixed costs containing step costs is depicted by figure 16.7, for which the table of figures is given below:-

No. of Units	Variable Cost	Step & Fixed Costs	Total Cost	Sales Revenue
	£	£	£	£
3,000	6,000	5,000	11,000	12,500
4,000	8,000	6,000	14,000	18,000
5,000	10,000	7,000	17,000	22,500

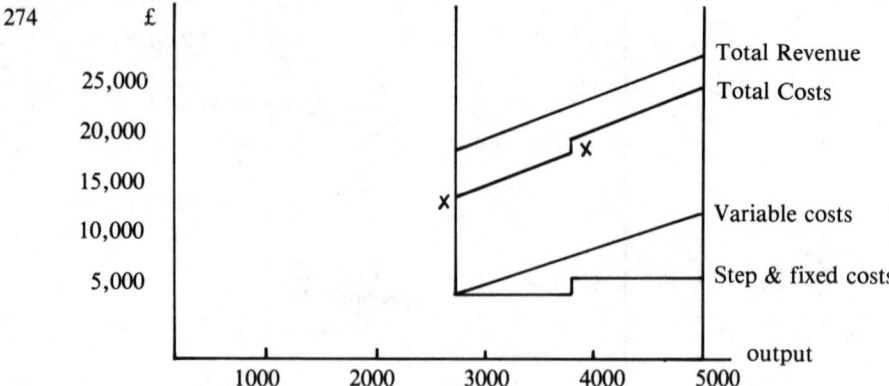

Figure 16.7. Break-even graph with step costs.

With these particular figures there is no break-even point. The firm is always operating at a profit. If this was the case history of a particular firm, it would be tempting to extrapolate the lines to the left in order to find the break-even point. As already stated, such an extrapolation must be viewed with extreme caution, since there are no recorded figures to support the extended lines. The cost behaviour of the firm to the left of the lower bound of production is a relatively unknown thing.

The usefulness of break-even charts

If the assumptions outlined above hold to some reasonable degree, these charts provide a useful means of presenting information. They are very helpful in the process of communicating data which is relevant to decisions about output. The nature of the analysis is clearly very simple, involving no more than the easiest of algebraic manipulation, as was demonstrated in the text.

When the assumptions are not all reasonably acceptable the break-even analysis really becomes inadequate. This particularly applies in the fairly usual situation of the firm which manufactures and sells several products, with possibilities of different sales mixes. Such a firm would have as many break-even points as it would have sales mixes.

Profit-volume graphs

Profit volume graphs can be used as an alternative to cost-volume-graphs and are considered briefly below. Figure 16.8 illustrates.

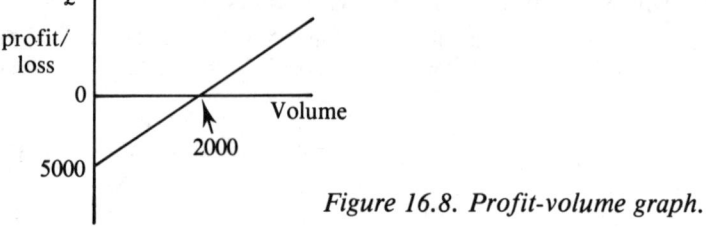

Figure 16.8. Profit-volume graph.

Figure 16.8 shows the Y axis measuring profit/loss and the X axis is volume of production and sales. The cost and revenues given below are reproduced from earlier in the chapter, when they were used to draw the first cost-volume-profit graph. A addition column has been added to show the profit/loss figure at each level.

No. of Units	Fixed Cost £	Variable Cost £	Total Cost £	Sales Revenue £	Profit/ loss £
0	5,000	0	5,000	0	(5,000)
1,000	5,000	2,000	7,000	4,500	(2,500)
2,000	5,000	4,000	9,000	9,000	0
3,000	5,000	6,000	11,000	13,500	2,500
4,000	5,000	8,000	13,000	18,000	5,000

The information about break-even points is now presented by a single line graph, whose slope is equal to the units contribution.

Chapter Summary

As the volume of sales and production increases, the revenue and total costs per unit will be altering. Given knowledge of the alterations, graphs of corresponding revenue and cost functions can be drawn and shown as the break-even model of the firm, according to the economists. In practice these functions are not easily ascertained and the accountant accordingly makes approximations.

The activities of the firm are known to move between upper and lower bands of activity and between these, it is assumed that selling prices and variable costs are constant per unit. This gives a straight line graph, which can be used to portray a very simple picture of the firm. This picture depends on a number of other assumptions, such as single products, no lack of resources, which make for a rather unreal model.

The techniques are worth studying though, because they provide a useful guide to presenting management information and the analysis is a good introduction to decision taking. In the next chapter, consideration is given to the choice between production possibilities where one or more resources are scarce. An understanding of cost-volume-profit relationships is a necessary pre-requisite to this next topic.

Exercises

Questions 16.1-16.5. (Answers provided)

16.1 The Star Product Company manufactures and sells a single product. The unit contribution is shown below:

	£
Selling price	40
Direct materials	15
Direct labour	10
Variable factory overhead	5
Variable selling overhead	3
	33
Unit contribution	7

Fixed overheads are £50,000 factory overhead and £10,000 selling and administration.

Required: calculation of:

a) the break-even point

b) the volume of sales required for profit of £20,000

c) the profit earned at a sales volume of £400,000

d) the increase in the break-even point given a material price increase of 20%.

16.2 The cost accountant of the Express Company has prepared the following estimates for manufacture of a new product at a newly erected factory:

$$\begin{aligned}
\text{raw material cost} &= 15 \times \\
\text{direct labour cost} &= 20 \times \\
\text{factory overhead cost} &= 10 \times + 50,000
\end{aligned}$$

where $\times$ = production in units.

Proposed selling price = £50.

Required:

a) graph the revenue and cost lines and find the break-even point.

b) read off the profit at 15,000 units of production and sales

c) the new break-even point if fixed overheads were estimated to be £70,000 and the selling price were raised to £55.

16.3 The Times Company manufactures card tables which it sells to clubs and retailers at an average price of £10. Variable costs of manufacture are £5 and fixed overheads are £400,000.

Required:

(a) the break-even point at these prices and costs

(b) the company is currently making and selling £54,000 tables which represents 60% of capacity. The sales director maintains that a price reduction of 20% would enable the factory to operate at 100%. Would this be worthwhile?

(c) a large chain store, previously not a customer, has offered to buy 40,000 chairs at £6 each. Should the company accept this offer?

16.4 The Guardian company has the following profit equations:

$$25 \times = 15 \times + 10,000 + I$$

where $\times$ = number of units produced and sold

I = profit

Required: a graph of unit average cost against units produced. Impose the selling prices and find the break-even point.

16.5 The Telegraph company has a cost structure which includes step
cost:

No. of Units	Variable Cost	Step Cost	Fixed Cost
1000	1000	2000	4000
2000	2000	2000	4000
3000	3000	3000	4000
4000	4000	4000	4000
5000	5000	5000	4000
6000	6000	5000	4000

The unit selling price is £3.

Required: the break-even point found graphically.

Questions 16.6-16.10. Answers not provided.

16.6 A company manufactures a range of products which it sells through
manufacturers' agents to whom it pays commission of 20% of the
selling price of the products.

Its budgeted profit and loss statement for 1978 is as follows:

	£	£
Sales		225,000
Production costs:		
Prime costs and variable overhead	78,750	
Fixed overhead	36,250	
		115,000
		110,000
Selling costs:		
Commission to manufacturers' agents	45,000	
Sales office expenses (fixed)	2,000	
		47,000
		63,000
Administration costs (fixed)		30,000
Profit		£33,000

Subsequent to the preparation of the above budgeted profit and loss
statement, the company is faced with a demand from its agents for
an increase in their commission to 22% of selling price.

As a result, the company is considering whether it might achieve
more favourable results if it were to discontinue the use of
manufacturers' agents and, instead, to employ its own sales force.

The costs that this would involve are budgeted as follows:

	£
Sales manager (salary and expenses)	7,500
Salesmen's expenses (excluding travelling costs)	2,000
Sales office costs (additional to present costs)	5,000
Interest and depreciation on sales department cars	3,500

4 salesment at a salary of £4,000 each plus commission of 5% on sales, plus car allowance of 10 pence per mile to cover all costs except interest and depreciation.

On the assumption that the company decides to employ its own sales force on the above terms, you are required to ascertain:

(a) What is the maximum average mileage per annum that salesmen could travel if the company is to achieve the same budgeted profit as it would have obtained by retaining the manufacturers' agents and granting them the increased commission they had requested.

Assume that sales in each case would be as budgeted.

(b) At what level of sales would the original budgeted profit be achieved if each salesman were to travel an average of 14,000 miles per annum.

Assume that all other assumptions inherent in the budgets were maintained.

(c) What is the maximum level of commission on sales that the company could afford to pay if it wished to achieve a 16% increase in its original budgeted profit and expected a 16% increase in sales (at budgeted selling prices) and an average of 16,000 miles per annum to be travelled by each salesman.

(Calculate your answer to one decimal place).

ICMA(CA2).

16.7 A company manufactures three products, X, Y and Z. The budgets are currently being prepared for 1977 and estimates have been submitted for sales, costs and output.

From the data provided below you are required to prepare two statements to show:

(i) the expected profit if the original budget is pursued;

(ii) the expected profit at maximum sales demand.

The standard cost per unit is as follows:

		Product	
X	Y	Z	
	£	£	£
Direct materials: Aye	8	6	6
Bee	2	4	2
Cee	6	2	4
Direct wages	8	10	12
Variable overhead	6	8	8
Fixed overhead	12	15	18

Fixed overhead is absorbed as a percentage of direct wages and is based on the original budget.

	Units	Units	Units
Budgeted output for 1977	8,000	6,000	10,000
Maximum sales demand (estimated)	10,000	7,500	12,500
	£	£	£
Sales price	40	50	60

ICMA(CA1).

16.8 The accountant of XYZ Ltd has produced the following statement of cost and profit for his company's product, the annual production/sales level of which is 50,000 units.

	£
Direct material	25
Direct labour	3
Variable overhead	2
Fixed overhead	5
Profit	15
Selling Price	50

You are required to:

(i) (a) prepare a chart from which the contribution and profit at levels of activity up to 50,000 units per annum, may be read;

   (b) show on your chart any adjustment(s) necessary to reflect an increase of 5% in direct material cost.

(ii) calculate the additional production/sales which would be necessary to maintain the company's annual profit, taking into account the additional cost referred to in (b) above, assuming there are no other changes in costs, or in selling price.

(iii) state and comment upon the assumptions inherent in charts of the type required in (i) above.

CA(AC2).

16.9 A company has decided that its profit on turnover is insufficient and after investigation, has concluded that it must attempt to change its mix of sales.

You are required to:

(a) present on graph paper a profit-volume (P/V) graph to show:

   (i) the results of the budgeted sales mix for the year; and

   (ii) the expected results if the sales mix were changed to that recommended by the sales director;

(b) comment on the results shown on your graph.

Budgeted data for the year:

	£'000
Total budgeted sales value	5,000
Total fixed overhead	800

Sales of individual products

Product	Mix %	Total variable costs £000
W	40	1,500
X	10	600
Y	30	1,200
Z	20	600

Proposed budget for the year:

The sales director is faced with severe competition in his market, so does not believe that he can increase total sales. However, he believes that if he discontinues product X, he can increase sales of the remaining products, so that the original total budgeted sales value would be unchanged. His recommendation is based on an estimate that the sales mix should be:

Product: %

W	40
Y	20
Z	40

ICMA(CA2).

16.10 Part Works Ltd. is a publishing company which specialises in the production of part work publications. The company recently introduced special single publications to enable it to extend the life of some of its more successful ventures. One such publication is to follow on from the extremely successful 'Silver Fingers' part work.

The costing for this single publication, which as yet is unnamed and referred to as Silver Fingers A, is as follows:

(i) Preparation costs, commissioning authors, photographers, composition, blocks, etc, for whatever quantity of the publication is produced, will be £3,000.

(ii) Printing costs £8 per hundred up to 25,000 and then £4 per hundred for any further copies. The reduction in costs coming abour because of less spoilt work and scrapping of paper during longer print runs.

(iii) Binding and other finishing costs £100 per 5,000 whatever quantity is produced.

The publication is to be sold direct to newsagents and similar retailers at a fixed price of 20p each, to retail at a price of 25p.

Required:

(a) A table showing the production costs for 15,000, 20,000, 25,000, 30,000 and 35,000 of Silver Fingers A, together with the average costs per 5,000 copies of each quantity. Show the marginal cost for each increment.

(b) Draw a breakeven chart for the publication and from this derive the breakeven point. Check the accuracy of your graph by calculating the breakeven point.

(c) Part Works Ltd. has already printed 35,000 copies of a publication with similar costs to Silver Fingers A. This has not sold as well as expected and the firm has 10,000 copies left which seem likely to remain unsold. A dealer, who specialises in market trading, offers to buy these for £600. What factors should be considered before deciding whether or not to accept the offer? What difference would it have made if the offer had been for £100?

CA(MA).

Seminar Problem 16

The A.J. Press company manufactures a range of soft drinks. For 19X5 the firm sold 900,000 litres, entirely in 1 litre bottles. Profit was as shown in the statement below:

*Profit and Loss Account for the
year ended 31/12/X5*

		£
Sales (900,000 bottles)		180,680
Cost:		
Raw materials	51,230	
Labour	25,160	
Other materials	30,200	
Manufacturing overhead	25,450	132,050
Gross profit		48,630
Selling expenses	19,240	
Administration expenses	20,160	39,400
		9,230

This profit is poor in comparison with other companies in the same line of business, both in terms of ratio of net profit to sales and return on capital employed.

The general manager is about to start an exercise of information gathering which will help him in planning a campaign to increase profits to around £20,000 per annum. From records of previous years he established a pattern of production and costs. This indicated that the mix of different types of drinks was stable and that 19X5 costs showed no unrepresentative features. The costs could reasonably be analysed into variable and fixed categories, with the following being classed as variable:

Raw materials	100%
Other materials	90%
Labour	50%

All other costs were fixed.

It should be possible to manufacture and sell 1,000,000 bottles without adding equipment or significantly altering unit variable costs or fixed overheads.

Required:

1) draw three charts, each showing production and sales at 1,000,000 bottles and profit at the required level of £50,000, assuming,

   a) that selling prices increase,

   b) that variable costs decrease and

   c) that fixed costs decrease. By how much do these factors change?

2) what assumptions have been made in preparing these charts? How useful are such charts?

Chapter 17

Accounting for Decisions

The relevant costs

The contribution that accountants make to management control systems is not usually in the form required for making decisions. Flexible budgets, variance analysis, unit costs are all required for the on-going control of the firm. When it comes to decisions about production, making or buying components, prices for special orders, buying new machinery and so on, the relevant accounting data emphasizes different features of cost. This chapter examines the nature of these relevant costs.

The question of decision making can conveniently be divided into two sections. Decisions on problems in which there is no capital expenditure required and those concerned with capital outlay. This chapter deals with the former type only and postpones consideration of investment decisions until chapter 19. A further assumption is that no resources are in short supply. This in turn is dealt with in the next chapter.

Costs for Decisions

Decisions are about future courses of action and figures put into the decision making model have to be predictions. These must always be uncertain by their very nature, but predictions can be and so should be, better than mere guesses. Reference to cost trends and changing circumstances in the future all help to improve the quality of forecast figures.

The question to ask about a decision is a simple one. How will this course of action affect future costs and revenues? Will the additional costs involved be greater than or less than the corresponding savings or revenues?

Differential costs

Differential costs are the key. Alternatively they may be referred to as incremental costs. These are the costs which are predicted to occur in the future, given some specified course of action. An illustration of this uses the information given in figure 17.1.

	Present Activity £		Proposed Change £	Incremental Revenue and cost £
Sales:				
$5000 \times £10$	50,000	$4800 \times £12$	57,600	7,600
Variable costs:				
$5000 \times £6$	30,000	$4800 \times £6$	28,800	(1,200)
Contribution	20,000		28,800	8,800
Fixed costs	10,000		10,000	—
	10,000		18,800	8,800

Figure 17.1

The current level of activity is to sell 5,000 units at £10 each. A price increase to £12 is forecast to reduce the demand in terms of units to 4,800, giving sales revenue of 57,600. There is no change in fixed costs and so the differential income forecast for this change is £8,800.

Note that the analysis is based on cost behaviour. The knowledge of how the costs behave in relation to sales is assumed. Without this knowledge there can be no meaningful data. Suppose the accounting model is a full or absorption cost type. Then the normal form of accounting report shown by such a system would give a unit cost of production which included a mix of unsegretated variable and fixed costs.

	Present Activity		Proposed Increase		Differential	
£/units	£	£/units	£	£/units	£	
Sales	10	50000	12	57600	2	7600
Costs	8	40000	8	38400	—	(1600)
Profit	2	10000	4	19200	2	9200

This analysis suggests that the income will increase by £9,200. Because it fails to differentiate between variable and fixed costs, it does not increase the unit share of fixed overheads. Of course, a firm operating full costing would be aware of this and would make the differential analysis according to cost behaviour. The point of the illustration is to emphasize the superiority of the variable cost model in terms of its versatility.

Other cost terms

Opportunity Cost

Since costs constitute a sacrifice of values, they can frequently be regarded as the acquisition price of goods and services, or in the case of depreciation as part of the acquisition price to be set against revenue. Sometimes a different view of cost can be taken. It can relate to some foresaken alternative. That is, it can be an *'opporunity' cost,* which should be considered when evaluating alternatives.

Example

A company warehouse is currently leased for £20,000 per annum and could be used in a project, which is estimated to produce annual profits of £50,000 before rent. Alternatively the warehouse could be sub-let to another firm for £40,000 per annum, with replacement premises available at an annual rent of £30,000. There are two possible courses of action which can be evaluated separately.

1) Accept the project and sub-let

	£
Net revenue after rent	30,000
Rent in-flow	40,000
	70,000
Rent-outflow	30,000
	40,000

2) Reject the project and sub-let:

	£
Net rent-in-flow	20,000

Rather than consider both possiblities in the manner shown, the best result comes from including the opportunity cost.

		£
Net revenue before rent		50,000
Rent of warehouse	£20,000	
Opportunity cost of		
not sub-letting:	10,000	30,000
		20,000

The opportunity cost reveals the net advantage or disadvantages of one choice over another. Here there is a net advantage of £20,000 in favour of accepting the project and sub-letting.

Sunk costs

Occasionally references are made to sunk costs. These consist of expenditure which has taken place in the past and cannot influence the decision under consideration. A common example is the cost of a special investigation to obtain the argument and figures for and against a particular course of action. Such a feasibility study is a *'sunk' cost*. The information given by the study may be relevant, but the cost of the study is not. Consider the following figures as a further example:

Existing plant — cost £1m — running cost £2m per annum.

This plant is no longer adequate and there are alternative ways of providing the necessary increase in capacity.

First — by extending the plant at a cost of £1m and increasing running costs by £½m per annum.

Second — by scrapping the plant and joining a consortium to provide a central capacity covering a wider area. Share of capital cost would be £0.5m with running costs £2.5m.

The cost of the existing plant is totally irrelevant to the decision. Other factors, such as problems which are not quantifiable are matters of policy and may heavily influence the final outcome.

Selling or further processing

In this type of situation a company may be faced with a choice between selling products at a certain stage or processing them more. In this example a company manufactures and sells three products from a joint process. The approach to allocation of the joint costs is to divide them on the bases of market values at the cut-off point.

Product	Production in units	Market Value/unit	Total Market Value	Joint costs
X	1,000	£1	£1,000	£500
Y	2,000	£1	£2,000	£1,000
Z	3,000	£2	£6,000	£3,000

In the case of product Z, this can be sold as shown at a price of £2 per unit. Alternatively, it can be processed further and sold as Z1 at a price of £4. The addition processing cost would be £1,000. The output from the process would be 2 units of Z1 from 3 units of Z.

The figures relating to the new course of action can be expressed as follows:-

		£
Differential revenue:		
Product Z1 2000 × £4		8,000
Product Z		6,000
		2,000
Differential costs:		
Further processing of Z1		1,000
Differential income		1,000

From the figures alone this is a very simple situation. But, as it has been so frequently said before, marketing and other commercial considerations may make it a very difficult one.

It is clear that the joint costs are not relevant.

If only Z1 is produced, then the £6,000 revenue from Z is an opportunity cost. Another way of arriving at the same result is to present both courses of action in full and independently of one another.

COURSE A:

Sell Z.

Predicted Results: £

Sales 6,000

COURSE B:

Sell Z1

Predicted Results:

	£
Sales	8,000
Costs	1,000
Income	7,000

Difference £1,000 in favour of selling as Z1.

The purpose of this second presentation is to demonstrate that by reporting on all available possibilities in this way, opportunity costs are automatically included.

Special Order decision

Many firms find themselves faced with the choice of accepting an order — usually quite significant in quantity — at a special price. The management knows that the firm must cover all its costs and make profits adequate for its finance, if it is to survive in the long run. This means that the prices obtainable for goods must exceed the 'full' costs of production, distribution etc. without regard to whether these behave in a variable of fixed relation to output. Accounting statements with this in view, would take the following from:

A Monthly Statement

	£	£
Sales (10,000 units)		26,100
Costs:		
Raw materials	7,600	
Primary packaging	2,500	
Direct Labour	2,800	
Factory overhead	2,700	
Distribution overhead	3,000	
Selling overhead	4,400	
Administration overhead	400	23,400
profit		2,700

There are no opening and closing stocks. However, suppose that the firm's management have been asked to supply a special order of 1,000 units per month at a price of £2.00. It could be, say, for the packaging of a commodity under a special 'own house' brand name. Clearly, there are many implications here, which will be touched on later. But what are the figures to help the management?

They are not readily available in the statement as shown. On first thought the management could dismiss the request on the grounds that the price tendered is below the full unit cost of production and distribution etc. Selling below unit cost will lose us money, they could argue. Is this true?

The answer cannot be given from the figures provided. A special investigation would be needed to re-present the figures in a new form. The result of such an exercise is now shown:

	Unit Price/ Cost	Total
Production 10,000 units		
Sales	2.61	26,100
Costs: raw materials	0.76	7,600
primary packaging	0.25	2,500
direct labour	0.28	2,800
factory overhead-variable	0.14	1,400
distribution overhead variable	0.16	1,600
selling overhead-variable	0.26	2,600
Total variable costs	1.85	18,500
Contribution margin	0.76	7,600
Fixed costs:		
factory	0.13	1,300
distribution	0.14	1,400
selling	0.18	1,800
administration	0.04	400
Total fixed costs	0.49	4,900
Net profit	0.27	2,700

The variable cost of producing the product is £1.85. Now it is possible to perform the differential analysis for the sale of 1,000 units at £2.00.

		£
Differential revenue	$1000 \times £2.00$	2,000
Differential costs		
raw material	1000×0.76	760
primary packaging	1000×0.25	250
direct labour	1000×0.28	280
factory overhead	1000×0.14	140
distribution	1000×0.16	160
selling	1000×0.26	260
		1,850
Differential income		150

This is assuming:

1) there are no alternative outlets for the additional 1,000 units

2) they can be produced without any change in fixed costs.

The incremental income of £150 is 5% of the original profit and, therefore not merely marginal. It seems a substantial addition to profits. The knowledge contained in the variable statement of costs is of considerable use in making short-run pricing decisions.

Such short-run decisions need to be made when there is spare capacity which cannot be utilised by expanding existing sales outlets. The provision of marginal analysis is an essential part of such a decision-making process.

It is not the only part though. Supplying goods to separate markets at special prices can damage existing customer relationships. Again there may be some 'leakage' between the special market and the main market. These commercial considerations are not quantified in the accountant's analyses, but clearly they cannot be ignored.

In addition to these commercial hazards, firms must avoid an indiscriminate and slavish use of marginal analyses. Too much attention to the marginal cost can reduce the awareness of the need to cover all fixed costs. Special agreements can represent the thin end of the wedge and develop into the standard pattern.

Finally, the ratio of variable costs to output is not constant in practice. In cases of reducing activity this is particularly true, for instance in the case of labour and their redundancy payments. Fixed costs too, are often step costs and have to be looked at carefully.

Notwithstanding these cautions, the use of variable costing is a useful aid to decision-making in the pricing area.

It should be added here that emphasising the role of variable costing in the short-term pricing decision, should not be taken to imply that it is deficient as a guide in the long-run.

Other Areas of Decision-making

Remember that we are dealing with cases in which no investment is involved and in which there are no scarce resources.

Make or buy

Backward integration of production exists to some extent in all firms and expanding or contraction the extent of this is a constantly recurring decision. Should the firm make the component itself or sub-contract the work? Part of the decision information is provided by the predicted incremental costs and it is important to present these correctly.

A firm is considering the possibilityt of sub-contracting the manufacture of component 'X' and the accountant prepares the following statement:

Cost of manufacture:

variable $3000 \times £3$	£9,000
avoidable fixed	2,000
opportunity cost	1,500
	12,500
Cost of buying	11,000
Advantage in buying	1,500

The items in this statement are worth looking at a little more closely. The variable costs have been explained previously. The avoidable fixed costs are ones which bear two distinct characteristics. They are fixed in the sense already explained and they would disappear in the event of sub-contracting the product. They are traceable to the manufacture of 'X' and are not shared costs. The opportunity cost would be the possible benefit of utilising the freed facilities. In the above example, the conditions would be met if 'X' were manufactured and wholly occupied separate premises, which if the circumstances arose, could be sub-let.

Choosing between using these premises for making or buying the component is more than a matter of the figures. It is in fact a complex one of considering many commercial factors. These include the pros and cons of specialist versus integrated firms and the relationship with existing suppliers for other components. A word of caution should also be included about the preparation of the figures themselves. Many firms have found that they have underestimated the cost of manufacture, particularly when the decision concerns a change from buying.

Adding products

Reasons for adding new products to a firm's range are always related to increasing profits or reducing risk. The nature of the addition is influenced by the existing product range. There may be gaps in complementary merchandise or at price levels. The life cycle of the firm's output may be a short one. Provided no investment is required then incremental analysis will provide a solution. The opportunity cost of the resources to be utilised must be taken into account. That is all possible uses for the facilities involved have to be considered.

Assume that a firm has some idle facilities and that it is looking for extra work. An opportunity presents itself in the form of a regular order for 10,000 units/month of a new product 'Y' at a price of £1 per unit. 'Y' can be made without any adaptation, by the other facilities. How should the cost accountant present the figures. By now the pattern should be familiar, since these decisions are made from the basic incremental costs.

Proposal to manufacture 'Y'

	£/unit	£
Cost of manufacture:		
Variable cost	0.75	7,500
Additional fixed overheads		1,500
Opporunity cost		Nil
		9,000
Sales 10,000 at £1		10,000
Contribution		1,000

The opportunity costs are nil because the facilities are idle and there are no other possibilities to be considered. The additional fixed overheads are the other side of the coin where avoidable overheads are concerned. They are in fact, the traceable and unavoidable extras of power and supervisor.

Dropping a Product

Again where no investment, or disinvestment, is involved, incremental analysis will suffice. Remember that the costs must be avoidable if they are included as cost reductions.

As in all other cases, commercial considerations enter the decision-making process. In addition, management have a variety of possiblities before them, ranging from closure thrdugh cost reduction, price change to replacement with a new product.

Suggestions that a product is not sufficiently profitable are often confirmed by the cost accountant's full cost analyses. For example, the product 'Z' has the following performance reported:

Sales:	$1000 \times £2.50$	£2,500
Cost of goods sold:		
Material	$1000 \times £0.50$	500
Labour	$1000 \times £0.25$	250
Variable overhead	$1000 \times £0.25$	250
fixed	$1000 \times £0.30$	300
		£1,300
Selling and administration:		
variable	$1000 \times £1.00$	1,000
fixed	$1000 \times £0.40$	400
		£2,700
Loss		£200

In order to make a more relevant report for the particular decision involved, it is necessary to analyse these expenses to identify how much could be avoided if the product were dropped and also to ascertain whether any other would be incurred. It could be that most of the fixed costs represent shared facilities with other products, manufacturing machinery and regional sales offices for example. An exception amounts to £100. Other variable overheads may be totally avoidable. The new analysis would take this form:

Sales:	£2,500
Variable costs:	
of goods sold	1,000
of selling and administration	1,000
Traceable fixed costs	100
	£2,100
Contribution to shared overheads:	£400

Pricing decisions

Setting the price for a product is a crucial one since it is one of the determinants of profit. In the long run every firm has to cover all its costs including the cost of its capital, if it is to survive. How the price is set is a very complicated process and results from a considerable number of factors. Some firms dominate and are price makers, whilst others are weak in comparison and have to take the price set by others. The level of sales is affected by price, but this is not the only factor which influences the demand for the product. Marketing effort, including notably advertising can play a significant role. So too does the real extent to which competition between firms exists. Although trading agreements are illegal insofar as they restrict competition, it is an accepted fact the the existing level of such competition is far below the level classed as perfect.

Since this chapter is concerned with costs and decisions, it is reasonable to concentrate here on the influence that cost information has on pricing policy. It must be pointed out, right at the start of this section, that there can be no question of setting a price solely in accordance with costs as arrived at by the business itself. Such a policy could lead to immediate failure if the price so determined, were wrong in market terms.

What cost information is of interest to the businessmen when they are reviewing prices and how may it be presented to them? In essence the information can be given in two ways:

1) As a mark up on cost.   2) As a return on investment.

Cost pricing

In turn this can be divided into three categories:

1) full cost

2) conversion cost pricing and   3) variable cost pricing.

By now the student has been introduced to all the costing terminology and it is a simple matter to illustrate these methods. Consider a firm that specialises in the manufacture of dresses. Contracts for specified designs and quantities are tendered for. When a specification is received it is given a price estimate along the following lines:

1) *Full cost*

	£
Materials	5
Labour	7
Factory overheads	5
Factory costs	17
Selling and administration:	
variable	2
fixed	1
Full cost	20
Profit mark-up (60%)	12
Selling price	32

2) *Conversion cost*   £

            Labour   7

            Factory overheads   5

                                            12

            Mark up (100%)   12

                                          24

            Material   5

            Selling and administration   3

            Selling price   32

3) *Variable cost*   £

                material   5

                labour   7

                factory   3

                selling   2

                                    17

            Mark up   15

            Selling price   32

These figures have all been chosen to illustrate that although the basis of each method is distinctive, the extent of the percentage mark-up can be varied to give the same final advisory figure for price. Whether the manager would tender say £30 as his firm's price for the contract would depend on many other considerations, some of which have been mentioned.

Return on Investment

In the example given above the mark-up percentages have been chosen, such that given normal volumes of production, an acceptable return on investment will be achieved. They will be firmly rooted in past experience and regular failure to achieve these percentages are a danger signal.

Arriving at a price from considerations of return on capital, is therefore, related to the previous methods outlined. Starting from the formula:

    Revenue = Total Cost + Profit

and substituting selling price/unit × volume for revenue and target % age × capital employed for profit, gives:

    Selling price × volume = Total Costs + % × capital employed

    Rearranging:

$$\text{Selling price} = \frac{\text{Total costs} + \% \times \text{capital employed}}{\text{Volume}}$$

Example

The company making Flumenite calculates that the cost of a new factory to produce 5m litres of fluid would be £1m. Annual total cost would be £0.5m and the company target rate of return is 10%.

	£(m)
Total cost of production	0.5
Target return on capital invested 10% × £1m	0.1
	0.6

Volume 5m litres
Selling price/litre 0.6/5 = £0.12

The problem with this type of price assessment is the one associated with identifying the quantity of capital employed with the product, since many aspects of capital are shared facilities.

Chapter Summary

The cost information required for helping in the decision making process is not included as part of the regular reporting output from the cost accounting system. Each decision is a unique affair requiring individual analysis. The basic ingredients of relevant reports have been identified in this chapter. These are the incremental revenues and costs which flow from the proposed course or courses of action. The amount of avoidability has to be measured for each cost class and all opportunities have to be incorporated into the analysis.

It has repeatedly been stressed that the cost figures are estimates and therefore, may be treated with appropriate reserve. Even more often, the not so easily quantifiable aspects of decision making have been stressed.

All the examples given assumed that there were no scarce resources and no capital outlays were required. These two major conditions are introduced into succeeding chapters.

Exercises

Questions 17.1-17.5. (Answers provided)

17.1 The Tribune Group of Companies is considering the alternative of buying a sub-assembly at present manufactured in one of its factories.

Total costs for the normal annual total of 50,000 are as follows:

	£
Direct Materials	75,000
Direct Labour	100,000
Variable cost of manufacture	25,000
Allocated share of factory overheads	150,000
	350,000

If the decision be made to buy the sub-assembly it would be expected that 90% of the variable costs and 20% of the fixed costs would be avoided. The quoted price for buying is £5 per unit.

Required: should the sub-assembly be made or purchased outside?

17.2 The Spectator (Spare Parts) Company makes and sells a single product and is currently operating at 60% capacity. Data per unit are:

	£
Selling price	20
Materials	7
Labour	5
Overheads	3

At 60% capacity the firm makes and sells 40,000 units. The overheads not absorbed are written off as a period cost.

An alternative plan for the firm is to take the sub-assemblies a stage further and use all the plant capacity. The new selling price would be £25. Material costs would increase by £1 per unit and labour by £2 per unit. Variable overheads would increase by £0.50 per unit and new quality control staff would cost £10,000 a year.

Required: should the manufacturing process be extended?

17.3 The Statesman (Shirt Manufacturers) has 2000 shirts included in its year end stocks at a cost of £2 each. However, they are of a distinctive style and cannot be sold at the price originally envisaged.

The following courses of action are available:

(a) Restyle the shirts at a cost of £1 each and sell them at their original price of £3.

(b) Restyle the shirts differently at a cost of £2 each and sell them for £4 each.

(c) Sell them as they are for £1 each.

In the case of alternatives (a) and (c) no selling and distribution expenses are involved. In the case of (b) it will be necessary to pay sales commission of 10%.

Which alternative do you see as the most desirable, basing your decision on the figures given only?

17.4 The Punch Company manufacturers a range of cleaning and polishing products. There is spare capacity for a new spray polish to be added to the product range. Estimates of sales volume, price and costs are as follows:

Sales volume	100,000 units
	£
Sales price	0.30 per unit
Direct materials	0.07 per unit
Direct labour	0.10 per unit
Variable manufacturing cost	0.03
Variable selling cost	0.03
Share of fixed cost:	
manufacturing	0.04
selling and administration	0.04

Required: an assessment of the new product's worthwhileness.

17.5 The Listener Company manufacturers hearing aids, operating in a factory with a normal capacity of 100,000 units.

Standard costs are as follows:

	£
Direct material	5.20
Direct labour	7.10
Variable manufacture	2.30
Fixed manufacture	4.00

The budget for the coming year estimates production and sales at 60,000 with fixed selling and administration expenses amounting to £100,000. Selling price is £20 per unit.

Currently, there are buyers from abroad who are negotiating to buy 40,000 units. What is the minimum special price that they can be offered, assuming that such a deal would not damage existing sales? At what price would the company break-even?

Questions 17.6-17.10. Answers not provided

17.6 Ayeco Limited, with a central organisation in Ayetown, has three manufacturing units. One is in Beetown, the second in Ceetown and third in Deetown. The company manufactures and sells an air-conditioner under the brand name of Ayecool at a price of £200. It is unable to utilise fully its manufacturing capacity.

Summarised profit and loss statements for the year are shown below:

	B	C	D	Total
Costs:	£000	£000	£000	£000
Direct materials	200	800	400	1,400
Direct wages	200	900	350	1,450
Production overhead:				
variable	50	300	150	500
fixed	200	600	300	1,100
Sub-total	650	2,600	1,200	4,450

Selling overhead:				
variable	25	200	100	325
fixed	75	250	150	475
Administration overhead	100	450	200	750
Sub-total	850	3,500	1,650	6,000
Central organisation costs	50	200	100	350
Total	900	3,700	1,750	6,350
Profit	100	300	250	650
Sales	1,000	4,000	2,000	7,000

The management of the company has to decide whether, or not, to renew the lease of the property at Beetown, which expires next year. The company has been offered an extension to the lease at an additional cost of £50,000 per annum. This situation concerning the lease has been known for some time, so the accountant has collected relevant information to aid the decision. It is estimated that the cost of closing down Beetown would be offset by the surplus obtained by the sale of plant, machinery and stock.

If Ayeco Limited does not renew the lease of the Beetown property it can:

1. accept an offer from Zeeco Limited, a competitor, to take over the manufacture and sales in the Beetown area and pay to Ayeco Limited a commission of £3 for each unit sold;

2. transfer the output at present made in Beetown to either Ceetown or Deetown. Each of these units has sufficient plant capacity to undertake the Beetown output but additional costs in supervision, salaries, storage and maintenance would be incurred. These additional costs are estimated as amounting yearly to £250,000 at Ceetown and to £200,000 at Deetown.

If the Beetown sales connections are transferred to either Ceetown or Deetown, it is estimated that additional transport costs would be incurred in delivering to customers in the region of Beetown, and that these would amount to £15 per unit and £20 per unit respectively.

You are required to:

(a) present a statement to the board of directors of Ayeco Limited to show the estimated annual profit which would arise from:

(i) continuing product at all three sites;

(ii) closing down production at Beetown and accepting the offer of the sales commission from Zeeco Limited;

(iii) transferring Beetown sales to Ceetown;

(iv) transferring Beetown sales to Deetown.

(b) comment on your statement, indicating any problems which may arise from the various decisions which the board may decide to take.   ICMA(CA2).

17.7 A company located in London acts as a distributor for a range of specialist products that it sells to retailers throughout the United Kingdom.

The products vary considerably, and order from retailers consist typically of a mixture of the products in the range. All despatches are made to retailers by hired road transport.

Hitherto the company has sent goods to retailers without charging for delivery, but due to increases in carriage costs it now proposes to place a bottom limit on free delivery orders. The limit proposed is £20 per order.

Data on the company's products are as follows:

Per Pack

Product	Selling price £	Direct cost £	Weight kilograms
A	1.50	0.75	1.0
B	7.50	5.50	6.0
C	6.50	4.20	13.5
D	15.00	8.50	12.0
E	16.00	11.60	16.0
F	4.50	3.50	4.0
G	3.50	3.00	5.0

Carriage costs per delivery for an average distance of 150 miles, are:

Weight kilograms	Cost £
10 or less	1.3
over 10 but not above 15	1.5
over 15 but not above 20	1.8
over 20 but not above 25	2.0
over 25 but not above 30	2.2
over 30 but not above 35	2.4
over 35 but not above 40	2.7
over 40 but not above 45	2.9

The company is considering making all sales to retailers in the North (200 or more miles from London) through a sub-distributor who has his own sales force. The company would make bulk deliveries fortnightly to the sub-distributor, but would continue to collect payment of accounts from retailers.

You are required to:

(a) show the percentage contribution to sales for each product and rank them in descending order;

(b) calculate, to one decimal place, the profits that would result from each of seven free delivery orders (for an average distance of 150 miles), the first being for £20's worth of product A, the second for £20's worth of B, the third for £20's worth of C, and so on through to the seventh order for £20's worth of G; (N.B. Assume that packs can be split to make a £20 order.)

(c) state for which products £20 would be a suitable limit for free delivery if the company's criterion is that carriage costs (for an average distance of 150 miles) should not exceed one-third of the contribution provided by that product;

(d) list the costs that the company would need to consider if it wished to decide what commission it could afford to pay to the sub-distributor in the North. ICMA(CA2)

17.8 Symbols Ltd manufactures three products, Alpha, Beta and Gamma, the standard costs of which are as follows:

	Alpha £	Beta £	Gamma £
Materials	21	14	21
Labour:			
Machinists*	6	9	3
Assemblers§	3	4	2

The company's fixed overheads for the forthcoming year commencing 1 January 1977 are expected to amount to £100,000.

The marketing direct has estimated that demand for the forthcoming year will be:

Alpha	6,000 at selling price of £50
Beta	10,000 at selling price of £45
Gamma	8,000 at selling price of £40

but the production director has pointed out that machine capacity is currently 88,000 hours per annum, although this will increase to 120,000 hours per annum when the new plant, already on order, is delivered, but this will not be during the year for which the budget is being prepared. However, the production director, anticipating the problem, has located a general engineering firm who are equipped to undertake work of appropriate quality and have quoted the following prices for production of the company's products on a sub-contracting basis:

Alpha	£40
Beta	£36
Gamma	£32

You are required to:

(a) advise the managing director how the services of the sub-contractor should be used to enable Symbols Ltd to meet the expected demand for its products in the most profitable manner, showing full details of the calculation upon which your advice is based;

(b) prepare a statement showing the profit to be expected if your advice is followed; and

(c) briefly explain the reasoning you have applied in making your recommendation.

*Machinists are paid £1.50 per hour.

§Assemblers are paid £1.00 per hour.

CA(AC2).

17.9 The Holee College teaches wholly through the correspondence method. This is done by the production of self-study packs which enables students to prepare for professional qualifications.

Each course of study was sold at the price of £15 last year and a total of 10,000 units were produced and sold. The production costs of the various courses offered by the College are the same.

The variable cost of producing a study course last year was:

	£
Direct materials	5.00
Direct labour	6.00
Other direct costs (mainly postage)	0.60
Variable overheads	0.40
Total variable cost	£12.00

The fixed overhead for the Holee College during the year was £20,000. During the coming year the costs of the organisation are expected to increase by the following:

	%
Direct materials	20.00
Direct labour	16.67
Other direct costs	67.00
Variable overhead	25.00
Fixed overhead	5.00

Market research has shown that when the company increases the price of its courses to its students, as long as the increase is kept below 17.5% this is unlikely to have an effect on the number of units sold. However, for every 1% prices are raised above a 17.5% increase, the number of units sold can be expected to fall by 2%.

Requried:

For the coming year:

(a) The selling price of the study courses if the number of study courses sold and the annual profits are to remain as before.

(b) The number of units that the organisation would have to sell if it did not change the price charged for these, but maintained the profit level attained in the previous year.

(c) A brief analysis of a situation where, when prices are changed the number of units sold is affected. The data provided in the above example can be used to illustrate your analysis.

CA(MA)

17.10 Asp Limited manufactures a simple garden tool. At present the company is working at full capacity producing the three components A, B and C, one of each being required for the assembly of the tool. All the machines are capable of making all the components. Current cost data concerning one hundred tools are as follows:

	Machine hours £	Variable £	Cost Fixed £	Total £
Components—A	10	26	10	36
—B	16	32	12	44
—C	20	32	32	64
Assembly	—	52	22	74
	46	142	76	218
Selling price				250

The management is engaged in preparing next year's budget and an increase in sales is to be provided for. The factory is already having to work at full machine capacity to meet current demand and no increase in the present machine capacity can be effected for over twelve months, though facilities involving variable costs can be increased at very short notice. It is decided that one of the components will have to be bought out. The following quotations have been received:

Component	£
A price per 100 tools	36
B price per 100 tools	46
C price per 100 tools	54

The sales manager feels sure that he can sell at least 50% more tools than at present and probably 75% more provided the factory capacity is available.

You are required:

(a) to prepare a report for management giving your recommendation as to which component should be ordered from outside suppliers for the coming year if production is increased by 50% and 75% respectively, and

(b) to explain the assumptions underlying your report.

ICAEW(MA).

Seminar Problem 17

J. Weeks and company maintains as part of its business, a small department specialising in the manufacture and maintenance of highly specialised drums used in distributing a substantial quantity of the firm's output.

The departmental cost statement for the year ended 31-12-X5 is shown below:

	£	£
Materials		9,000
Labour		12,000
Overheads:		
manager's salary	5,000	
rent	1,000	
depreciation-machinery	1,000	
maintenance of machinery	1,500	
miscellaneous	700	9,200
Share of general administration		2,000
		32,200

The General Manager has been considering the possibility of subcontracting the work. He has just received a quotation from an independent company, which is willing to provide the necessary number of drums for an annual sum of £20,000. There will be an additional and separate contract to maintain the drums for £5,000 per annum.

A decision has to be made from three possible courses of action.

Required:

1) identify the possible courses of action

2) assess the cost of each course. In order to do this, examine each cost and discuss its relevance. Finally make an assumption about each cost and base your figures on these assumptions

3) what other considerations would you apply to the decision?

Chapter 18

Accounting for decisions — the problem of scarce resources

The central problem for all organisations is to obtain the best output from a given set of inputs, whilst at the same time being conscious of constraining influences and developing a policy to deal with them. How to make the most efficient use of the resources available, which comprise a wide ranging group of assets and human skills. These available resources are capable of being used in production and other functions in so many combinations that the search for the most efficient way assumes complex proportions.

This chapter introduces a technique which can help in this search for efficiency, but which does not provide all the answers to management problems. Linear programming is a mathematical approach for determining the best way of using scarce resources in combination. The principles of the problem solving technique will be examined, but students should refer to more specialised literature, if they wish to study linear programming to a more advanced level.

A preliminary illustration

Here are production costs for simple situation involving two products X and Y. Assume that the firm can sell all that it can make and there are no long term problems or product interdependencies.

	X	Y
	£	£
Selling price/unit	20	10
Variable cost/unit	18	9
Contribution	2	1
Labour hrs/unit	4	1

The total of labour hours available is 400. This labour force is easily switched from one product to the other and the same machines can be used. The factor limiting output is the availability of labour hours. All other factors are present and in no shortage in relation to the output capacity of the existing labour force.

Given all these assumptions, it is a very simple matter to plan the production in order to maximise the contribution to overhead and profit. Limiting manufacture to units of Y gives a total contribution of $400 \times £1$, whereas concentrating entirely on X gives $400/4 \times £2$ equals £200 contribution.

In this case there is only one input limiting production, that is the quantity of labour. The best plan is to be obtained by ranking the products in terms of contribution per unit of the limiting factor. Here this gives £2/4 = 0.50p for X and £1/1 = £1 for Y. Y. ranks higher than X, therefore concentrate production on Y.

An Extended Illustration

The extension is to increase the number of inputs that are scarce up to two. Now the rule of ranking the products in terms of contribution per unit of limiting factor of input no longer applies.

Some figures are needed with which to explain the points under discussion.

	Product	
	X	Y
	£	£
Selling price	34	25
Variable costs		
Material	4	5
Direct labour	20	10
	24	15
Contribution	10	10
Number of components/unit	4	5
Number of labour hours/unit	20	10
Total number of components available	= 100	
Labour hours available	= 320	

The figures relate to a small manufacturing unit that can make and sell products X and Y. The sales of X and Y at the prices shown are limited by the quantities produced. In turn production is limited by the scarcity of components and labour. The problem is to establish what production of X and Y will give the optimum result.

The costs shown as variable have been specially computed for the purpose of this product decision. So, for example, the labour force does not have special skills such that it would be undesirable in slack periods to dispense with their services, on the grounds that it may be difficult to re-engage them when demands improved. (Since the example is dealing in a simple situation a simple view of labour relations may be taken).

There are two scarce resources comparied to one in the previous example. Is it possible to decide on a production mix which looks reasonable, based on some information about contribution? For each scarce resource the contributions are as follows:-

	Components	Labour Hours
	Contribution/unit	Contribution/unit
X	£10/4 = £2.5	£10/20 = £0.5
Y	£10/5 = £2.0	£10/10 = £1.0

Unfortunately this does not help. Making X's seems advantageous from the point of view of utilising available components, since each component used in X manufacture contributes more than if used in manufacturing Y.

Looking at labour though, suggests making Y as being the better course of action, because each labour hour utilised making Y contributes £1.0, against £0.5 for X.

The solution would appear to be some combination of X and Y rather than making all X or all Y. This solution is to be found by using the mathematical technique of linear programming.

A Graphical Solution

The problem is to maximise the contributions from production of X and Y. That is maximise

$$Z = 10X + 10Y$$

where X and Y are the number of units produced of products X and Y respectively and each unit contributes £10 to fixed overheads and profit.

Z is referred to as the objective function which is to be maximised. This is a simple mathematical expression of what is to be done.

There are constraints on manufacture which can also be expressed in mathematical terms. For components

$$4X + 5Y \leqslant 100$$

which simply expresses that components used cannot exceed 100.

For labour

$$20X + 10Y \leqslant 320$$

which does a similar thing for labour hours which are limited to 320.

Bringing these relationships together, gives:

$$
\begin{aligned}
\text{maximise} \quad & Z = 10X + 10Y \\
\text{subject to} \quad & 4X + 5Y \leqslant 100 \\
& 20X + 10Y \leqslant 320 \\
& X \geqslant 0 \\
& Y \geqslant 0
\end{aligned}
$$

These last two simply state that the solution must express X and Y as zero or positive numbers.

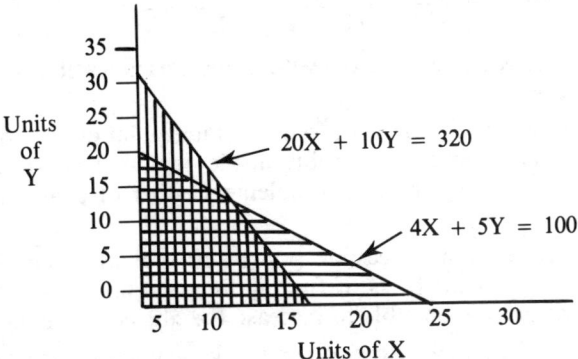

First, imagine that there are no constraints. Any part of the space could be chosen to give a combination of X and Y and, no matter where, such a combination could be improved upon. But the terms of the problem are that constraints exist. These are expressed by the relationships given above.

Components available for a period cannot exceed 100. As far as possible the object is to utilise all available inputs, so think in terms of:

$$4Y + 5Y = 100$$

that is take the upper boundary of the equality rather than the range offered by the inequality. This is drawn on the graph as shown.

Since all negative solutions are excluded, the required answer must be within the area shaded horizontally. This is the area bounded by:

$$X = Y$$
$$Y = 0$$
$$4X + 5Y = 100$$

For example $X = 20$, $Y = 15$ lies outside the area. This would require $20 \times 4 + 15 \times 5$ components, which equals 155, that is well more than the number available.

The constraint for labour is:

$$20X + 10Y = 320$$

This is also drawn on the graph. The area which is feasible for the solution is now reduced to the common part, which is shaded both horizontally and vertically. This is reproduced below:

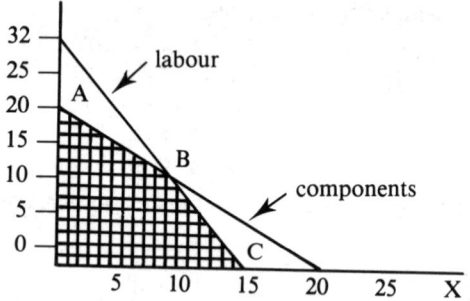

Any combination of X's and Y's from within this area is feasible and could provide the solution.

The optimal solution, though, is to be found at some point on the boundary of the feasibility area: since any point inside represents a production schedule which is not using the full complement either of components or labour hours.

A process of starting at any feasible point and moving from there to improved answers forms the basis of finding the solution. At the optimal combination it will not be possible to increase the objective function.

As a start, consider the possible solution given by the point at the origin. Its practical interpretation is to do nothing and this is certainly feasible, but is it optimal or could it be improved upon? Certainly it can, either by making Y's only or by making X's only. In either case each unit produced contributes £10 to fixed overheads and profit.

If the decision is to make Y's, then this means choosing points on the Y axis by moving upwards until a limit is reached. This limit is given by running out of available labour or components. In this case it will be the components; when 20 Y's at 5 a unit will use up all the available component supply. This is the point A on the graph.

Next move down towards the point B. This is the component constraint line. It represents all the combinations of X and Y which use a 100 components. As progress is made along this line components are being transferred from the manufacture of Y to the manufacture of X.

At the start of this process there are:

Y	X	Contribution	Components used
20	0	£200	100

transferring one component gives

Y	X	Contribution	
		£(198 + 2.5)	$19.8 \times 5 + 4 \times 0.25$
19.80	0.25	= £200.5	= 100

for the same number of components there has been an increase in contribution. Each transfer of one component increases the total contribution by £0.5. This is difference between the contribution per unit of component to X (£2.5) and to Y (£2.0) (See above).

The point B represents the end of that part of the component constraint line that forms part of the feasible solution. The next step is to move along the labour constraint line, so transferring units of labour from production Y to X. Each unit transferred reduces the total contribution by £0.5. This time because the contribution per unit of labour is less when producing X than when producing Y. Progress along this line until C is reached.

From the point C, it is only feasible to reduce the production of X, production of Y being zero. This returns to the point of origin, reducing the total contribution all the way.

The maximum contribution was at the point B. At that point on the boundary of the feasibility area which best combines the uses of available labour and components.

At point B, $X = 10$ and $Y = 12$, giving $Z = £220$.

The iso-contribution line

As an alternative the solution point can be found graphically by introducing a set of parallel iso-contribution lines. These lines give the same contribution from any point on them, that is from any combination of X and Y satisfying the line equation. All that is needed is the largest contribution given by any isocontribution line within the feasible solution area.

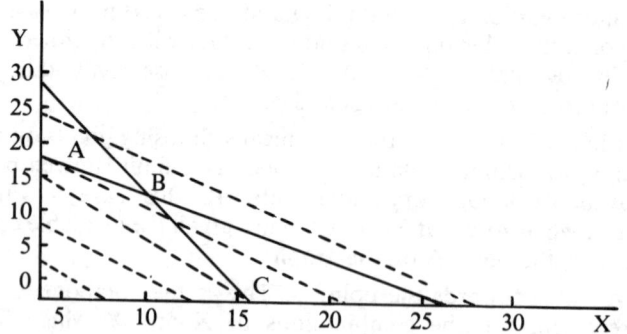

Choose a small contribution first say £50 provided by production of 5 units of Y and 0 units of X. Insert in the equation:

$$Z = 10 X + 10 Y$$

gives $Z = 50$.

Similarly 0 units of Y and 5 units of X produce $Z = 50$. These two points (0, 5) and (5,0) identify a line which always gives a contribution of £50.

The graph given above shows a series of such lines drawn parallel to each other and moving away from the origin. The lines are parallel because they are all given by the equation:

$$Z = 10 X + 10 Y$$

where Z is given increasing values. The gradient of the line is -1 given by regrouping the variables:

$$Y = -X + 0.1 Z$$

Some of the lines shown are entirely within the feasible region, others are partly in it and the remainder lie entirely outside. The line which satisfies the tests of largest contribution and being within the feasible range, is the one which touches the boundary tangentially. In the example that would be at B.

If the tangential line coincides with one of the boundary lines, then there would be a series of solutions.

Alternative Methods of Solution

The illustrative problem used in this chapter has been, naturally enough, a simple one. It was solved graphically, because this treatment analyses the problem and leads to the appropriate problem solving technique. As a further alternative, algebraic methods could have been used. The object is to maximise $Z = 10 X + 10Y$

subject to:

$$4X + 5Y \leqslant 100$$
$$20X + 10Y \leqslant 320$$
$$X \geqslant 0$$
$$Y \geqslant 0$$

It has been established that the solution for X, Y giving a maximum Z, lies on the boundary of the feasible area. The problem then is to establish which point by solving four pairs of equations and testing the resulting value for Z.

The four corners of the feasible solution area are given by solving the appropriate pairs of equations;

0 is given by $X = 0$,

$\quad\quad\quad\quad\quad Y = 0$

$\left.\begin{array}{l} \end{array}\right\}$ $X = 0, Y = 0$

A is given by $X = 0$

$\quad\quad 4X + 5Y = 100$

$\left.\begin{array}{l} \end{array}\right\}$ $X = 0, Y = 20.$

B is given by $4X + 5Y = 100$

$\quad\quad 20X + 10Y = 320$

$\left.\begin{array}{l} \end{array}\right\}$ $X = 10 \ Y = 12$

C is given by $20X + 10Y = 100$

$\quad\quad Y = 0$

$\left.\begin{array}{l} \end{array}\right\}$ $X = 5 \ Y = 0$

substituting these point in turn into $Z = 10X + 10Y$, gives the maximum value for X at the point B. At the origina $Z = 0$, at A $Z = 200$, at B $Z = 220$ and at C $Z = 50$.

Thus, a simple problem can be solved graphically and algebraically. However, the important point to be made is that as the number of unknowns grows beyond two, there must be a move from graphical solutions to more advanced mathemtical methods. The most well known of these is the simplex method and the interested student is recommended to consult a suitable elementary text dealing with such techniques.

Assumptions

A mathematical programming technique used to solve problems of this nature, needs data which is precisely formulated. In order to give such input, it is usually necessary to make assumptions.

In this case assumptions have been made about the linearity of selling price and costs, about the split between variable and fixed costs, about the constraints, about the division of X and Y into fractional parts and about the relationship between X and Y.

The assumptions about sales are that all output can be sold at the price quoted; but the optimal solution may involve quantities to be offered for sale which would require some flexibility in pricing. The same with costs. As production schedules increases there is a possibility that the unit cost will rise, implying a non-linear relationship. In the opposite way, there may be savings on material costs as a result of larger orders being placed. Linearity also implies a constant level of efficiency in terms of output per unit of material, labour and overhead put in.

The division between variable and fixed costs has been examined in Chapter 14. There it was seen that the division was not an easy matter and could be blurred through lack of adequate quantitics of data. There is no provision for steps costs in the solution, but, in practice, it may be necessary to do something about these. This would be in cases where the solution range included a break in step costs. The problem could be solved with a maximum output equal to the top limit of the step cost and then solved again wtih the next pair of limits. Solutions would be adjusted manually for the step costs.

The constraints used in the problem are given as fixed, but, once again, this is an assumption which is not totally realistic. By organisational means and by paying different prices for the inputs, it is possible to alter these constraints.

Solving the problem in the way shown, admits the possibility of producing and selling fractional parts. In most manufacturing situations this is a harmless if wrong assumption. Where large numbers of units are the norm, it is a simple matter to round off the answer. In cases of small numbers, rounding off may not give a reasonable approximation to the optimal result. Such cases call for special methods.

Lastly, in the section about assumptions, there should be mention of the possibility of interdependence between X and Y. They may be complementary products for example, such that it would not be feasible to vary the proportions of X and Y production beyond a certain range. As with the question of whole number solutions, this interdependence between X and Y requires special methods.

Although a lengthy catalogue of limitations can be drawn up, linear programming is still a very powerful decision-making aid. It is being used more and more in business to-day. This is because there are many cases where the assumptions dealt with in the text above, apply within reasonable degrees of tolerance.

Finally, it is often said of decision models that they are of little value because of the uncertainty of future events. One way of takling this problem is to perform a sensitivity analysis. This gives the effect of changing input figures on the optimum result. It will show up which estimates need to be considered with more care. In linear programming this type of analysis is easy to undertake once the basic model has been formulated and set up for solving. It simply required a re-run with alternative figures.

Dual or Shadow Prices

These synonymous terms represent the marginal contribution to fixed costs and profit, made by each resource. The dual (or shadow) prices is the amount by which total contribution would rise or fall if one unit of a scarce resource were added or removed.

In the problem previously discussed the available number of components was 100 and of labour hours 320. The dual prices of these resources will be calculated and their significance discussed.

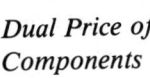 *Dual Price of Components*

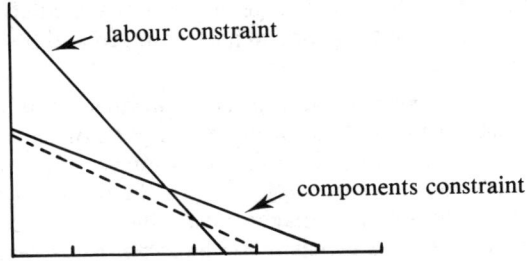

The dash line represents the downward movement of components to 99. It has not been drawn to scale and so no units are shown on the axes. The new optimal solution is given by the intersection of

$$4X + 5Y = 99$$
$$20X + 10Y = 320$$

giving

$$X = 11.67$$
$$Y = 10.17$$

and

$$Z = 10X + 10Y = 116.7 + 101.7 = 218.4$$

The original solution to the problem was $Z = 220$. So the dual price of one unit of component is £(220 − 218.4) = £1.16.

Dual Price of Labour

Keeping components at availability 100 and reducing labour to 319, gives these two equations as the solution.

$$4X + 5Y = 100$$
$$10X + 10Y = 319$$

giving

$$Y = 12.07$$
$$X = 9.92$$

and

$$Z = 120.7 + 99.2 = 219.9$$

The dual price of one unit of labour hours is £(220 − 219.9) = £0.1.

The Use of Dual Prices

The dual price is the amount by which the contribution changes according to unit changes in resources. If one additional component comes available it can contribute £1.6 to fixed costs and profits. It should not be used on activities which produce less than this figure, unless there are clear reasons resulting from other policy.

A dual price is the excess of the internal over external opportunity cost. The wage and related expense is the external opportunity cost. The dual price represents the maximum amount a firm is willing to pay for one extra unit.

The dual price can be used as an indicator of which resources are constraints to be relieved. Such relief will increase contribution per unit of input added. But in each case a point will be reached when the resource is no longer a constraining one. Once a change in resource available is greater than marginal, the terms of the problem have changed and the original dual price no longer applies.

Sometimes a firm has arrived at a set of production decisions based on an L.P., but wishes to give some autonomy to parts of the organisation. It can do this by charging the division (or whatever segment of the firm is involved) with the full opportunity cost of the resources granted to it. This means that the divisional manager most adhere to the original plan or use the resources at least as efficiently if he is not to be reported as failing to cover all the costs. In this way the sub-optimal use of resourcecs is reduced.

Chapter Summary

When the accountant is providing data for managerial decisions, he should be aware of the type of decision making model that is being used. In this chapter there has been an emphasis on the problem involving scarce resources.

If one resource is in short supply, it is a simple matter to rank the products in terms of contribution per unit of the limiting factor. However, this fails to provide a solution when there are two or more constraints. It is then necessary to set out the problem as shown and employ more sophisticated mathematical models. The basic idea of linear programming has been explained, but for more information about methods such as the simplex, it is necessary to consult some appropriate text on analytical techniques.

Dual prices were explained as the marginal contribution to fixed costs and profit, made by each resource. One advantage of the simplex method is that it automatically gives the dual prices as part of the solution.

Exercises

Questions 18.1-18.6. (Answers provided)

18.1 Mr. Green operates a small business turning out two product based on different mixes of three basic materials.

	Product		Material available
Material	X	Y	
1 (units)	3	2	90 units
2 (units)	4	5	150 units
3 (units)	1	3	60 units

Profit contribution for X is £1.00 per unit and for Y £1.50 per unit. Calculate the mix to maximise profit.

18.2 The Black and White Games Company manufactures two similar games using the same materials. Contributions and limiting factors are set out below:

	Game	
	1	2
Material (£)	2	3
Labour (£)	4	3
Labour hours	4	3
Labour available =		420
Machine hours	1	2
Machine hours available		150
Selling price (£)	12	12

Required: the maximum contribution obtainable.

18.3 Brown and Company manufactures two products, one a deluxe version of the other. They involve two simple processes of Wedging and Squedging.

	Process time in hours		Product
	W	S	cost/unit
Standard	1¼	1	15
Deluxe	1¼	2	20

An agreement with labour stipulates that at least 2000 hours operating time must be applied to each process. There is one regular contract for 1000 units of the standard version which must be met. Any other production can be sold.

Required: the *minimum cost* at which these requirements may be met.

(Hint — the feasibility polygon is now to the right of each line).

18.4 Francis Grey runs a small company with the following production model:

	Process		
	X	Y	Available
Input 1	3	2	300
Input 2	6	8	960
Input 3	4	8	800

The unit contributions are X£4 and Y£3.

Required: the dual prices for inputs 1, 2 and 3. What is their significance?

18.5

Labour type	Product X	Y	Z	Available man-hours/ period
A	1	3	3	3600
B	2	2	2	2800
C	2	2	1	3000
selling price	£9.00	£11.00	£10.00	per unit
total variable cost	£7.16	£9.34	£8.65	per unit

Fixed cost for the period are expected to be £2,900, including £1,000 for depreciation of machinery used in the manufacture of X and Y. Labour costs/hour are £2.00, £2.10, and £2.20 respectively for A, B and C.

Required: formulation of the linear programming model. (Do not solve).

Questions 18.6-18.10. Answers not provided.

18.6 Industrial Fitments Ltd. Product three types of shelving viz 'Factory', 'Stores' and 'Office', which are made from the same basic material, viz. mild steel, which costs £1 per square metre. The standard unit cost of the three products are as follows:

	'Factory' p	'Stores' p	'Office' p
Direct material:			
Mild Steel	84	78	75
Attachments	14	25	30
Direct labour:			
Machining	10	15	19
Spraying	4	7	6
Unit selling prices are:	175	186	190

Sales expectations for the forthcoming month are:

	Units
'Factory'	2,000
'Stores'	2,400
'Office'	1,600

Owing to an industrial dispute, suppliers of mild steel have intimated that they will be able to supply only 2,500 square metres during the month.

You are required to:

(a) prepare a statement which will enable you to advise management on the most profitable production pattern to pursue;

(b) mention briefly the matters which should receive the attention of management when confronted with the type of situation described above.

CA(AC2).

18.7 For LP Limited the following data are relevant to its products L and P:

	Product L	Product P
Per unit	£	£
Selling price	200.00	240.00

	Product L	Product P
Costs:	£	£
Direct materials	45.00	50.00
Direct wages:		
Department: 1	16.00	20.00
2	22.50	13.50
3	10.00	30.00
Variable overhead	6.50	11.50

Fixed overhead is budgeted at £275,000 per annum.

Relevant data for each department are:

	Number of employees	Hours per employee per week	Wage rate per hour £
Department: 1	20	40	2.00
2	15	40	2.25
3	18	40	2.50

In the present environment, it is not possible to engage any more employees.

You are required to:

(a) show mathematically the objective function and the constraints;

(b) show on a graph the mix of products which will optimise the contribution of LP Limited;

(c) state the production required to obtain the largest contribution and the amount of that contribution.

ICMA(CA2).

18.8 A factory owned by your company consists of two departments: 1. machining and 2. finishing. Two products, X and Y, are manufactured. The sales mix of the products has in the past varied considerably with demand but currently there is little difficulty in selling output irrespective of the available mix. However, serious difficulties are now being experienced in the supply of raw materials for product Y and the result is that production of Y will have to be limited to a maximum of 1,800 units per week.

The maximum output from each department per week is as follows:

Department 1 (machining)   4,000 units of product X, or 2,000 units of product Y, or a proportionate mix of both products.

Department 2 (finishing) 2,400 units of product X, or 4,000 units of product Y, or a· proportionate mix of both products.

Financial data are as follows:

		£
Selling price, per unit:	Product X	18.00
	Product Y	20.00
Variable costs, per unit:	Product X	16.00
	Product Y	17.50
Fixed costs	£1,200 per week.	

You are required to prepare:

(a) a graph illustrating the various constraints on production;

(b) a weekly profitability statement to indicate the production mix producing most profit. Workings should be shown.

ICMA(MA1).

18.9 Alfred Ltd is preparing its plans for the coming month. It manufactures two products, the flaktrap and the saptrap. Details are as follows:

Product	flaktrap	saptrap	Price/wage rate
Amounts per unit:			
Selling price (£)	125	165	
Materials used (kg)	6	4	£5 per kg.
Labour hours—skilled	10	10	£3 per hour
—semi-skilled	5	25	£2 per hour

The Company's overhead recovery rate is £2 per hour (for both skilled and semi-skilled labour) of which £1 relates to variable costs and £1 to fixed costs. The supply of skilled labour is limited to 2,000 hours per month and the supply of semi-skilled labour is limited to 2,500 hours per month. At the selling prices indicated, maximum demand for flaktraps is expected to be 150 units per month and maximum demand for saptraps is expected to be 80 units per month. The directors of Alfred believe that demand for each product could be increased by advertising.

You are required to:

(a) find the product mix which will maximise Alfred's profit,

(b) find the maximum monthly expenditure on advertising which would be worthwhile if it increased the demand for flaktraps by 50 units per month, and

(c) explain the meaning of the expression "dual price" (or "shadow price") and comment briefly on the usefulness of a knowledge of dual prices.

ICAEW(EFD).

18.10 A company has an assured market for any quantities of two products, which are processed on one machine and then finished by hand. The products are not complementary and may be produced independently in varying quantities. Planned output is 600 units per week of each product, a combination chosen because it fully utilises machine and labour capacities. Maximum utilisation is the rule-of-thumb strategy used by the management as most likely to yield maximum profit.

Machine capacity is 1,200 units per week of either product or a combination of the two; no time is lost in changing over from one product ot the other. Machine operators cannot be discharged and their wages are included in fixed overhead. Finishing-labour supply is limited to 2,400 direct hours per week. Finishing labour is a fixed cost in the short run as no other work is available if machine output is delayed for any reason. Standard product costs and selling prices are as follows:

	Product A	Product B
	£	£
Standard product costs:		
Materials	2	2
Finishing labour—£3 per hour	9	3
Fixed overhead—⅓ labour cost	3	1
	14	6
Selling price	16	8

Last week the factory manager scheduled production of only 500 units of each product, as an overhaul of the machine, which would reduce available machine capacity to 1,000 units, was unavoidable. As a result, the finishing staff was idle for most of one day while the operators carried out the overhaul.

You are required:

(a) using graphical methods, to show
   (i) whether the normal rule-of-thumb strategy optimises contribution to profit, and if not what strategy would do this;
   (ii) how many units of each product would have optimised contribution to profit during the overhaul; and

(b) to calculate
   (i) standard net profit under the optimum strategy you recommend in (a) (i);
   (ii) how much, if any, contribution to profit was lost by the factory manager's decision on product mix during the overhaul.

ICAEW(MA).

Seminar Problem 18

Annapurna Ltd is drawing up production plans for the coming year. Four products are available with the following financial characteristics:

Product	A	B	C	D
Amounts per unit:				
Selling price	£55	£53	£97	£86
Cost of materials	£17	£25	£19	£11
Labour hours—Grade A	10	6	—	—
—Grade B	—	—	10	20
—Grade C	—	—	12	6
Variable overheads	£6	£7	£5	£6

Fixed overheads of the firm amount to £35,500 per annum. Each grade of labour is paid £1.50 per hour but skills are specific to a grade so that an employee in one grade cannot be used to undertake the work of another grade. The annual supply of each grade is limited to the following maximum: Grade A, 9,000 hours; Grade B, 14,500 hours; Grade C, 12,000 hours. There is no effective limitation on the volume of sales of any product.

You are required to:

(a) calculate the product mix which will maximise profit for the year and state the amount of the profit (you may use a graphical method, the simplex method or any other method which gives the optimum);

(b) calculate the minimum price at which the sale of product A would be worthwhile;

(c) calculate the amount by which profit could be increased if the supply of Grade A labour were increased by 1 hour; and

(d) describe shortly the limitations of the technique you have used in answering (a).

ICAEW(EFD).

Chapter 19

Investment Decisions — I

In the long run, a firm's survival depends upon a successful set of investment decisions being made. The replacement of plant and machinery, expansion into new areas, introducing new technology and many other types of investment, all call for major decisions on the part of management. Not all the criteria given to the decision makers is in financial terms, but accountant's make a major contribution to the information available.

This chapter examines the methods employed in evaluating the worthwhileness of proposed projects. As is so often the case when developing models, it is necessary to set out a list of assumptions. Without these, the students is unable to approach the subject in an ordered fashion and fails to stay the course because of his early bewilderment. These assumptions though, are not so unrealistic as to entirely invalidate the results obtained from the simplified model. Nonetheless it is adviseable to always bear in mind the fact that relaxing the assumptions and extending the model can usually bring about an improvement in its usefulness.

The first thing assumed is that there is complete confidence in the accuracy of future revenues and costs. This is to say that no recognition is given to the problems of risk and uncertainty. The second is that the cost of capital of the company concerned is easily ascertained. This cost of capital is the rate required to satisfy the demands of those who provide funds, eg. debenture holders and shareholders. It is the rate at which future cash flows must be discounted in order to assess the outcome of the project in terms of its present value. Thirdly, there will be no consideration of situations in which there is a shortage of funds relative to the total outlay of all the possible opportunities available to the firm for investment. Nor are there to be any other scarce resources. Finally two important elements in the form of inflation and taxation will be ignored in this early treatment.

Methods of Evaluating Projects

Four ways of measuring the worthwhileness of a proposal will be considered. The first two are usually referred to as the traditional methods, which means that they have been replaced by new techniques which are conceptually sounder. These traditional techniques ignore the time value of money, whereas the other two discount the cash flows.

a) Payback period

This is the best known of the traditional methods. It has been extensively used in the past as the sole basis for deciding on a project. it is still widely used as a supplement to discounting methods.

The approach is to ask a basic question. How long is the period between the start of the project and recouping the original outlay? This simple example will illustrate. It sets out the net cash returns from five possible investments, all with the same outlay. In every case the project is completed after four years.

Project no.	Outlay (£)	net receipts (£) year 1	year 2	year 3	year 4
1	10,000	6,000	4,000	4,000	5,000
2	10,000	4,000	6,000	3,000	3,000
3	10,000			10,000	12,000
4	10,000			5,000	5,000
5	10,000			5,000	10,000

The company directors may decree a cut off period of two years.

In the example given all but projects 1 and 2 would be rejected since the outlay of £10,000 is not recovered in the first two years. It ignores project 3 which could be a good investment. It makes no distinction between projects 1 and 2, even though they have different cash flows in years 3 and 4.

b) Return on Investment

This method calculates an average annual profit and an average book value, expressing the first as a percentage of the second. It is an attempt to incorporate profitability into the assessment.

Example—Outlay   £1,000   at time t_0
       Net cash flows: £200   at time t_1
                        400   at time t_2
                        600   at time t_3
       proceeds from sale of asset   100   at time t_3

This data indicates that the project is completed within three years, the original asset being sold for £100 at the end of year three.

	year 1	year 2	year 3
Opening value	1,000	700	400
Depreciation	300	300	300
Written down value	700	400	100

Average investment in the period $= \dfrac{1000 + 100}{2} = £550$

Profits:

	year 1	year 2	year 3
Cash flow	200	400	600
Depreciation	300	300	300
Net profit	− 100	100	300

Average annual profit $= (- 100 + 100 + 300)/3 = £100$

Return $= \dfrac{100}{550} = 18.2\%$ per annum.

Assessment of a) and b)

The major criticism that applies to both of these methods, is that they ignore the timing of cash flows. This is illustrated in the payback example which gave the same ranking to projects 1 and 2, although the division of the cash flows between the years was different and clearly favoured the first.

There is a preference for cash now rather than later, since this gives possibilities of earlier re-investment or repayment of borrowing. Alternatively it gives a choice of earlier consumption. The discounting methods described later are designed to take this factor into account.

Additional drawbacks to the two methods are that payback ignores profit and the return method is subject to all the usual problems connected with profit measurement.

Discounting Methods

These methods attempt to account for the timing of cash flows by discounting the cash flows at an appropriate rate. The discounting factors used presents the firms collective rate which equates money at one point in time with an amount of money at another. It means that the firm is indifferent between having £100 (say) now and £110 (say) exactly one year later. If the return on a single year investment is greater than £110, the firm will invest, if less that £110 it will not.

The technique relies on the compound interest formula:-

$$S = P(1+r)^n$$

$$\text{or } P = \frac{S}{(1+r)^n}$$

where P = present value.
S = future sum
r = annual rate of interest expressed as a decimal
n = number of years ahead relating to the future sum.

Suppose the following cash flows were to be available at the times given.

Outlay $£x_0$ at time to = the present
Net receipt $£x$, at time t_1 = the end of the first year.
Net receipt $£x_2$, at time t_2 = the end of the second year.
Such a cash flow can be given a present value by inserting the figures for each year into the formula for P.

$$P = x_0 + \frac{x_1}{(1+r)} + \frac{x_2}{(1+r)^2} \text{---------------}$$

$$\text{or NPV} = \sum_{j=0}^{n} x_j \cdot (1+r)^{-j}$$

Net Present Value

The application of the simple formula just developed, to the expected cash flows, gives a single result. This is the net present value of the cash stream. When applied to a single project this net present value technique gives a positive or negative result. If the answer is positive it means that the firm will benefit in financial terms if the project is undertaken. The result is the opposite if the net present value is negative. The extent of the benefit would be equal to the net present value and would be after satisfying the demands of the provision of capital.

Suppose that an investment opportunity occurs with the following profile. Invest £800 now and receive £400 per annum for three years, payments to be made at the end of each year. The person to whom this investment possibility is presented has no money, but can borrow at 10% per annum. First calculate the net present value:

$$\text{n.p.v.} = -£800 + \frac{400}{(1+0.1)} + \frac{400}{(1+0.1)^2} + \frac{400}{(1+0.1)^3} = £195$$

On the strength of this calculation, it should be possible to borrow enough for the investment and the additional benefit, knowing that the £400 annuity will satisfy the loan and the interest charges at 10%.

Amount borrowed at to:	£995
Interest at t_1 (10%)	99.5
	1094.5
Repayment at t_1	400.0
	694.5
Interest at t_2 (10%)	69.5
	764.0
Repayment at t_2	400.0
	364.0
Interest at t_3 (10%)	36.0
	400.0
Repayment at t_3	400.0
	—

The project is immediately worth £195, that is now not at the end of the three years. This is illustrated by the fact that the amount that could be borrowed was not simply £800, but included the overall benefit.

The next example deals with a more varied style of cash flow.

Example

A firm is considering an investment in a project with an initial cost of £4,000. The life of the project is expected to be three years. Estimated revenue and cost figures are:

Year	Revenue	Cost	Net inflow
1	5,000	4,000	1,000
2	6,000	3,000	3,000
3	7,000	3,000	4,000

The firm's discount rate is 10%.

Putting these figures into the net present value calculation gives:

$$NPV = -400 + \frac{1000}{(1+0.1)} + \frac{3000}{(1+0.1)^2} + \frac{4000}{(1+0.1)^3}$$

With the aid of a calculator this can be evaulated by the standard arithmetical process. Where there is no calculator available tables can be used. These give factors to replace $\frac{1}{(1.1)}, \frac{1}{(1.1)^2}$ etc.

These tables are reproduced as appendices A and B. The one referred to here is usually described as the 'present value of £1, to be received n periods hence, interest rate i per period'. The symbol with these table if V_i^n.

(See Appendix A). So, $V_{.10}^2 = \frac{1}{(1+0.1)^2}$

In the example the discount factors are included in the table below:-

Year	Cash Flow	Discount Factor	Discounted Value
0	(4000)	1.0000	(4000)
1	1000	0.9091	909
2	3000	0.8265	2480
3	4000	0.7513	3005
		NPV.	£2394

There are three points to note here:-

1) The positive net present value indicates that the firm would increase its net worth if the investment opportunity were accepted.

2) All cash flows have been taken as though occurring on the last date of each year. This is a convenient approximation which does not seriously affect the results.

3) Depreciation is not included as part of the yearly cash flows, because the whole cost of the asset acquired have already been included in the calculations. Usually this is at time to, but this is not necessarily so.

Sometimes the figures in the analysis are in the form of regular yearly receipts, in which case annuity tables can be used. Example.

Outlay at to $= £4,000$
Receipts for
years $t_1 - t_3$ $= £3,000$ per annum
Discount rate 10%

$$n.p.v. = -4000 + \frac{3000}{(1+.1)} + \frac{3000}{(1+.1)^2} + \frac{3000}{(1+.1)^3}$$

$$= -4000 + 3000. \ a_{\overline{3}|.10}$$

where the factor $a_{\overline{3}|.10}$ is given in the table entitled 'present value of an annuity of £1 for n periods, interest rate i per period'. (Appendix B). In this example the factor is 2.4869.

$$= -4000 + 3000 \times 2.4869$$
$$= £3461.$$

Internal Rate of Return

This is a second application of the discounting formula. Under net present value calculations the discounting rate is put into the equation and the net present value is the unknown to be found. A positive result is favourable. The internal rate of return method puts the net present value at nil and treats the discount rate as unknown. In other words the technique is to find the discount rate at which it is just beneficial to accept the project.

The formular becomes:

$$0 = x_0 + \frac{x_1}{(1+r)} + \frac{x_2}{(1+r)^2} \text{------------} \frac{x_n}{(1+r)^n}.$$

When the rate is found it can then be compared with a hurdle or cut-off figure, which represents the minimum acceptable return. If it is below the minimum then the project is rejected.

Example

Use the cash flows given for the example of net present value calculations:

$$0 = -4000 + \frac{1000}{1+r} + \frac{3000}{(1+r)^2} + \frac{4000}{(1+r)^3}$$

Equations such as these, being high order equations, are not easily solved. Trial and error procedures have to be used. It is possible to establish an approximate region for the answer and start from there. However, as a general rule, try a figure and raise or lower it until the net present value becomes zero. If the rate used gives a positive result, then try a higher rate. If the converse is true, then lower the rate. It is not sound to interpolate between a rate above and a rate below the required answer.

Try r = 30%, this gives:

$$-4000 + 1000 \times 0.7696 + 3000 \times 0.5921 + 4000 \times 0.4561$$
$$= £373$$

which is not a high enough rate of interst.

Net try 35%, this gives:

$$-4000 + 1000 \times 0.7407 + 3000 \times 0.5487 + 4000 \times 0.4064 = £12$$

This is approximately the answer. 36% would give $-£52$.

This return is then compared with the firm's cut off rate. If it is above, it is acceptable.

In order to illustrate n.p.v. the technique comprehensively, a more complex problem will be considered next.

Example

An investment opportunity in mining has the following data forecast:

1) The survey costs were £200,000. The survey is now complete.

2) The initial investment before extraction could begin, would be £200,000.

3) The estimated quantity of extractable mineral is 600,000 tons. The selling price of the mineral is £20/ton.

4) Present wage rates are £3.00/hour and labour costs/ton extracted are expected to be £10.

5) The site cost £500,000 ten years ago. It is currently valued at £1,500,000.

6) The site would have to be restored after mining and it is estimated that this would cost £100,000.

7) The residual value of equipment bought for the project would be £50,000.

8) The combination of machinery bought and labour available would restrict output to 100,000 tons per annum.

Take the cost of capital of the firm as 10%.

Required

Calculate whether it is worthwhile to undertake this proposal.

Solution

It is useful to set out the solution to problems such as these in a standard way. Draw up a table of incomings and outgoings on a year by year basis. Then apply the appropriate discount rate to each year to arrive at the net present value. Figures in '000s.

Item/years	0	1	2	3	4	5	6
	£	£	£	£	£	£	£
Survey (1)			not relevant				
Investment	2,000						
Revenue		2,000	2,000	2,000	2,000	2,000	2,000
Labour		1,000	1,000	1,000	1,000	1,000	1,000
Site cost (2)	1,500						
Restoration (3)							100
Sale of equipment							50
Net cash flow	(3,500)	1,000	1,000	1,000	1,000	1,000	1,050
Discount factor	1.00	.909	.826	.751	.683	.621	.564
Present value	3,500	909	826	751	683	621	592
Net present value	1,882						

Notes:

1. The survey cost is a sunk cost, gone forever and no longer relevant to a decision.

2. This site cost is the opportunity to sell the site for £1,500,000. The net present value of the project must exceed this amount if it is to be worthwhile. Otherwise the site could be sold and a better return obtained.

3. Strictly speaking this should be shown as taking place in year 7, but since placing all annual cash flows together at the end of the year is an approximation, it is assumed here that the restoration work will be done quickly after closing the mine will be nearer to the end of year 6.

These figures are chosen for ease of illustration. As such, being largely annuities, they could have been presented more directly, namely:

$npv = 3,500 + 1000a_{\overline{3}|.10} + 1050 \text{ v } 10^6$, but the purpose of the illustration was to show the more general method.

Net Present Value Versus Internal Rate of Return

These similar methods do not always give the same result and some preference has to be indicated for one or the other. The examples given to illustrate the methods, have been simple situations with a standard pattern of cash outflow by net inflows. Further, they have involved a choice between acceptance or rejection. In these circumstances NPV and IRR give the same advice. However, project selection is not always concerned with cases like these.

Mutually exclusive investments

One situation which can lead to a conflict between NPV and IRR is the case of mutually exclusive investments with project characteristics which are outside the pattern described in the paragraph above. Mutually exclusive investments are competing one where a choice of one from two or more possibilities has to be made. Two examples will be given, the first showing investment opportunities of different size of outlay. The second has the same outlay, but different timing of cash flows.

Example

One of the three possible investments has to be chosen. They are mutually exclusive.

	Annual Income	Present value of income	Outlay	Net Present Value	Internal Rate of Return
	£	£m	£m	£m	%
A	500,000	5	2	3	25
B	900,000	9	4	5	22.5
C	1,500,000	15	8	7	18.75

The annual income represents a perpetuity and the discount rate is 10%. The internal rate of return is found by expressing the annual income as a percentage of the outlay, since the new net present value is to be nil.

According to the NPV test, C should be chosen, as it has the highest net present value. On the other hand the I.R.R. has reverse ranking. The internal rate of return is giving a percentage figure based on average investment and is ignoring the absolute size of the investment returns. Given that there are no constraints on the capital available and that risk is not a factor, then investment C must be preferable. An alternative way of looking at these investments is to move from opportunity A to B and then to C, using the incremental approach. It is clear that each additional amount of investment is worthwhile, although the size of the return is diminishing.

	Annual Income £	Present Value £m	Outlay £m	Net Present Value £m	Internal Rate of Return %
A	500,000	5	2	3	25
B	900,000	9	4	5	22.5
Increment (B-A)	400,000	4	2	2	20*
C	1,500,000	15	8	7	19.75
Increment C-B	600,000	6	4	2	15*

*newly calculated

Example

Two mutually exclusive ivestments have the same outlay but different styles of cash flows.

		A			B	
Period	Cash Flows £	Present Value Factor (8%)	Present Value £	Cash Flows £	Present Value (Factor) (8%)	Present Value £
0	(5000)	1.00	(5000)	(5000)	1.00	(5000)
1	500	0.93	465	2881	0.93	2679
2	5500	0.86	4730	2881	0.86	2478
			195			157

If the internal rate of return for both investments is calculated it turns out to be identical at 10% for both cases. Using the firm's cost of capital of 8%, the NPV method prefers investment A, whereas the internal rate of return method gives an answer of indifference between the two.

Multiple solutions

The equation solved for the internal rate of return is of the type described as polynominal. There are as many solutions as there are powers of the unknown. This does not present a problem when the standard pattern of a cash outlay followed by cash inflows is present. This is because there is only one real root, the rest coming into the classification that mathematicians have termed imaginery. In other cases there may be more than one solution. Investments of this kind are not difficult to find. Any form of mineral extraction which requires that the site should be made good at the end of the operation would qualify.

Example

The following cash flow for an investment A requires a terminal expenditure.

Project A

Period	Cash Flow
0	(1000)
1	5000
2	(5000)

For A, using IRR

$$0 = -1000 + \frac{5000}{1+r} - \frac{5000}{(1+r)^2}$$

multiplying by $\dfrac{(1+r)^2}{1,000}$ and rearranging gives:

$$r^2 - 3r + 1 = 0$$

giving $r = 3 \pm 5/2$,

which is not a unique solution and could present problems of interpretation.

Which to choose?

Given the provisions set out above in terms of the style of the cash flow, comparability between investments in terms of size and life, then I.R.R. and N.P.V. give the same results. In practice the list should be extended to include no shortage of capital and no need to take investment opportunities of later periods into account now. The questions then becomes one of choosing between conflicting results.

What, then is the basic difference between the two methods? Earlier in this chapter the net present value was calculated for an investment of £800 which provided an income of £400 per annum for three years. The money for the investment was borrowed at 10%. The result of the calculation was £195 and this was demonstrated to be equal to the immediate benefit of the investment. Now calculate the I.R.R. for the same investment opportunity. By trial and error the answer for the internal rate of return is marginally above 23%. As before, calculate the interest payments and returns over three years to demonstrate the validity of the result.

Sum borrowed to	800
interest at 23% t_1	184
	984
annuity at t_1	400
	584
interest at 23% t_2	134
	718
annuity at t_2	400
	318
interest at 23% t_3	73
	391
annuity at t_3	400

The figures do not quite amount to zero at the end, because the 23% is an approximation.

In the N.P.V. calculation it was assumed that the cash flows are earning or being re-invested at the cost of the capital, in this case borrowed at 10%. Under I.R.R. the assumption made is that the flows are capable of being re-invested at the higher rate of 23%. Choice between the N.P.V. and I.R.R. then becomes one of deciding which of these assumptions is more valid. Where the marginal cost of capital is constant and the firm is accepting all investment opportunities which according to their internal rate of return rank above this marginal cost, then N.P.V. should prevail. Put another way, it means that the firm is investing in order of rank down to the last acceptable investment. The cash flows are additional, or more correctly, replacement sources of investment capital and as such are saving the cost of the replaced capital. However, the two assumptions made above do not always hold. Firstly, the firm may be short of capital and thus unable to accept all the investment opportunities and secondly the marginal cost of capital may be increasing significantly. In these cases the cash flows will be replacing investment capital which has a higher cost and use of N.P.V. is at least an understatement.

Finally, it should be said that many firms use IRR. Mainly, it is supposed because senior managers more readily accept conclusions presented as a percentage rather than they would a net present value. It is also true that the difference between the calculated rate and the cut off figure gives an indication of how big a margin or error there is in the discount rate used. This second point is useful as part of a general examination of the sensitivity of the analysis to the estimate used for costs, revenues and so on. This will be looked at in the next chapter. On its own though, it is not enought to justify giving preference to IRR over NPV.

Exercises

Questions 19.1-19.5 (Answers provided)

19.1 Calculate the payback period for each of the investment possibilities detailed below:

Investment		Cash Flows (In)			
	Outlay	Year 1	Year 2	Year 3	Year 4
1	10,000	3,000	4,000	4,000	5,000
2	8,000	4,000	2,000	1,000	1,000
3	15,000	6,000	5,000	5,000	4,000

19.2 The Ince Company accountant has drawn together two profiles for possible but mutually exclusive investment opportunities:

Investment		Cash Flows	
I	t_0	t_1	t_2
1	$-10,000$	7,000	8,000
2	$-10,000$	4,000	11,000

Both investments are complete at t_2 and there are no residual proceeds from sales of assets.

Required: the return on investment of both projects. Which would you recommend?

19.3 Bickershaw and Company are considering the following investment opportunity

period	Cash Flow
	£
0	(9,000)
1	1,000
2	5,100
3	9,300

The company has a cost of capital of 10%.

Required: calculate the net present value and the internal rate of return.

19.4 The Orrell Company is considering whether to continue with the manufacture of one of its component parts, or to buy them for £20 each.

The part is made using a machine which originally cost £35,000 and now has a book value of £20,000. It could be sold immediately for £5,000. There are no alternative uses.

Manufacture takes place in a self-contained shed which could be rented out for £12,000 per year.

The company accountant has provided other cost information as follows:

	£
Direct material	3
Direct labour	5
Variable overhead	2
Fixed overhead	2 (note: £1000 directly traced)
	12 per unit

Annual usage is 2000 parts a year and this is expected to continue for three years, by which time the part will no longer be used.

Required: the make or buy decision assuming company cost of capital at 10%. Ignore taxation.

19.5 Explain the basic methods of evaluating investment opportunities. Which would you recommend your company to adopt and why?

Graph net present value versus cost of capital for normal investment flows. How does the internal rate of return relate to this graph?

Questions 19.6-19.10. Answers not provided.

19.6 The estimated investment and net resultant annual cash flow of each of four mutually exclusive projects are shown below (negative items are in brackets):

	A	B	C	D
Project years	£	£	£	£
Year 0	(150,000)	(300,000)	(300,000)	(75,000)
Year 1	30,000	105,000	—	34,500
Year 2	30,000	105,000	—	30,000
Year 3	30,000	105,000	—	15,000
Year 4	30,000	105,000	—	15,000
Year 5	30,000	105,000	—	—
Year 6	30,000	—	300,000	—
Year 7	30,000	—	300,000	—
Year 8	30,000	—	300,000	—
Year 9	30,000	—	300,000	—
Year 10	30,000	—	300,000	—

The management have calculated the internal rate of return on each as: 15% 22% 20% 12%

and have announced their decision to undertake B as its return is highest and covers the company's cost of capital of 10%.

You are required to state, with reasons, whether you consider this procedure to be satisfactory and, if you consider that it is not, to provide an alternative calculation and explain to the management briefly but clearly the reasoning underlying your choice of method.

ICAEW(MA).

19.7 A company making motor car components uses three separate machines to undertake the turning, boring and grinding operations. The present machines are old and unreliable and the factory engineer has put forward two alternative proposals for their replacement by:

(i) three new individual machines; or

(ii) a combined special purpose machine.

From the data given below, you are required to:

(a) evaluate both of these proposals, and

(b) write a short appraisal of your analysis making a firm recommendation on the replacement action to be taken.

	Present machines		Proposed machines	
Machine type	Original capital cost	Operating expenses per year	Capital cost	Operating expenses per year
	£	£	£	£
Turning	25,000	20,000	50,000	7,000
Boring	35,000	21,000	53,000	8,000
Grinding	20,000	12,000	31,000	6,000
Multi-purpose	—	—	147,000	17,000

The economic life of all the new machines is eight years and by that time it is estimated their salvage value will be equal to their dismantling cost.

You may ignore all taxation and investment allowances in the calculations.

The company normally expects new capital investment to provide a 14% D.C.F. return.

ICMA(MA2).

19.8 For more than ten years Carbon Ltd. has invested £1,000 per annum in new fixed assets. Each investment has been appraised as a separate project using discounted cash flow principles. The forecasted internal rate of return has been exactly 20 per cent per annum of a life of 10 years for all projects accepted. Moreover, actual results have always exactly equalled forecasts. Net cash inflows from each project have increased at the rate of 20 per cent per annum over the project life — i.e., net cash inflows from any project have been $A(1.20)$ in the first year and $A(1.20)^n$ in year n where A is some constant. The working capital of Carbon is negligible. The firm incurs no fixed costs (i.e., all costs are attributable to individual projects) and holds no assets other than those acquired from the annual investment of £1,000. The annual cash surplus is distributed as a dividend. For financial accounting purposes, depreciation is provided on a straight line basis.

You are required to:

(a) calculate the annual accounting rate of return by Carbon in aggregate (i.e. the ratio of total net profit to balance sheet value of capital employed at the start of the year),

(b) explain for the benefit of someone who is unfamiliar with investment appraisal techniques why accounting rate of return differs from the internal rate of return, and

(c) discuss the alternatives available to the directors of a firm wishing to change its accounting rate of return without changing accounting policies.

Ignore taxation. ICAEW(EFD)

19.9 Your client Egbert Ltd has been negotiating with Beornwulf Ltd for the purchase of one of its manufacturing divisions. The profit and loss account for the year just ended and the current balance sheet are summarised as follows:

Profit and Loss Account	£'000	£'000
Sales—all to external customers		376
Less —Materials and Components—external	52	
Materials and Components—internal	43	
Manufacturing Labour	124	
Depreciation of Plant and Equipment	15	
Other Manufacturing Overheads incurred in Division	64	
Administrative Overheads incurred in Division	38	
Share of Head Office Costs	24	
		360
Net Profit		16

Balance Sheet

	£'000
Plant and Equipment—cost less depreciation	34
Stock at cost—Finished Goods	72
—Raw Materials	26
Trade Debtors	54
	186
Less Trade Creditors	32
Head Office Capital Employed	154

You are given the following additional information:

(1) "Materials and Components—internal" represents items transferred from another division. Under Beornwulf's transfer pricing policy, these items are prices at variable cost pluys 30 per cent to cover fixed overheads. Egbert would manufacture the items concerned itself under similar conditions to Beornwulf as regards costs.

(2) Egbert would take over all the assets of the division and discharge the creditors. However, the plant and equipment is believed to be obsolete. It would be sold for scrap at £10,000 and replaced by equipment leased on an annual contract for an initial rent of £25,000 per annum.

(3) Egbert believes that stocks of finished goods could be reduced to one half of their present level. The reduction would be effected by a special sale immediately following the acquisition to realise £40,000.

(4) "Share of Head Office Costs" represents an allocation of administrative costs on the basis of divisional sales. The acquisition would cause Egbert's costs of general management to increase by £8,000 in the first year.

(5) It is expected that all items of cost and revenue for the division and all working capital items would increase at 15 per cent per annum, in step with the retail price index for the indefinite future. Egbert requires a rate of return of 21 per cent per annum on new investments.

You may assume that all receipts and payments arise at annual intervals.

You are required to:

(a) prepare a calculation to guide Egbert in deciding on the maximum sum it should pay for the division of Beornwulf, and

(b) add a brief note on the other factors which might influence the decision in practive.

Ignore taxation.   ICAEW(EFD).

19.10 The following information is given relating to a proposed capital expenditure project:

	£
Cost of project	350,000
Cash inflow per annum, prior to tax	80,000
Scrap/residual value	nil
Working capital requirements:	
At commencement of project	10,000
After one year, a further	10,000
All released at end of the seventh year	20,000

Tax assumptions:

(i) corporation tax is at the rate of 50%

(ii) the first allowance is at the rate of 100% and there are sufficient corporate profits available from other activities to absorb the whole amount of this allowance in the first year;

(iii) tax payments are made and allownces are received in the year following that to which they relate.

Grant:

A 20% tax free regional development grant is available and it is expected that this will be received one year after the purchase and installation of capital equipment.

Expected life of equipment	6 years
Company cut-off rate	18% after tax

You are required to:

(a) compile a discounted cash flow (DCF) statement to ascertain whether or not the project is acceptable;

(b) calculate the approximate DCF rate of return (internal rate of return) for the project.

ICMA(MA1).

Seminar Problem 19

Congo Ltd is considering the selection of one of a pair of mutually exclusive investment projects. Both would involve purchase of machinery with a life of five years.

Project 1 would generate annual cash flows (receipts less payments) of £200,000; the machinery would cost £556,000 and have a scrap value of £56,000.

Project 2 would generate annual cash flows of £500,000; the machinery would cost £1,616,000 and have a scrap value of £301,000.

Congo uses the straight line method for providing depreciation. Its cost of capital is 15 per cent per annum. Assume that annual cash flows arise on the anniversaries of the initial outlay, that there will be no price changes over the project lives and that acceptance of one of the projects will not alter the required amount of working capital.

You are required to:

(a) calculate for each project:

    (i)   the accounting rate of return (ratio, over project life, of average accounting profit to average book value of investment) to nearest one per cent,

    (ii) the net present value,

    (iii) the internal rate of return (D.C.F. yield) to nearest one per cent, and

    (iv) the payback period to one decimal place and,

(b) state which project you would select for acceptance, if either, giving reasons for your choice of criterion to guide the decision.

Ignore taxation.   ICAEW(EFD).

Chapter 20

Investment Decisions — continued

In the previous chapter ways of evaluating possible capital programmes, were examined. In circumstances of constant marginal cost of capital and no capital rationing, the net present value technique gives the best result. The whole chapter depended upon a number of assumptions and the purpose of this chapter is to relax these. It is worthwhile repeating what the assumptions were: absence of taxation and inflation, no risk or uncertainty, known cost of capital and no shortage of capital.

Taxation

The rules concerning taxation are of application to both the formulation of cash flows and in assessing the cost of capital. In this section the first of these only, will be considered. When money is spent on investment, it has two affects on the cash flows. Firstly as an outgoing and secondly as a saving in taxation of profits. To understand how this is so, it is necessary to look at the appropriate tax procedures.

A firm's expenditure on new assets is allowed as a deduction from profits for tax relief purposes. The deduction is made in accordance with the current regulations contained in the Finance Acts and are in place of the accounting depreciation. In this way the govenment of the day can use the capital allowances as a part of its fiscal policy.

This can be explained as follows:

	£
Profit after deducting depreciation	1000
Add: depreciation	200
	1200
Deduct: capital allowances	320
Taxable profit	880

Over the years, the method of calculating each years entitlement to capital allowances has varied considerably. It has been one of the instruments used by governments as part of their policy to encourage industrial investment. The principle is that at least the cost of the asset should be allowed as a deduction, according to some specified formula, the formula itself being something that has changed frequently over the years.

Although the rates in force have varied from year to year, the pattern of capital allowances has been either to give tax relief on the whole cost over a number of years or to give tax relief plus a bonus. These latter have been referred to as investment grants.

An example of the first type is given below. As a general supposition let the expenditure on machines of a specified category be allowed by deducting 40% in the first year and 25% per annum thereafter on a reducing balance basis.

Example:

A firm buys such a machine for £1000 and sells it after 3 years for £300

Year		£
1	Cash	1000
	Allowance	400
2		600
	Allowance	150
3		450
	Sales proceeds	300
	Balancing allowance	150

The total of the allowance is £(400 + 150 + 150) = 700 which in turn equals the cost less the sales proceeds. Note that the last allowance is a balancing figure. Had the sales proceeds been £500 then there would have been a balancing *charge* of £50.

For an example of investment allowances, use the same figures but make an investment allowance of 20% in the first year.

Year		£
1	Cash	1000
	Investment allowance	200
	First year allowance	400
		600

the second and third years are as before, including the balancing allowance. This means that the original capital expenditure is allowed over its lifetime as a deduction from profit and, in addition, 20% of the capital cost is deducted from the taxable profits relating to the first year.

In recent years the system of fiscal inducements to investment have grown in a variety of ways. Differentials are now made to help particular industries and to encourage a diversification to the regions. As well as being attracted by capital these grants now relate to labour as well.

The next point to make concerns the timing of these tax allowances. There is a fairly simple way of calculating when a firm is due to pay its tax bill. For firms incorporated after the introduction of Corporation Tax, the tax due is usually payable nine months after the end of the accounting year.

For companies which were operating when income tax (as opposed to corporation tax) applied, the ascertainment of the due date is done differently. The rule is that payment is due on the 1st January of the income tax year following the income tax year in which the relevant accounting year ends. This latter provision applies to a majority of firms.

Example

A firm's accounting year ends on 30th September 19X5. This is in the income tax year from 6th April 19X5 — 5th April 19X6, referred to as the 19X5/X6 tax year. The following tax year is 19X6/X7 and the due date for tax is 1st January 19X7.

With knowledge of the specific tax rules in force it is relatively easy to work out the appropriate cash flows.

Example

The firm in the example above buys a machine for £45,000 on 1st June 19X5. The rate of corporation tax is 50% and the company would claim a first year capital allowance of 100% and taxable profits would exceed this allowance in the first year.

$$\begin{array}{ll} \text{The cost would be at } t_0 & = \pounds 45000 \\ \text{Tax saving at } t_2 \text{ at } 50\% & = \pounds 22500 \end{array}$$

The time t_0 is 1st June 19X5 and t_2 is 31st May 19X7. This date being substituted for the real date of 1st January 19X7, since all cash flows are assumed to take place at the year end.

Inflation

In times of changing price levels, an individuals marginal rate of time preference will reflect his expectation of the rate of change of prices. When evaluating projects the firm will, likewise, use a higher rate if it is thought that inflation will prevail. The discounting rate may be thought of as having two components, one an allowance for inflation and the other which may be the real point of indifference between investing and no investing.

It is clear that if the rate allows for inflation, then so should the cash flows used in the calculation.

This seems to be the simplest way of handling the problem, even though it does add the additional estimate of inflation rates for the future. An alternative way would be to deal with real cash flows. This has the disadvantages that it does not allow for differing price movements for labour and material, say. It still leaves the problem of what is the real element of the discount rate, after allowing for inflation. An example will help to make things clearer:

Example

A firm is considering a project with the following cash flows, all at todays prices: $t_0 = -500; t_1 = 300; t_2 = 200; t_3 = 500.$

the real discount rate is 10%. Prices are expected to increase at an annual rate of 5% and the money rate of interest is $15\frac{1}{2}\%$.

1) Use real flows and the real discount rate

$$\text{npv} = -500 + \frac{300}{1.10} + \frac{200}{1.10^2} + \frac{500}{1.10^3} = 312$$

ii) Use cash flows allowing for inflation and the money cost of capital

$$npv = -500 + \frac{300(1+0.5)}{1.155} + \frac{200(1+0.5)}{1.155^2} + \frac{500(1+0.5)}{1.155^3} = 312$$

The answer is the same in both cases because the two expressions reduce to the same. The expression $1.05/1.155 = 1.00/1.10$ which demonstrates the equivalence of the two expressions.

In general terms, if 'm' is the money rate of interest, 'r' is the rate of inflation and 'i' is the real rate of interest, then:

$$\frac{1+r}{1+m} = \frac{1}{1+i} \quad \text{or rearranging } (1+m) = (1+r)(1+i)$$

Finally in this section, here is an illustration of differing inflation rates.

Example

A firm is considering an investment of £75,000 on a machine with a life of four years and nil residual value. This machine will produce a product to sell at £60 for a quantity of 1000 units. The estimated cost of each unit manufactured would be:

	£
Materials	10.00
Labour (10 hrs at £2.00/hr)	20.00
Variable overhead (10 hrs at £0.50/hr)	5.00
	35.00

The discount rate to be used is 20% in money terms. Material costs, overheads and selling prices are expected to increase at the rate of 15% per annum and labour costs are expected to increase at the rate of 20% per annum.

Is the purchase of the new machine worthwhile in terms of its net present value?

Solution

The method is to calculate the cash flows for the factors according to their individual inflation rates. In this example this can be facilitated by grouping together material, overhead and revenue which are all expected to increase at 15% per annum.

Cash flow subject to 15% inflation—

	£
Materials	10
overhead	5
	15
revenue	60
net difference	45
units	1000

Cash flow subject to 20% inflation—
labour   £20 per unit

Combined cash flow

year n.		1	2	3	4
net revenue	$1000 \times 45 \times 1.15^n$	51750	59512	68439	78705
Labour	$1000 \times 20 \times 1.20^n$	24000	28800	34560	41472
		27750	30712	33879	38233
Discount factor 20%		.83	.69	.59	.48
Present value		23032	21191	19989	17872

Net present value £(82084 – 75000) = £7084.

The problem has been solved by calculating the equivalent money flows of items subject to the differing inflation rates. These have been brought together for discounting. The n.p.v. of the project is positive.

Risk and Uncertainty — Sensitivity analysis

The figures that have been put into these net present value calculations are not usually known with certainty. Is it possible to take any steps to minimise the doubts that arise from this?

One way is to examine the individual estimates in order to ascertain how sensitive the overall result is to errors. Consider the following expression of the net present value calculation—

$$npv = x_0 + \frac{x_1}{(1+i)} + \frac{x_2}{(1+i)^2} + \frac{x_3}{(1+i)^3} + \frac{x'_3}{(1+i)^3}$$

Where x_0 is the initial outlay

x_1 x_2 and x_3 are net cash flows for each year, with x'_3 being the residual value in the final year.

Examine x_0 first. Set $npv = 0$ and obtain

$$0 = x_0 + \frac{x_1}{(1+i)} + \frac{x_2}{(1+i)^2} + \frac{x_3}{(1+i)^3} + \frac{x'_3}{(1+i)^3}$$

and x_0 is found. If the new value of the outlay giving $npv = 0$ is not much different to the original estimate, then the calculation of the npv is sensitive to the accuracy of the estimate of the outlay. Repeating this for each element will suggest the estimates which need the most careful compilation.

Example

Kingslake Products Limited is studying the feasibility of introducing a new product. It has been estimated that the special equipment needed would cost £10,000 and to have a useful life of five years. Its resale value then would be nil. The product would also have a five year life span, by which time it would be obsolete. Annual sales would be of 1000 units at a unit price of £25. The variable cost would amount to £23 per unit. The cost of capital is 10% per annum.

Is the project worthwhile? How sensitive is the calculation to errors in the given estimates?

Solution

$$
\begin{aligned}
\text{n.p.v.} \quad &= -10{,}000 + 25 \times 1000 \times a_{\overline{5}|.10} - 23 \times 1000 \times a_{\overline{5}|.10} \\
&= -10{,}000 + 25 \times 1000 \times 3.79 - 23 \times 1000 \times 3.79 \\
&= -10{,}000 + 94750 - 87170 \\
&= -2420
\end{aligned}
$$

In this case the figures suggest that the new product is not worthwhile. The fact that a negative conclusion is reached does not mean that no further investigation is necessary. It is just as important to ensure that good opportunities are not missed as it is to avoid eventual losses on apparently profitable ventures.

There are four estimates which can be investigated for sensitivity. The equipment cost, the volume of units sold per annum, the unit profit margin and the life span of the product and machine.

Equipment cost:

set the n.p.v. $= 0$ and calculate the equipment cost which gives this result.

$$
\begin{aligned}
0 &= x + 25{,}000\, a_{\overline{5}|.10} - 23{,}000\, a_{\overline{5}|.10} \\
0 &= x + 94750 - 87170 \\
x &= 7580
\end{aligned}
$$

This means that the initial outlay would have to drop to 7580 before the project broke-even. In percentage terms, the required change would be

$$
\frac{(10{,}000 - 7580)}{10{,}000} \times 100 = \frac{242{,}000}{10{,}000}
$$

$$
= 24.2\%
$$

A substantial requirement such as this represents, indicates that there is little point in concentrating on this factor in the first instance.

volume:

again setting n.p.v. $= 0$

$$
\begin{aligned}
0 &= -10{,}000 + x \times (25 - 23)\, a_{\overline{5}|.10} \\
x &= \frac{10{,}000}{2 \times 3.79} = 1319
\end{aligned}
$$

and the percentage change is $\dfrac{319 \times 100}{1000} = 31.9\%$

Profit margin:

$$
\begin{aligned}
0 &= -10{,}000 + X \times 1000 \times a_{\overline{5}|.10} \\
X &= \frac{10}{3.79} = 2.6
\end{aligned}
$$

giving a percentage change of $\dfrac{0.6 \times 100}{2} = 30\%$

However, this could be obtained by increasing the selling price to £25.6, decreasing the variable cost to £22.4 or some amalgamation of changes in these factors. In these cases the percentage changes become much more modest. For sales, for example, it becomes $\dfrac{0.6}{25} \times 100 = 2.4$.

Life span:
$$0 = -10,000 + 25 \times 1000 \times a_{\overline{3}|.10} - 23 \times 1000 \times a_{\overline{3}|.10}$$
$$= -10,000 + 2,000\, a_{\overline{3}|.10}$$
$$a_{\overline{3}|.10} = 5$$

and from the table this gives approximate 8 years. It means an increase in life of $\dfrac{3}{5} \times 100 = 60\%$.

Calculations such as these can given useful clues as to the safety of the estimates and hence the amount of confidence that can be attached to them. As a result of such analysis it is often possible to double check or provide independent checks for the critical points.

Probability Distributions

A second approach is to introduce probability distributions and measures of dispersion. A project is given the following estimates:

Outlay at t_0 = 100
Receipt at t_1 $100 < x < 133$
Discount rate 10%

The receipts at t_1 are forecast to be within the range £110 – £133. Suppose that by observing the results of a large number of comparable projects, a probability distribution, can be estimated:

n p v	probability
£	p
100	.20
110	.60
120	.20
	1.00

then the expected net present value will be
$$100 \times 0.20 + 110 \times 0.60 + 120 \times 0.20 = 110.$$

Now compare with a second project which has the same estimates in terms of net present values but has a different probability distribution:

n p v	probability
£	p
100	.30
110	.40
120	.30

Here the expected value is $100 \times .30 + 110 \times .40 + 120 \times .30 = 110$ again.

For both projects, the expected net present value is the same. Even so, given a choice between the two, it is possible to make a decision. The first project can be seen to have the weight of probabilities centred on the result nearest the expected value of 110. The probabilities of being substantially off this value are less than in the second project. For somebody who prefers to avoid risk, project 1 would be the more acceptable. For a person with some preference for taking risks, project 2 would be acceptable because of the higher chance of achieving an expected value of £120.

These observations can be replaced by calculations of the standard deviation in each case:

For project 1 it is: $\{(-10^2 \times .20) + (10^2 \times .20)\}^{\frac{1}{2}}$
$$= 6.32$$

For project 2 it is:- $\{(-10^2 \times .30) + (10^2 \times .30)\}^{\frac{1}{2}}$
$$= 7.74$$

The project with the less risk attached has the smaller standard deviation associated with it.

Introduce a third project which has the same probability distribution as the previous one, but has different cash flows:

n p v	p
105	.30
110	.40
115	.30

The expected value is $105 \times .30 + 110 \times .40 + 115 \times .30 = 110$ yet again. This time the results give a standard deviation of $(-5^2 \times .30 + 5^2 \times .30)^{\frac{1}{2}}$
$$= 3.88$$

The project which seems to bear the least risk has the lowest standard deviation. This is because the concept of risk is in accordance with the standard deviation measurement. The greater the spread of possible net present values and the less concentrated the probabilities about the expected value, then the greater the risk.

In practice it is often not possible to fit a probability distribution. Nor is it a practicable proposition at the present time to quantify attitudes to risk as displayed by a management group. Even so the technique can be considered as having some prospects for useful developments.

Cost of Capital

Where there are long-term borrowings in the form of debentures etc., there is a contractual relationship which determines income flows.

$$W_0 = \frac{K}{(1-i)} + \frac{K}{(1+i)^2} \dots \frac{K}{(1+i)^n} + \frac{W}{(1+i)^n}$$

where W_0 is the current price

$\quad$ K $\;$ is the interest payment

$\quad$ W $\;$ is the amount repayable on redemption.

i is the cost of debt capital and represents the cost of continuing to use the existing source of finance, rather than redeeming it at the market price.

The calculation of the cost of capital for equity is not so easy. The current price of equity shares is known, but not the future stream of income. One suggested model is to start with the last paid dividend and estimate shareholders expectations of the future growth in dividends. This would give

$$V_0 = \frac{D_0(1+g)}{(1+i)} + \frac{D_0(1+g)^2}{(1+i)^2} \;\dots\dots$$

where $\quad V_0$ = the current market value

$\quad D_0$ = the last dividend paid

$\quad$ g $\;$ = expected rate of growth

$\quad$ i $\;$ = cost of equity capital

The expression above is a geometric progression with the ratio equal to $(1+g)/(1+i)$.

$$V_0 = \frac{D_0 (1+g)}{(1+i)} \bigg/ \left(1 - \frac{1+g}{1+i} \right)$$

$$= \frac{D_0 (1+g)}{(i-g)}$$

$$\text{and } i = \frac{D_0 (1+g)}{V_0} + g$$

Putting some figures in to illustrate, if a company share has a current market value of £2.00, an expected growth rate of 5% per annum and the last dividend was 10p per share then—

$$i \quad = \frac{0.10(1+0.05)}{2.00} + 0.05$$

$$= 0.1025$$

$$= 10.25\%$$

Where a company has both equity and debt, then a weighted average cost of capital can be calculated, using the normal arithmetic process. Suppose a company had—

$$\text{2,000 share of market value £1}$$
$$\text{1,000 debentures of market value £1}$$

and cost of equity and debt capital equal to 10% and 5% respectively.

Then, the weighted average cost of capital would be

$$\frac{2,000 \times .1 + 1000 \times .05}{2000 + 1000}$$

$$= 0.083 = 8\tfrac{1}{3}\%$$

In this sketchy account of the cost of capital, it has not been possible to deal with all available forms of finance. For further treatment, students are referred to more specialist texts on finance.

Current investigations into firms cost of capital do not give rise to a set of consistent results such that any formulated model can be chosen and used with confidence. However, such calculations can form part of the basis for arriving at discount rates to be used.

Capital Rationing

This situation occurs when the total cost of opportunities for profitable investment exceed the funds available. Theoretically such situations should not exist, because of the ability to raise extra funds to meet the cost of all the investment possibilities. In practice, though, either because the assumed cost of capital is too low or because of administrative limitations, capital rationing does happen.

The problem is one of 'choosing an optimum set of investments given a limited amount of capital. It can be illustrated with these figures:-

project	t_0 £	t_1 £	t_2 £	t_3 £	n.p.v.
A	− 3000	− 2000	4000	3000	770
B	− 2000	− 4000	4000	4000	720
C	− 2000	− 4000	4000	5000	470
D	− 400	− 2000	4000	4000	520
	− 11000	− 12000	16000	16000	
available capital	7000	15000			

The example shows a simple capital rationing situation, with an insufficient quantity of funds available at time t_0.

Assume that it is possible to divide these projects into fractional parts. Once again a difficult subject is being simplified in order to make an orderly presentation of the problem and give indications of methods of solving them. In this text it will not be feasible to do more than this and as students increase their knowledge they will need to refer to more advanced texts.

The figures given show a problem of a single constraining factor. With investments capable of being undertaken in fractional parts, the optimal selection can be obtained by ranking the present values per £ of investment. This process would give:

A: 3000/770 = £3.9
B: 2000/720 = £2.8
C: 2000/470 = £4.3
D: 4000/520 = £5.7

The ranking is D, C, A and B. The solution is given by accepting D and C in full and A to the extent of one-half. This would fully utilise the capital of £7000. This ranking of present values per unit of investment fails when there are more than one limiting factor. A more universally applicable method is to be found in mathematical programming. As an introduction to this idea, formulate the above problem in mathematical terms.

Maximise

$$770 \, x_1 + 720 \, x_2 + 470 \, x_3 + 520 \, x_4$$

subject to:

$$3000 \, x_1 + 2000 \, x_2 + 2000 \, x_3 + 4000 \, x_4 \leqslant 7000$$

$$x_1, x_2, x_3, x_4, \leqslant 1$$

$$x_1, x_2, x_3, x_4, \geqslant 0$$

this says in simple mathematical terms what the problem is.

x_1, x_2, x_3, x_4 are the fraction of projects A, B, C, D respectively which are to be accepted under an optimal under an optimal solution. The object is to maximise the net present value of the accepted combination.

In the likely event of the divisible assumption not being applicable, the simple linear programming solutions would have to be extended to take in integer programming. This would give a solution to accept projects B and C, which can easily be verified with such simple numbers to operate as in the example.

Mathematical programming continues to provide correct solutations as the problem intensifies with additional limiting factors. Suppose that in the illustration used, the capital available at t_1 was £10,000, so giving a shortage of money at times t_0 and t_1. Ranking methods are no use here and the formulation and solution of the problem have to be mathematical. Again assume divisible investments.

The mathematical representation becomes:

Maximise:

$$770 \, x_1 + 720 \, x_2 + 470 \, x_3 + 520 \, x_4$$

subject to:

$$3000 \, x_1 + 2000 \, x_2 + 200 \, x_3 + 4000 \, x_4 \leqslant 7000$$

$$2000 \, x_1 + 4000 \, x_2 + 400 \, x_3 + 2000 \, x_4 \leqslant 10000$$

$$\text{and } 0 \leqslant x_{1-4} \leqslant 1$$

and again, given indivisible projects, the solution lies in integer programming techniques.

Chapter Summary

Examining potential projects for a firm is an exercise of major importance. As was examined in an earlier chapter on control, this selection has to be done within a system involved in initiating and examining as well as selecting the successful candidates for inclusion in the capital programme. This chapter has been concerned, along with the preceding one, with one technical aspect of this process. The fact that discounting techniques are indeed but a part of the whole process is to be emphasized.

The main thrust of this chapter has been to examine ways in which the assumptions of the preliminary treatment may be relaxed. To a large extent the solutions have been tentative and have been pointers towards further study rather than exhaustive discussions of the points involved.

Exercises

Questions 20.1-20.5. (Answers provided)

20.1　The Alpha Trading Company is considering the purchase of a new computer system for £150,000. An alternative proposal is to lease the system for yearly payments in advance of £30,000. If the machine is bought then the company would operate it for five years, by which time it would have a sale value of £40,000.

Both the purchase price and the lease payments are fully allowed for tax purposes.

Company cost of capital is 10%, taxation 50%.

Required: a recommendation as to which course of action should be taken.

20.2　The Beta Company has an investment opportunity with the following characteristics:

Life product	— 5 years
Selling price	— £5
Total variable cost	— £3
Initial investment	— £60,000
Volume of sales	— 10,000 per year

These are current prices. It is expected that inflation will continue throughout the five years at a steady rate of 10%. The firm's cost of capital in money terms if 15%. No other factors are relevant.

Required: your evaluation of the project.

20.3　Use the same data as set out in question 20.2, with the alteration that the total variable cost has elements which are subject to differing rates of inflation.

Material cost	£1
Conversion cost	2
	£3

The conversion cost and the selling price will respond to the 10% inflation rate, but material costs will be subject to a lower rate of inflation of 5%.

Required: your evaluation of the project in these new circumstances.

20.4 The Gamma Company is about to introduce a new product. The net present value calculation is made from the equation given below, where x is the number of units to be made and sold and the amounts are in pounds.

$$npv = -50,000 + 10 \times a_{\overline{5}|.10} - 5x\, a_{\overline{5}|.10} + 5,000\, V_{\overline{5}|.10}$$

The selling price is £10 as shown and the other items are initial, unit and residual costs and values. x = 4000.

Required: an assessment of the sensitivity of the npv to the individual factors.

20.5 The Delta Company has the following investments competing for limited funds totalling £380,000.

	A	B	C	D
Initial investment	60,000	200,000	150,000	70,000
Annual cash flows	25,000	40,000	35,000	20,000
Life in years	3	9	7	5
Cost of capital 10%				

These projects are of such a nature that they can be accepted in part form.

Required: how would you set about choosing the optimal investment programme? (Formulate the model but do no solve).

Questions 20.6-20.7. Answers not provided.

20.6 A bus and coach company has decided to introduce an express service between a main line railway station and a nearby town. Fares will be 15p single and 30p return. The company is considering the purchase of either 32 or 50 seat buses to which the following estimates relate:

	32 seat	50 seat
Number of buses to be purchased	6	4
Useful life	5 years	5 years
Purchase price of each bus (paid on delivery)	£6,000	£10,000
Mileage per gallon	10	7½
Disposable value at end of useful life	£800	£1,000
Driver's hourly wage	£2	£2
Price per gallon of petrol	80p	80p
Other running costs, annual total for all buses together	£4,000	£3,000

During the four rush hours each day all buses will be in service and are expected to operate at full capacity in both directions of the route, each bus covering the route 12 times (six round trips) during the four hours. During the remainder of the 16 hour day, 500 passengers will be carried on single trips and the company at the Traffic Commissioners' insistence will operate four buses on the route. Part-time drivers will be employed for the extra hours during the rush hour periods. A bus travelling the route all day will cover 480 miles. A bus travelling only during the rush hours will cover 120 miles a day. There are 260 working days in the year. The company's annual cost of capital is 20%.

You are required to determine whether the company should purchase six 32 seaters or four 50 seaters. For simplicity assume that all operating cash flows occur entirely on the last day of the year to which they relate. Ignore taxation.

ICAEW(MA).

20.7 Everest Ltd is considering the replacement of a group of machines used exclusively for the manufacture of one of its products, the Yeti. The existing machines have a book value of £65,000 after deducting straight line depreciation from historical cost; however, they could be sold only for £45,000. The new machines would cost £100,000. Everest expects to sell Yeties for four more years. The exististing machines could be kept in operation for that period of time if it were economically desirable to do so. After four years, the scrap value of both the existing machines and the new machines would be zero.

The current costs per unit of manufacturing Yetis on the existing machines and the new machines are as follows:

	Existing machines			New machines
	£	£		
Materials	22.00			20.00
Labour (32 hours @ £1.25)	40.00	(16 hours @ £1.25)		20.00
Overehads (32 hours @ £0.60)	19.20	(16 hours @ £1.80)		28.80
Total cost		81.20		68.80

Overheads are allocated to products on the labour hour rate method. The hourly rates of 60p and £1.80 comprise 25p asnd 62.5p for variable overheads and 35p and £1.175 for fixed overheads, including depreciation.

Current sales of Yetis are 1000 units per annum at £90 each; if the new machines were purchased, output would be increased to 1200 units and selling price would be reduced to £80.

Everest requires a minimum rate of return on investment of 20 per cent per annum in money terms. Materials costs, overheads and selling prices are expected to increase at the rate of 15 per cent per annum, in step with the index of retail prices. Labour costs are expected to increase at the rate of 20 per cent per annum. Assume that annual receipts and payments would arise annually on the anniversary of the installation of the new machinery.

You are required to:

(a) give calculations to show whether purchase of the new machines would be worthwhile, and

(b) explain shortly your treatment of inflation.

Ignore taxation. ICAEW(EFD)

20.8 Fluorine Ltd is choosing which investment to undertake during the coming year. The following table has been prepared, summarising the main features of available projects:

Project	Cash Outlays		Cash Receipts	
	Time 0 £'000	Time 1 £'000	Time 1 £'000	Time 2 £'000
Sodium	20	50	20	80
Magnesium	40	35	40	55
Aluminium	50	35	10	115
Silicon	40	15	10	75
Phosphorus	30	40	20	80

There will be no cash flows on any of the projects after time 2. All projects are regarded as being of equal risk. Fluorine uses only equity sources of finance at an estimated cost of 20 per cent per annum.

Cash flows given above represent estimated results for maximum possible investment in each project; lower levels of investment may be undertaken in which case all cash flows will be reduced in proportion.

You are required to:

(a) prepare calculations to identify the optimal set of investments assuming that capital available is limited to £100,000 at time 0, and £200,000 at time 1; assume for the purpose of this requirement only that the Aluminium project and the Silicon project are mutually exclusive.

(b) explain what calculations you would undertake to identify the optimal set of investments assuming that capital available is limited to £100,000 at time 0, and to £40,000 at time 1; give reasons for your choice of method but do not give calculations, and

(c) draft short notes for a reply to a director of Fluorine who has seen your proposals, has commended that the use of sophisticated methods of calculation is unjustified in view of the uncertainty of the estimates of cash flows and has expressed his opinion that the payback method is generally to be preferred.

Ignore taxation. ICAEW(EFD)

20.9 Your company is reconsidering its methods of capital expenditure appraisal. At present, only single value forecasts are prepared irrespective of the risk factors involved.

As management accountant you are requested to prepare a paper for the board of directors explaining the various methods which the company could adopt to incorporate factors of risk into the appraisal process.

ICMA(MA1).

20.10 The XYZ Company Limited is considering the acquisition of new plant and equipment as part of an expansion programme. The estimated cost of the equipment is £80,000 and the terms of purchase require payment of 50% with order, and the remainder 30 days after delivery and installation. Delivery and installation is expected three months after receipt of the order and production will start one month after delivery and installation. It is estimated that sales of products which the new equipment will produce will be as follows:

Annual Sales	Probability
10,000 units	0.1
15,000 units	0.2
20,000 units	0.3
25,000 units	0.3
30,000 units	0.1

The estimated selling price and variable costs of these product is as follows:

Average Selling Price		£5
Avereage Variable Cost—Material	£2	
Labour	1	
	—	
	3	
Contribution		£2

Total fixed costs excluding depreciation are estimated at £10,000 per annum. Debtors will take on average one month pay and the company will take two months credit from its material suppliers. Apart from the production required to meet sales there will be an investment in stocks of £20,000. It is company practice in assessing projects to assume that only 90% of investment in stock and debtors is recovered.

In addition to the expenditure included above the sales forecast is based on the assumption that there will be special sales promotion at the beginning of the first two sales years of £10,000 and £12,000 respectively. If this sales-promotion expenditure is not incurred it is estimated that sales will be as follows:

Annual Sales	Probability
10,000 units	0.3
15,000 units	0.3
20,000 units	0.2
25,000 units	0.2
30,000 units	0.0

Although the equipment has an estimated technical life of ten years the sales life of the product is uncertain and the market research department can only given general guidance that it will almost certainly be longer than six years and less than ten. The company's long-run projected capital structure on which the cost of capital is based is as follows:

Type	Estimated Net Cost	Amount
Equity	17%	£10,000,000
Loans	14%	5,000,000

You are required to advise on the suitability or otherwise of embarking on this project assuming

(a) a life of six years and (b) a life of nine years.

Note 1

Taxation can be ignored.

Note 2

	14%	15%	16%	17%	18%
The present value of £1 now—					
The present value of £1 in 1 Year	0.877	0.870	0.862	0.855	0.847
2 Years	0.769	0.756	0.743	0.731	0.718
3 Years	0.675	0.658	0.641	0.624	0.609
4 years	0.592	0.572	0.552	0.534	0.516
5 years	0.519	0.497	0.476	0.456	0.437
6 years	0.456	0.432	0.410	0.390	0.370
7 years	0.400	0.376	0.354	0.333	0.314
8 years	0.351	0.327	0.305	0.285	0.266
9 years	0.308	0.284	0.263	0.243	0.225
10 years	0.270	0.247	0.227	0.208	0.191
11 years	0.237	0.215	0.195	0.178	0.162

CA(FM)

Seminar Problem 20

Lithium Ltd is a mining company. It has just discovered a mineral deposit and its directors have to decide on the worthwhileness of mining operations. The following information has been discovered in the course of preliminary investigations:

(1) Costs of £225,000 have been incurred on surveys to locate the deposit and estimate its volume. On average, these costs were incurred one year ago.

(2) At the commencement of mining, it would be necessary to incur outlays of £864,000 for tunnelling and development of the site and of £328,000 on mining equipment.

(3) The quantity of mineral in the deposit is estimated to be 500,000 tons. The price of the mineral at the present time is £16 per ton and the price is expected to increase at the rate of 25 per cent per annum over the next five years because of the scarcity of the mineral. (If mining commenced immediately, the first output would be sold after one year fo £20 per ton).

(4) Mining would require three hours of labour per ton. Present wage rates are £2 per hour. There is a scarcity of labour with the necessary skills and consequently all employees would have to be transferred from a nearby site owned by Lithium. The company would have to accept a loss of cash contribution from its other operations of £1 per hour (allowing for inflation) on labour transferred from the other site. However, the labour shortage is expected to last for only one year. Other variable costs of mining would be £3 per ton. Wage rates and other costs are expected to increase at 20 per cent per annum.

(5) Lithium purchased the site on which the mineral deposit is located for £50,000 five years ago. It has recently been offered £550,000 for the site by a company which wishes to develop it for an alternative project.

(6) On average, two out of every three surveys undertaken by Lithium are abortive. The directors believe that each successful project should be charged with three times its actual survey costs to make sure that the company covers its costs overall.

(7) On completion of mining, the company would need to make the site good at a cost of £450,000. The mining equipment would have a life of 10 years., It could be transferred to another site in five years time and would save costs having a value of £150,000 at that time. Both of these estimates include an allowance for inflation.

(8) The cost of capital of Lithium is estimated at 20 per cent per annum in money terms; the index of retail prices is expected to increase at 15 per cent per annum over the next few years.

One director believes that it would be preferable to delay either the mining or the sale of the mineral to take advantage of expected increases in selling prices. If mining is carried out according to the original schedule but sale is postponed, additional storage and handling costs would amount to £2 per ton per annum (allowing for inflation).

Assume that annual receipts and payments arise at the end of each year. You are required to:

(a) prepare calculations to estimate whether it is worthwhile for Lithium to proceed immediately with the proposed mining project, assuming an extraction rate of 100,000 tones per annum,

(b) prepare calculations to show whether it would be worthwhile to postpone (i) the extraction or (ii) the sale of 50,000 tons from year one to year two, and

(c) explain, briefly, your treatment of survey costs in the light of the information given in paragraph (6).

Ignore taxation.   ICAEW(EFD).

Appendix A
Present value of 1

Period	1%	2%	3%	4%	5%	6%	7%	8%	9%	10%	12%	14%	15%
1	0.990	0.980	0.971	0.961	0.952	0.943	0.935	0.926	0.917	0.909	0.893	0.877	0.870
2	0.980	0.961	0.943	0.925	0.907	0.890	0.873	0.857	0.842	0.826	0.797	0.769	0.756
3	0.971	0.942	0.915	0.889	0.864	0.840	0.816	0.794	0.772	0.751	0.712	0.675	0.658
4	0.961	0.924	0.889	0.855	0.823	0.792	0.763	0.735	0.708	0.683	0.636	0.592	0.572
5	0.951	0.906	0.863	0.822	0.784	0.747	0.713	0.681	0.650	0.621	0.567	0.519	0.497
6	0.942	0.888	0.838	0.790	0.746	0.705	0.666	0.630	0.596	0.564	0.507	0.456	0.432
7	0.933	0.871	0.813	0.760	0.711	0.665	0.623	0.583	0.547	0.513	0.452	0.400	0.376
8	0.923	0.853	0.789	0.731	0.677	0.627	0.582	0.540	0.502	0.467	0.404	0.351	0.327
9	0.914	0.837	0.766	0.703	0.645	0.592	0.544	0.500	0.460	0.424	0.361	0.308	0.284
10	0.905	0.820	0.744	0.676	0.614	0.558	0.508	0.463	0.422	0.386	0.322	0.270	0.247
11	0.896	0.804	0.722	0.650	0.585	0.527	0.475	0.429	0.388	0.350	0.287	0.237	0.215
12	0.887	0.788	0.701	0.625	0.557	0.497	0.444	0.397	0.356	0.319	0.257	0.208	0.187
13	0.879	0.773	0.681	0.601	0.530	0.469	0.415	0.368	0.326	0.290	0.229	0.182	0.163
14	0.870	0.758	0.661	0.577	0.505	0.442	0.388	0.340	0.299	0.263	0.205	0.160	0.141
15	0.861	0.743	0.642	0.555	0.481	0.417	0.362	0.315	0.275	0.239	0.183	0.140	0.123
16	0.853	0.728	0.623	0.534	0.458	0.394	0.339	0.292	0.252	0.218	0.163	0.123	0.107
17	0.844	0.714	0.605	0.513	0.436	0.371	0.317	0.270	0.231	0.198	0.146	0.108	0.093
18	0.836	0.700	0.587	0.494	0.416	0.350	0.296	0.250	0.212	0.180	0.130	0.095	0.081
19	0.828	0.686	0.570	0.475	0.396	0.331	0.276	0.232	0.194	0.164	0.116	0.083	0.070
20	0.820	0.673	0.554	0.456	0.377	0.319	0.258	0.215	0.178	0.149	0.104	0.073	0.061
25	0.780	0.610	0.478	0.375	0.295	0.233	0.184	0.146	0.116	0.092	0.059	0.038	0.030
30	0.742	0.552	0.412	0.308	0.231	0.174	0.131	0.099	0.075	0.057	0.033	0.020	0.015

Period	16%	18%	20%	24%	28%	32%	36%	40%	50%	60%	70%	80%	90%
1	0.862	0.847	0.833	0.806	0.781	0.758	0.735	0.714	0.667	0.625	0.588	0.556	0.526
2	0.743	0.718	0.694	0.650	0.610	0.574	0.541	0.510	0.444	0.391	0.346	0.309	0.277
3	0.641	0.609	0.579	0.524	0.477	0.435	0.398	0.364	0.296	0.244	0.204	0.171	0.146
4	0.552	0.516	0.482	0.423	0.373	0.329	0.292	0.260	0.198	0.153	0.120	0.095	0.077
5	0.476	0.437	0.402	0.341	0.291	0.250	0.215	0.186	0.132	0.095	0.070	0.053	0.040
6	0.410	0.370	0.335	0.275	0.227	0.189	0.158	0.133	0.088	0.060	0.041	0.029	0.021
7	0.354	0.314	0.279	0.222	0.178	0.143	0.116	0.095	0.059	0.037	0.024	0.016	0.011
8	0.305	0.266	0.233	0.179	0.139	0.108	0.085	0.068	0.039	0.023	0.014	0.009	0.006
9	0.263	0.226	0.194	0.144	0.108	0.082	0.063	0.048	0.026	0.015	0.008	0.005	0.003
10	0.227	0.191	0.162	0.116	0.085	0.062	0.046	0.035	0.017	0.009	0.005	0.003	0.002
11	0.195	0.162	0.135	0.094	0.066	0.047	0.034	0.025	0.012	0.006	0.003	0.002	0.001
12	0.168	0.137	0.112	0.076	0.052	0.036	0.025	0.018	0.008	0.004	0.002	0.001	0.001
13	0.145	0.116	0.093	0.061	0.040	0.027	0.018	0.013	0.005	0.002	0.001	0.001	0.000
14	0.125	0.099	0.078	0.049	0.032	0.021	0.014	0.009	0.003	0.001	0.001	0.000	0.000
15	0.108	0.084	0.065	0.040	0.025	0.016	0.010	0.006	0.002	0.001	0.000	0.000	0.000
16	0.093	0.071	0.054	0.032	0.019	0.012	0.007	0.005	0.002	0.001	0.000	0.000	
17	0.080	0.060	0.045	0.026	0.015	0.009	0.005	0.003	0.001	0.000	0.000		
18	0.069	0.051	0.038	0.021	0.012	0.007	0.004	0.002	0.001	0.000	0.000		
19	0.060	0.043	0.031	0.017	0.009	0.005	0.003	0.002	0.000	0.000			
20	0.051	0.037	0.026	0.014	0.007	0.004	0.002	0.001	0.000	0.000			
25	0.024	0.016	0.010	0.005	0.002	0.001	0.000	0.000					
30	0.012	0.007	0.004	0.002	0.001	0.000	0.000						

Appendix B
Present value of Annuity of 1 per period

Period	1%	2%	3%	4%	5%	6%	7%	8%	9%	10%
1	0.990	0.980	0.971	0.962	0.952	0.943	0.935	0.926	0.917	0.909
2	1.970	1.942	1.913	1.886	1.859	1.833	1.808	1.783	1.759	1.736
3	2.941	2.884	2.829	2.775	2.723	2.673	2.624	2.577	2.531	2.487
4	3.902	3.808	3.717	3.630	3.546	3.456	3.387	3.312	3.240	3.170
5	4.853	4.713	4.580	4.452	4.329	4.212	4.100	3.993	3.890	3.791
6	5.795	5.601	5.417	5.242	5.076	4.917	4.766	4.623	4.486	4.355
7	6.728	6.472	6.230	6.002	5.786	5.582	5.389	5.206	5.033	4.868
8	7.652	7.325	7.020	6.733	6.463	6.210	5.971	5.747	5.535	5.335
9	8.566	8.162	7.786	7.435	7.108	6.802	6.515	6.247	5.985	5.759
10	9.471	8.983	8.530	8.111	7.722	7.360	7.024	6.710	6.418	6.145
11	10.368	9.787	9.253	8.760	8.306	7.887	7.499	7.139	6.805	6.495
12	11.255	10.575	9.954	9.385	8.863	8.384	7.943	7.536	7.161	6.814
13	12.134	11.348	10.635	9.986	9.394	8.853	8.358	7.904	7.487	7.103
14	13.004	12.106	11.296	10.563	9.899	9.295	8.745	8.244	7.786	7.367
15	13.865	12.849	11.938	11.118	10.380	9.712	9.108	8.559	8.060	7.606
16	14.718	13.578	12.561	11.652	10.838	10.106	9.447	8.851	8.312	7.824
17	15.562	14.292	13.166	12.166	11.274	10.477	9.763	9.122	8.544	8.022
18	16.398	14.992	13.754	12.659	11.690	10.828	10.059	9.372	8.756	8.201
19	17.226	15.678	14.324	13.134	12.085	11.158	10.336	9.604	8.950	8.365
20	18.046	16.351	14.877	13.590	12.462	11.470	10.594	9.818	9.128	8.514
25	22.023	19.523	17.413	15.622	14.094	12.783	11.654	10.675	9.283	9.077
30	25.808	22.397	19.600	17.292	15.373	13.765	12.409	11.258	10.274	9.427

Period	12%	14%	16%	18%	20%	24%	28%	32%	36%
1	0.893	0.877	0.862	0.847	0.833	0.806	0.781	0.758	0.735
2	1.690	1.647	1.605	1.566	1.528	1.457	1.392	1.332	1.276
3	2.402	2.322	2.246	2.174	2.106	1.981	1.868	1.766	1.674
4	3.037	2.914	2.798	2.690	2.589	2.404	2.241	2.096	1.966
5	3.605	3.433	3.274	3.127	2.991	2.745	2.532	2.345	2.181
6	4.111	3.889	3.685	3.498	3.326	3.020	2.759	2.534	2.339
7	4.564	4.288	4.089	3.812	3.605	3.242	2.937	2.678	2.455
8	4.968	4.639	4.344	4.078	3.837	3.421	3.076	2.786	2.540
9	5.328	4.946	4.607	4.303	4.031	3.566	3.184	2.868	2.603
10	5.650	5.216	4.833	4.494	4.193	3.682	3.269	2.930	2.650
11	5.988	5.453	5.029	4.656	4.327	3.776	3.335	2.978	2.683
12	6.194	5.660	5.197	4.793	4.439	3.851	3.387	3.013	2.708
13	6.424	5.842	5.342	4.910	4.533	3.912	3.427	3.040	2.727
14	6.628	6.002	5.468	5.008	4.611	3.962	3.459	3.061	2.740
15	6.811	6.142	5.575	5.092	4.675	4.001	3.483	3.076	2.750
16	6.974	6.265	5.669	5.162	4.730	4.033	3.503	3.088	2.758
17	7.120	5.373	5.749	4.222	4.775	4.059	3.518	3.097	2.763
18	7.250	6.467	5.818	5.273	4.812	4.080	3.529	3.104	2.767
19	7.366	6.550	5.877	5.316	4.844	4.097	3.539	3.109	2.770
20	7.469	6.623	5.929	5.353	4.870	4.110	3.546	3.113	2.772
25	7.843	8.873	6.907	5.467	4.948	4.147	3.564	3.122	2.776
30	8.055	7.003	6.177	5.517	4.979	4.160	3.569	3.124	2.778

Solutions

1.1 (a) $(1,000 + 10,000 - 1,500) = 9,500 + 25,000 + 45,000 = 79,500$
(b) $9,500 + 25,000 + 45,000 + 15,000 - 17,000 + 77,500$
(c) $10,000 + 77,500 - 8,000 = 79,500$.

1.2 Drs Raw materials 5,700, Work-in-progress 3,400, 4,500 man. o/h 2,000, 4,500; Crs Raw materials 3,4000, man. o/h 7,000. Subsidiary acs, drs A 2,000, B 2,500, C 1,200, WIPI, 1,600, 2,000, 2,000, WIP2, 1,800, 2,500, 5,000 ind. lab. 2,000, ind. mat. 500, depn 2,500, utilities 2,000.

1.3 Cost of production (nil + 70,000 - 1,000 + 1,000 - 9,000) + (20,000 + 5,000 + 15,000 + 1,000 + 4,000 - 1,000) + 100,000 = 205,000.
 Cost of goods produced nil + 205,000 - 15,000 = 190,000
 Cost of goods sold nil + 190,000 - 5,000 = 185,000.
 Gross profit 320,000 - 185,000 = 135,000. Net profit 135,000 - 40,000 = 95,000.

1.4 depn. adj: cost account deduction 5,000 + 5,125 = 10,125, so deduct 125 from finance. Rent deduct 500. W.I.P. increase deduct 800. Add finance expenses, 5,000. Net difference 3,575.

1.5 Debit balances: fixed assets 55,000, debtors 70,000 raw materials 13,000, factory o/h 5,000, selling o/h 17,500, admin. 10,000 W.I.P.A. 4,000, W.I.P.B. 3,500, finished goods 85,000 c.o.g.s. 140,000.. Credit balances capital 100,000, bank o/d 33,000, crs 93,000, sales 174,000, provn. for depn. 3,000. Trial bal. total 403,000 gross profit 174,000 - 140,000 = 34,000.

2.1 (i) c, (ii) f, (iii) g, (iv) j, (v) d, (vi) i.

2.2 (i) fixed (ii) step (iii) variable (iv) production or manufacture (v) variable (vi) fixed (vii) period (viii) full, variable.

2.3 $4,000 + 55,000 - 7,000 = 52,000$ (cost of raw material) $+ 48,000 + 2,000 + 30,000 = 132,000$.

2.4 $(8,000 + 260,000 - 12,000) = 256,000 + 572,000 + 290,000 + (12,000 - 20,000) = 1,110,000 + (100,000 - 1,110,000 \div 555,000) = 1,090,100 + 100,000 = 1,190,000 + 60,000 + 20,000 + 40,000 = 1,310,100$ (total cost) operating profit 189,900.

2.5 period 1 $15,000 \times (7 - 3 - 1) - 45,000 =$ nil. period 2 $20,000 \times 3 - 45,000 = 15,000$. period 3 $25,000 \times 3 - 45,000 = 30,000$.

3.1 Stocks at Jan 1 $50 \times 3.00 = 150.00$, Jan 7 $50 \times 3.00 + 50 \times 3.02 + 301.00$, Jan 10 $10 \times 3.00 + 50 \times 3.02 = 181.00$, Jan 14 $10 \times 3.00 + 100 \times 3.02$, $= 332.00$, Jan 17 $40 \times 3.02 + 50 \times 3.03 = 172.30$, Jan 24 $10 \times 3.03 = 30.30$, Jan 28 $10 \times 3.03 + 50 \times 3.04 = 182.30$.

3.2 Stocks at Jan 7 $50 \times 3.00 + 50 \times 3.02 = 301.00$, Jan 10 $50 \times 3.00 + 10 \times 3.02 = 180.20$, Jan 14 $50 \times 3.00 + 60 \times 3.02 = 331.20$, Jan 17 $40 \times 3.00 = 120.00$. Jan 21 $40 \times 3.00 + 50 \times 3.03 = 171.50$, Jan 24 $10 \times 3.00 = 30.00$, Jan 28 $10 \times 3.00 + 50 \times 3.04 = 182.00$.

3.3 Stocks at Jan 7 $100 \times 3.01 = 301.00$, Jan 10 $60 \times 3.01 = 180.60$, Jan 14 $110 \times 3.014 = 331.60$, Jan 17 $40 \times 3.014 = 120.62$, Jan 21 $90 \times 3.023 = 272.12$, Jan 24 $10 \times 3.023 = 30.23$, Jan 28 $60 \times 3.037 = 182.23$.

3.4 Stocks at Jan 1 $50 \times 3.00 = 150.00$, Jan 7 $50 \times 3.02 + 50 \times 3.02$ after revaluation $= 302.00$, Jan 10 $60 \times 3.02 = 181.20$ Jan 14 $50 \times 3.02 + 60 \times 3.02 = 332.20$, Jan 17 revalue 110 at 3.03 less 70 issued $= 40 \times 3.03 = 121.20$, Jan 21 $90 \times 3.03 = 272.70$, Jan 24 revalue 90 at 3.04 less 80 issued $= 10 \times 3.04 = 30.40$, Jan 28 $60 \times 3.04 = 182.40$.

3.5 (i) $1,000 + 8,000 - 1,000 = 8,000 + 40,000 - 3,000$ (loss) $= 45,000$ sales.
(ii) $5,000 + 8,000 + 40,000 - 6,000 = 47,000 - 2,000$ (loss) $= 45,000$.
(iii) $5,000 + 8,000 + 40,000 - 5,000 = 48,000 - 3,000$ (loss) $= 45,000$.
(iv) $5,000 + 8,000 + 40,000 - 5,889 = 47,111 - 2,111$ (loss) $= 45,000$.

4.1 R, 70. S, 73. T, 60.

4.2 U, 128. V, 104. W. 86.4.

4.3 U, 120. V, 106⅔. W, 90.

4.4 Excess over std. $28,000 - 420 \times 60 = 2,800$ gives 10%. X earns 42 $(1.5 + 7.5\%$ of 1.5$) = 67.725$. Y $= 80.41$. Z $= 60.20$.

4.5

time taken	30	40	50	60
bonus	50	44	28	0

5.1

	P_1	P_2	P_3	S_1	S_2	
Rent	1,500	1,500	1,500	750	750	floor space
Heating	923	923	692	231	231	c.c
Power	5,000	2,000	1,000	1,667	333	machine h.p.
Depn.	2,000	800	800	1,200	5,200	machine values
Labour	4,000	4,000	6,000	2,000	2,000	labour hours
Misc.	667	667	1,000	333	333	labour hours

5.2 $S_1 \rightarrow P_1$ 2,472 P_2 1,236 P_3 1,236 S_2 1,237 $= 6,181$
$S_2 = 8,847 + 1,237 \rightarrow P_1$ 3,361 P_2 3,361 P_3 3,362.

5.3 P_1 19,923 $+ P_2$ 14,487 $+ P_3$ 15,590 $= 50,000$.

5.4 Absorbed ohs $= £115,500$, rate $= £2.1$ per unit, production $= 115,000 \div 2.1 = 55,000$.

5.5 (a) $50,000 - (40,000 + 4,000) = 6,000$. (b) $50,000 - (40,000 + 300 + 4,000) = 5,700$.

6.1 Dr Job 2-104 £455 Cr Material accounts 300 and 20, wages 75, overhead absorbed 60.

6.2 Dr Material 60,000 Cr creditors 60,000; dr wages 72,000, cr wages due (or cash + deductions) 72,000; cr material 65,000, dr work-in-progress 65,000; cr materials 5,000 dr overhead 5,000; dr overhead (or via indirect labour cost) 40,000, cr wages due 40,000; dr overhead 50,000 cr cash + creditors 50,000; dr work-in-progress 90,000 cr overhead 90,000.

6.3 materials cr 8,400; labour cr 2,440; overhead control dr 3,750 cr 3,660; job no 100 dr 1,200, 400, 600 cr 2,200; job no 101 dr 1,600, 500, 750 cr 2,850; job no 102 2,100, 540, 810 cr 2,850; job no 102 2,100, 540, 810 cr 3,450; job no 103 2,500, 580, 870 cr 3,950; job no 104 dr 1,000, 420, 630; fin. goods dr 12,450 cr 5,050; c.o.g.s. dr 5,050; sales cr 7,000 debtors dr 7,000.

6.4 profit before adj. Jan/Dec costs as shown 445,100 + 15,000 = 460,100. Revenue value 515,000 + stocks 73,400. Profit 128,300.

6.5 profit 476,000 − 375,000 = 401,000. Assumed profit 75% of (350,000/430,000) × 401,000 = 244,796.

7.1 Unit cost for January 63,350/9,050 = 7. Transfer 1,500 units at (6+7)2, 7,500 at 7, w.i.p. valued at 7.

7.2 material cost (42,000 + 186,000) ÷ (140,000 + 62,0000) = 30p Conversion cost (11,240 + 70,000) ÷ (70,000 + 607,000) = 12p.

7.3 process 1. transfer cost 50,636, work-in-progress 8,864. process 2 transfer cost 90,044, work-in-progress 13,592.

7.4 process 1. transfer cost 49,527, work-in-progress 8,748. process 2, transfer cost 89,525, work-in-progress 13,481.

7.5 Transfer to process 2, 4,500, to process 3, 1,500 Transfer to finished goods from process 2, 4,886, closing stock process 2, 2,314. Transfer from 3 to finished goods 3,200.

8.1 411 000

8.2 o/s 192,000 cost of production 160,650 + 2,142,000 + 252,000 c/s 263,200 cost of goods sold 2,554,650 profit 195,350.

8.3 gross profit 12,600; net profit 3,980. Balance sheet lease 14,250, f + f 4,500, cash 10,000, drs. 8,730, stock 9,480 total 46,960. Capital 43,370, drawings (18,000), profit 3,980, creditors 7,610, loan 10,000 total 46,960.

8.4 gross profit 40,000, net profit 7,900, transfer to reserve 4,140, nil balance c/f. Balance Sheet, fixed assets 11,600 less 3,500, stock 25,000, drs 16,667, cash 2,782; share capital 6,000, reserves 12,140, debentures 2,000, current liabilities 29,250, corporation tax due 3,160.

9.1 Price 1,000 A; usage 2,000 A.

9.2 Skilled rate 10 A, efficiency 20 A; semi-skilled 25 A and 15 F; unskilled 20 A and 30 A.

9.4 price cronium 500 A Draconium 1,000 F; mix 8,000 A and 4,000 F; yield 3,400 F.

9.5 Men rate 70 A, mix 100 A, efficiency 70 A, overtime 25 A, idle 70 A (treating o/t as unplanned). Women rate 65 A, mix 75 F, efficiency 105 A, idle 30 A.

10.1 630 + 510 + 1,150 + 360 + 500 + 400 + 600 = 4,150; variable rate = 2.05 fixed rate = 2.05, absorption = 4,305.

10.2 100 A, 124 A, 21 F. Budget overheads = 3000 × 2.1.

10.3 variable rate 5.5, fixed rate 1450/1000; 300 A, 275 A, 72.5F.

10.4 Price 3,000 A volume 4,000 F (using margins).

10.5 price X 21, A, Y 42 A, Z nil; mix 35 F, 105 F, 126 A, volume 25 A, 75 A, 30 A.

11.1 Dr Material control 2000, price variance 200, cr. creditors 2200. Dr W.I.P. 1530, use variance 100, cr material control 1630.

11.2 Dr W.I.P. 6000, rate variance 130, efficiency variance 400 cr. wages control 6530.

11.3 Dr overhead spending variance ac. 510, volume variance 990, overhead control 12500, cr. W.I.P. 14000.

11.4 actual hours 1000, actual rate 1.2, standard 1.0, standard hours 900.

11.5 Actual price 1.99, actual quantity 1000, material used 900, standard material 850, standard price 2.00.

13.1 141, 2411.

13.2 60, 12.

13.3 100, 20.

13.4 3520, 4600, 4640, 7180, 9220, 11000.

13.5 2560, (3090), (1340), 4040, 9230, 14530.

14.2 (b) 18, 28, $1 \to 2 \to 4 \to 5$

14.3 $1 \to 2 \to 4 \to 6$; none; 2 days.

14.4 AEJ; BFJ.

15.1 See 15.3

15.2 $y = 8.2x + 45$

15.3 $y = 9.3x + 30$; 0.99 a good fit showing a strong relationship between the production and costs.

15.4 $y = 0.08468x + 949$ giving 1796 for 10 000 units.

15.5 variable approx 19450, gives $y = 38.9 + 5650$, $x =$ machine hours.

16.1 (a) 8,571 (b) 11,429 (c) 10 000 (d) increase to 15,000.

16.2 (a) 10,000 (b) 25,000 (c) 7,000.

16.3 (a) 80,000 (b) new production level is 10,000 units above new breakeven point (c) no if (b) is operating, otherwise is could reduce overall loss by 120,000.

16.4 1000

16.5 Two at 3500 and 4000.

17.1 The incremental cost of buying is smaller by 50,000.

17.2 Yes. Incremental revenue less expenses is 50,000.

17.3 Alternative (a) with net incremental revenue 4,000 is best.

17.4 Net incremental revenue is 6,000 assuming fixed costs are not incremental.

17.5 14.60; 19.

18.1 Intersection $2y = 90 - 3x$ and $5y = 150 - 4x$.

18.2 $78 \times 6 + 36 \times 6 = 684$.

18.3 Make 500 Deluxe and 1,000 standard.

18.4 (1) 1.25 (2) nil (3) .06.

18.5 $1.84X + 1.66Y + 1.35 Z$ s.t. $X + 3Y + 3Z \leqslant 3,600$, $2x + 2Y + 2Z \leqslant 2,800$, $2x + 2Y + Z \leqslant 3,000$, x, y, z. $\geqslant 0$.

19.1 2.75; 4; 2.80

19.2 Aug. return = $2\frac{1}{2}\%$ per annum both projects. Recommend use of npv, here favours project 1

19.3 npv = 3111 JRR = 12.6%.

19.4 Make has smaller np cost by 12,933.

20.1 Buy with advantage of 9,857 in npv terms.

20.2 npv = 27,688.

20.3 npv = 33,159.

20.4 Percentage changes: 57.8, 49.7, 52, 38.2, 931. Not sensitive to any.

20.5 Using an L.P. Max 2 172 A + 30360 B + 20394 C + 5816 D. s.t. 60A 200 B + 150 C + 70D $\leqslant$ 380; 0 $\leqslant$ A, B, C, D, $\leqslant$ 1. Since single constraint the present value index will give solution, 100% B, 100% C, 3/7ths D.

Index